THE LONDON CIGARETTE CARD COMPANY

CIGARETTE CARD CATALOGUE

2009 edition

FIRST CATALOGUE PRODUCED IN 1929

ISBN 978-1-906397-03-6

Compiled by
IAN A. LAKER

Published by
THE LONDON CIGARETTE CARD COMPANY LTD
Sutton Road, Somerton, Somerset, England TA11 6QP

Telephone: 01458-273452
Fax: 01458-273515
International Calls: Telephone: ++ 44 1458-273452
Fax: ++ 44 1458-273515
E-Mail: cards@londoncigcard.co.uk

Web Site: www.londoncigcard.co.uk

Cards illustrated on the front cover are from the series:

Gallaher Ltd. Trains of The World 1937
John Player & Sons. Footballers 1928-29
Gallaher Ltd. Portraits of Famous Stars 1935
John Player & Sons. Uniforms of The Territorial Army 1939

Back cover:

R & J Hill Ltd. Famous Ships 1939
W.D. & H.O. Wills. Garden Flowers 1933
Ardath Tobacco Ltd. Proverbs 1936
Godfrey Phillips Ltd. Beauties of Today 2nd Series 1940

THE CIGARETTE CARD VIDEO

On 7 January 1993, history was made when the first ever television programme devoted entirely to cigarette cards was broadcast by HTV. And now you can buy the video, called

'Miniature Masterpieces'

Introduced by the well-known West Country personality Fred Wedlock, whose grandfather played football for Bristol City and who is featured in Ogden's 1905 series of Famous Footballers, the programme concentrates on the heyday of cigarette cards. In visits to the Wills' tobacco factory and the printers Mardon Son & Hall, we meet Eric Sampson, one of the artists who were employed in the top floor studios during the 1930s, and see some of his work. Text writer, Geoff Bennett, tells us about one of his mistakes which led to the issue of a corrected card, and we observe a modern artist, Eric Bottomley, at work on the recent series of Britain's Motoring History. Charlie Watkins, retired foreman printer at Mardons, shows us how cards were printed by chromolithography and letterpress. We see cards from many different periods — The Boer War, World War I, the 1920s and '30s, through to the famous Air Raid Precautions series, among the last to be printed by Mardons before their Caxton Works was destroyed in the blitz.

The cameras visit the London Cigarette Card Company in Somerton, and Frank Doggett demonstrates some of the more unusual cartophilic items such as silks, cards in metal frames and a record cigarette card which somehow the sound engineers actually manage to play. The film sound track cleverly uses music and historic recordings to recreate the essence of the period.

This fascinating tape was made by the production company Forum Television and plays for approximately 25 minutes. It is now available exclusively from the London Cigarette Card Company.

This is a unique opportunity to obtain a fascinating film which really does do justice to the subject — you will be impressed.

Published at £10.50   **Special Offer Price £7.50** post free to UK (overseas at cost)

HOW TO USE THE CATALOGUE

This catalogue is published in three sections. Section 1 covers the cigarette card issues of British Tobacco Manufacturers for the home market together with certain export series (indicated by 'export' in brackets). Section 2 deals with cards issued outside the United Kingdom. Section 3 covers reprinted series.

In each section manufacturers are featured in alphabetical order, and the issues of each firm are catalogued alphabetically within suitable sub-divisions, such as, in Section 1, 'Pre-1919 Issues', 'Post-1920 Issues', 'Silks', 'Miscellaneous' and, in Section 2, 'With Brand Name', 'Without Brand Name', 'Silks', etc. Where a brand name but no maker's name is shown on the card, reference should be made to the appropriate Index of Brands. Anonymous series, that is those with printed backs but no brand or maker's name, are listed under the firms to which the issue has been attributed. Anonymous British issues are also listed at the end of Section 1.

Information is given in the columns from left to right as follows:

Size
(a) British issues and reprints series: the code letter refers to the size of the card as indicated in the chart on page x. A number 1 or 2 after the letter means that the card is slightly larger or smaller than shown.
(b) Foreign issues: the absence of a code letter indicates that the series is of standard size. A code letter 'L' defines the card as being large (about 80 × 62 mm). Other codes are 'K' = smaller than standard, 'M' = between standard and large, and 'EL' = larger than large.

Printing
(a) British issues and reprint series: the code indicates the printing on the front of the card. 'BW' = black-and-white; 'C' = coloured; 'CP' = colour photograph; 'P' = photograph; 'U' = uncoloured (monochrome).
(b) Foreign issues: the letter 'P' is used to show that a series consists of photographs.

Number in Set
This figure gives the number of cards in the series. A question mark alongside shows the exact number is unknown.

Title and Date
Where a series title is printed on the cards, this is used in the catalogue. For cards which do not exhibit a series title, an 'adopted' title is shown (indicated by an asterisk in the British section). Where a firm issued more than one series with the same title, these are distinguished by the addition of 'Set 1', 'Set 2', etc. or a code letter. The date of issue, where known, is shown in brackets, otherwise an approximate date is shown prefixed by 'C'.

Reference Code
(a) British issues: un-numbered series, series issued by more than one manufacturer, and different series of the same title issued by a single firm, have been given an 'H' or 'Ha' number cross-referencing to Handbooks Parts I and II respectively, which provide further information. In some cases it might be necessary to follow the 'H' number through to Handbook Part II, the updated British Tobacco Issues Handbook 2003 edition, and also the World Tobacco Indexes (i.e. H.189 in Handbook Part I, Ha.189 in Handbook Part II, and XI/H.189 in World Index).
(b) Foreign issues: 'RB18' or 'RB 21' followed by a number refers to the Tobacco War reference book or the British American Tobacco reference book respectively. 'WI' and 'WII' refer to World Tobacco Index Part I and Part II respectively. A reference number following a Wills series relates to the Wills Reference Book (details of these publications will be found on page viii).

Prices
The last two columns show the London Cigarette Card Company's selling prices for odd cards and complete sets in very good condition. Where no price is shown, this does not necessarily mean that the Company are permanently unable to supply, and if you require items in this category please request a quotation enclosing a self-addressed envelope either with an International Reply Coupon or ready-stamped for posting in Britain.

HOW TO ORDER

Availability
We have one of the world's largest stocks of cigarette cards and the chances are that we will be able to supply your requirements for most series at the prices shown in the catalogue. However, certain odd cards, particularly from rarer series, may not be available in top condition and in such cases it is helpful if you indicate whether cards of a lower standard are acceptable at reduced prices. If a complete set is not in stock, we may be able to offer a part set, with one or two cards missing, at the appropriate fraction of full catalogue price. In some instances we can supply sets on request in fair to good condition at half catalogue price. If in doubt, please write for a quotation, enclosing a stamped, self-addressed envelope.

End Numbers
When ordering 'end' numbers, for example Nos. 1 and 50 of a set of fifty, please note that the following applies. For series catalogued up to £1 per card, end cards are charged at treble price. For series catalogued from £1 to £3 per card, end cards are charged at £3 per card. And for series catalogued at more than £3 per card there is no additional charge for end numbers.

Postage
Inland second class post is included in all prices quoted. Overseas postage is charged at cost.

Ordering and Payment
Please ensure that your name and full address are clearly shown. State the maker's name and the set title required (with 'first series', 'second series', date of issue, etc. as appropriate). For odds, please list each individual number wanted. Make your crossed cheque or postal order payable to The London Cigarette Card Company Limited and enclose with order. Notes and coins should be registered. Overseas payments can only be accepted by Sterling cheque drawn on a British bank or by credit/debit card. Please note we are unable to accept orders under £2.00. We accept Mastercard, Visa, American Express, Switch and Maestro credit/debit cards. Quote your card number and the card security code (which is the last three numbers in the signature strip), expiry date (and, for Switch and Maestro cards, the issue number if one is shown, or start date). Please allow 14 days for delivery. Send your order to:

The London Cigarette Card Co. Ltd.
Sutton Road, Somerton, Somerset TA11 6QP, England

24-Hour Telephone Order Line
For the convenience of customers, an answering machine is in operation to receive orders when the office is closed. Just leave your order, name and address with credit or debit card number and expiry date, and it will be dealt with as soon as possible. Please note that we can only deal with odds orders and general enquiries in office hours. Telephone number: 01458-273452 (International ++44 1458-273452).

Fax Machine
Our fax machine is on 24 hours a day to receive orders. Just place your order stating your name, address, credit or debit card number and expiry date. The fax number is 01458-273515 (International ++44 1458-273515).

E-Mail & Website
Our e-mail address is cards@londoncigcard.co.uk . Orders can also be placed using our secure website through the special requests page (www.londoncigcard.co.uk).

Remember that your cards will look their best when displayed in one of our albums: please see pages x and xi. Value Added Tax where applicable is included in all prices shown, at the current rate of 17½%.

Shop
For further information about the shop, including opening times, please see page v. Odd cards for collectors' wants lists are not stocked at the shop, but are available from our headquarters in Sutton Road on Mondays to Fridays from 9.30am to 1pm and 2pm to 4.30pm.

Guarantee
In the unlikely event that you, the collector, are not satisfied with the cards supplied, we guarantee to replace them or refund your money, provided the goods are returned within 14 days of receipt. This guarantee does not affect your statutory rights.

VISIT OUR SHOP
L.C.C.C., West Street, Somerton, Somerset TA11 7PR

Visit our shop in the centre of Somerton and you will be amazed at the selection of cards on display, with a superb range covering all kinds of subjects. You are welcome to browse, and you can sit at tables to view cards in comfort.

MORE THAN 4,500 DIFFERENT SETS ON DISPLAY • PRICES FROM £2.00

Albums, leaves, books, catalogues, new issues and frames
Large displays of framed cards from £10.00 etc

SPECIAL OFFERS TO VISITORS

Luxury Albums with 30 leaves on special offer at £9.50
Large Trade Card Albums with 30 leaves on special offer at £12.50

☆ **Saving £2.00 per Album** ☆

Save up to 50% off catalogue prices with our large selection of

☆ **Trade Card Sets at only £2.00** ☆

The Shop is conveniently located in Somerton town centre at the entrance to the main Brunel car park (free parking)

SHOP OPENING TIMES:

Monday, Tuesday, Thursday and Friday 9.30 to 1.00 and 2.00 to 5.00
Wednesday and Saturday 9.30 to 1.00
Telephone: 01458-274148 (shop only)
General enquiries, mail order department and 24-hour order line on 01458-273452

Please note that wants lists for odd cards cannot be dealt with at our shop. Collectors who require odd cards are most welcome to call at our head office in Sutton Road, Somerton (not open on Saturdays, telephone 01458-273452) which is only ⅓rd of a mile away.

OUR WEBSITE

www.londoncigcard.co.uk

OVER 4,500 SERIES NOW LISTED

We have completely updated and revised our website and this continues to be updated every month. The number of Thematic Lists in the Cards section has been increased, with a new feature being that each list now has a search button – so if, for instance, on the Football List you are searching for Arsenal Football sets, you just type in the word 'Arsenal' and all the sets that have the word Arsenal in the title will be displayed; similarly on the Sci-Fi list, typing 'Doctor Who' will display all the Doctor Who series.

OVER 4,000 SERIES ILLUSTRATED

On the Thematic Lists there are over 4,000 view buttons which link to sample illustrations.

Subjects covered:

American Football, Baseball etc	Native North American Indians
Animals and Wildlife	Pop Stars & Singers
Aviation, Space Travel & Astronomy	Railways
Birds, Butterflies & Moths	Reprints
Boxing	Royalty
Brook Bond Issues	Rugby League & Union
Cricket	Sci-Fi, plus Films & TV
Dinosaurs	Sci-Fi Star Trek
Dogs & Pets	Sci-Fi Star Wars
Film & Stage Stars 1920-40 Issues	Ships, Shipping & Naval
Fish, Fishing & the Ocean	Speedway
Flags, Arms & Maps	Sports General
Flowers, Trees & Gardening	Tennis
Football	Wrestling
Golf	Miscellaneous Cigarette Card Issues
Horses & the Turf	Miscellaneous Trade Card Issues
Military	Selection of Cigarette Card Sets £20 & under
Motoring	Selection of Trade Card Sets under £5

The website has over 4,500 series that can be bought through the 'buy' buttons, which can all be ordered securely through the **secure Thawte Certified Server ordering system**. There are also over 80 Sets of the Month, each with descriptions and illustrations. Plus special offers pages changed each month.

OTHER PAGES ON THE WEBSITE

New Issues	Reference Books	Magazine
Frames	Catalogues	Our Shop
Albums		Valuing and Selling

There is also an auction page which each month describes the forthcoming monthly auction and also has illustrations of some of the lots.

GIVE THE WEBSITE A VISIT – YOU WILL NOT BE DISAPPOINTED!

www.londoncigcard.co.uk

THE MAGAZINE FOR CARD COLLECTORS OLD & NEW

Over 150 sets offered each month at bargain discount prices to subscribers

CARD COLLECTORS NEWS

MONTHLY MAGAZINE
Now in its 76th Year

Cigarette Card News, launched in 1933, has been published continuously through peace-time and in war. In 1965 the title was changed to Cigarette Card News and Trade Card Chronicle in recognition of the growing importance of trade cards in the modern collecting world. Now, to mark the new millennium, our magazine is re-named 'Card Collectors News', retaining the initials 'CCN' familiar to generations of cartophilists. Today's magazine maintains the traditions established in the 1930s whilst giving full coverage to all the latest new card series and developments in the hobby.

Join subscribers all over the world who find Card Collectors News keeps them in touch with what's going on, and saves them money too!

Your subscription will cover 12 magazines posted monthly to your address

PLUS

- *Save £s with Subscribers' Special Offers with up to 25% off the catalogue price of selected sets*
- *FREE monthly 400-lot auction catalogue. Postal bidding open to collectors from around the world. Lots to suit every collector and pocket (many lots under £10)*
- *FREE sample card with every issue*
- *Set of the Month with up to 25% off the catalogue price*
- *Details of new series available from stock*

Inside the magazine itself you will find information about new card series, special commemorative features, interesting articles by expert contributors, research information by collectors and the compilers etc.

All this for just £22.00 a year (Europe £31.00, outside Europe £37.00)
Individual specimen copies £1.85 each

We also supply **Special Magazine Binders** each designed to hold 12 copies in a choice of attractive blue or maroon covers with gold lettering.
Price £7.50 each

Available only from
THE LONDON CIGARETTE CARD CO. LTD., SUTTON ROAD, SOMERTON, SOMERSET, ENGLAND TA11 6QP

CARTOPHILIC REFERENCE BOOKS

British Tobacco Issues Handbook. (Updated Edition 2003), 369 pages with over 2,600 cards illustrated, updates the original Handbooks Parts I & II, but excludes Ogden, Wills and The Godfrey Phillips Group of Companies **£23.50**

Handbook Part II (1920 to 1940) British Tobacco Issues. Updated by the above book, but includes Godfrey Phillips Silks listings. 164 pages, illustrated. Published at £12.00
.... **Special Offer Price £6.00**

World Tobacco Issues Part I. (Updated Edition 2000), issuers A to K, 344 pages **£22.50**

World Tobacco Issues Part II. (Updated Edition 2000), issuers L to Z, plus Anonymous, 362 pages **£22.50**

The above two books, updated to 31st August 2000, are a revision of the World Tobacco Indexes Parts I to V combined (but not the Handbooks) with many additions & amendments. They do not contain the Handbook and therefore do not have subject listings.

World Tobacco Card Index and Handbook Part I. 701 pages and nearly 2,000 cards illustrated .... **Out of Print**

World Tobacco Card Index Part II. Supplement to Index I, 452 pages with approximately 3,600 cards illustrated .... **Out of Print**

World Tobacco Card Index Part III. Supplement to Index I and II, 504 pages with more than 650 cards illustrated **£25.00**

World Tobacco Card Index Part IV. Supplement to Index I, II and III, 688 pages, illustrated .. **£18.50**

World Tobacco Card Index Part V. Supplement to Index I, II, III and IV, 552 pages with approximately 1,300 cards illustrated **£18.50**

Handbook of Worldwide Tobacco and Trade Silk Issues. 342 pages, illustrated. **£50.00**

Australian and New Zealand Card Issues. Over 300 pages with 600 cards illustrated ... **Out of Print**

Australian and New Zealand Card Issues Part II. 257 pages, more than 550 cards illustrated .. **£15.50**

The Card Issues of Abdulla/Adkin/Anstie. 20 pages **£4.00**

The Card Issues of Ardath Tobacco. 28 pages **£4.00**

The Card Issues of Churchman. 36 pages with 29 cards illustrated **£4.00**

The Card Issues of Faulkner. 12 pages **£4.00**

The Card Issues of Gallaher. 40 pages **£4.00**

The Card Issues of Hill. 28 pages **£4.00**

The Card Issues of Lambert & Butler. 32 pages with 25 cards illustrated **£4.00**

The Card Issues of Ogdens. (Updated Edition 2005), 330 pages with 815 illustrations **£20.00**

The Card Issues of Godfrey Phillips. 40 pages with 225 cards illustrated **£4.00**

The Card Issues of John Player. 44 pages with 26 cards illustrated **£4.00**

The Card Issues of Taddy. 32 pages with 30 cards illustrated **£4.00**

The New Tobacco War Reference Book. 236 pages, 2,330 cards illustrated **£20.00**

The Card Issues of Wills and BAT combined. 402 pages, illustrated **£20.00**

Guide Book No. 1, Ty-Phoo Tea Cards. 36 pages with 68 cards illustrated **£4.00**

Guide Book No. 2, F. & J. Smith Cards. 36 pages with 79 cards illustrated **£4.00**

Guide Book No. 3, A & BC Gum Cards. 44 pages with 29 cards illustrated (3rd edition 2004) .. **£4.00**

British Trade Card Index Part I. Pre-1945 issues .... **Out of Print**

British Trade Card Index Part II. 1945-1968 issues .... **Out of Print**

British Trade Card Index Part III. 1968-1986 issues, 400 pages with 480 cards illustrated ... **£12.50**

British Trade Card Index Part IV. 1986-1994 issues, 411 pages with 550 cards illustrated **£20.00**

British Trade Card Index Issues up to 1970. (Updated Edition 2006), 516 pages **£25.00**

British Trade Card Index Handbook Issues up to 1970. (Updated Edition 2006), 542 pages .. **£25.00**

Directory of British Tobacco Issuers. 36 pages with 16 cards illustrated **£4.00**

Glossary of Cartophilic Terms. 40 pages with 27 cards illustrated **£4.00**

BOOKS FOR THE COLLECTOR

Trade Card Catalogue, 2009 edition with **colour illustrations**. This is the only major catalogue devoted to trade cards. It gives details of a magnificent selection of over 6,000 different series issued by non-tobacco companies, with prices for sets, odd cards and makers' albums. The new 34th edition features the issues of Brooke Bond, Bassett, Topps, Typhoo, Inkworks, Rittenhouse, Comic Images and hundreds of other firms, with prices from £2.25 a set. Contains eight-page section with 61 colour illustrations. **£5.50**

Liebig Card Catalogue, 2009 edition. This price guide (not illustrated) lists over 1500 of these fascinating sets issued in different European languages (all except the earliest) by this manufacturer. It includes a brief history of the company, an English translation of each set title, together with Fada reference, the number in each set and date of issue from 1891 to 1973. . . . . **£4.50**

Brooke Bond Tea Cards Reference Book. The definitive reference book with 319 colour illustrations of cards and albums including overseas issues and the story of the company's first hundred years from one shop to market leader. **£12.50**

Brooke Bond Picture Cards "The First Forty Years". This invaluable 72-page reference book detailing all the issues of Brooke Bond Tea from 1954 to 1994. It includes British issues as well as overseas issues with illustrations. **£7.00**

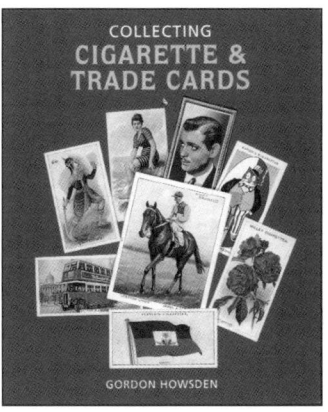

Collecting Cigarette & Trade Cards by Gordon Howsden. Traces the history and development of cards from their beginning to the present day and includes the background of the issuing firms, thematic collecting, printing and production, grading, pricing and so on. Authoritatively written in an easy-to-read style and beautifully illustrated in colour, the book approaches the subject from a fresh angle which will appeal to seasoned collectors and newcomers alike. Cigarette & Trade Cards is not only an indispensable reference work but also a joy to read or just browse through. 152 large-format pages with 220 colour illustrations featuring 750 cards and related ephemera. **£17.00**

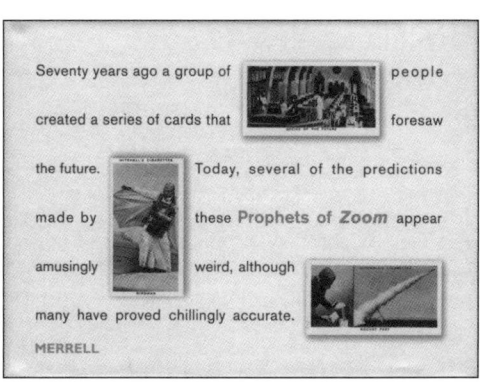

Prophets of Zoom. This hardback book reproduces the front and back of each card in Mitchell's 1936 series of 50 The World of Tomorrow, opposite which is pictured a modern equivalent. **£7.95**

All books are post-free to UK addresses.
Overseas orders postage at cost.

LUXURY ALBUMS

LUXURY BINDER WITH 30 LEAVES £11.50
MATCHING SLIP-CASE £5.00 (only supplied with binder)
EXTRA LEAVES 16p EACH
☆ GREY CARD INTERLEAVES — 30 FOR £3.50 ☆
(POST FREE TO UK ADDRESSES OR COLLECT FROM OUR SHOP)

Full display, front and back, is given to your cards in top quality transparent leaves held in a luxurious binder. The leaves are made from a tough, clear optical film. Binders are available in a choice of blue or maroon covers (with matching slip-cases as an optional extra) and each is supplied complete with 30 leaves, of which various sizes are available as listed below.

Page Ref.	Suitable for	Pockets Per Page	Pocket size (mm) wide × deep
A	Standard size cards	10	43 × 83
M	Medium size cards	8	55 × 83
D	Doncella/Grandee/Typhoo size cards	6	111 × 55
L	Large size cards	6	73 × 83
X	Extra large cards	4	111 × 83
P	Postcards	2	111 × 170
C	Cabinet size cards, booklets etc.	1	224 × 170
K	Miniature size cards	15	43 × 55

Remember to state which colour (blue or maroon) and which page reference/s you require.

Order by telephone (01458-273452), fax (01458-273515), e-mail (cards@londoncigcard.co.uk)
or through our website (www.londoncigcard.co.uk) 24 hours a day, 7 days a week
using your credit or debit cards, or you can order by post.

ALBUMS FOR LARGE TRADE CARDS

☆ An album designed specifically for modern trade cards like Skybox, Comic Images, Rittenhouse, Inkworks, Topps etc
☆ The ideal way to display your large modern trade cards to their best advantage
☆ 3-ring luxury padded binders in a choice of maroon or blue
☆ There are two types of leaves:
              9 pockets per sheet size 91 × 68mm, reference LT
              6 pockets per sheet size 138 × 66mm, reference WV
☆ Post free to UK addresses or collect from our shop (overseas postage at cost)

**COMPLETE ALBUM WITH 30 LEAVES
IN A CHOICE OF "LT" OR "WV" LEAVES £14.50 • EXTRA LEAVES 20p EACH**

☆ COLLECTORS' ACCESSORIES ☆

A neat and tidy way for you to deal with incomplete sets is to use our
numbered, printed 'wants' lists

30 adhesive lists numbered 1 to 50 .... 75p

The professional way to wrap sets for safe storage is with our translucent
glascine wrapping strips

200 strips size 123 × 68 mm for standard size cards £3.50
200 strips size 175 × 83mm for large cards £4.00
200 strips size 228 × 83mm for extra-large cards £4.50

FRAMES FOR YOUR CARDS

Why not select cards on the subject of your choice and frame them to make an interesting decorative feature for your home or workplace? Ideal also as a 'personal interest' gift for friends and relatives. Frames also enable you to display a themed selection or a complete set as an alternative to storing them away in an album. Using top quality materials to give a really professional finish, our frames are designed with glass on both sides so that the cards can be placed in the mount to display both fronts and backs without risk of damage.

COMPLETE FRAMES

Complete kit includes wooden frame, mounting board, two sheets of glass, spring clips, etc, ready for wall display in the following sizes:

Standard Size Cards 36 × 68mm		Large Size Cards 62 × 80mm		Modern Large Size Cards 64 × 89mm	
50 cards	£35.00	25 cards	£35.00	12 cards	£24.00
25 cards	£24.00	24 cards	£35.00	10 cards	£24.00
15 cards	£20.00	20 cards	£35.00	6 cards	£17.00
10 cards	£16.00	15 cards	£30.00		
3 cards	£9.50	12 cards	£24.00		
1 card	£9.50	9 cards	£20.00		
		6 cards	£17.00		

1 postcard size card (104 × 151mm) £9.50   1 postcard size card (89 × 140mm) £9.50

Mounting board colours as shown below

SEPARATE MOUNTING BOARDS AVAILABLE

Mounting boards can be purchased separately in green, black, brown or maroon as follows:

Standard Size Cards 36 × 68mm		Large Size Cards 62 × 80mm		Modern Large Size Cards 64 × 89mm	
50 cards	£5.00	25 cards	£5.00	12 cards	£3.50
25 cards	£3.50	24 cards	£5.00	10 cards	£3.50
15 cards	£3.00	20 cards	£5.00	6 cards	£2.50
10 cards	£2.50	15 cards	£5.00		
3 cards	£2.50	12 cards	£3.50		
1 card	£2.50	9 cards	£3.00		
		6 cards	£2.50		

1 postcard size card (104 × 151mm) £2.50   1 postcard size card (89 × 140mm) £2.50

FRAMES OF CARDS MAKE IDEAL PRESENTS
POST FREE TO UK ADDRESSES, OR COLLECT FROM OUR SHOP
THE LONDON CIGARETTE CARD COMPANY LIMITED
Mail order telephone 01458-273452 (24 hrs), fax 01458-273515 or e-mail cards@londoncigcard.co.uk

2009 AUCTIONS

WE HAVE BEEN AUCTIONING FOR OVER 70 YEARS
CARDS TO SUIT EVERY COLLECTOR

Monthly 400-lot postal auctions of cigarette and trade cards and associated items with estimated values from as little as £1 up to many hundreds. Lots to interest every collector and suit their pocket.

Postal Auctions for 2009 are as follows:

Friday,	2nd January
Saturday,	31st January
Saturday,	28th February
Saturday,	28th March
Saturday,	25th April
Saturday,	30th May
Saturday,	27th June
Saturday,	25th July
Saturday,	29th August
Saturday,	26th September
Saturday,	31st October
Saturday,	28th November

Each postal auction finishes at midnight on the above dates.

A guide to how we assess condition and how to bid can be found on our bidding sheet so it couldn't be easier if you are an 'auction beginner'.

There are no additional charges to bidders for buyer's premium so bidding is straightforward, with no 'hidden extras'.

Each lot is described with an estimate of its value reflecting the condition of the cards, ranging from poor right through to mint condition, and for over 70 years collectors have bid with complete confidence, knowing that every effort is made to describe the lots accurately.

Each auction contains a selection of rare sets, rare and scarce individual cards, pre-1918 issues, 1920-40 series, old and modern trade issues including Brooke Bond, errors and varieties, silks, albums, books, Liebigs, cigarette packets etc – in fact plenty to interest everyone.

Auction catalogues are available <u>FREE OF CHARGE</u>, 4 weeks before the date of sale from The London Cigarette Card Company Limited, Sutton Road, Somerton, Somerset TA11 6QP
Telephone: 01458 273452   Fax: 01458 273515
E-mail: auctions@londoncigcard.co.uk

The Auction Catalogue can be found on our website, which contains a preview of each auction as well as facilities for on-line bidding – visit www.londoncigcard.co.uk for further details.

Also a copy of the auction catalogue is automatically sent each month to subscribers to our magazine *Card Collectors News* (subscription details on page vii of this catalogue).

REGIMENTAL BOOKS

The following series of books featuring the different Regiments and Corps of the British Army illustrated on Cigarette and Trade cards, contain History, Uniforms, Badges, Regimental Colours, Victoria Cross Winners and Personalities. Approximately 200 illustrations in each book, 56 pages with 16 in full colour, all produced by David J. Hunter.

The Coldstream Guards	£8.50
The Gordon Highlanders	£8.50
Queen's Own Highlanders (Seaforth & Camerons)	£8.50
The Queen's Royal Lancers	£8.50
The Regiments of Wales (The Welsh Guards, The Royal Welsh Fusiliers & The Royal Regiment of Wales)	£8.50
The Royal Army Medical Corps	£8.50
The Royal Marines	£8.50
The Royal Regiment of Fusiliers — Part 1 (The Royal Northumberland Fusiliers & The Royal Warwickshire Regiment)	£8.50
The Royal Regiment of Fusiliers — Part 2 (The Royal Fusiliers (City of London Regiment) & The Lancashire Fusiliers)	£8.50
The Scotts Guards	£8.50
The Worcestershire & Sherwood Foresters Regiment	£8.50

All books are post-free to UK addresses. Overseas orders postage at cost.

GREETING CARDS
A CARD FOR EVERY OCCASION

Only £1.25 each

Choose from 72 subjects

Greetings cards which feature cigarette cards on all manner of different subjects, beautifully printed in colour, and with the bonus of early packet designs from the firms which issued the cards reproduced on the back. The insides are blank so that they can be used for any and every occasion. This is a brilliant idea for collectors. Send them to friends or relatives, include them with gifts, or just collect them yourself.

Aesop's Fables	Aircraft	Alpine Flowers	Astronomy
Aviators	Bats	Batsmen	Bowling
Boxing	Boy Scouts	Brahms & Liszt	Butterflies
Cars	Celebrated Oils	Cinema Stars	Composers
Cycling (Lady Cyclists)	Cycling (3 Profiled Bikes)	Deer	Derby Winners
Dogs (Hounds)	Dogs (Terriers)	Elizabethan Mis-Quotes	Film Stars
Fire Appliances	Firefighters	Flowering Trees	Flowers in Pots
Freshwater Fish	Frogs and Toads	Gilbert & Sullivan	Golfers
Grand National Winners	Hares & Rabbits	Highland Regiments	Highway Code
Jovial Golfers (Humorous)	Keep Fit	Lighthouses	Lizards
Marine Life (Jellyfish etc)	Marine Life (Penguin etc)	Marine Mammals	Medals
Merchant Ships	Mice	Mis-Quotes	Motor Cycles
Mythology	Newts	Old English Flowers	Owls
Parrots	Polar Exploration	Poultry	Predatory Mammals
Proverbs	Railway Engines	Red Indians (Pocahontas)	Red Indians (Geronomo)
Roses	Rowing	Sea Shells	Small Mammals
Snakes	Speed Boats	Teaching	Tennis (Men's Shots)
Warships	Wicketkeeping	Wild Flowers	Wildlife (Badger etc)

TOP QUALITY, DISTINCTIVE AND EYE-CATCHING CARDS WHICH STAND OUT FROM ALL THE OTHERS AS SOMETHING COMPLETELY DIFFERENT — SIZE 150 x 100mm ONLY £1.25 EACH INCLUDING ENVELOPE

See them all in our West Street shop, or order direct from
**THE LONDON CIGARETTE CARD COMPANY LIMITED
SUTTON ROAD, SOMERTON, SOMERSET TA11 6QP**

CARD SIZES (Applies to British issues only)

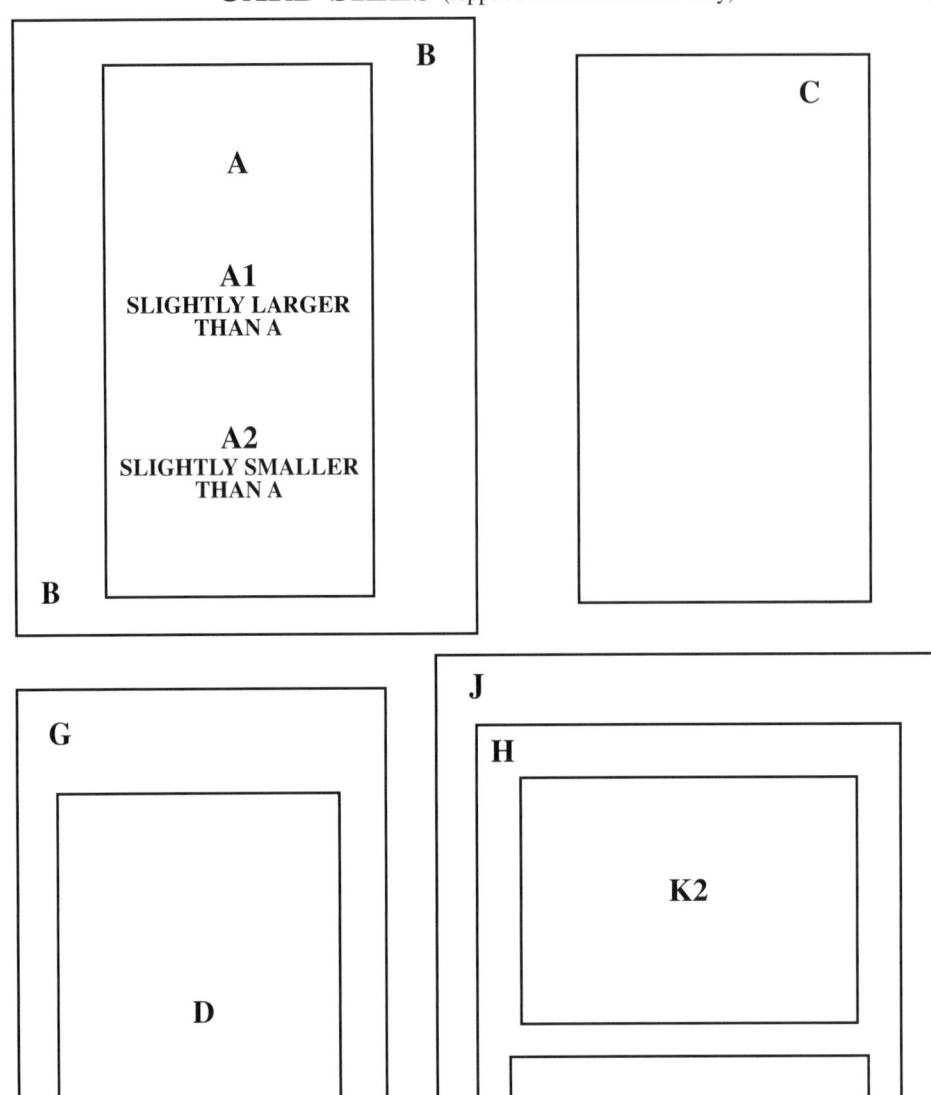

SECTION I

BRITISH CIGARETTE CARDS

INDEX OF BRANDS

The following is a list of the cases so far known where cards appear without the name of issuer, but inscribed with a brand name or other indication which is the collector's only clue to the identity of the issuer.

A   INDEX OF BRANDS and initials found on British issues of cards or silks

Airmail Cigarettes — see Hill
All Arms Cigarettes — see Ray & Co.

BDV Cigarettes — see Godfrey Phillips
Bandmaster Cigarettes — see Cohen, Weenen & Drapkin
Big Gun Cigarettes — see Sandorides
Black Cat Cigarettes — see Carreras
Blush of Day Cigarettes — see Robinson & Barnsdale
Borneo Queen Cigars — see B. Morris
Broadway Novelties — see Teofani
The Buffs — see Drapkin
Bulldog Cigars — see Elliot

Cake Walk Cigarettes — see Pezaro
Caps The Lot — see Bewlay
Casket and Critic Cigarettes — see Pattreiouex
Castella Cigars — see W.D. & H.O. Wills
Chairman Cigarettes — see R.J. Lea
The Challenge Flat Brilliantes — see Gloag
Citamora Cigarettes — see Gloag
Club Member Cigarettes — see Pattreiouex
Club Mixture Tobaccos — see Continental Cigarette Factory
Colin Campbell Cigars — see Robinson & Barnsdale
Crowfoot Cigarettes — see Hill
Cymax Cigarettes — see Coudens

Double Ace Cigarettes — see Ardath

Eldona Cigars — see Drapkin & Millhoff
Erinmore Cigarettes — see Murray
Explorer Cigars — see Drapkin & Millhoff

The Favourite Magnums Cigarettes — see Teofani
The Flor de Dindigul Cigar — see Bewlay
Forecasta — see B. Morris
Four Square — see Dobie
Fresher Cigarettes — see Challis

GP — see Godfrey Phillips
Gainsborough Cigarettes — see Cohen Weenen
Gala Cigarettes — issuers unknown, see under Miscellaneous
General Favourite Onyx — issuers unknown, see under Anonymous
Gibson Girl Virginia, Madrali Turkish and Hungarian — see Golds
Gold Flake Cigarettes — see Hill
Gold Flake, Honeydew and Navy Cut Medium Cigarettes — see Hill
The Greys Cigarettes — see United Kingdom Tobacco Co.
Guards Cigarettes — see Carreras

Hawser, Epaulet and Honey Flake Cigarettes — see Wholesale Tobacco Supply Syndicate
Heart's Delight Cigarettes — see Pritchard & Burton

Imperial Tobacco Limited (Castella) — see W.D. & H.O. Wills

Jersey Lily Cigarettes — see Wm. Bradford
Cigarette Job — see Societe Job
Junior Member Cigarettes — see Pattreiouex

Kensitas Cigarettes — see J. Wix

King Edward VII Cigarettes — see Cabana

Leon de Cuba Cigars — see Eldons
Levant Favourites — see B. Morris
Life Ray Cigarettes — see Ray & Co.
Lucana Cigarettes — see Sandorides

Manikin Cigars — see Freeman
Matossian's Cigarettes — see Henley & Watkins
Max Cigarettes — see A. & M. Wix
Mayblossom Cigarettes — see Lambert & Butler
Mills — see Amalgamated

New Orleans Tobacco — see J. & T. Hodge

1a, 27 & 33 Leigh Road, Eastleigh — see Ingram's
Oracle Cigarettes — see Tetley

Park Drive — see Gallaher
Pibroch Virginia — see Fryer
Pick-Me-Up Cigarettes — see Drapkin & Millhoff
Pinnace — see Godfrey Phillips
Pioneer Cigarettes — see Richmond Cavendish
Polo Mild Cigarettes — see Murray
Private Seal Tobacco — see Godfrey Phillips

QV Cigars — see Webster

RS — see Robert Sinclair
Reina Regenta Cigars — see B. Morris
De Reszke Cigarettes — see Millhoff and Godfrey Phillips
Ringers Cigarettes — see Edwards, Ringer & Bigg
Roseland Cigarettes — see Glass

St Dunstan's — see Carreras
Senior Service Cigarettes — see Pattreiouex
Spinet Cigarettes or The Spinet House — see Hill
The Spotlight Tobaccos — see Hill
Star of the World Cigarettes — see JLS
State Express Cigarettes — see Ardath
Summit — see International Tobacco Co.
Sunripe Cigarettes — see Hill
Sunspot Cigarettes — see Theman
Sweet Alva Cigarettes — see Drapkin

TSS — see Tobacco Supply Syndicate
Tatley's Cigarettes — see Walker's Tobacco Co.
Three Bells Cigarettes — see J. & F. Bell
Tipsy Loo Cigarettes — see H.C. Lloyd
Topsy Cigarettes — see Richards & Ward
Trawler, Critic and King Lud Cigarettes — see Pattreiouex
Turf Cigarettes — see Carreras

WTC — see Walker's Tobacco Co.

B INDEX OF INSCRIPTIONS found on British issues of cards

'The Cigarettes with which these Picture Cards are issued are manufactured in England and are Guaranteed Pure' — see Hill
'England expects that Every Man will do his duty — By Purchasing these Cigarettes you are supporting British labour' — issuers unknown, see Anonymous
'Issued with these Famous Cigarettes' — see Teofani
'Issued with these Fine Cigarettes' — see Teofani
'Issued with these High Grade Cigarettes' — see Teofani
'Issued with these Well-known Cigarettes' — see Teofani
'Issued with these World Famous Cigarettes' — see Teofani
'Presented with these well-known choice cigarettes' — see Teofani
'Smoke these cigarettes always' — see Teofani
'These Cigarettes are Guaranteed Best British Manufacture' — see Hill.

C INDEX OF OTHER INDICATIONS found on British Tobacco issues

THE B.I. Co. — see Burnstein Isaacs
Chantler & Co., Bury — see Lea
'Eagle, Cork' — see Lambkin
Agnes D. Eld, Dudley — see Lea
L. & Y. Tobacco Co. -— see Lancs. and Yorks. Tobacco Manufacturing Co.
Orient Line Steamships — see Singleton & Cole
PO Box 5764, Johannesburg — see A. & M. Wix
S.C. Peacock Sales Co. — see Lea

Size	Printing	Number in set		Handbook reference	Price per card	Complete set

ABDULLA & CO. LTD, London

20 page reference book (combined with Adkin & Anstie) — £4.00

A EXPORT ISSUES POST-1920

Size	Print	No.	Title	Ref	Price	Set
A	BW	50	Beauties of To-Day (1938)	Ha.514	£3.60	—
A	C	25	British Butterflies (1935)	Ha.517-1	£1.20	£30.00
A	P	52	Cinema Stars Set 1 (c1933)	Ha.515-1B	£4.00	—
A2	U	30	Cinema Stars Set 2 (c1933)	Ha.515-2	£5.00	—
A2	U	30	Cinema Stars Set 3 (c1933)	Ha.515-3	£4.00	—
A2	U	32	Cinema Stars Set 4 (c1933)	Ha.515-4	£2.50	£80.00
A2	C	32	Cinema Stars Set 5 (c1933)	Ha.515-5	£2.50	£80.00
A2	C	30	Cinema Stars Set 6 (c1933)	Ha.515-6	£3.60	—
D	C	25	Feathered Friends (1935)	Ha.516	£1.20	£30.00
A2	C	50	Film Favourites (1934)	Ha.517-2	£4.00	—
A	C	50	Film Stars (1934)		£8.00	—
—	C	24	*Film Stars (128 × 89mm) (c1934)	Ha.517-3	£8.00	—
A	C	25	Old Favourites (1936) (Flowers)	Ha.517-4	80p	£20.00
A	C	40	Screen Stars (1939):			
			A Normal Abdulla back		£1.25	£50.00
			B 'Issued by the Successors to ...' back		£2.50	—
A2	C	50	Stage and Cinema Beauties (1935)	Ha.517-5	£4.00	—
A	U	30	Stars of the Stage and Screen (c1934)		£4.00	—

B MISCELLANEOUS

Size	Print	No.	Title	Ref	Price	Set
		? 4	Bridge Rule Cards (various sizes) (c1935)		£16.00	—
—	C	2	Commanders of the Allies (127 × 67mm) (c1915)		£75.00	—
	BW	3	Great War Gift Packings Cards (1916)		£75.00	—
A	U	18	Message Cards (letters of the alphabet) (c1936)		£12.00	—
K2	U	18	Message Cards (letters of the alphabet) (c1936)		£12.00	—

ADCOCK & SON, Norwich

POST-1920 ISSUE

Size	Print	No.	Title	Ref	Price	Set
A1	U	12	Ancient Norwich (1928)		—	£140.00
			11/12 Ancient Norwich (No. 6 missing)		£3.00	£33.00

ADKIN & SONS, London

20 page reference book (combined with Abdulla & Anstie) — £4.00

A PRE-1919 ISSUES

Size	Print	No.	Title	Ref	Price	Set
D	BW	25	*Actresses — French. Nd. 126-150 (c1898)	H.1	£180.00	—
A	C	15	*Beauties 'PAC' (c1898)	H.2	£300.00	—
A2	C	12	Character Sketches:	H.3		
			A Black printing on back (1901)		£7.50	£90.00
			B Green printing on back (1902)		£7.50	£90.00
A2	C	12	A Living Picture (c1901):	H.5		
			A 'Adkin & Sons' at top back			
			(i) crimson		£7.50	£90.00
			(ii) scarlet		£7.50	£90.00
			B 'These cards are ...' at top back		£7.50	£90.00
A	BW	25	Notabilities (1915)	H.6	£5.00	£125.00
A1	C	12	Pretty Girl Series (Actresses) (c1897)	H.7	£60.00	—
A2	C	12	*Pretty Girl Series 'RASH' (1897):	H.8		
			A Calendar back		£60.00	—
			B Advertisements back		£35.00	—
			C Figure and verse back		£35.00	—
D	C	12	A Royal Favourite (1900)	H.9	£12.00	£145.00

Size	Print-ing	Number in set		Handbook reference	Price per card	Complete set

ADKIN & SONS, London *(continued)*

A	BW		Soldiers of the Queen (1899-1900):	H.10		
			A Series of 50:			
		24	(a) Nos. 1-24 '... and exclusively with'		£27.00	—
		50	(b) Nos. 1-50 and variety '... and issued with ...'		£5.00	£250.00
		59	B Series of 60, plus No. 61 (Nos 28, 33 not issued)		£4.50	
A	BW	31	*Soldiers of the Queen and Portraits (1901)	H.11	£5.50	£170.00
A	C	30	Sporting Cups and Trophies (1914)		£17.00	—
A	BW	25	War Trophies (1917)		£5.00	£125.00

B POST-1920 ISSUES

A	C	50	Butterflies and Moths (1924)	H.80	£1.90	£95.00
A	C	50	Wild Animals of the World (1922)	H.77	£1.70	£85.00

C MISCELLANEOUS

—	C	12	Character Sketches (premium issue) (c1901)	H.3	£100.00	—
—	C	4	*Games — by Tom Browne, postcard back (135 × 85mm) (c1900)	H.4	£300.00	—
—	C	12	A Living Picture (premium issue) (c1900)	H.5	£100.00	—

AIKMAN'S, Montrose

PRE-1919 ISSUE

D	C	30	*Army Pictures, Cartoons, etc. (c1916)	H.12	£110.00	—

H.J. AINSWORTH, Harrogate

PRE-1919 ISSUE

D	C	30	*Army Pictures, Cartoons, etc (1916)	H.12	£110.00	—

ALBERGE & BROMET, London

PRE-1919 ISSUES

A	C		*Boer War and General Interest (c1900):	H.13		
		? 11	A 'Bridal Bouquet' and 'El Benecio' wording on green leaf design back		£100.00	—
		? 2	B 'La Optima' and 'Federation' wording on green leaf design back		£150.00	—
		? 8	C 'Bridal Bouquet' and 'El Benecio' wording on brown leaf design back		£100.00	—
Dl	C	40	*Naval and Military Phrases (c1904):	H.14		
			A 'Bridal Bouquet' and 'El Benecio'		£100.00	—
			B 'La Optima' and 'Federation'		£100.00	—
Dl	C	30	*Proverbs (c1903)	H.15	£100.00	—

PHILLIP ALLMAN & CO. LTD, London

POST-1940 ISSUES

A	C	50	Coronation Series (1953)		90p	£45.00
			Pin-up Girls (1953):	H.851		
A1	C		A First 12 subjects:			
		12	Ai Unnumbered, 'For men only'		£5.00	£60.00
		12	Aii Numbered, 'Ask for Allman always'		£4.00	£50.00
		12	Aiii Unnumbered, 'Ask for Allman always'		£4.00	£50.00
A1	C	12	B Second 12 subjects		£5.00	—
A1	C	24	C Inscribed '1st series of 24'		£8.00	—
—	C	24	D Large size (75 × 68mm)		£4.00	—

AMALGAMATED TOBACCO CORPORATION LTD ('Mills' Cigarettes)

A POST-1940 ISSUES

—	C	25	Famous British Ships 'Series No. 1' (75 × 48mm) (1952)		20p	£3.50

Size	Printing	Number in set		Handbook reference	Price per card	Complete set

AMALGAMATED TOBACCO CORPORATION LTD ('Mills' Cigarettes) *(continued)*

—	C	25	Famous British Ships 'Series No. 2' (75 × 48mm) (1952)		20p	£3.50
—	C	50	History of Aviation (75 × 48mm) (1952):			
			A Nos. 1 to 16, 18 to 25 and 27		£2.00	—
			B Nos. 17, 26 and 28 to 50		24p	£6.00
A	C	25	Kings of England (1954)		£1.60	£40.00
A	C	25	Propelled Weapons (1953)		20p	£4.00

B EXPORT ISSUES

A	C	25	Aircraft of the World (1958)	H.852	80p	£20.00
A	C	25	Animals of the Countryside (1957)	H.853	30p	£7.50
A	C	25	Aquarium Fish (1961)	H.854	20p	£4.00
A	C	25	Army Badges — Past and Present (1961)		90p	£22.50
A	C	25	British Coins and Costumes (1958)	H.855	36p	£9.00
A	C	25	British Locomotives (1961)	H.856	40p	£10.00
A	C	25	British Uniforms of the 19th Century (1957)	H.857	90p	£22.50
A	C	25	Butterflies and Moths (1957)	H.858	30p	£7.50
A	C	25	Cacti (1961)	H.859	50p	£12.50
A	C	25	Castles of Britain (1961)	H.860	£1.20	£30.00
A	C	25	Coins of the World (1961)	H.861	20p	£3.50
A	C	25	Communications (1961)	H.862	£1.00	£25.00
A	C	25	Dogs (1958)	H.863	70p	£17.50
A	C	25	Evolution of the Royal Navy (1957)	H.864	60p	£15.00
A	C	25	Football Clubs and Badges (1961)	H.865	£1.40	
A	C	25	Freshwater Fish (1958)	H.866	24p	£6.00
A	C	25	Guerriers à Travers les Ages (French text) (1961)	H.882	80p	£20.00
A	C	25	Historical Buildings (1959)	H.867	80p	£20.00
A	C	25	Histoire de l'Aviation, 1st series (French text) (1961)	H.868	20p	£5.00
A	C	25	Histoire de l'Aviation, 2nd series (French text) (1962)	H.868	£1.00	£25.00
A	C	25	Holiday Resorts (1957)	H.869	20p	£3.00
A	C	25	Interesting Hobbies (1959)	H.870	40p	£10.00
A	C	25	Into Space (1958)	H.871	28p	£7.00
A	C	25	Les Autos Moderns (French text) (1961)	H.875	50p	£12.50
A	C	25	Medals of the World (1959)	H.872	24p	£6.00
A	C	25	Merchant Ships of the World (1961)	H.873	60p	£15.00
A	C	25	Merveilles Modernes (French text) (1961)	H.876	40p	£10.00
A	C	25	Miniature Cars and Scooters (1959)	H.874	£1.20	£30.00
A	C	25	Nature (1958)	H.877	20p	£3.00
A	C	25	Naval Battles (1959)	H.878	40p	£10.00
A	C	25	Ports of the World (1957)	H.869	20p	£3.00
A	C	25	Ships of the Royal Navy (1961)	H.879	50p	£12.50
A	C	25	Sports and Games (1958)	H.880	£1.20	£30.00
A	C	25	Tropical Birds (1959)	H.881	£1.20	—
A	C	25	Weapons of Defence (1961)	H.883	£1.00	£25.00
A	C	25	Wild Animals (1958)	H.884	20p	£5.00
A	C	25	The Wild West (1960)	H.885	90p	£22.50
A	C	25	World Locomotives (1959)	H.886	£1.20	£30.00

THE ANGLO-AMERICAN CIGARETTE MAKING CO. LTD, London——

PRE-1919 ISSUE

A	C	20	Russo-Japanese War Series (1906)	H.100	£375.00	—

THE ANGLO CIGARETTE MANUFACTURING CO., London——

A PRE-1919 ISSUES

A	C	36	Tariff Reform Series (1909)	H.16	£30.00	—

Size	Print-ing	Number in set		Handbook reference	Price per card	Complete set

E. & W. ANSTIE, Devizes

20 page reference book (combined with Abdulla & Adkin) — £4.00

A PRE-1919 ISSUES
A	C	16	*British Empire Series (1904)	H.17	£12.50	£200.00
—	C	8	Puzzles (26 × 70mm) (1902)	H.18	£160.00	—
—	C	5	Royal Mail (70 × 50mm) (1899)	H.19	£250.00	—

B POST-1920 ISSUES
A2	C	25	Aesop's Fables (1934)	H.518	£3.00	£75.00
A	BW	40	Nature Notes (1939)		£10.00	—
A	U	50	People of Africa (1926)		£3.50	£175.00
A	U	50	People of Asia (1926)		£3.50	£175.00
A	U	50	People of Europe (1925)		£3.50	£175.00
A2	BW	40	Places of Interest (1939):			
			A Varnished front		90p	£36.00
			B Unvarnished front		£3.00	—
A	C	50	*Racing Series (1922):			
			1-25 — Racing Colours		£5.00	—
			26-50 — Horses, Jockeys, Race-courses, etc		£6.50	—
A	C	50	Scout Series (1923)		£3.50	£175.00
A2	C		Sectional Series:			
		10	Clifton Suspension Bridge (1938)	H.519-1	£2.50	£25.00
		10	Stonehenge (1936)	H.519-2	£2.50	£25.00
		10	The Victory (1936)	H.519-3	£4.00	—
		20	Wells Cathedral (1935)	H.519-4	£2.50	£50.00
		20	Wiltshire Downs (1935)	H.519-6	£2.50	£50.00
		10	Windsor Castle (1937)	H.519-5	£2.50	£25.00
A2	BW	40	Wessex (1938)		£1.50	£60.00
A	U	50	The World's Wonders (1924)		£1.60	£80.00

C SILKS. Anonymous unbacked woven silks. Width sizes only are quoted as the silks were prepared in ribbon form and length sizes are thus arbitrary.

—	C	10	*Flags, large (width 95mm) (c1915)	H.495-1	£11.00	—
—	C	36	*Flags, small (width 42mm) (c1915)	H.495-1	£1.80	—
—	C	85	*Regimental Badges (width 32mm) (c1915)	H.495-3	From £2.00	—
—	C		*Royal Standard and Portraits (c1915):	H.495-2		
		1	Royal Standard (width 61mm)		—	£15.00
		1	King George V:			
			(a) Large (width 71 mm), black frame		—	£70.00
			(b) Large (width 71mm), gold frame		—	£60.00
			(c) Small (width 15mm)		—	£70.00
		1	Queen Mary:			
			(a) Large (width 71 mm)		—	£60.00
			(b) Small (width 35mm)		—	£75.00
		1	Lord French (width 71mm)		—	£85.00
		1	Lord Kitchener (width 71mm)		—	£20.00

H. ARCHER & CO., London

PRE-1919 ISSUES
C	C		*Actresses — Selection from 'FROGA A and B' (c1900):	H.20		
		? 20	A 'Golden Returns' back		£65.00	—
		? 13	B 'M.F.H.' back		£65.00	—
C			*Beauties — 'CHOAB' (c1900):	H.21		
	U	50	A 'Bound to Win' front		£28.00	—
	C	? 4	B 'Golden Returns' back		£70.00	—
	C	? 5	C 'M.F.H.' back		£70.00	—
C	C	20	*Prince of Wales Series (c1912)	H.22	£30.00	—

Size	Print-ing	Number in set		Handbook reference	Price per card	Complete set

ARDATH TOBACCO CO. LTD, London

28 page reference book — £4.00

A PRE-1919 ISSUES. All export

Size	Print	Num	Description	Ref	Price	Set
—	U	30	Boucher Series (77 × 62mm) (c1915)		£3.00	—
A1	U	40	Franz Hals Series, Dutch back (c1916)		£15.00	—
—	U	30	Gainsborough Series (77 × 62mm) (c1915)	H.714	£3.00	—
A1	U	50	Great War Series (c1916)		£6.00	—
A1	U	50	Great War Series 'B' (c1916)		£6.00	—
A1	U	50	Great War Series 'C' (c1916)		£6.00	—
			Hollandsche Oude Meesters, Dutch back (70 × 60mm) (c1916):			
—	U	25	A First 25 subjects		£15.00	—
—	U	25	B Second 25 subjects		£15.00	—
—	U	30	Raphael Series (77 × 62mm) (c1915)		£3.00	—
—	U		Rembrandt Series (1914):			
		30	A Large size (77 × 62 mm), English back		£3.50	—
		40	B Large size (77 × 62mm), Dutch back		£16.00	—
		30	C Extra-large size (101 × 62mm)		£6.00	—
—	U	30	Rubens Series (77 × 61 mm) (c1915):			
			A English 'State Express' back		£3.00	—
			B English 'Winfred' back		£15.00	—
			C Dutch back		£15.00	—
			D New Zealand 'State Express' back		£15.00	—
—	C	12	Types of Smokers (c1910):	H.716		
			A Size 77 × 64mm		£75.00	—
			B Size 102 × 64mm		£75.00	—
—	U	30	Valasquez Series (c1915):			
			A Large size (77 × 62mm)		£3.50	—
			B Extra-large size (101 × 62mm)		£5.00	—

B POST-1920 NON-PHOTOGRAPHIC ISSUES

Size	Print	Num	Description	Ref	Price	Set
A1	C	50	*Animals at the Zoo (export) (c1924):	H.520		
			A Back with descriptive text		£2.50	—
			B Back without description, 'Double Ace' issue		£15.00	—
A	C	96	Ardath Modern School Atlas (export) (c1935)		£1.60	—
A	C	25	Big Game Hunting (export) (c1930):			
			A Back in blue		£4.00	—
			B Back in black		£15.00	—
A	U	50	Britain's Defenders (1936)		80p	£40.00
	U	50	British Born Film Stars (export) (1934):			
A2			A Small size, back white semi-glossy		£1.60	—
A2			B Small size, back cream matt		£1.60	—
—			C Medium size (67 × 53mm)		£2.70	—
	U		Camera Studies (c1939):	H.644		
—		36	A Small size (70 × 44mm)		£1.25	£45.00
—		45	B Large size (79 × 57mm)		£1.00	£45.00
—	C	25	Champion Dogs (95 × 67mm) (1934)		£1.80	£45.00
A	C	50	Cricket, Tennis and Golf Celebrities (1935):			
			A Home issue, grey back		£1.40	£70.00
			B Export issue, brownish-grey back, text revised		£2.50	£125.00
—	U	25	Dog Studies (95 × 68mm) (1938)		£5.00	£125.00
A	C	25	Eastern Proverbs (export) (c1930)	H.521	£1.80	£45.00
A	C	48	Empire Flying-Boat (sectional) (1938)		£1.60	£80.00
A	C	50	Empire Personalities (1937)		80p	£40.00
A	C	50	Famous Film Stars (1934)		£1.00	£50.00
A	C	50	Famous Footballers (1934)		£1.60	£80.00
A	C	25	Famous Scots (1935)		£1.40	£35.00
—	C	25	Fighting and Civil Aircraft (96 × 68mm) (1936)		£2.40	£60.00

Size	Printing	Number in set		Handbook reference	Price per card	Complete set

ARDATH TOBACCO CO. LTD, London *(continued)*

Size	Print	Num	Description	H.Ref	Price	Set
A	C	50	Figures of Speech (1936)		£1.20	£60.00
A	C	50	Film, Stage and Radio Stars (1935)		£1.10	£55.00
—	C	25	Film, Stage and Radio Stars (96 x 68mm) (1935)		£1.20	£30.00
—	BW	?17	Film Stars (postcard size) (c1935)	H.645	£25.00	—
—	C	50	From Screen and Stage (96 x 65mm) (1936)		£1.20	£60.00
A	U	50	Life in the Services (1938):			
			A Home issue, adhesive		70p	£35.00
			B Export issue, non-adhesive		£1.20	£60.00
A	C	50	National Fitness (1938):			
			A Home issue, adhesive		60p	£30.00
			B Export issue, non-adhesive		£1.00	£50.00
A	U	50	Our Empire (export) (c1937)	H.522	£1.40	£70.00
A	C		Proverbs (c1936):			
		25	A Home issue Nos 1-25		£1.40	£35.00
		25	B Export issue Nos 26-50		£3.00	—
	U	100	Scenes from Big Films (export) (1935):			
A			A Small size, white back		£2.00	—
A			B Small size, cream back		£4.00	—
—			C Medium Size (67 x 52mm)		£4.00	—
A	C	50	Silver Jubilee (1935)		70p	£35.00
A	C	50	Speed — Land, Sea and Air (1935):			
			A Home issue, 'Issued with State Express'		£1.50	£75.00
			B Export issue, Ardath name at base		£2.00	—
—	C	25	Speed — Land, Sea and Air (95 x 68mm) (1938)		£1.60	£40.00
A	C	50	Sports Champions (1935):			
			A Home issue, 'State Express' at base		£1.10	£55.00
			B Export issue, 'Ardath' at base		£1.80	£90.00
A	C	50	Stamps — Rare and Interesting (1939)		£1.30	£65.00
A	C	50	Swimming, Diving and Life-Saving (1937) (export) ..	H.523	£2.00	—
A	C	50	Tennis (1937) (export)	H.524	£2.00	—
A	C	48	Trooping the Colour (sectional) (1939)		£1.80	£90.00
A	C	50	Who is This? (1936) (Film Stars)		£1.80	£90.00
—	BW	24	World Views (No. 13 not issued) (95 x 68mm) (1937) .		40p	£10.00
A	C	50	Your Birthday Tells Your Fortune (1937)		60p	£30.00
C	***POST-1920 PHOTOGRAPHIC ISSUES***					
A2	P	54	Beautiful English Women (1928) (export)		£3.50	—
A2	P	35	Hand Shadows (c1930) (export)		£30.00	—
A2	CP	50	New Zealand Views (1928) (export)		£2.50	—
H	P		Photocards — Numbered Series (1936)*:			
		110	'A' — Football Clubs of North West Counties		£1.80	£200.00
		110	'B' — Football Clubs of North East Counties		£2.00	—
		110	'C' — Football Clubs of Yorkshire		£1.50	£165.00
		165	'D' — Football Clubs of Scotland		£1.20	£200.00
		110	'E' — Football Clubs of Midlands		£1.80	£200.00
		110	'F' — Football Clubs of London and Southern Counties		£1.50	£165.00
		99	'Z' — General Interest (Sports):			
			Nos. 111-165		70p	£38.00
			Nos. 166-209 (Cricket etc)		70p	£32.00
		11	'A.s' (1), 'C.s' (2-3), 'E.s' (4-10), 'F.s' (11) — Football Clubs (supplementary)		£4.00	£45.00
H	P		Photocards — 'A Continuous Series of Topical Interest' (1937):	H.525		
		22	Group A — Racehorses and Sports		£1.00	£22.00
		22	Group B — Coronation and Sports		—	£35.00
			21 Different (minus Walter Neusel)		80p	£16.00
		22	Group C — Lancashire Personalities		—	£45.00
			21 Different (minus Gracie Fields)		£1.25	£25.00

Size	Print-ing	Number in set		Handbook reference	Price per card	Complete set

ARDATH TOBACCO CO. LTD, London *(continued)*

Size	Print-ing	Number in set	Description	Handbook reference	Price per card	Complete set
		22	Group D — Sports and Miscellaneous		£1.35	£30.00
		22	Group E — Film Stars and Sports		£1.25	£27.00
		22	Group F — Film Stars and Sportsmen		£1.35	£30.00
		66	'G.S.' — Miscellaneous subjects (export)		£2.40	—
H	P		Photocards — 'A Continuous Series of General interest', with album offer (1938):	H.526		
		11	Group G — Australian Cricketers		£18.00	—
		22	Group H — Film, Radio and Sporting Stars		£1.25	£27.00
		22	Group I — Film Stars and Miscellaneous		£1.25	£27.00
	P		Photocards — 'A Continuous Series of General Interest', without album offer — uncoloured (1938):	H.527		
H		22	Group J — Film Stars and General Interest		£1.10	£24.00
H		22	Group K — Film, Radio and Sporting Stars:			
			1 With 'Kings' Clause		£1.25	£27.00
			2 Without 'Kings' Clause (export)		£1.50	—
H		44	Group L — Film Stars and Miscellaneous		70p	£30.00
		45	Group M — Film Stars and Miscellaneous:			
C			1 Small size		90p	£40.00
—			2 Large size (80 × 69 mm), with 'Kings' Clause		90p	£40.00
—			3 Large size (80 × 69mm), without 'Kings' Clause		90p	£40.00
	P	45	Group N — Film, Stage and Radio Stars:			
C			1 Small size		90p	£40.00
—			2 Large size (80 × 69mm)		90p	£40.00
H	CP		Photocards — 'A Continuous Series of General Interest', without album offer — Hand coloured (export) (1938):	H.528		
		22	Group 1 — Views of the World		90p	£20.00
		22	Group 2 — Views of the World		90p	£20.00
		22	Group 3 — Views of the World		80p	£17.50
			Real Photographs:			
	P	45	Group O — 'A Continuous Series of General Interest' — Films, Stage and Radio Stars (1939)	H.529	70p	£32.00
C	P	45	'1st Series of 45' — Film and Stage Stars (1939)		£1.00	—
C	P	54	'2nd Series of 54' — Film and Stage Stars (1939)		£1.00	—
J2	P	18	'First Series' — Views (1937)		£2.50	—
J2	P	18	'Second Series' — Film and Stage Stars (1937)		£2.50	—
J2	P	18	'Third Series' — Views (1937)		£2.50	—
J2	P	18	'Fourth Series' — Film and Stage Stars (1937)		£2.50	—
J2	P	18	'Fifth Series' — Views (1938)		£2.50	—
J2	P	18	'Sixth Series' — Film and Stage Stars (1938)		£2.50	—
H	P	44	'Series One' 'G.P.1' — Film Stars (export) (1939)		90p	£40.00
H	P	44	'Series Two' 'G.P.2' — Film Stars (export) (1939)		45p	£20.00
H	P	44	'Series Three' 'G.P.3' — Film Stars (export) (1939)		£3.00	—
H	CP	44	'Series Three' 'C.V.3' — Views (export) (1939)		80p	£35.00
H	CP	44	'Series Four' 'C.V.4' — Views (export) (1939)		35p	£15.00
J2	P	36	'Series Seven' — Film and Stage Stars (1938)		£1.00	—
J2	P	54	'Series Eight' — Film and Stage Stars (1938)		80p	£45.00
	P	54	'Series Nine' — Film and Stage Stars (1938):			
H			A Medium size		80p	£45.00
J2			B Extra-large size		80p	£45.00
	P	54	'Series Ten' — Film and Stage Stars (1939):			
—			A Large size (80 × 69mm)		80p	£45.00
J2			B Extra-large size		80p	£45.00
	P	54	'Series Eleven' — Film and Stage Stars (1939):			
—			A Large size (80 × 69mm)		80p	£45.00
J2			B Extra-large size		£1.20	—

Size	Printing	Number in set		Handbook reference	Price per card	Complete set

ARDATH TOBACCO CO. LTD, London *(continued)*

Size	Printing	Number in set	Description	Handbook reference	Price per card	Complete set
—	P	54	'Series Twelve' — Film and Stage Stars (80 × 69mm) (1939)		80p	£45.00
—	P	54	'Series Thirteen' — Film and Stage Stars (80 × 69mm) (1939)		80p	£45.00
	P	36	'Of Famous Landmarks' (1939):			
—			A Large size (80 × 69 mm), titled 'Real Photographs'		£3.50	—
	J2		B Extra-large size, titled 'Real Photographs of Famous Landmarks'		£1.50	£55.00
	P	36	'Of Modern Aircraft' (1939):			
—			A Large size (80 × 69mm)		£4.00	—
J2			B Extra-large size		£3.00	—

D MISCELLANEOUS

Size	Printing	Number in set	Description	Handbook reference	Price per card	Complete set
—	C	1	Calendar for 1937 (silk) (138 × 102mm)	H.508	—	£100.00
—	C	1	Calender for 1938 (silk) (160 × 102mm)	H.508	—	£100.00
—	C	30	Girls of All Nations (78 × 66mm) (c1916)		£17.00	—
		25	Historic Grand Slams (folders) (101 × 70mm) (c1935)		£27.00	—
J2	U	48	How to Recognise the Service Ranks (holed for binding) (c1939)	H.642	£5.00	—
			Industrial Propaganda Cards (c1942):	H.914		
H1	C	2	A Black background		£7.50	£15.00
H1	C	4	B Coloured fronts		£7.50	£30.00
J2	BW	11	C White fronts		£4.00	£45.00
J2	U	?171	Information Slips (holed for binding) (1938)	H.643	£3.00	—
			Ministry of Information Cards (1941-3):			
J2	U	5	A Calendar — 'It all depends on me'		£4.00	£20.00
			B Greeting Card — 'It all depends on me'		£6.00	—
—	C	24	C 'It all depends on me' (80 × 63mm)	H.913	£1.25	£30.00
—	C	1	D Union Jack Folder (60 × 46mm)		—	£10.00
—	C	1	E 'On the Cotton Front' (80 × 63mm)	H.913	—	£2.50
—	BW	1	F 'On the Kitchen Front' (70 × 55mm)	H.913	—	£2.50
—	BW		Ships of The Royal Navy (Double Ace Cigarettes Slides) (c1955)	H.887	£12.00	—
J2	U	?5	Wonderful Handicraft (c1935)	H.717	£35.00	—

THE ASSOCIATED TOBACCO MANUFACTURERS LTD

POST-1920 ISSUES

Size	Printing	Number in set	Description	Handbook reference	Price per card	Complete set
C2	C	25	Cinema Stars (export) (c1926):	H.530		
			A 'Issued with Bond Street Turkish Cigarettes'		£30.00	—
			B 'Issued with John Bull Virginia Cigarettes'		£30.00	—
			C 'Issued with Club Virginia Cigarettes'		£30.00	—
			D 'Issued with Heliopolis Turkish Cigarettes'		£30.00	—
			E 'Issued with Sports Turkish Cigarettes'		£30.00	—

A. ATKINSON, London

PRE-1919 ISSUE

Size	Printing	Number in set	Description	Handbook reference	Price per card	Complete set
D	C	30	*Army Pictures, Cartoons, etc (c1916)	H.12	£110.00	—

AVISS BROTHERS LTD, London

PRE-1919 ISSUE

Size	Printing	Number in set	Description	Handbook reference	Price per card	Complete set
D1	C	40	*Naval and Military Phrases (c1904)	H.14	£140.00	—

J.A. BAILEY, Swansea

PRE-1919 ISSUE

Size	Printing	Number in set	Description	Handbook reference	Price per card	Complete set
D1	C	40	*Naval and Military Phrases (c1904)	H.14	£200.00	—

Size	Print-ing	Number in set		Handbook reference	Price per card	Complete set

A. BAKER & CO. LTD, London

PRE-1919 ISSUES

A	BW	20	*Actresses — 'BLARM'(c1900):	H.23		
			A Long design back (64mm)		£30.00	—
			B Design altered and shortened (58mm)		£30.00	—
A	BW	10	*Actresses — 'HAGGA' (c1900)	H.24	£30.00	£300.00
	BW		*Actresses 'Baker's 3-sizes' (c1900):	H.25		
A		25	Small cards		£30.00	—
		25	Medium cards (56 × 75mm)		£50.00	—
		25	Extra large cards (67 × 127mm)		£225.00	—
C	BW	?41	*Baker's Tobacconists' Shops (c1901):	H.26		
			A 'Try our 3½d Tobaccos' back		£220.00	—
			B 'Cigar, Cigarette, etc. Manufacturers' back		£120.00	—
C	C	25	Beauties of All Nations (c1900):	H.27		
			A 'Albert Baker & Co. (1898) ...' back		£20.00	£500.00
			B 'A. Baker & Co. ...' back		£15.00	£375.00
C	BW	16	*British Royal Family (c1902)	H.28	£50.00	—
A1	BW	20	Cricketers Series (1901)	H.29	£275.00	—
A1	C	25	*Star Girls (c1898)	H.30	£180.00	—

BAYLEY & HOLDSWORTH

PRE-1919 ISSUE

A	C	26	*International Signalling Code (c1910)		£160.00	—

E. C. BEESTON, Wales

PRE-1919 ISSUE

D	C	30	*Army Pictures, Cartoons etc (c1916)	H.12	£110.00	—

BELFAST SHIPS STORES CO. LTD, Belfast

PRE-1919 ISSUE

	C	1	*Dickens' Characters (79 × 40mm) (c1895)	H.31	£700.00	—

J. & F. BELL LTD, Glasgow

PRE-1919 ISSUES

A	BW	10	*Actresses — 'HAGGA' ('Three Bells Cigarettes') (c1900)	H.24	£70.00	—
C	C	25	*Beauties — Tobacco Leaf Back (c1898):	H.32		
			A 'Bell's Scotia Cigarettes' back		£110.00	—
			B 'Three Bells Cigarettes' back		£110.00	—
A	C	25	Colonial Series (c1901)		£40.00	—
A	BW	30	*Footballers (c1902)		£65.00	—
A	C	25	Scottish Clan Series No. 1 (c1903)	H.33	£14.00	£350.00

B. BELLWOOD, BRADFORD

PRE-1919 ISSUE

C	C	18	Motor Cycle Series (c1912)	H.469	£100.00	—

RICHARD BENSON LTD, Bristol

POST 1920 ISSUE

	U	24	Old Bristol Series:			
—			A Original issue (80 × 70mm) (c1925):			
			i 23 different, minus No. 8		£3.00	£70.00
			ii Number 8		—	£30.00
—			B Reprint (88 × 78-83mm) (1946)		£2.00	£50.00

Size	Print-ing	Number in set		Handbook reference	Price per card	Complete set

BENSON & HEDGES, London

POST-1940 ISSUE

| A2 | C | 1 | Advertisement Card, The Original Shop (1973) | | — | £2.00 |
| B | C | 10 | B.E.A. Aircraft (1958) | H.888 | £10.00 | — |

FELIX BERLYN, Manchester

PRE-1919 ISSUE

	C	25	Golfing Series (Humorous) (c1910):			
A1			A Small size		£400.00	—
—			B Post card size (139 × 87mm)		£500.00	—

BERRY, London

PRE-1919 ISSUE

| D | U | 20 | London Views (c1905) | H.34 | £200.00 | — |

BEWLAY & CO. LTD, London

PRE-1919 ISSUES

D1	U		Bewlay's War Series (Generals, etc) (c1915):	H.477		
		12	A 'Caps the Lot' Smoking Mixture		£12.00	—
		6	B Try Bewlay's 'Caps the Lot' Mixture		£12.00	—
		6	C Try Bewlay's 'Modern Man' Mixture		£12.00	—
D1	U	25	Bewlay's War Series (Photogravure War Pictures) (c1915):	H.35		
			A 'Modern Man' Mixtures etc		£12.00	—
			B 'Modern Man' Cigarettes		£12.00	—
			C 'Two Great Favourites'		£12.00	—
A	C	6	*Comic Advertisement Cards (1909)	H.36	£200.00	—
—	C	6	*Comic Advertisement Cards (140 × 88mm) (c1909)	H.36	£90.00	—

W.O. BIGG & CO., Bristol

PRE-1919 ISSUES

A	C	37	*Flags of All Nations (c1904):	H.37		
			A 'Statue of Liberty' back, 4d oz		£8.00	—
			B As A:— (a) altered to 4½d by hand		£8.00	—
			(b) 4½d red seal over 4d		£8.00	—
			C Panel design 'New York' Mixture		£8.00	—
A	C	50	Life on Board a Man of War (c1905)	H.38	£10.00	£500.00

JAS. BIGGS & SONS, London

PRE-1919 ISSUES

C	C	26	*Actresses — 'FROGA A' 'Two Roses' in white (c1900)	H.20	£40.00	—
C	C	52	*Actresses — 'FROGA A & B' 'Two Roses' in black (c1900)	H.20	£55.00	—
A	C		*Beauties, with frameline — 'CHOAB' (c1900):	H.21		
		25	A Blue typeset back		£70.00	—
		50	B Overprinted in black on Bradford cards		£65.00	—
C	C		*Beauties, no framelines — selection 'BOCCA' (c1900):	H.39		
		25	A Blue back		£70.00	—
		25	B Black back		£70.00	—
C	C	30	*Colonial Troops (c1901)	H.40	£30.00	—
C	C	30	*Flags and Flags with Soldiers (c1903)	H.41	£28.00	—
A1	C	25	*Star Girls (c1900)	H.30	£200.00	—

Size	Printing	Number in set		Handbook reference	Price per card	Complete set

J. S. BILLINGHAM, Northampton

PRE-1919 ISSUE
| D | C | 30 | *Army Pictures, Cartoons etc (c1916) .... | H.12 | £110.00 | — |

R. BINNS, Halifax

POST-1920 ISSUE
| A | U | 15 | *Halifax Footballers (c1924) .... | H.531 | £150.00 | — |

BLANKS CIGARETTES

POST-1920 ISSUE
| A | C | 50 | Keystrokes in Break-Building (c1935) .... | H.647 | £350.00 | — |

THE BOCNAL TOBACCO CO., London

POST-1920 ISSUES
| A2 | U | 25 | Luminous Silhouettes of Beauty and Charm (1938) ... | | £2.60 | £65.00 |
| A2 | C | 25 | Proverbs Up-to-Date (1938)...................... | | £2.40 | £60.00 |

ALEXANDER BOGUSLAVSKY LTD, London

POST-1920 ISSUES
—	C	12	Big Events on the Turf (133 × 70mm) (1924)		£45.00	—
A2	C	25	Conan Doyle Characters (1923):			
			A Back in black, white board		£7.00	—
			B Back in grey, cream board		£7.00	—
			C Back in green		£7.00	—
A2	C	25	Mythological Gods and Goddesses (1924)		£2.80	£70.00
A	C	25	*Sports Records, Nd. 1-25 (1925)		£2.00	£50.00
A	C	25	Sports Records, Nd. 26-50 (1925)		£2.00	£50.00
	C	25	Winners on the Turf (1925):			
A			A Small size, captions 'sans serif'		£3.20	£80.00
A			B Small size, captions with 'serif'		£5.00	—
B			C Large size		£5.50	—

R. & E. BOYD LTD, London

POST-1920 ISSUES
—	U	25	Places of Interest (c1938):			
			A Size 67 × 35mm		£60.00	—
			B Size 71 × 55mm		£60.00	—
—	U	25	Wild Birds at Home (75 × 57mm) (c1938)	H.626	£60.00	—

WM. BRADFORD, Liverpool

PRE-1919 ISSUES
C	C	50	*Beauties 'CHOAB' (c1900)	H.21	£32.00	—
D	U	?7	Beauties — 'Jersey Lily Cigarettes' (c1900)	H.488	£375.00	—
D2	BW	20	Boer War Cartoons (c1901)	H.42	£100.00	—

T. BRANKSTON & CO., London

PRE-1919 ISSUES
C	C	30	*Colonial Troops (c1901):	H.40		
			A Golf Club Mixture		£30.00	—
			B Red Virginia		£30.00	—
			C Sweet as the Rose		£30.00	—
A2	C	12	*Pretty Girl Series 'RASH' (c1900)	H.8	£250.00	—

Size	Printing	Number in set		Handbook reference	Price per card	Complete set

BRIGHAM & CO., Reading

PRE-1919 ISSUES

B	U	16	Down the Thames from Henley to Windsor (c1912) ..		£140.00	—
A	U	16	Reading Football Players (c1912)		£350.00	—
—	BW	3	Tobacco Growing in Hampshire (89 × 79mm) (1915) ..	H.470	£16.00	£50.00

BRITANNIA ANONYMOUS SOCIETY

PRE-1919 ISSUE

—	C	? 29	*Beauties and Scenes (60 × 40mm) (c1914)	H.532	£80.00	—

BRITISH & COLONIAL TOBACCO CO., London

PRE-1919 ISSUE

A1	C	25	*Armies of the World (c1900)	H.43	£160.00	—

J.M. BROWN, Derby

PRE-1919 ISSUE

D	C	30	*Army Pictures, Cartoons etc (c1916)	H.12	£110.00	—

JOHN BRUMFIT, London

POST-1920 ISSUE

A	C	50	The Public Schools' Ties Series (Old Boys) (1925) ...		£4.00	£200.00

G.A. BULLOUGH, Castleford

PRE-1919 ISSUE

D	C	30	*Army Pictures, Cartoons etc (c1916)	H.12	£110.00	—

BURSTEIN, ISAACS & CO., London

(The BI-CO Company, B.I. & Co. Ltd)

POST-1920 ISSUES

D	BW	25	Famous Prize-Fighters, Nd. 1-25 (1923)		£6.00	—
D	BW	25	Famous Prize-Fighters, Nd. 26-50 (1924)		£6.00	—
D	P	28	London View Series (1922)		£4.00	—

BYRTWOOD & CO., Bristol

PRE-1919 ISSUE

A2	U	? 30	*Pretty Girl Series — 'BAGG' (c1900)	H.45	£120.00	—

CABANA CIGAR CO., London

PRE-1919 ISSUE

—	BW	2	Advertisement Card — 'Little Manturios' (63 × 49mm) (1905)	H.719	£300.00	—
A2	C	40	*Home and Colonial Regiments (c1900)	H.69	£300.00	—

PERCY E. CADLE & CO. LTD, Cardiff

PRE-1919 ISSUES

A1	BW	20	*Actresses 'BLARM' (c1900)	H.23	£35.00	—
C	U	26	*Actresses — 'FROGA A' (c1900):	H.20		
			A Printed Back		£35.00	—
			B Rubber — Stamped Back		£160.00	—
C	C	26	*Actresses — 'FROGA B' (c1900)	H.20	£50.00	—
C	BW	12	*Boer War and Boxer Rebellion Sketches (c1901)	H.46	£50.00	—
C	BW	10	*Boer War Generals — 'FLAC' (c1901)	H.47	£65.00	—
A	BW	20	*Footballers (c1904)	H.4	£65.00	—

Size	Print-ing	Number in set		Handbook reference	Price per card	Complete set

CARRERAS LTD, London

A   PRE-1919 ISSUES

Size	Print.	No.	Title	Handbook	Price	Complete
—	C		*Flags of the Allies (shaped) (c1915):	H.49		
		1	Grouped Flags:'Black Cat' Cigarettes		£45.00	—
		5	Allies Flags: 'Black Cat' Cigarettes		£45.00	—
A	C	140	Raemaeker's War Cartoons (1916):			
			A 'Black Cat' Cigarettes		£1.10	£155.00
			B Carreras Cigarettes		£3.50	—
A	C	50	The Science of Boxing (c1916):			
			A 'Black Cat' back		£3.00	£150.00
			B 'Carreras Ltd' back		£5.00	—
A	C	80	Types of London (1919)		£1.50	£120.00
A	C	50	Women on War Work (c1916)		£6.50	£325.00

B   POST-1920 ISSUES. Mostly home issues, export only issues indicated.

Size	Print.	No.	Title	Handbook	Price	Complete
A	CP	24	Actresses and Their Pets (1926) (export)	H.648	£5.00	—
	C	48	Alice in Wonderland (1930):			
A			A Small size, rounded corners		£1.50	£75.00
A			B Small size, square corners		£3.00	—
B2			C Large size		£1.80	£90.00
		1	D Instruction Booklet		—	£18.00
A	C	50	Amusing Tricks and How to Do Them (1937)		£1.30	£65.00
	C		Battle of Waterloo (1934):	H.533		
C		1	1 Paper insert, with instructions		—	£12.00
—		15	*2 Soldiers and Guns, large size (67 × 70mm)		£4.00	—
A			*3 Soldiers and Guns, small size:			
		10	Soldiers — Officers' Uniforms		£2.00	—
		12	Soldiers and Guns		£2.00	—
C1	C	50	Believe it or Not (1934)		70p	£35.00
A	C	50	Birds of the Countryside (1939)		£1.00	£50.00
A	C	50	Britain's Defences (1938)		70p	£35.00
	C	25	British Costumes (1927):			
C2			A Small size		£1.40	£35.00
B2			B Large size		£1.40	£35.00
A	P	27	British Prime Ministers (1928) (export)		£1.50	£40.00
A1	C	1	Calendar for 1934		—	£25.00
A	C	50	Celebrities of British History (1935):			
			A Brown on cream back (two shades of ink)		90p	£45.00
			B Pale brown on bluish back		90p	£45.00
A	C	25	Christie Comedy Girls (1928) (export)		£2.00	£50.00
A	U		Cricketers (1934):			
		30	A 'A Series of Cricketers'		£3.30	£100.00
		50	B 'A Series of 50 Cricketers':			
			1 Front in brown and white		£3.50	£175.00
			2 Front in black and white		£35.00	—
A	BW	50	Dogs and Friend (1936)		50p	£25.00
A	C	50	Do You Know? (1939)		30p	£15.00
A	C	50	Famous Airmen and Airwomen (1936)		£1.70	£85.00
	C		Famous Escapes (1926):			
A		25	A Small size		£1.60	£40.00
B2		25	B Large size		£1.40	£35.00
—		10	C Extra-large size (133 × 70mm)		£3.00	£30.00
A2	C	96	Famous Film Stars (1935)	H.534	£1.20	£115.00
A	C		Famous Footballers (1935):			
		48	A Set of 48		£1.40	£70.00
		24	B Nos. 25-48 redrawn		£1.80	£45.00
A	C	25	Famous Men (1927) (export)		£1.40	£35.00

Size	Printing	Number in set		Handbook reference	Price per card	Complete set

CARRERAS LTD, London *(continued)*

Size	Printing	Number in set	Title	Handbook reference	Price per card	Complete set
B2	P	24	Famous Naval Men (1929) (export)		£1.75	£42.00
—	C	6	Famous Posters (folders) (65 × 41mm) (1923)	H.606	£25.00	—
B2	P	12	Famous Soldiers (1928) (export)		£5.50	£65.00
A	P	27	Famous Women (1929) (export)		£1.20	£32.00
A	C	25	Figures of Fiction (1924)		£2.00	£50.00
	P	54	Film and Stage Beauties (1939):			
A2			A Small size		50p	£27.00
—			B Medium size (70 × 60mm):			
			(a) Without full point after 'Carreras Ltd'		65p	£35.00
			(b) With full point after 'Carreras Ltd.'		80p	£42.00
	P	36	Film and Stage Beauties:			
B1			A Large size (1939)		£1.00	£36.00
J2			B Extra-large size (1938)		£1.50	£55.00
A	C	50	Film Favourites (1938)		£1.40	£70.00
A	P	54	Film Stars — 'A Series of 54' (1937)		85p	£45.00
	P	54	Film Stars (1938):			
A			A Small size, 'Second Series of 54'		50p	£27.00
—			B Medium size (68 × 60mm), 'A Series of 54'		£1.00	£55.00
J2	P		Film Stars (export):			
		36	'A Series of 36' (c1935)		£2.50	—
		36	'Second Series of 36' (c1936)		£2.50	—
		36	'Third Series of 36' (c1937)		£2.50	—
		36	'Fourth Series of 36' (c1938)		£2.50	—
A2	C	50	Film Stars, by Florence Desmond (1936)		90p	£45.00
—		72	Film Stars, oval (70 × 30mm) (1934):			
	P		A Inscribed 'Real Photos'		£2.50	—
	U		B Without 'Real Photos'		£1.50	£110.00
A	C	50	Flowers (1936)		50p	£25.00
A2	C	75	*Footballers (1934):			
			A 'Carreras Cigarettes' on front 27mm long		£2.00	£150.00
			B 'Carreras Cigarettes' on front 26mm long		£2.00	£150.00
	C	36	'Fortune Telling' (1926):			
A			A Small size:			
			1 Card inset		50p	£18.00
			2a Head inset, black framelines		40p	£14.00
			2b Head inset, brown framelines		75p	£27.00
B2			B Large size:			
			1 Card inset		40p	£15.00
			2 Head inset		50p	£18.00
		1	C Instruction Booklet:			
			1 Address 23 New North Street		—	£20.00
			2 Address 12 Bath Street		—	£11.00
	P		Glamour Girls of Stage and Films (1939):			
A2		54	A Small size		55p	£30.00
—		54	B Medium size (70 × 60mm)		65p	£35.00
—		36	C Large size (76 × 70mm)		£1.00	£36.00
J2		36	D Extra-large size		£1.25	£45.00
	C	50	'Gran-Pop' by Lawson Wood (1934):			
C1			A Small size		50p	£25.00
B			B Large size		40p	£20.00
	C	52	Greyhound Racing Game (1926):			
A			A Small size		25p	£12.50
B2			B Large size		25p	£12.50
		1	C Instruction Leaflet		—	£11.00
	C	48	Happy Family (1925):			
A1			A Small size		36p	£18.00
B2			B Large size		36p	£18.00

Size	Print-ing	Number in set		Handbook reference	Price per card	Complete set

CARRERAS LTD, London *(continued)*

Size	Print-ing	Number in set	Description	Handbook reference	Price per card	Complete set
A	C	25	Highwaymen (1924)		£2.40	£60.00
A	C	50	History of Army Uniforms (1937)		£1.20	£60.00
A	C	50	History of Naval Uniforms (1937)		90p	£45.00
	C		Horses and Hounds (1926)			
A		25	A Small size		£2.00	£50.00
B2		20	B Large size		£2.00	£40.00
—		10	C Extra-large size (133 × 70mm)		£4.00	£40.00
	C	50	Kings and Queens of England (1935):			
A			A Small size		£1.60	£80.00
B2			B Large size		£2.40	£120.00
A	U	50	A 'Kodak' at the Zoo 'Series of Fifty' (1924)		70p	£35.00
A	U	50	A 'Kodak' at the Zoo '2nd Series' (1925)		70p	£35.00
A	P	27	Malayan Industries (1929) (export)		80p	£20.00
	P	24	Malayan Scenes (1928):			
A			A Small size		£3.00	—
—			B Medium size (70 × 60mm)		75p	£18.00
—	C	53	*Miniature Playing Cards (44 × 32mm) (c1935)	H.535-1A	20p	£9.00
	C	50	The 'Nose' Game (1927):			
A			A Small size		50p	£25.00
B2			B Large size		50p	£25.00
		1	C Instruction Leaflet		—	£11.00
	C	50	Notable MPs (1929):			
A			A Small size		£1.20	£60.00
—			B Medium size (69 × 60mm)		60p	£30.00
A	P	25	Notable Ships — Past and Present (1929) (export)		£1.40	£35.00
	C		Old Staffordshire Figures (1926):			
A		24	A Small size		£1.25	£30.00
—		12	B Extra-large size (134 × 71mm)		£3.00	£36.00
B	C	24	Old Staffordshire Figures (different subjects) (1926) ...		£1.50	£36.00
	C	24	Orchids (1925):			
A			A Small size		£1.00	£25.00
B			B Large size		£1.00	£25.00
—			C Extra-large size (133 × 70mm)		£3.40	—
A	C		Our Navy (1937):	Ha.536		
		20	A Thick card, selected numbers		£1.20	£24.00
		50	B Thin card		£1.20	£60.00
C1	C	50	Palmistry (1933)		60p	£30.00
A	P	27	Paramount Stars (1929) (export)		£1.70	£45.00
A	C	25	Picture Puzzle Series (1923)	H.649	£1.40	£35.00
—	C	53	Playing Cards (68 × 42mm) (c1925)	H.535-1B	£1.20	—
	C		*Playing Cards and Dominoes (1929):	H.535-1C		
C		52	A Small size — (a) Numbered		50p	—
			(b) Unnumbered		50p	—
—		26	B Large size (77 × 69mm):			
			(a) Numbered		80p	£20.00
			(b) Unnumbered		80p	£20.00
A	C	48	Popular Footballers (1936):			
			A White back		£1.10	£55.00
			B Cream back		£1.10	£55.00
—	C		Popular Personalities, oval (70 × 30mm) (1935):	H.629		
		72	1 Normal issue		85p	£60.00
		10	2 Replaced subjects (Nos. 1-10) for issue in Eire ...		£20.00	—
	C		Races — Historic and Modern (1927):			
A		25	A Small size		£2.40	£60.00
B		25	B Large size		£2.40	£60.00
—		12	C Extra-large size (133 × 69mm)		£5.00	£60.00

Size	Print-ing	Number in set		Handbook reference	Price per card	Complete set

CARRERAS LTD, London *(continued)*

Size	Print-ing	Number in set	Description	Handbook reference	Price per card	Complete set
	C		Regalia Series (1925):			
A		25	A Small size		50p	£12.50
B		20	B Large size		60p	£12.00
—		10	C Extra-large size (135 × 71mm)		£2.00	£20.00
—	C	50	'Round the World' Scenic Models (folders) (83 × 73mm) (c1930)		80p	£40.00
	C		School Emblems (1929):			
A		50	A Small size		90p	£45.00
B		40	B Large size		75p	£30.00
—		20	C Extra-large size (134 × 76mm)		£2.25	£45.00
C1	C	48	Tapestry Reproductions of Famous Paintings (sectional) (1938)		70p	£35.00
A	C	50	Tools — And How to Use Them (1935)		£1.80	£90.00
A	P	27	Views of London (1929) (export)		40p	£11.00
A	P	27	Views of the World (1927) (export)		75p	£20.00
A	C	25	Wild Flower Art Series (1923)		£1.20	£30.00

C POST-1940 TURF SLIDE ISSUES

Size	Print-ing	Number in set	Description	Handbook reference	Price per card	Complete set
A	U	50	British Aircraft (1953)		£1.40	£70.00
A	U	50	British Fish (1954)		60p	£30.00
A	U	50	British Railway Locomotives (1952)		£1.40	£70.00
A	U	50	Celebrities of British History (1951)		£1.20	£60.00
A	U	50	Famous British Fliers (1956)		£5.00	—
A	U	50	Famous Cricketers (1950)		£5.00	—
A	U	50	Famous Dog Breeds (1952)	H.889	£1.60	£80.00
A	U	50	Famous Film Stars (1949)		£3.00	—
A	U	50	Famous Footballers (1951)		£4.50	—
A	U	50	Film Favourites (1948)		£4.00	—
A	U	50	Film Stars (1947)		£3.00	—
A	U	50	Footballers (1948)		£4.50	—
A	U	50	Olympics (1948)		£5.00	—
A	U	50	Radio Celebrities (1950)		£1.20	£60.00
A	U	50	Sports Series (1949)		£3.50	—
A	U	50	Zoo Animals (1955)		50p	£25.00

(N.B. These prices are for the full slides. If only the cut slides are required these will be half Catalogue price.)

D POST-1940 ISSUES

Size	Print-ing	Number in set	Description	Handbook reference	Price per card	Complete set
A	C	50	British Birds (1976)		20p	£3.75
A	C	50	Flowers All the Year Round (1977)		20p	£10.00
A	C	50	Kings and Queens of England (1977)		30p	£15.00
A	C	50	Military Uniforms (1976)		20p	£4.00
A	C	50	Palmistry (1980)		£1.00	—
A	C	50	Sport Fish (1978)		20p	£3.75
A	C	50	Vintage Cars (1976):			
			A With word 'Filter' in white oval:			
			i Thin card, bright red oblong at top		20p	£9.00
			ii Thick card, bright red oblong at top		20p	£7.50
			iii Thin card, dull red oblong at top		40p	—
			B Without word 'Filter' in white oval		20p	£5.00

E MISCELLANEOUS PRE-1919 ISSUES

Size	Print-ing	Number in set	Description	Handbook reference	Price per card	Complete set
D1	BW	200	The Black Cat Library (Booklets) (c1910)		£12.00	—
D1	BW	5	The Handy Black Cat French-English Dictionary (Booklets) (1915)		£22.00	—
—	—	? 104	*Lace Motifs* (c1915) (various sizes)	H.506	From £8.00	—

F MISCELLANEOUS POST-1940 ISSUES

Size	Print-ing	Number in set	Description	Handbook reference	Price per card	Complete set
A	C	60	Flags of All Nations (unissued) (c1960)		50p	£30.00

Size	Print-ing	Number in set		Handbook reference	Price per card	Complete set
CARRERAS LTD, London *(continued)*						
—	C	4	Guards Series (68 × 50mm): A Military Mug Series (1971)		£1.00	—
		8	B Order Up the Guards (1970)		£1.00	—
		16	C Send for the Guards (1969)		£1.00	—
—	C	7	Millionaire Competition Folders (68 × 30mm) (1971)		£2.00	—
A	U	50	Radio & Television Favourites (unissued) (c1955)		£8.00	—
G	**SILKS**					
—	C	12	Miscellaneous Series Cabinet size (1915)	H.505-18	£180.00	—

CARRICK & CO., Hull

PRE-1919 ISSUE

D	C	12	*Military Terms (1901)	H.50	£70.00	—
—	U	1	Queen Victoria Jubilee 1887 (105 × 67mm)	H.720	—	£300.00

P. J. CARROLL & CO. LTD, Dundalk, Glasgow and Liverpool

A PRE-1919 ISSUES

D	C	25	British Naval Series (c1915)	H.51	£40.00	
A	P	20	County Louth G.R.A. Team and Officials (1913)		£30.00	
D	BW	25	*Derby Winners (1914-15):	H.52		
			A Back in black		£100.00	—
			B Back in green		£100.00	—

B POST-1920 ISSUES

D	C	25	Ship Series (1937)		£8.00	£200.00
D	U	24	Sweet Afton Jig-Saw Puzzles (1935)	H.650	£18.00	—

C MISCELLANEOUS

D	C	25	Birds (prepared but not issued) (c1940)	H.537	70p	£17.50

THE CASKET TOBACCO & CIGARETTE CO. LTD, Manchester

PRE-1919 ISSUES

A2	U	? 1	Bowling Fixture Cards, Coupon Back (1907)	H.53	£450.00	—
A2	U	? 4	Cricket Fixture Cards, Coupon back (1905-06)	H.53	£400.00	—
A2	U	? 2	Cyclists Lighting-up Table (1909-10)		£400.00	—
A2	U	? 17	*Football Fixture Cards, Coupon back (1905-11)	H.53	£500.00	—
A2	BW	? 7	Road Maps (c1910)	H.54	£400.00	—

S. CAVANDER & CO., London and Portsea

PRE-1919 ISSUE

D	BW	50	*Beauties — selection from 'Plums' (1898)	H.186	£375.00	—

CAVANDERS LTD, London and Glasgow

POST-1920 ISSUES

A	C	25	Ancient Chinese (1926)		£1.60	£40.00
A	C	25	Ancient Egypt (1928)		£1.60	£40.00
B	C	25	Ancient Egypt (different subjects) (1928)		£1.40	£35.00
A	P	36	Animal Studies (1936)		40p	£14.00
	CP	50	Beauty Spots of Great Britain (1927):			
A			A Small size		40p	£20.00
—			B Medium size (76 × 52mm)		40p	£20.00
	CP		Camera Studies (1926):			
A		54	A Small size		20p	£11.00
—		56	B Medium size (77 × 51mm)		25p	£12.50
A	C	30	Cinema Stars — Set 6 (1934)	Ha.515	£1.20	£36.00

Size	Print-ing	Number in set		Handbook reference	Price per card	Complete set

CAVANDERS LTD, London and Glasgow *(continued)*

Size	Print-ing	Number in set	Description	Handbook reference	Price per card	Complete set
—	CP	30	The Colonial Series (77 × 51mm) (1925):			
			A Small caption, under 1mm high		50p	£15.00
			B Larger caption, over 1mm high		50p	£15.00
—	C	25§	Coloured Stereoscopic (77 × 51mm) (1931)		60p	£30.00
D	C	25	Feathered Friends or Foreign Birds (1926):	Ha.516		
			A Titled 'Feathered Friends'		£2.40	—
			B Titled 'Foreign Birds'		£1.40	£35.00
—	C	25§	Glorious Britain (76 × 51mm) (1930)		60p	£30.00
			The Homeland Series (1924-26):	Ha.539		
A			Small size:			
	CP	50	A Back in blue		£1.00	£50.00
	CP	50	B Back in black, glossy front		£1.00	£50.00
	CP	54	C Back in black, matt front		40p	£20.00
			Medium size (77 × 51mm):			
	CP	50	D Back inscribed 'Hand Coloured Real Photos'		30p	£15.00
	CP	56	E As D, with 'Reprinted …' at base		50p	£28.00
	CP	56	F Back inscribed 'Real Photos'		50p	£28.00
	P	56	G Back inscribed 'Real Photos'		50p	£28.00
A	C	25	Little Friends (1924)	Ha.540	£1.20	£30.00
—	C	25	The Nation's Treasures (77 × 51mm) (1925)		50p	£12.50
	P		Peeps into Many Lands — 'A Series of …' (1927):			
D		36§	A Small size		50p	£36.00
—		36§	B Medium size (75 × 50mm)		80p	£55.00
—		36	C Extra-large size (113 × 68mm)		£2.00	—
	P	36§	Peeps into Many Lands — 'Second Series …' (1928):			
D			A Small size		£1.00	£75.00
—			B Medium size (75 × 50mm)		£1.00	£75.00
	P	24§	Peeps into Many Lands — 'Third Series …' (1929):			
D			A Small size		40p	£20.00
			B Medium size (75 × 50mm)		90p	£45.00
—			C As B, but inscribed 'Reprinted by Special Request'		£1.50	£75.00
	P	24§	Peeps into Prehistoric Times — 'Fourth Series …' (1930):			
D			A Small size		90p	£45.00
—			B Medium size (75 × 50mm)		£1.20	£60.00
—	P		*Photographs (54 × 38mm) (1924):	Ha.541		
		30	1 Animal Studies		£1.50	—
		3	2 Royal Family		£3.30	—
—	C	48	Regimental Standards (76 × 70mm) (c1924)	Ha.502-7	£12.00	—
C	C	25	Reproductions of Celebrated Oil Paintings (1925)	Ha.542	£1.20	£30.00
	CP	108	River Valleys (1926):			
A			A Small size		30p	£32.00
—			B Medium size (75 × 50mm)		33p	£35.00
A	C	25	School Badges (1928):	Ha.543		
			A Back in dark blue		£1.00	£25.00
			B Back in light blue		£1.00	£25.00
—	CP	30	Wordsworth's Country (76 × 51mm) (1926)		80p	£24.00

§ Stereoscopic series, consisting of a Right and a Left card for each number, a complete series is thus **double** the number shown.

R.S. CHALLIS & CO. LTD, London

POST-1920 ISSUES

Size	Print-ing	Number in set	Description	Handbook reference	Price per card	Complete set
D1	C	50	Comic Animals (1936)		70p	£35.00
A	BW	44	Flickits (Greyhound Racing Flickers) (1936)	Ha.589-1	£40.00	—

Size	Printing	Number in set		Handbook reference	Price per card	Complete set

R.S. CHALLIS & CO. LTD, London *(continued)*

D1	U	36	Wild Birds at Home (1935):	H.626		
			A Inscribed 'Issued with Baldric Cigarettes'		60p	£22.00
			B Above wording blocked out in black		£1.25	£45.00

H. CHAPMAN & Co.

PRE-1919 ISSUE

D	C	30	*Army Pictures, Cartoons, etc (c1916)	H.12	£175.00	—

CHARLESWORTH & AUSTIN LTD, London

PRE-1919 ISSUES

C	U	50	*Beauties — 'BOCCA' (c1900)	H.39	£30.00	—
C	BW	16	*British Royal Family (1902)	H.28	£45.00	—
C	C		Colonial Troops (c1900):	H.40		
		50	A Black back		£35.00	—
		30	B Brown back		£35.00	—
A1	BW	20	Cricketers Series (1901)	H.29	£320.00	—
C	C	30	*Flags and Flags with Soldiers (c1903)	H.41	£32.00	—

CHESTERFIELD CIGARETTES

POST-1940 ISSUE

—	C	6	Chesterfield Collection (76 × 45mm) (1979)		£3.00	—
—	C	6	Cocktails (76 × 45mm) 1980		50p	£3.00

CHEW & CO., Bradford

PRE-1919 ISSUE

D	C	30	*Army, Pictures, Cartoons etc (c1916)	H.12	£110.00	—

W.A. & A.C. CHURCHMAN, Ipswich

36 page reference book — £4.00

A ***PRE-1919 ISSUES***

C	C	26	*Actresses — 'FROGA A' (c1900)	H.20	£32.00	—
C	C	26	*Actresses — 'FROGA B' (c1900)	H.20	£40.00	—
C	U	24	*Actresses, 'For the Pipe' back (c1900)	H.55	£75.00	—
A	C	25	Army Badges of Rank (1916)	H.56	£5.00	£125.00
A	C	12	*Beauties — 'CERF' (1904)	H.57	£55.00	—
			*Beauties — 'CHOAB' (c1900):	H.21		
—	C	3	I Circular cards, 55mm diameter		£900.00	—
C	C	25	II Five different backs		£120.00	—
C	U	25	*Beauties — 'FECKSA' (c1902)	H.58	£85.00	—
C	C	25	*Beauties — 'GRACC' (c1900)	H.59	£85.00	—
A	C	50	Birds and Eggs (1906)	H.60	£6.00	£300.00
D	BW	20	*Boer War Cartoons (c1901)	H.42	£95.00	—
		20	*Boer War Generals' — 'CLAM' (c1901):	H.61		
A2	BW		A Black front		£35.00	—
A	U		B Brown front		£35.00	—
A	C	50	Boy Scouts (1916)	H.62	£7.00	£350.00
A	C	50	Boy Scouts, 2nd series (1916)	H.62	£7.00	£350.00
A	C	50	Boy Scouts, 3rd series (1916):	H.62		
			A Brown back		£7.00	£350.00
			B Blue back		£10.00	—
D	P	41	*Celebrities — Boer War Period (c1901)	H.63	£18.00	—
A	C	38	Dogs and Fowls (1908)	H.64	£7.50	—

Size	Print-ing	Number in set		Handbook reference	Price per card	Complete set
W.A. & A.C. CHURCHMAN, Ipswich *(continued)*							
A		50	East Suffolk Churches:			
	BW		A Black front, cream back (1912)		£2.00	£100.00
	BW		B Black front, white back (1912)		£2.00	£100.00
	U		C Sepia front (1917)		£2.00	£100.00
A	C	50	Fish and Bait (1914)	H.65	£6.50	£325.00
A	C	50	Fishes of the World (1911):	H.66	—	£250.00
			30 cards as re-issued 1924		£1.65	£50.00
			20 cards not re-issued		£10.00	—
A	C	50	Flags and Funnels of Leading Steamship Lines (1912)	H.67	£6.50	—
A	C	50	Football Club Colours (1909)	H.68	£10.00	£500.00
A	U	50	*Footballers — Photogravure Portraits (c1910)		£30.00	—
A	C	50	Footballers — Action Pictures & Inset (1914)		£15.00	£750.00
C	C	40	*Home and Colonial Regiments (1902)	H.69	£45.00	—
A	C	50	Interesting Buildings (1905)	H.70	£7.00	£350.00
A	C	50	*Medals (1910)	H.71	£7.00	£350.00
A	C	50	*Phil May Sketches (1912):	H.72		
			A 'Churchman's Gold Flake Cigarettes'		£7.00	£350.00
			B 'Churchman's Cigarettes'		£8.00	—
A	C	50	*Regimental Colours and Cap Badges (1911)	H.73	£6.00	£300.00
A	C	50	Sectional Cycling Map (1913)	H.74	£6.00	£300.00
A	C	50	Silhouettes of Warships (1915)		£8.00	—
A	C	50	A Tour Round the World (1911)	H.75	£6.50	£325.00
A1	C	25	*Types of British and Colonial Troops (c1900)	H.76	£45.00	—
A	C	50	Wild Animals of the World (1907)	H.77	£7.00	£350.00
B	**POST-1920 ISSUES**							
—	C	48	Air-Raid Precautions (68 × 53mm) (1938)	H.544	40p	£20.00
A	U	50	Association Footballers (1938)		70p	£35.00
A	U	50	Association Footballers, 2nd series (1939)		£1.20	£60.00
A	C	25	Boxing (1922)	H.311	£6.00	—
A	U	50	Boxing Personalities (1938)		£1.80	£90.00
A	U	25	British Film Stars (1934)		£2.00	£50.00
A	C	55	Can You Beat Bogey at St Andrews? (1933):			
			A Without overprint		£3.00	—
			B Overprinted in red 'Exchangeable'		£3.00	—
	U		Cathedrals and Churches (1924):	H.545		
A		25	A Small size		£2.00	£50.00
J		12	B Extra-large size		£10.00	—
A	C	50	Celebrated Gateways (1925)	H.347	£2.00	£100.00
A	C	25	Civic Insignia and Plate (1926)		£1.80	£45.00
A	C	50	Contract Bridge (1935)		80p	£40.00
A	C	50	Cricketers (1936)		£3.40	—
	C		Curious Dwellings:			
A		25	A Small size (1926)		£2.00	£50.00
B		12	B Large size (1925)		£4.50	—
A	C	25	Curious Signs (1925)		£2.00	£50.00
	C		Eastern Proverbs:	H.521		
			A Small size:			
A		25	1 'A Series of 25' (1931)		80p	£20.00
A		25	2 '2nd Series of 25' (1932)		£1.20	£30.00
			B Large size:			
B		12	1 'A Series of 12' (1931)		£4.00	—
B		12	2 '2nd Series of 12' (1933)		£2.50	£30.00
B		12	3 '3rd Series of 12' (1933)		£2.25	£27.00
B		12	4 '4th Series of 12' (1934)		£1.50	£18.00
A	C	50	Empire Railways (1931)		£2.40	£120.00
A	C	25	Famous Cricket Colours (1928)		£3.80	£95.00

Size	Printing	Number in set		Handbook reference	Price per card	Complete set

W.A. & A.C. CHURCHMAN, Ipswich *(continued)*

Size	Print.	No.	Description	Hbk	Price	Set
	U		Famous Golfers:			
A		50	A Small size (1927)		£9.00	—
			B Large size:			
B		12	1 'A Series of 12' (1927)		£25.00	—
B		12	2 '2nd Series of 12' (1928)		£25.00	—
	C		Famous Railway Trains:			
A		25	A Small size (1929)		£2.60	£65.00
			B Large size:			
B		12	1 'Series of 12' (1928)		£6.00	—
B		12	2 '2nd Series of 12' (1929)		£6.00	—
A	C	52	'Frisky' (1935)		£3.50	—
A	C	50	History and Development of the British Empire (1934)		£1.80	£90.00
—	U	48	Holidays in Britain (Views and Maps) (68 × 53 mm) (1937)		40p	£20.00
—	C	48	Holidays in Britain (views only) (68 × 53mm) (1938) ..		50p	£25.00
A	C	25	The Houses of Parliament and Their Story (1931)		£1.80	£45.00
	C		Howlers:			
A		40	A Small size (1937)		30p	£12.00
B		16	B Large size (1936)		50p	£8.00
A	C	25	The Inns of Court (1932)		£2.80	£70.00
A	C	25	Interesting Door-Knockers (1928)		£2.40	£60.00
A	C	25	Interesting Experiments (1929)		£1.40	£35.00
A	C	50	'In Town To-night' (1938)		40p	£20.00
B	C	12	Italian Art Exhibition, 1930 (1931)		£2.00	£24.00
B	C	12	Italian Art Exhibition, 1930 — '2nd Series' (1931) ...		£2.00	£24.00
	C		The King's Coronation (1937):			
A		50	A Small size		22p	£11.00
B		15	B Large size		80p	£12.00
A	U	50	Kings of Speed (1939)		60p	£30.00
	C		Landmarks in Railway Progress:			
A		50	A Small size (1931)		£2.80	£140.00
			B Large size:			
B		12	1 '1st Series of 12' (1932)		£5.00	£60.00
B		12	2 '2nd Series of 12' (1932)		£5.00	£60.00
	U		Lawn Tennis (1928):	H.546		
A		50	A Small size		£3.50	£175.00
B		12	B Large size		£10.00	—
	C		Legends of Britain (1936):			
A		50	A Small size		90p	£45.00
B		12	B Large size		£1.50	£18.00
	C		Life in a Liner (1930):			
A		25	A Small size		£1.60	£40.00
B		12	B Large size		£5.00	—
	C		Men of the Moment in Sport:			
A		50	A Small size (1928)		£5.00	£250.00
			B Large size:			
B		12	1 '1st Series of 12' (1929)		£8.00	—
B		12	2 '2nd Series of 12' (1929)		£8.00	—
—	C	48	Modern Wonders (68 × 53mm) (1938)		32p	£16.00
A	C	25	Musical Instruments (1924)	H.547	£3.40	£85.00
	C		Nature's Architects (1930):			
A		25	A Small size		£1.40	£35.00
B		12	B Large size		£2.25	£27.00
—	U	48	The Navy at Work (68 × 53mm) (1937)		50p	£24.00
A	C	25	Pipes of the World (1927)		£3.00	£75.00

Size	Printing	Number in set			Handbook reference	Price per card	Complete set

W.A. & A.C. CHURCHMAN, Ipswich *(continued)*

Size	Print.	No.		Title	Handbook	Price	Complete
	C			Prominent Golfers (1931):			
A		50	A	Small size		£8.00	—
B		12	B	Large size		£20.00	—
	C			The 'Queen Mary' (1936):			
A		50	A	Small size		£1.50	£75.00
B		16	B	Large size		£3.00	£50.00
A	C	50		Racing Greyhounds (1934)		£2.60	£130.00
—	C	48		The RAF at Work (68 × 53mm) (1938)		90p	£45.00
	C			Railway Working	H.548		
			A	Small size:			
A		25		1 'Series of 25' (1926)		£3.60	£90.00
A		25		2 '2nd Series of 25' (1927)		£2.40	£60.00
			B	Large size:			
B		12		1 'Series of 12' (1926)		£9.00	—
B		13		2 '2nd Series, 13' (1927)		£9.00	—
B		12		3 '3rd Series, 12' (1927)		£9.00	—
A	BW	50		Rivers and Broads (1922):			
			A	Titled 'Rivers & Broads'		£6.00	—
			B	Titled 'Rivers & Broads of Norfolk & Suffolk' ..		£5.00	—
A	C	50		Rugby Internationals (1935)		£1.80	£90.00
A	C	50		Sporting Celebrities (1931)		£3.00	£150.00
	C			Sporting Trophies (1927):			
A		25	A	Small size		£2.40	£60.00
B		12	B	Large size		£6.00	—
A	C	25		Sports and Games in Many Lands (1929)	H.651	£5.00	£125.00
	C			The Story of London (1934):			
A		50	A	Small size		£1.50	£75.00
B		12	B	Large size		£3.00	£36.00
	C			The Story of Navigation:			
A		50	A	Small size (1936)		40p	£20.00
B		12	B	Large size (1935)		£1.25	£15.00
A	C			3 Jovial Golfers in search of the perfect course (1934):			
		36	A	Home issue		£3.50	—
		72	B	Irish issue, with green over-printing		£7.00	—
	C			Treasure Trove:			
A		50	A	Small size (1937)		40p	£20.00
B		12	B	Large size (1935)		£1.50	£18.00
	C			Warriors of All Nations:			
A		25	A	Small size (1929)		£2.80	£70.00
			B	Large size:			
B		12		1 'A Series of 12' (1929)		£4.00	£50.00
B		12		2 '2nd Series of 12' (1931)		£4.00	£50.00
	C			Well-known Ties (1934):			
A		50	A	Small size		80p	£40.00
			B	Large size:			
B		12		1 'A Series of 12'		£1.75	£21.00
B		12		2 '2nd Series of 12'		£1.75	£21.00
A	C	50		Well-known Ties, '2nd Series' (1935)		70p	£35.00
A	U	25		Wembley Exhibition (1924)		£2.40	£60.00
A	U	50		West Suffolk Churches (1919)		£1.80	£90.00
—	C	48		Wings Over the Empire (68 × 53mm) (1939)		40p	£20.00
	C			Wonderful Railway Travel (1937):			
A		50	A	Small size		50p	£25.00
B		12	B	Large size		£1.50	£18.00

C MISCELLANEOUS

	BW	1	Christmas Greetings Card (68 × 53mm) (1938)	—	£2.00

Size	Printing	Number in set		Handbook reference	Price per card	Complete set

W.A. & A.C. CHURCHMAN, Ipswich *(continued)*

Size	Printing	Number in set		Handbook reference	Price per card	Complete set
—	U	55	Olympic Winners Through The Years (Package Designs, 30 small, 25 large) (1960)	H.891	£2.00	—
—	C	48	Pioneers (68 × 53mm) (Prepared but not issued) (c1940)		—	—
—	U	40	The World of Sport (Package Designs, 30 small, 10 large) (1961)	H.892	£2.00	—
A	C	50	World Wonders Old and New (prepared but not issued) (c1955)		40p	£20.00

WM. CLARKE & SON, Dublin

PRE-1919 ISSUES

Size	Printing	Number in set		Handbook reference	Price per card	Complete set
A	C	25	Army Life (1915)	H.78	£12.00	£300.00
A1	BW	16	*Boer War Celebrities — 'CAG' (c1901)	H.79	£25.00	—
A	C	50	Butterflies and Moths (1912)	H.80	£8.00	£400.00
A	BW	30	Cricketer Series (1901)		£150.00	—
A1	BW	66	Football Series (1902)	H.81	£30.00	—
A	C	25	Marine Series (1907)		£13.00	£325.00
A	C	50	Royal Mail (1914)	H.82	£11.00	£550.00
	C	50	Sporting Terms (38 × 58mm) (c1900):	H.83		
			14 Cricket Terms		£45.00	—
			12 Cycling Terms		£45.00	—
			12 Football Terms		£45.00	—
			12 Golf Terms		£45.00	—
—	C	20	*Tobacco Leaf Girls (shaped) (c1898)	H.84	£450.00	—
—	C	25	Well-known Sayings (71 × 32mm) (c1900)	H.85	£24.00	£600.00

J. CLAYTON, Wakefield

PRE-1919 ISSUE

Size	Printing	Number in set		Handbook reference	Price per card	Complete set
—	C	? 6	*Play Up Sporting Shields (c1895)	H.718	£175.00	—

J.H. CLURE, Keighley

PRE-1919 ISSUES

Size	Printing	Number in set		Handbook reference	Price per card	Complete set
D	C	30	*Army Pictures, Cartoons, etc (c1900)	H.12	£110.00	—
A	U	50	War Portraits (1916)	H.86	£80.00	—

J. LOMAX COCKAYNE, Sheffield

PRE-1919 ISSUE

Size	Printing	Number in set		Handbook reference	Price per card	Complete set
A	U	50	War Portraits (1916)	H.86	£80.00	—

COHEN WEENEN & CO. LTD, London

A ***PRE-1919 ISSUES***

Size	Printing	Number in set		Handbook reference	Price per card	Complete set
—	P	40	*Actresses, Footballers and Jockeys (26 × 61mm) (c1901)	H.87	£50.00	—
A1	U	26	*Actresses — 'FROGA A' (c1900)	H.20	£65.00	—
A	C	25	*Beauties — selection from 'BOCCA' (c1900)	H.39	£75.00	—
A1	C	25	*Beauties — 'GRACC' (c1900)	H.59	£90.00	—
D2	BW	25	*Boxers (c1912):	H.721		
			A Black back		£14.00	—
			B Green back		£11.00	£275.00
			C *Without Maker's Name*		£17.00	—
A	BW		*Celebrities — Black and white (1901):	H.88		
		65	A 'Sweet Crop, over 250 ...' back		£5.00	—
		? 19	B 'Sweet Crop, over 500 ...' back		£10.00	—

Size	Print-ing	Number in set		Handbook reference	Price per card	Complete set

COHEN WEENEN & CO. LTD, London *(continued)*

Size	Print-ing	Number in set	Description	Handbook ref.	Price per card	Complete set
A	C	45	*Celebrities — Coloured (1901): I 1-45 Boer War Generals etc. 'Sweet Crop, over 100 ...' back:	H.89	—	£225.00
			A Toned back		£5.00	—
			B White back		£5.00	—
			C Plain Back		£8.00	—
		121	II 1-121 Including Royalty, etc. 'Sweet Crop, over 250 ...' back:			
			1-45 as in I		£8.00	—
			46-121 additional subjects		£5.00	—
—	C		*Celebrities — 'GAINSBOROUGH I' (1901):	H.90		
—		? 16	A In metal frames (46 × 67mm)		£100.00	—
D2		39	B 'Sweet Crop, over 250 ...' back		£40.00	—
D		30	C 'Sweet Crop, over 400 ...' back		£11.00	£330.00
		2	D 1902 Calendar Back gilt border to front		£100.00	—
D1		39	E Plain Back		£12.00	£475.00
—	P	? 172	*Celebrities — 'GAINSBOROUGH II' (c1901):	H.91		
			A In metal frames (46 × 67mm)		£15.00	—
			B Without frames showing Frame Marks		£5.00	—
			C Without Frames no Frame Marks (as issued) ...		£10.00	—
A2	C	20	*Cricketers, Footballers, Jockeys (c1900):	H.92		
			A Caption in brown		£20.00	£400.00
			B Caption in grey-black		£20.00	£400.00
D	C	40	Fiscal Phrases (c1905):	H.93		
			A 'Copyright Regd.' on front		£11.00	£440.00
			B Without 'Copyright Regd.'		£11.00	£440.00
A2	C	60	Football Captains, 1907-8 — Series No. 5	H.94	£14.00	—
A2	BW	100	*Heroes of Sport (c1898)	H.95	£75.00	—
A	C	40	*Home and Colonial Regiments (c1901):	H.69		
			A 'Sweet Crop, over 100 ...' back		£9.00	£360.00
			B 'Sweet Crop, over 250 ...' back		£13.00	—
			C 1902 Calendar Back Gilt Border		£120.00	—
A2	C	20	*Interesting Buildings and Views (1902):	H.96		
			A No Framelines		£10.00	£200.00
			B Gilt Framelines 1902 Calendar back		£100.00	—
K2	C	52	*Miniature Playing Cards — Bandmaster Cigarettes (c1910)		£4.00	—
D2	C		*Nations (c1902):	H.97		
		20	A Blue back		£12.00	£240.00
		20	B Plain back — gilt border		£100.00	—
		1	C 1902 Calender back		£100.00	—
D	C	40	Naval and Military Phrases (c1904):	H.14		
			A Red back, 'Series No. 1'		£16.00	£640.00

			B 'Sweet Crop, over 250 ...' back:
			  i) White Border ....
			  ii) Gilt Border ....
					£28.00
					£100.00
						—
						—

D2	C	50	Owners, Jockeys, Footballers, Cricketers — Series No. 2 (c1906)	H.98	£13.00	£650.00
D2	C	20	Owners, Jockeys, Footballers, Cricketers — Series No. 3 (c1907)	H.99	£14.00	£280.00
D	C	30	*Proverbs, 'Sweet Crop, over 400 ...' back (c1905) ...	H.15	£15.00	—
A	C	20	Russo-Japanese War Series (1904)	H.100	£18.00	—
A	BW	25	*Silhouettes of Celebrities (c1905)	H.101	£12.00	£300.00
D1	C	50	Star Artistes — Series No. 4 (c1905):	H.102		
			20 With stage background		£11.00	£220.00
			30 No stage, plain background		£10.00	£300.00

26

Size	Print-ing	Number in set		Handbook reference	Price per card	Complete set

COHEN WEENEN & CO. LTD, London *(continued)*

D	C	50	V.C. Heroes (of World War I), Nd. 51-100 (1915):			
			51-75 — dull greyish card		£10.00	£250.00
			Without Maker's Name on back		£12.00	—
			76-100 — glossy white card		£10.00	£250.00
D	U	50	*War Series (World War I) (1915):	H.103		
			1-25 Admirals and Warships:			
			A Thick card		£10.00	£250.00
			B Thin card		£10.00	£250.00
			26-50 Leaders of the War:			
			A Maker's Name on back		£10.00	£250.00
			B *Without Maker's Name on back*		£12.00	—
D1	C	30	Wonders of the World — 'Series No. 6' (c1908)	H.104	£7.00	£210.00

B POST-1920 ISSUES

D2	U	25	*Cricketers (1926)		£15.00	—
D2	C	20	Nations (1923)	H.97	£4.50	£90.00
D1	C	30	Wonders of the World (1923)	H.104	£2.70	£80.00

C SILKS

—	C	16	*Victoria Cross Heroes II (72 × 70mm)			
			(paper-backed) (c1915)	Ha.504-2	£40.00	—

T. H. COLLINS, Mansfield

POST-1920 ISSUES

A1	U	25	Homes of England (1924)		£6.00	£150.00
A	C	25	Sports and Pastimes — Series I (1923)	H.225	£7.00	£175.00

F. COLTON Jun., Retford

PRE-1919 ISSUES

D	C	30	*Army Pictures, Cartoons, etc (c1916)	H.12	£110.00	—
A	U	50	War Portraits (1916)	H.86	£80.00	—

T. W. CONQUEST, London

PRE-1919 ISSUE

D	C	*30	Army Pictures, Cartoons etc (c1916)	H12	£110.00	—

THE CONTINENTAL CIGARETTE FACTORY, London

POST-1920 ISSUES

A	C	25	Charming Portraits (c1925):	H.549		
			A Back in blue, with firm's name		£5.00	—
			B Back in blue, inscribed 'Club Mixture Tobacco'		£7.00	—
			C Back in brown, inscribed 'Club Mixture Tobacco'		£9.00	—
			*D *Plain back*		£5.00	—

COOPER & CO'S STORES LTD, London

PRE-1919 ISSUES

A	BW	25	*Boer War Celebrities — 'STEW' (c1901):	H.105		
			A 'Alpha Mixture' back		£130.00	—
			B 'Gladys Cigars' back		£130.00	—

CO-OPERATIVE WHOLESALE SOCIETY LTD, Manchester

A *PRE-1919 ISSUES*

A2	C	? 6	*Advertisement Cards (c1915)	H.106	£350.00	—
A	C	25	Boy Scout Series (c1915)		£32.00	—

Size	Printing	Number in set		Handbook reference	Price per card	Complete set

CO-OPERATIVE WHOLESALE SOCIETY LTD, Manchester *(continued)*

Size	Pr	Num	Title	Ref	Price	Set
A	C	50	British Sport Series§ (c1914)	H.112	£28.00	—
A	C	28	*Co-operative Buildings and Works (c1914)	H.107	£13.00	£365.00
A	C	25	Parrot Series (1910)		£35.00	—
A	C	18	War Series (c1915)		£28.00	—

§Note: Cards advertise non-tobacco products, but are believed to have been packed with cigarettes and/or tobacco.

B POST-1920 ISSUES

Size	Pr	Num	Title	Ref	Price	Set
A	C	24	African Types (1936)		50p	£12.00
—	U	50	Beauty Spots of Britain (76 × 51mm) (1936)		35p	£17.50
A2	C	50	Boy Scout Badges (1939)		£1.40	£70.00
A	C	48	British and Foreign Birds (1938)		70p	£35.00
D	C	25	*Cooking Recipes (1923)		£2.20	£55.00
A	C	24	English Roses (1924)		£4.00	£100.00
A	C	50	Famous Bridges (48 + 2 added) (1937)		90p	£45.00
A	C	48	Famous Buildings (1935)		70p	£35.00
A2	C	25	How to Do It (1924):	Ha.550		
			A 'Anglian Mixture' back		£2.60	—
			B 'Equity Tobacco' back		£2.60	—
			C 'Jaycee Brown Flake' back		£2.60	—
			D 'Raydex Gold Leaf' back		£2.60	—
A	C	48	Musical Instruments (1934)		£3.80	£190.00
A	C	48	Poultry (1927)		£7.00	£350.00
A	C	48	Railway Engines (1936)		£3.20	£160.00
A	C	24	Sailing Craft (1935)		£1.40	£35.00
A2	C	48	Wayside Flowers, brown back (1923)		£2.00	£100.00
A2	C	48	Wayside Flowers, grey back (1928)		80p	£40.00
A2	C	48	Wayside Woodland Trees (1924)		£2.50	£125.00

C POST-1940 ISSUE

Size	Pr	Num	Title	Ref	Price	Set
A	C	24	Western Stars (1957)		65p	£16.00

COPE BROS. & CO. LTD, Liverpool

A PRE-1919 ISSUES

Size	Pr	Num	Title	Ref	Price	Set
	BW	20	*Actresses — 'BLARM' (c1900):	H.23		
A1			A Plain backs. Name panel ¼" from border		£35.00	—
A1			B Black design back. Name ¼" from border		£35.00	—
D			C Black design back. Name panel ⅟₁₆" from border		£35.00	—
A	U	? 6	*Actresses — 'COPEIS' (c1900)	H.108	£225.00	—
A	U	26	*Actresses 'FROGA A' (c1900)	H.20	£90.00	—
D1	P	50	*Actresses and Beauties (c1900)	H.109	£14.00	—
KI	P	? 46	*Beauties, Actors and Actresses (c1900)	H.110	£26.00	—
A	C	52	*Beauties — P.C. inset (c1898)	H.111	£45.00	—
A	C	15	*Beauties 'PAC' (c1898)	H.2	£75.00	—
A1	C	50	Boats of the World (c1910)		£14.00	£700.00
D2	BW	126	Boxers (c1915):			
			1-25 Boxers		£18.00	£450.00
			26-50 Boxers		£15.00	£375.00
			51-75 Boxers		£15.00	£375.00
			76-100 Boxers		£20.00	£500.00
			101-125 Army Boxers		£14.00	£350.00
			126 'New World Champion'		—	£40.00
A1	C	35	*Boy Scouts and Girl Guides (c1910)	H.132	£12.00	£420.00
D	BW	25	British Admirals (c1915)	H.103	£12.00	£300.00
A2	C	50	British Warriors (c1912):			
			A Black on white backs		£7.50	£375.00
			B Grey on toned backs		£9.00	£450.00

Size	Print-ing	Number in set		Handbook reference	Price per card	Complete set

COPE BROS. & CO. LTD, Liverpool *(continued)*

Size	Print-ing	Number in set	Description	Handbook reference	Price per card	Complete set
A	C	50	Characters from Scott (c1900):			
			A Wide card		£12.00	£600.00
			B Narrow card — officially cut		£12.00	—
	U	115	Chinese Series (c1903):	H.113		
A1			Nos 1-20		£11.00	—
A1			Nos 21-40		£11.00	—
			Nos 41-65:			
D			A Thick brown card		£11.00	—
A1			B Re-drawn, smaller format		£11.00	—
A2			Nos 66-115		£11.00	—
A	C	50	Cope's Golfers (1900):			
			A Wide card		£80.00	—
			B Narrow card — officially cut		£80.00	—
A	C	50	Dickens' Gallery (1900)		£10.00	£500.00
A	C	50	Dogs of the World (by Cecil Aldin) (c1910)		£13.00	£650.00
A	C	25	Eminent British Regiments Officers' Uniforms (c1908):		—	£300.00
			A Yellow-brown back		£12.00	—
			B Claret back		£12.00	—
A2	C	30	*Flags of Nations (c1903):	H.114		
			A 'Bond of Union' back		£12.00	£360.00
			B *Plain back*		£9.00	—
D	C	24	*Flags, Arms and Types of Nations (c1904):	H.115		
			A Numbered		£7.00	£175.00
			B Unnumbered		£90.00	—
—	U	20	*Kenilworth Phrases (80 × 70mm) (c1910)	H.116	£300.00	—
A2	C	50	Music Hall Artistes (c1910):			
			A Inscribed 'Series of 50'		£35.00	—
			B Without the above		£11.00	£550.00
A	U	472	Noted Footballers — 'Clips Cigarettes' (c1910):	H.474		
			1 Unnumbered — Wee Jock Simpson		—	£50.00
			120 Series of 120:			
			A Greenish-blue frame		£18.00	—
			B Bright blue frame		£18.00	—
			162 Series of 282:			
			A Greenish-blue frame		£18.00	—
			B Bright blue frame		£18.00	—
			471 Series of 500. Bright blue frame		£18.00	—
D	P	195	Noted Footballers — 'Solace Cigarettes' (c1910)	H.474	£18.00	—
A	C	24	*Occupations for Women (1897)	H.117	£90.00	—
A	C	52	*Playing Cards. Blue backs (c1902):	H.118		
			A Rounded Corners		£16.00	—
			B Square Corners		£12.00	—
—	C	24	Photo Albums for the Million (c1898):	H.119		
			12 Buff cover (25 × 39mm)		£16.00	—
			12 Green cover (25 × 39mm)		£16.00	—
—	C	7	The Seven Ages of Man (114 × 78mm) (c1885)	H.726	£300.00	—
A	C	50	Shakespeare Gallery (c1900):			
			A Wide card		£12.00	£600.00
			B Narrow card — officially cut		£12.00	—
A1	C	25	*Uniforms of Soldiers and Sailors (c1900):	H.120		
			A Circular Medallion back, wide card		£28.00	—
			B Square Medallion back, wide card		£50.00	—
			C Square Medallion back, narrow card, officially cut		£22.00	—
D	BW		VC and DSO Naval and Flying Heroes:			
		50	Unnumbered (1916)	H.121	£9.00	£450.00
		25	Numbered 51-75 (1917)		£10.00	£250.00
D	BW	20	*War Pictures (1915)	H.122	£12.50	£250.00

Size	Print-ing	Number in set		Handbook reference	Price per card	Complete set

COPE BROS. & CO. LTD, Liverpool *(continued)*

Size	Print-ing	Number in set		Handbook reference	Price per card	Complete set
D	BW	25	*War Series (War Leaders and Warships) (c1915)	H.103	£13.00	—
A1	C	25	Wild Animals and Birds (c1908)		£16.00	—

B POST-1920 ISSUES

Size	Print-ing	Number in set		Handbook reference	Price per card	Complete set
D	BW	25	Boxing Lessons (1935)		£4.00	£100.00
—	C	25	Bridge Problems (folders) (85 × 50mm) (1924)		£25.00	—
A1	U	25	Castles§ (1939)		£1.20	£30.00
A1	U	25	Cathedrals§ (May, 1939)		£1.40	£35.00
—	C	25	Dickens' Character Series (75 × 58mm) (1939)		£1.00	£25.00
—	C	25	The Game of Poker§ (75 × 58mm) (1936)		50p	£12.50
—	C	50	General Knowledge§ (70 × 42mm) (1925)		£4.00	—
—	BW	32	Golf Strokes (70 × 45mm) (1923)		£14.00	—
A1	C	60	'Happy Families' (1937)		£1.50	£90.00
—	C	50	Household Hints§ (advertisement fronts) (70 × 45mm) (1925)		£1.60	£80.00
C	BW	30	Lawn Tennis Strokes (1924):			
			A Numbers 1 to 25		£6.00	—
			B Numbers 26 to 30		£20.00	—
—	U	50	Modern Dancing (folders) (74 × 43mm) (1926)		£14.00	—
A2	C	25	Pigeons (c1926)		£8.00	£200.00
A2	C	25	Song Birds (c1926)		£7.00	£175.00
A1	C	25	Sports and Pastimes (1925)	H.551	£4.00	£100.00
—	C	25	Toy Models (The Country Fair) (73 × 66mm) (c1930) ..	H.552	40p	£10.00
A	C	25	The World's Police (c1935)		£4.60	£115.00

§Joint Cope and Richard Lloyd issues.

E. CORONEL, London

PRE-1919 ISSUE

Size	Print-ing	Number in set		Handbook reference	Price per card	Complete set
A	C	25	*Types of British and Colonial Troops (1900)	H.76	£60.00	—

DAVID CORRE & CO., London

PRE-1919 ISSUE

Size	Print-ing	Number in set		Handbook reference	Price per card	Complete set
—	C	1	Advertisement Card — The New Alliance (70 × 42mm) (c1915)		—	£350.00
D	C	40	*Naval and Military Phrases (1900):	H.14		
			A With border		£75.00	—
			B Without border		£75.00	—

JOHN COTTON LTD, Edinburgh

POST-1920 ISSUES

Size	Print-ing	Number in set		Handbook reference	Price per card	Complete set
—	C	50	*Bridge Hands (folders) (82 × 66mm) (1934)		£10.00	—
A1	U	50	*Golf Strokes — A/B (1936)		£8.00	—
A1	U	50	*Golf Strokes — C/D (1937)		£9.00	—
A1	U	50	*Golf Strokes — E/F (1938)		£13.00	—
A1	U	50	*Golf Strokes — G/H (1939)		£500.00	—
A1	U	50	*Golf Strokes — I/J (1939)		£500.00	—

A. & J. COUDENS LTD, London

POST-1920 ISSUES

Size	Print-ing	Number in set		Handbook reference	Price per card	Complete set
A1	P	60	British Beauty Spots (1923):	H.553		
			A Printed back, numbered		£1.50	£90.00
			B Printed back, unnumbered		£2.50	—
			*C Back rubber stamped 'Cymox Cigarettes ...' ...		£4.00	—
			*D *Plain back*		£4.00	—

Size	Print-ing	Number in set		Handbook reference	Price per card	Complete set

A. & J. COUDENS LTD, London *(continued)*

| A | P | 60 | Holiday Resorts in East Anglia (1924) .... | | £1.25 | £75.00 |
| A2 | BW | 25 | Sports Alphabet (1924) .... | H.551 | £8.00 | £200.00 |

THE CRAIGMILLAR CREAMERY CO. LTD, Midlothian

PRE-1919 ISSUE

| H | C | 1 | *Views of Craigmillar (c1901) .... | H.727 | — | £700.00 |

W.R. DANIEL & CO., London

PRE-1919 ISSUES

A2	C	30	*Colonial Troops (c1902):	H.40		
			A Black back		£90.00	—
			B Brown back		£90.00	—
A2	C	25	*National Flags and Flowers — Girls (c1901)	H.123	£140.00	—

W.T. DAVIES & SONS, Chester

A   PRE-1919 ISSUES

A	C	50	*Actresses — 'DAVAN' (c1902)	H.124	£85.00	—
A	C	25	Army Life (1915)	H.78	£12.00	—
A	BW	12	*Beauties (1903)	H.125	£50.00	—
A	C	50	Flags and Funnels of Leading Steamship Lines (1913)	H.67	£12.00	—
A	BW	? 12	Newport Football Club (c1904)	H.126	£400.00	—
A	BW	5	Royal Welsh Fusiliers (c1904)	H.127	£400.00	—

B   POST-1920 ISSUES

A2	U	42	Aristocrats of the Turf (1924):	H.554		
			1 Nos 1-30 — 'A Series of 30'		£6.00	—
			2 Nos 31-42 — 'A Series of 42'		£20.00	—
A2	U	36	Aristocrats of the Turf, Second Series (1924)	H.554	£5.50	—
A	C	25	Boxing (1924)	H.311	£4.40	£110.00

S. H. DAWES, Luton

PRE-1919 ISSUE

| D | C | 30 | *Army Pictures, Cartoons, etc (c1916) .... | H.12 | £110.00 | — |

J.W. DEWHURST, Morecambe

PRE-1919 ISSUE

| D | C | 30 | *Army Pictures, Cartoons, etc (c1916) .... | H.12 | £110.00 | — |

R.I. DEXTER & CO., Hucknall

PRE-1919 ISSUE

| D2 | U | 30 | *Borough Arms (1900) .... | H.128 | £1.30 | £40.00 |

A. DIMITRIOU, London

POST-1920 ISSUE

| — | C | ? 3 | Advertisement Cards (100 × 65mm) (c1930) .... | | £125.00 | — |

GEORGE DOBIE & SON LTD, Paisley

A   POST-1920 ISSUES

| — | C | ? 22 | Bridge Problems (folders) (circular 64mm diam.) (c1933) .... | | £35.00 | — |
| A | C | 25 | Weapons of All Ages (1924) .... | | £6.00 | £150.00 |

B   POST-1940 ISSUE

| — | C | 32 | Four-Square Book (Nd 1-32) (75 × 50mm) (1963) .... | | £2.00 | — |

Size	Print-ing	Number in set		Handbook reference	Price per card	Complete set

GEORGE DOBIE & SON LTD, Paisley *(continued)*

—	C	32	Four-Square Book (Nd 33-64) (75 × 50mm) (1963) . . .		£2.00	—
—	C	32	Four-Square Book (Nd 65-96) (75 × 50mm) (1963) . . .		£1.50	£50.00

DOBSON & CO. LTD ─────────────────────────────

PRE-1919 ISSUE

A	C	8	The European War Series (c1917)	H.129	£40.00	—

THE DOMINION TOBACCO CO. (1929) LTD, London ─────────────

POST-1920 ISSUES

A	U	25	Old Ships (1934)		£2.40	£60.00
A	U	25	Old Ships (Second Series) (1935)		80p	£20.00
A	U	25	Old Ships (Third Series) (1936)		80p	£20.00
A	U	25	Old Ships (Fourth Series) (1936)		£1.80	£45.00

JOSEPH W. DOYLE LTD, Manchester ────────────────────

POST-1920 ISSUES

—	P	18	*Beauties, Nd X.1-X.18 (89 × 70mm) (c1925)	H.653	£12.00	—
D	P	12	Dirt Track Riders Nd. CC.A.1-CC.A.12 (c1925)	H.635	£50.00	—
D	P	12	Views Nd. CC.B.1-CC.B.12 (c1925)	H.635	£28.00	—
D	P	12	Views Nd CC.C.1-CC.C.12 (c1925)	H.635	£28.00	—
D	P	12	*Beauties Nd. CC.D.1-CC.D.12 (c1925)	H.635	£28.00	—
D	P	12	*Beauties Nd CC.E.1-CC.E.12 (c1925)	H.635	£28.00	—

MAJOR DRAPKIN & CO., London ─────────────────────

A PRE-1919 ISSUES

D	BW	12	*Actresses 'FRAN' (c1910)	H.175	£7.50	—
—	BW	? 1	*Army Insignia (83 × 46mm) (c1915)	H.130	£400.00	—
—	—	? 111	'Bandmaster' Conundrums (58 × 29mm) (c1910)	H.131	£10.00	—
A2	BW	? 32	Boer War Celebrities 'JASAS' — 'Sweet Alva Cigarettes' (c1901)	H.133	£150.00	—
A1	P		*Celebrities of the Great War (1916):	H.135		
		36	A Printed back		70p	£25.00
		34	B *Plain back*		£1.00	£34.00
—	BW	96	Cinematograph Actors (42 × 70mm) (1913)	H.134	£13.00	—
A	C	25	How to Keep Fit — Sandow Exercises (c1912):	H.136		
			A 'Drapkin's Cigarettes'		£15.00	£375.00
			A1 'Drapkin's Cigarettes' short cards, cut officially		£15.00	—
			B 'Crayol Cigarettes'		£15.00	£375.00
D	U	48	Photogravure Masterpieces (1915)	H.137	£10.00	—
—	C	25	*Soldiers and Their Uniforms, die cut (1914):	H.138	—	£80.00
			A 'Drapkin's Cigarettes'		From £1.00	
			B 'Crayol Cigarettes'		From £1.00	—
D	BW		*Views of the World (c1912):	H.176		
		12	A Caption in two lines		£5.00	£60.00
		8	B Caption in one line		£30.00	—
D	BW	8	*Warships (c1912)	H.463	£12.00	—

B POST-1920 ISSUES

C	C	8	*Advertisement Cards (c1925):	Ha.555		
			1 Packings (4)		£7.50	£30.00
			2 Smokers (4)		£6.50	£26.00

Size	Printing	Number in set		Handbook reference	Price per card	Complete set

MAJOR DRAPKIN & CO., London *(continued)*

Size	Printing	Number in set	Description	Handbook reference	Price per card	Complete set
	BW	50	Around Britain (1929) (export):			
C			A Small size		£1.30	£65.00
B1			B Large size		£2.50	—
	C	50	Around the Mediterranean (1926) (export):	Ha.610		
C			A Small size		£1.50	£75.00
B1			B Large size		£2.50	—
A2	P	40	Australian and English Test Cricketers (1928)		£1.85	£75.00
A1	U	25	British Beauties (1930) (export)		£2.80	£70.00
	C	15	Dogs and Their Treatment (1924):			
A			A Small size		£5.50	£85.00
B2			B Large size		£6.50	£100.00
A	C	40	The Game of Sporting Snap (1928)		£4.00	—
			Instruction Leaflet		—	£11.00
	C	50	Girls of Many Lands (1929):			
D			A Small size		£4.00	—
—			B Medium size (76 × 52mm)		50p	£25.00
A2	BW	54	Life at Whipsnade Zoo (1934)	Ha.556	50p	£27.00
D2	C	50	'Limericks' (1929):	Ha.557		
			A White card		£1.40	£70.00
			B Cream card		£1.40	£70.00
A2	P	36	National Types of Beauty (1928)	Ha.558	75p	£27.00
	C	25	Optical Illusions (1926):			
A			A Small size. Home issue, name panel (23 × 7mm)		£3.20	£80.00
A			B Small size. Export issue, name panel (26 × 10mm)		£3.00	£75.00
B2			C Large 'size. Home issue		£3.40	£85.00
	C	25	Palmistry:			
A			A Small size (1927)		£3.00	£75.00
B			B Large size (1926)		£3.00	£75.00
	C	25	Puzzle Pictures (1926):			
A			A Small size		£3.60	£90.00
B			B Large size		£4.00	£100.00
A2	P	36	Sporting Celebrities in Action (1930) (export)		—	£300.00
			35 different (No. 18 withdrawn)		£5.00	£175.00
C	**SILKS**					
—	C	40	Regimental Colours and Badges of the Indian Army (70 × 50mm) (paper-backed) (c1915):	H.502-5		
			A The Buffs' back		£5.00	—
			B No brand back		£35.00	—
D	**MISCELLANEOUS**					
A	C	1	'Grey's' Smoking Mixture Advertisement Card (plain back) (c1935)		—	£7.00

DRAPKIN & MILLHOFF, London

PRE-1919 ISSUES

Size	Printing	Number in set	Description	Handbook reference	Price per card	Complete set
A	U		*Beauties 'KEWAI' (c1898):	H.139-1		
		? 2	A 'Eldona Cigars' back		£225.00	—
		? 1	B 'Explorer Cigars' back		£225.00	—
A	BW	25	*Boer War Celebrities — 'PAM' (c1901):	H.140		
			A With PTO on front 'Pick-Me-Up Cigarettes'		£30.00	—
			B Without PTO on front 'Pick-Me-Up Cigarettes' .		£30.00	—
			C Plain back		£50.00	—
C	C	30	*Colonial Troops (c1902)	H.40	£50.00	—
—	BW	? 7	*'Pick-me-up' Paper Inserts (112 × 44mm) (c1900) ...	H.141	£200.00	—
—	U	? 2	*Portraits (48 × 36mm) (c1900)	H.461	£200.00	—
A2	U	? 3	*Pretty Girl Series — 'BAGG' (c1900)	H.45	£225.00	—

Size	Print-ing	Number in set		Handbook reference	Price per card	Complete set

J. DUNCAN & CO. LTD, Glasgow

A PRE-1919 ISSUES

D1	C	48	*Flags, Arms and Types of Nations (c1910):	H.115		
			A Back in Blue		£27.00	—
			B Back in Green		£50.00	—
A	C	20	Inventors and Their Inventions (c1915)	H.213	£50.00	—
A	C	30	Scottish Clans, Arms of Chiefs and Tartans (c1910):	H.142		
			A Back in black...........................		£125.00	—
			B Back in green		£17.00	—
—	C		Scottish Gems: (58 × 84mm):	H.143		
—	C	72	1st series (c1912)		£13.00	—
—	C	50	2nd series (c1913)		£13.00	—
—	C	50	3rd series (c1914)...........................		£13.00	—
D	C	25	*Types of British Soldiers (c1910)	H.144	£45.00	—

B POST-1920 ISSUES

D1	C	50	'Evolution of the Steamship' (c1925)	H.559	—	£75.00
			47/50 ditto		75p	£35.00
			'Olimpia II'		£25.00	—
			'Castalia' and 'Athenia'		£7.50	—
H1	BW	50	Scottish Gems (known as '4th Series') (c1925)	H.143	50p	£25.00

G. DUNCOMBE, Buxton

PRE-1919 ISSUE

D	C	30	*Army Pictures, Cartoons, Etc (c1916)	H.12	£110.00	—

ALFRED DUNHILL LTD, London

POST-1940 ISSUE

—	U	25	Dunhill Kingsize Ransom (75 × 45mm) (1985)		£1.60	—

EDWARDS, RINGER & CO., Bristol

PRE 1919 ISSUE

—	BW	50	How to Count Cribbage Hands (79 × 62mm) (c1908) ..		£150.00	—

EDWARDS, RINGER & BIGG, Bristol

A PRE-1919 ISSUES

A	U	25	Abbeys and Castles — Photogravure series (c1912):			
			A Type-set back............................		£8.00	£200.00
			B 'Statue of Liberty' back		£8.00	£200.00
			C 'Stag Design' back		£8.00	£200.00
A	U	25	Alpine Views — Photogravure series (c1912):			
			A 'Statue of Liberty' back		£8.00	£200.00
			B 'Stag Design' back		£8.00	£200.00
A	C	12	*Beauties — 'CERF' (1905)	H.57	£60.00	—
A	U	25	*Beauties — 'FECKSA', 1900 Calendar back	H.58	£37.00	—
A	C	50	*Birds and Eggs (1906)	H.60	£12.00	£600.00
A	BW	? 2	Boer War and Boxer Rebellion Sketches (c1901)	H.46	£120.00	—
A	BW	25	*Boer War Celebrities — 'STEW' 1901 Calendar back	H.105	£40.00	—
A	C	1	Calendar for 1899	H.730	—	£400.00
A	C	1	Calendar (1905), Exmore Hunt Stag design back	H.730	—	£350.00
A	C	2	Calendar (1910)	H.730	£350.00	—
A	U	25	Coast and Country — Photogravure series (1911):			
			A 'Statue of Liberty' back		£8.00	£200.00
			B 'Stag Design' back		£8.00	£200.00
A	C	23	*Dogs series (1908):	H.64		
			A 'Exmoor Hunt' back		£9.00	—
			B 'Klondyke' back		£4.50	£105.00

Size	Print-ing	Number in set		Handbook reference	Price per card	Complete set

EDWARDS, RINGER & BIGG, Bristol *(continued)*

Size	Print	Num	Description	Ref	Price	Set
A	C	3	Easter Manoeuvres of Our Volunteers (1897)	H.146	£300.00	—
A	C	25	Flags of All Nations, 1st series (1906)	H.37	£7.00	£175.00
A	C	12	Flags of All Nations, 2nd series (1907)	H.37	£11.00	£135.00
A	C	37	*Flags of All Nations (1907):	H.37		
			A Globe and Grouped Flags back		£7.00	—
			B 'Exmoor Hunt' back:			
			i 4½d per oz		£7.00	—
			ii Altered to 5d by hand		£7.00	—
			iii 5d label added		£9.00	—
			C 'Stag' design back		£7.00	£260.00
			D Upright titled back		£7.00	—
A	C	50	Life on Board a Man of War (1905)	H.38	£10.00	—
—	C	1	'Miners Bound for Klondyke' (41 × 81mm) (1897)		—	£500.00
A	C	10	Portraits of His Majesty the King in Uniforms of the British and Foreign Nations (1902)	H.147	£38.00	£380.00
A	C	50	A Tour Round the World (Mar. 1909)	H.75	£10.00	£500.00
A	C	56	War Map of the Western Front (1916)		£10.00	—
A	U	54	War Map of the Western Front, etc Series No. 2 (1917):			
			A 'Exmoor Hunt' back		£10.00	—
			B 'New York Mixture' back		£10.00	—

B POST-1920 ISSUES

Size	Print	Num	Description	Ref	Price	Set
A	C	25	British Trees and Their Uses (1933)	H.654	£2.60	£65.00
A	C	50	Celebrated Bridges (1924)	H.346	£2.40	£120.00
	U		Cinema Stars (1923):			
A2		50	A Small size		£1.50	£75.00
—		25	B Medium size (67 × 57mm)		£1.80	£45.00
A	C	25	Garden Life (1934)	H.449	£3.20	£80.00
A	C	25	How to Tell Fortunes (1929)		£3.60	£90.00
A	C	50	Mining (1925)	H.450	£2.40	£120.00
A	C	25	Musical Instruments (1924)	H.547	£3.60	£90.00
A	C	25	Optical Illusions (1936)	H.560	£3.00	£75.00
A	C	25	Our Pets (1926)	H.561	£2.40	£60.00
A	C	25	Our Pets, 2nd series (1926)	H.561	£2.40	£60.00
A	C	25	Past and Present (1928)		£3.20	£80.00
A	C	25	Prehistoric Animals (1924)		£5.00	£125.00
A	C	25	Sports and Games in Many Lands (1935)	H.651	£5.00	£125.00

S. EISISKI, Rhyl

PRE-1919 ISSUES

Size	Print	Num	Description	Ref	Price	Set
D	U	? 25	*Actresses 'ANGOOD' (c1900)	H.187	£300.00	—
A	U	? 6	*Actresses — 'COPEIS' (c1900)	H.108	£300.00	—
A	U	? 23	*Beauties — 'FENA' (c1900)	H.148	£300.00	—
A	U	? 2	*Beauties — 'KEWA I', back inscribed 'Eisiski's New Gold Virginia Cigarettes' (c1900)	H.139	£300.00	—
A	U	? 2	*Beauties — 'KEWA I', back inscribed 'Eisiski's Rhyl Best Bird's Eye Cigarettes' (c1900)	H.139	£300.00	—
A	U	? 2	*Beauties — 'KEWA I' Rubber-stamped back (c1900)	H.139	£300.00	—

ELDONS LTD

PRE-1919 ISSUE

Size	Print	Num	Description	Ref	Price	Set
A1	C	30	*Colonial Troops — 'Leon de Cuba' Cigars (c1900)	H.40	£150.00	—

R. J. ELLIOTT & CO. LTD, Huddersfield

PRE 1919 ISSUE

Size	Print	Num	Description	Ref	Price	Set
A2	C	? 2	Advertisement Card — Bulldog (c1910)		£250.00	—

Size	Print-ing	Number in set		Handbook reference	Price per card	Complete set

EMPIRE TOBACCO CO., London

PRE-1919 ISSUE
| D | C | ? 6 | Franco-British Exhibition (c1907) .... | H.471 | £250.00 | — |

THE EXPRESS TOBACCO CO. LTD, London

POST-1920 ISSUE
| — | U | 50 | 'How It is Made'(Motor Cars) (76 × 51mm) (1931) ... | | £3.00 | — |

L. & J. FABIAN, London

POST-1920 ISSUE
—	P		The Elite Series (Beauties) (c1935):			
D1		24	A Numbered LLF 1 to 24		£35.00	—
A1		? 47	B Plain Numerals		£35.00	—

FAIRWEATHER & SONS, Dundee

PRE-1919 ISSUE
| A | C | 50 | Historic Buildings of Scotland (c1914) .... | | £45.00 | — |

W. & F. FAULKNER, London

12 page reference book — £4.00

A PRE-1919 ISSUES
C	C	26	*Actresses — 'FROGA A' (c1900)	H.20	£45.00	—
D2	C	12	*'Ation Series (1901)		£22.00	—
C	C	25	*Beauties (c1898)	H.150	£70.00	—
A	U	49	*Beauties — 'FECKSA' (1901)	H.58	£22.00	—
A	BW	16	*British Royal Family (1901)	H.28	£35.00	—
D2	C	12	*Coster Series (1900)	H.151	£30.00	—
A	BW	20	Cricketers Series (1901)	H.29	£250.00	—
D2	C	12	Cricket Terms (1899)	H.152	£75.00	—
D2	C	12	Football Terms, 1st Series (1900)	H.153	£30.00	—
D2	C	12	Football Terms, 2nd Series (1900)	H.153	£30.00	—
D2	C	12	*Golf Terms (1901)	H.155	£90.00	—
D2	C	12	Grenadier Guards (1899)	H.156	£25.00	—
A2	C	40	*Kings and Queens (1902)	H.157	£22.00	—
D2	C	12	Kipling Series (1900)	H.158	£25.00	—
D2	C	12	The Language of Flowers (1900):	H.159		
			A 'Grenadier' Cigarettes		£30.00	—
			B 'Nosegay' Cigarettes		£30.00	—
D2	C	12	*Military Terms, 1st series (1899)	H.50	£24.00	—
D2	C	12	*Military Terms, 2nd series (1899)	H.160	£24.00	—
D2	C	12	*Nautical Terms, 1st series (1900)	H.161	£20.00	—
D2	C	12	*Nautical Terms, 2nd series (1900):	H.162		
			A 'Grenadier' Cigarettes		£20.00	—
			B 'Union Jack Cigarettes'		£22.00	—
D2	C		'Our Colonial Troops' (1900):			
			A Grenadier Cigarettes:			
		30	i With copyright Nos 1-30		£30.00	—
		90	ii Without copyright Nos 1-90		£14.00	—
		60	B Union Jack Cigarettes Nos 31-90		£17.00	—
A	C	20	Our Gallant Grenadiers, 1-20:	H.163		
			A Without ITC Clause (1901):			
			i Thick card		£16.00	£320.00
			ii Thin card		£16.00	£320.00
			B With ITC Clause, thin card (1902)		£27.00	£540.00
A	C	20	Our Gallant Grenadiers, 21-40 (1903)		£25.00	£500.00

Size	Print-ing	Number in set		Handbook reference	Price per card	Complete set
W. & F. FAULKNER, London *(continued)*						
D2	C	12	*Policemen of the World (1899):	H.164		
			A 'Grenadier' Cigarettes		£150.00	—
			B 'Nosegay' Cigarettes		£32.00	—
D2	C	12	*Police Terms (1899)	H.165	£27.00	
D2	C	12	*Puzzle series (1897):	H.166		
			A 'Grenadier Cigarettes		£160.00	—
			B 'Nosegay Cigarettes		£65.00	—
A	BW	25	*South African War Scenes (1901)	H.167	£16.00	£400.00
D2	C	12	Sporting Terms (1900)	H.168	£32.00	—
D2	C	12	Street Cries (1902)	H.169	£24.00	—
B	***POST-1920 ISSUES***					
A	C	25	Angling (1929)	H.655	£7.50	—
A	C	50	Celebrated Bridges (1925)	H.346	£2.50	£125.00
A	C	25	Old Sporting Prints (1930)	H.563	£3.60	£90.00
A	C	25	Optical Illusions (1935)	H.560	£3.00	£75.00
A	C	25	Our Pets (1926)	H.561	£3.00	£75.00
A	C	25	Our Pets, 2nd series (1926)	H.561	£2.80	£70.00
A	C	25	Prominent Racehorses of the Present Day (1923)		£3.20	£80.00
A	C	25	Prominent Racehorses of the Present Day, 2nd series (1924)		£5.00	£125.00

FIELD FAVOURITES CIGARETTES

PRE-1919 ISSUE

D	P	? 1	*Footballers (c1895)	H.731	£1800.00	—

FINLAY & CO. LTD, Newcastle-on-Tyne and London

PRE-1919 ISSUES

D1	BW	? 28	Our Girls (c1910)	H.170	£125.00	—
A	U	30	World's Aircraft (c1912)		£65.00	—

FLYNN, Dublin

PRE-1919 ISSUE

A	C	26	*Beauties — 'HOL' (c1900)	H.192	£400.00	—

C. D. FOTHERGILL, St Helens

PRE-1919 ISSUE

—	C	? 1	*'Play Up' Sporting Shields (c1895)	H.718	£175.00	—

FRAENKEL BROS., London

PRE-1919 ISSUES

A2	C	? 2	*Beauties — 'Don Jorg (c1898)	H.733	£700.00	—
A	U	? 23	*Beauties — 'FENA' (c1898)	H.148	£100.00	—
A	C	25	*Beauties — 'GRACC' (c1898)	H.59	£150.00	—
A	U	24	*Beauties — 'HUMPS' (c1900)	H.222	£120.00	—
A	U	26	*Music Hall Artistes (c1900):	H.171		
			A Pink card		£90.00	—
			B White card		£90.00	—
A2	C	25	*Types of British and Colonial Troops (c1900)	H.76	£65.00	—

FRANKLYN, DAVEY & CO., Bristol

A PRE-1919 ISSUES

A	C	12	*Beauties — 'CERF' (1905)	H.57	£65.00	—
D2	C	50	*Birds (c1895)		£65.00	—

Size	Printing	Number in set		Handbook reference	Price per card	Complete set

FRANKLYN, DAVEY & CO., Bristol *(continued)*

Size	Print	Num	Description	Ref	Price	Set
A2	BW	10	*Boer War Generals — 'FLAC' (1901)	H.47	£85.00	—
A	C	25	Ceremonial and Court Dress (Oct. 1915)	H.145	£10.00	—
A	C	50	*Football Club Colours (1909)	H.68	£15.00	£750.00
A	C	50	Naval Dress and Badges (1916)	H.172	£12.00	—
A	C	25	*Star Girls (c1898)	H.30	£220.00	—
A	C	10	Types of Smokers (c1898)		£55.00	£550.00
A	C	50	Wild Animals of the World (c1902)	H.77	£12.00	£600.00

B POST-1920 ISSUES

Size	Print	Num	Description	Ref	Price	Set
A	C	25	Boxing (1924)	H.311	£3.20	£80.00
A	C	50	Children of All Nations (1934)	H.656	90p	£45.00
A	C	50	Historic Events (1924)	H.464	£2.50	£125.00
A	U	25	Hunting (1925)		£1.00	£25.00
A	U	50	Modern Dance Steps (1929)		£5.00	£250.00
A	U	50	Modern Dance Steps, 2nd series (1931)		70p	£35.00
A	C	50	Overseas Dominions (Australia) (1923)	H.451	£4.50	£225.00

C MISCELLANEOUS

Size	Print	Num	Description	Ref	Price	Set
—	C	? 1	Comic Dog Folder (opens to 183 × 65mm) (1898)	H.490	—	£500.00

A.H. FRANKS & SONS, London

PRE-1919 ISSUES

Size	Print	Num	Description	Ref	Price	Set
D1	BW	56	*Beauties — 'Beauties Cigarettes' (c1900)	H.173	£70.00	—
D	C	24	*Nautical Expressions (c1900)	H.174	£75.00	—
A1	C	25	*Types of British and Colonial Troops (c1900)	H.76	£60.00	—

J.J. FREEMAN, London

PRE-1919 ISSUES

Size	Print	Num	Description	Ref	Price	Set
D	BW	12	*Actresses — 'FRAN' (c1912)	H.175	£40.00	—
D	BW	12	*Views of the World (c1910)	H.176	£40.00	—

J. R. FREEMAN, London

A POST-1920 ISSUE

Size	Print	Num	Description	Ref	Price	Set
—	U	12	*'Manikin' Cards (77 × 49mm) (c1920)	H.481	£75.00	—

B POST-1940 ISSUE

Size	Print	Num	Description	Ref	Price	Set
C1	U	33	Football Challenge (1969)		£6.00	—

C. FRYER & SONS LTD, London

A PRE-1919 ISSUES

Size	Print	Num	Description	Ref	Price	Set
A2	C		*Boer War and General Interest: (c1900)	H.13		
		? 10	A Brown leaf design back		£140.00	—
		? 5	B Green leaf design back		£140.00	—
		? 2	C Green daisy design back		£140.00	—
D	C	40	*Naval and Military Phrases (c1905)	H.14	£60.00	—
A2	BW	? 13	*'Vita Berlin' series (c1902)	H.177	£350.00	—

B POST-1920 ISSUE

Size	Print	Num	Description	Ref	Price	Set
—	—	50	Clan Sketches (101 × 74mm) (paper folders with wording only) — 'Pibroch Virginia' (c1930)	Ha.628	£13.00	—

FRYER & COULTMAN, London

PRE-1919 ISSUES

Size	Print	Num	Description	Ref	Price	Set
D	BW	50	*Beauties — PLUMS (c1900)	H.186	£500.00	—
—	C	12	*French Phrases, 1893 Calendar back (96 × 64 mm)	H.178	£450.00	—

Size	Print-ing	Number in set		Handbook reference	Price per card	Complete set

J. GABRIEL, London

PRE-1919 ISSUES
A	BW	10	*Actresses — 'HAGG A' (1900)	H.24	£70.00	—
A2	C	25	*Beauties — 'GRACC' (c1898)	H.59	£140.00	—
A	BW	20	Cricketers series (1901)	H.29	£400.00	—
A	C	40	*Home and Colonial Regiments (c1902)	H.69	£80.00	—
A	U	? 52	*Pretty Girl series — 'BAGG' (c1898)	H.45	£70.00	—
A2	C	25	*Types of British and Colonial Troops (c1900)	H.76	£65.00	—

GALA CIGARETTES

PRE-1919 ISSUE
D1	U	? 1	Stamp Card c1910	H.589	—	£150.00

GALLAHER LTD, Belfast and London

40 page reference book — £4.00

A PRE-1919 ISSUES
D	P	110	*Actors and Actresses (c1900)	H.179	£5.00	—
D	C	25	The Allies Flags: (1914):			
			A Toned card		£5.00	—
			B White card		£5.00	—
D	C	100	Association Football Club Colours (1910):			
			A Grey border		£8.00	—
			B Brown border		£8.00	—
A	C	52	*Beauties (c1900):	H.180		
			A Without inset		£12.00	—
			B With Playing Card inset		£12.00	—
D	C	50	*Birds and Eggs (c1905):	H.60		
			A 'Gallaher Ltd' Label		£45.00	—
			B 'Manufactured by Gallaher' Label		£8.00	—
D	C	100	Birds' Nests and Eggs series (1919):			
			A White card		£1.50	£150.00
			B Toned card		£1.50	—
D	C		Boy Scout series Grey-green back (1911):	H.630		
		100	A 'Belfast and London'		£2.40	£240.00
		86	B 'London and Belfast'		£2.60	—
D	U	50	British Naval series (1914)		£5.00	£250.00
D	P	100	English and Scotch Views (c1910)		£3.20	£320.00
D	C	100	Fables and Their Morals, (1912):			
			A Numbered Outside Set Title Panel		£1.60	£160.00
			B & C Later printings, see Post-1920 issues			
D	C	100	The Great War series (1915)		£2.40	£240.00
D	C	100	The Great War series — Second Series (1916)		£2.40	£240.00
D	C		The Great War, Victoria Cross Heroes (1915-16):	H.735		
		25	1st series 1-25		£4.40	£110.00
		25	2nd series 26-50		£4.40	£110.00
		25	3rd series 51-75		£4.40	£110.00
		25	4th series 76-100		£4.40	£110.00
		25	5th series 101-125		£4.40	£110.00
		25	6th series 126-150		£4.40	£110.00
		25	7th series 151-175		£4.40	£110.00
		25	8th series 176-200		£4.40	£110.00
D	C	100	How to do it (1916)		£3.50	£350.00
D			Irish View Scenery (c1910):	H.181		
	BW	400	1-400, matt:			
			A Numbered on back		£2.00	—
			B Unnumbered, plain back		£3.00	—

Size	Print-ing	Number in set		Handbook reference	Price per card	Complete set

GALLAHER LTD, Belfast and London *(continued)*

	P	400	1-400, glossy — see H.181-A			
			A Black photo		90p	£360.00
			B Brown photo		£3.00	—
			C As A, but series title and No. omitted		£2.00	—
			D Numbered 1-200 plain back		£3.00	—
	P	600	1-600, glossy — see H.181-B			
			A Nos 1 to 500		90p	£450.00
			B Nos 501 to 600		£4.00	—
D	C	100	'Kute Kiddies' series (1916)		£3.75	£375.00
D	P	50	Latest Actresses (1910):			
			A Black photo		£13.00	—
			B Chocolate photo		£18.00	—
A	C	50	*Regimental Colours and Standards (Nd 151-200) (1899)		£6.50	£325.00
A	C	50	Royalty series (1902)		£6.50	£325.00
A	C	111	The South African series (Nd 101-211) (1901):			
			A White back		£5.50	—
			B Cream back		£5.50	—
D	C	100	'Sports' series (1912)		£6.50	£650.00
D	U	? 98	*Stage and Variety Celebrities (collotype) (c1898):	H.182		
			A 'Gallager' back		£80.00	—
			B 'Gallaher' back		£80.00	—
			C As B but larger lettering, etc		£80.00	—
D	C	100	Tricks and Puzzles series, green back (1913)		£5.00	£500.00
A	C	50	*Types of the British Army — unnumbered (1897):	H.183		
			A 'Battle Honours' back		£9.00	—
			B 'The Three Pipe ...' — green back		£9.00	—
A	C	50	*Types of the British Army — Nd 1-50 (1898):	H.183		
			A 'The Three Pipe ...' — brown back		£8.00	—
			B 'Now in Three ...' — brown back		£8.00	—
A	C	50	*Types of British and Colonial Regiments — Nd 51-100 (1900):			
			A 'The Three Pipe ...' — brown back		£8.00	—
			B 'Now in Three ...' — brown back		£8.00	—
D	C	100	Useful Hints series (1915)		£3.00	£300.00
D	U	25	Views in North of Ireland (1912)		£50.00	—
D	C	50	Votaries of the Weed (1916)		£6.00	£300.00
D	C	100	'Why is it?' series (1915):			
			A Green back		£3.20	£320.00
			B Brown back		£3.20	£320.00
D	C	100	Woodland Trees series (1912)		£5.00	£500.00

B POST-1920 ISSUES

D	C	48	Aeroplanes (1939)		90p	£45.00
A2	C	25	Aesop's Fables (1931):	H.518		
			A Inscribed 'A Series of 25'		£1.20	£30.00
			B Inscribed 'Series of 50'		£1.20	£30.00
D	C	100	Animals and Birds of Commercial Value (1921)		80p	£80.00
D	C	48	Army Badges (1939)		70p	£35.00
—	U	24	Art Treasures of the World (76 × 56mm) (1930)		80p	£20.00
—	P	48	Beautiful Scotland (77 × 52mm) (1939)	H.564-1	90p	£45.00
D	C	100	Boy Scout Series brown back (1922)	H.630	£2.00	£200.00
D	C	48	British Birds (1937)		50p	£25.00
D	C	100	British Birds by Rankin (1923):	H.537		
			A 'By Rankin'		£16.00	—
			B 'By George Rankin'		£1.40	£140.00

Size	Printing	Number in set		Handbook reference	Price per card	Complete set

GALLAHER LTD, Belfast and London *(continued)*

Size	Printing	Number in set	Description	Handbook reference	Price per card	Complete set
D	C	75	British Champions of 1923 (1924)		£1.80	£135.00
D	C	48	Butterflies and Moths (1938)		40p	£20.00
D	C	25	Champion Animals & Birds of 1923 (1924)		£1.80	£45.00
D	C	48	Champions (1934):			
			A Front without letterpress		90p	£45.00
			B Front with captions, subjects re-drawn		80p	£40.00
D	C	48	Champions, 2nd Series (1935)		60p	£30.00
D	C	48	Champions of Screen & Stage (1934):			
			A Red back		70p	£35.00
			B Blue back, 'Gallaher's Cigarettes' at base		£1.20	£60.00
			C Blue back, 'Gallaher Ltd' at base		£2.00	£100.00
D	U	100	Cinema Stars (1926)	H.658	£1.60	£160.00
—	P	48	Coastwise (77 × 52mm) (1938)	H.564-2	£1.00	£50.00
	C	24	Dogs (1934):			
			A Captions in script letters:			
D			1 Small size		£2.00	£50.00
B			2 Large size		£2.00	£50.00
			B Captions in block letters:			
D			1 Small size		£1.00	£24.00
B			2 Large size		£1.25	£30.00
D	C	48	Dogs (1936)		60p	£30.00
D	C	48	Dogs Second Series (1938)		45p	£22.00
D	C	100	Fables and Their Morals:			
			A First printing, pre-1919 issues			
			B & C numbered in set title panel			
			B Thin numerals (1922)			
			1 White card		80p	£80.00
			2 Yellow card		80p	£80.00
			C Thick numerals (1922)		80p	£80.00
D	U	100	Famous Cricketers (1926)		£2.75	£275.00
D	C	48	Famous Film Scenes (1935)		70p	£35.00
D	U	100	Famous Footballers, green back (1925)		£2.20	£220.00
D	C	50	Famous Footballers, brown back (1926)		£2.40	£120.00
D	C	48	Famous Jockeys (1936)		£1.20	£60.00
D	C	48	Film Episodes (1936)		70p	£35.00
D	C	48	Film Partners (1935)		80p	£40.00
—	P	48	Flying (77 × 52mm) (1938)	H.564-3	£1.50	—
D	C	100	Footballers, red back (1928):	H.659		
			1 Nos. 1-50 — Action pictures		£2.80	£140.00
			2 Nos. 51-100 — Portraits		£3.00	£150.00
D	C	50	Footballers in Action (1928)		£2.80	£140.00
D	C	48	Garden Flowers (1938)		20p	£10.00
D		100	Interesting Views:			
	P		A Uncoloured, glossy (1923)		£1.60	£160.00
	CP		B Hand-coloured, matt (1925)		£2.25	£225.00
B2	P	48	Island Sporting Celebrities (Channel Islands) (1938)		£2.50	—
D	C	50	Lawn Tennis Celebrities (1928)		£4.50	—
A	C	24	Motor Cars (1934)		£4.50	£110.00
D	C	48	My Favourite Part (1939)		60p	£30.00
D	C	48	The Navy (1937):			
			A 'Park Drive ...' at base of back		60p	£30.00
			B 'Issued by ...' at base of back		£1.20	£60.00
—	P	48	Our Countryside (72 × 52mm) (1938)	H.564-4	£1.25	—
D	C	100	Plants of Commercial Value (1923)		80p	£80.00
D	C	48	Portraits of Famous Stars (1935)		£1.00	£50.00
D	C	48	Racing Scenes (1938)		60p	£30.00

Size	Print-ing	Number in set		Handbook reference	Price per card	Complete set

GALLAHER LTD, Belfast and London *(continued)*

Size	Print	Num	Title	H.ref	Price	Complete
D	C	100	The Reason Why (1924)		75p	£75.00
D	C	100	Robinson Crusoe (1928)		£1.70	£170.00
B2	P	48	Scenes from the Empire (1939) (export)	H.565	30p	£15.00
—	P	24	Shots from the Films (77 × 52mm) (1936)	H.566	£3.50	—
D	C	48	Shots from Famous Films (1935)		60p	£30.00
D	C	48	Signed Portraits of Famous Stars (1935)		£2.50	—
D	C	48	Sporting Personalities (1936)		40p	£20.00
D	C	48	Stars of Screen & Stage (1935):			
			A Back in green		60p	£30.00
			B Back in brown		£1.60	£80.00
D	C	48	Trains of the World (1937)		£1.00	£50.00
D	C	100	Tricks & Puzzles Series, black back (1933):			
			Nos. 1-50		£1.00	£50.00
			Nos. 51-100		£1.00	£50.00
D	C	48	Wild Animals (1937)		30p	£15.00
D	C	48	Wild Flowers (1939)		60p	£30.00
D	C	100	The 'Zoo' Aquarium (1924)		£1.20	£120.00
D	C	50	'Zoo' Tropical Birds, 1st Series (1928)		£1.40	£70.00
D	C	50	'Zoo' Tropical Birds, 2nd Series (1929)		£1.40	£70.00

C   POST-1940 ISSUES

C1	C	20	Silk Cut Advertisements (1993)		£1.50	—
G2	C	5	Telemania (1989)		£2.00	—

D   SILKS

—	C	25	Flags — Set 1 (68 × 48mm) (paper-backed) (1916)	H.501-1	£7.50	—

SAMUEL GAWITH, Kendal

POST-1920 ISSUE

—	BW	25	The English Lakeland (90 × 70mm) (1926)		£20.00	—

F. GENNARI LTD, London

PRE-1919 ISSUE

A	U	50	War Portraits (1916)	H.86	£90.00	—

LOUIS GERARD LTD, London

POST-1920 ISSUES

D1	U	50	Modern Armaments (1936):	H.567		
			A Numbered		£1.00	£50.00
			B Unnumbered		£1.20	£60.00
D1	U	24	Screen Favourites (1937):	H.568		
			A Inscribed 'Louis Gerard & Company'		£3.50	—
			B Inscribed 'Louis Gerard Limited'		£3.50	—
D1	C	48	Screen Favourites and Dancers (1937)	H.569	£2.40	£120.00

W.G. GLASS & CO. LTD, Bristol

PRE-1919 ISSUES

A	BW	20	*Actresses — 'BLARM' (c1900)	H.23	£70.00	—
A2	BW	10	*Actresses — 'HAGG A' (c1900)	H.24	£70.00	—
A	U	25	*Beauties — 'FECKSA' (c1901)	H.58	£110.00	—
D1	BW	20	*Boer War Cartoons ('Roseland Cigarettes') (c1901)	H.42	£120.00	—
A	BW	25	*Boer War Celebrities — 'STEW' (c1901)	H.105	£80.00	—
A	BW	16	*British Royal Family (1901)	H.28	£70.00	—
A2	BW	20	Cricketers Series (1901)	H.29	£350.00	—
D	C	40	*Naval and Military Phrases (c1902)	H.14	£90.00	—
A	BW	19	*Russo-Japanese Series (1904)	H.184	£60.00	—

Size	Print-ing	Number in set		Handbook reference	Price per card	Complete set

R. P. GLOAG & CO, London

(Cards bear advertisements for 'Citamora' and/or 'The Challenge Flat Brilliantes' without maker's name)

PRE-1919 ISSUES

A2	U	? 9	*Actresses — 'ANGLO' (c1896):	H.185		
			A 'Citamora' on front		£350.00	—
			B 'The Challenge Flat' on front		£350.00	—
D			*Beauties — Selection from 'Plums' (c1898):	H.186		
	BW		A 'The Challenge Flat' front:			
		60	(a) front in black and white		£90.00	—
	U	? 10	(b) front in brown printed back		£200.00	—
	U	? 10	(c) front in brown, plain back		£200.00	—
	BW	? 10	B 'Citamora' front in black and white		£130.00	—
A	C	40	*Home and Colonial Regiments (c1900)	H.69	£45.00	—
D	C	30	*Proverbs (c1901)	H.15	£90.00	—
A2	C	25	*Types of British and Colonial Troops (c1900)	H.76	£55.00	—

GLOBE CIGARETTE CO.

PRE-1919 ISSUE

D	BW	25	*Actresses — French (c1900)	H.1	£300.00	—

GOLDS LTD, Birmingham

PRE-1919 ISSUES

A2	BW	1	Advertisement Card (Chantecler) (c1905)	H.737	—	£600.00
C	C	18	Motor Cycle Series (c1914):	H.469		
			A Back in blue, numbered		£50.00	—
			B Back in grey, numbered		£60.00	—
			C Back in grey, unnumbered		£60.00	—
—	BW	? 21	*Prints from Noted Pictures (68 × 81mm) (c1908)	H.216	£120.00	—

T. P. & R. GOODBODY, Dublin and London

A PRE-1919 ISSUES

—	U	? 4	*Actresses — 'ANGOOD' (36 × 60mm) (c1898)	H.187	£250.00	—
A2	U	? 10	*Beauties — 'KEWA' (c1898)	H.139	£200.00	—
D	BW		*Boer War Celebrities — 'CAG' (1901)	H.79		
		25	See H.79 — Fig. 79-B		£32.00	—
		16	See H.79 — Fig. 79-C		£35.00	—
		16	See H.79 — Fig. 79-D		£35.00	—
		16	See H.79 — Fig. 79-E		£35.00	—
	C	50	Colonial Forces (c1900):	H.188		
A2			A Brown back		£70.00	—
A2			B Black back		£70.00	—
—			C Size 80 × 50mm		£300.00	—
—	U	? 67	*Dogs (nine printings) (1910) (36 × 60mm)	H.189	£90.00	—
C	C	26	Eminent Actresses — 'FROGA A' (c1900):	H.20		
			A Front 'Goodbody' at base		£45.00	—
			B Front 'Goodbody' at top		£200.00	—
C	C	20	Irish Scenery (Five Printings) (c1905)	H.190	£40.00	—
A2	U	? 18	*Pretty Girl Series — 'BAGG' (c1898):	H.45		
			A Red stamped back		£200.00	—
			B Violet stamped back		£200.00	—
A	C	25	Types of Soldiers (c1914)	H.144	£60.00	—
D	U	20	*War Pictures (c1915)	H.122	£32.00	—
C	C	12	'With the Flag to Pretoria' (c1901)	H.191	£110.00	—

B POST-1920 ISSUES

D	C	50	Questions & Answers in Natural History (1924)		£2.60	£120.00
A	C	25	Sports & Pastimes — Series 1 (1925)	H.225	£6.00	£150.00

Size	Print-ing	Number in set		Handbook reference	Price per card	Complete set

GORDON'S, Glasgow

PRE-1919 ISSUE
A2　BW　? 4　Billiards — By George D. Gordon (c1910) ....　　£800.00　—

F. GOUGH, Blackley

PRE-1919 ISSUE
—　C　? 1　*Play Up Sporting Shields (c1895) ....　H.718　£125.00　—

GRAVESON, Mexboro'

PRE-1919 ISSUES
A2　C　30　*Army Pictures, Cartoons, Etc (c1916) ....　H.12　£120.00　—
A　U　50　War Portraits (1916) ....　H.86　£75.00　—

FRED GRAY, Birmingham

PRE-1919 ISSUE
A　C　25　*Types of British Soldiers (c1914) ....　H.144　£125.00　—

GRIFFITHS BROS., Manchester

POST-1920 ISSUE
—　P　18　*Beauties (89 × 70mm) (c1925) ....　H.653　£100.00　—

W. J. HARRIS, London

PRE-1919 ISSUES
A2　C　26　*Beauties 'HOL' (c1900) ....　H.192　£34.00　—
C　C　30　*Colonial Troops (c1900) ....　H.40　£90.00　—
A1　C　25　*Star Girls (c1899) ....　H.30　£250.00　—

JAS. H. HARRISON, Birmingham

PRE-1919 ISSUE
C　C　18　Motor Cycle Series (c1914) ....　H.469　£85.00　—

HARVEY & DAVEY, Newcastle-on-Tyne

PRE-1919 ISSUES
D1　C　50　*Birds and Eggs (c1905) ....　H.60　£4.50　£225.00
A1　C　35　*Chinese and South African Series (c1901) ....　H.193　£125.00　—
C　C　30　*Colonial Troops (c1900) ....　H.40　£75.00　—
A1　C　25　*Types of British and Colonial Troops (c1901) ......　H.76　£90.00　—

HARVEY'S NAVY CUT

PRE-1919 ISSUE
—　C　? 3　*Play Up Sporting Shields (c1895) ....　H.718　£125.00　—

W. & H. HEATON, Birkby

PRE-1919 ISSUE
—　BW　? 6　Birkby Views (70 × 39mm) (c1912) ....　H.226　£350.00　—

HENLY & WATKINS LTD, London

POST-1920 ISSUES
A1　C　25　Ancient Egyptian Gods — 'Matossian's
　　　　　　Cigarettes' (1924)　　　　　　　　　　　　H.570
　　　　　　　*A　Plain back ....　　　£7.00　£175.00
　　　　　　　　B　Back in blue ....　　　£7.00　£175.00

Size	Printing	Number in set		Handbook reference	Price per card	Complete set

HIGNETT BROS. & CO., Liverpool

A PRE-1919 ISSUES

Size	Printing	Number in set	Title	Handbook reference	Price per card	Complete set
C	C	26	*Actresses — 'FROGA A' (c1900)	H.20	£60.00	—
A2	U	25	*Actresses — Photogravure (c1900)	H.194	£27.00	—
D1	BW	28	*Actresses — 'PILPI I' (c1901)	H.195	£20.00	—
D1	P	50	*Actresses — 'PILPI II' (c1901)	H.196	£12.00	—
—	C	? 3	Advertisement Cards. (c1885)		£500.00	—
—	C	60	Animal Pictures ... (38 × 70mm) (c1900)	H.197	£32.00	—
D	U	50	*Beauties — gravure (c1898):	H.198		
			A 'Cavalier' back		£75.00	
			B 'Golden Butterfly' back		£75.00	
C	C	? 25	*Beauties — 'CHOAB' (c1900)	H.21	£200.00	—
—	C	? 16	Beauties — Postcard Size (c1900)	H.708	£350.00	—
A1	C	19	Cabinet, 1900	H.199	£90.00	—
A	C	25	Cathedrals and Churches (1909)	H.545	£4.40	£110.00
A	C	25	Company Drill (1915)		£4.40	£110.00
—	BW	6	Diamond Jubilee 1897 (156 × 156mm)	H.740	£500.00	—
A	C	25	Greetings of the World (1907 — re-issued 1922)		£3.00	£75.00
A	C	50	Interesting Buildings (1905)	H.70	£6.00	£300.00
—	C	40	*Medals (34 × 72mm) (1901):	H.200		
			A 'Butterfly Cigarettes'		£25.00	—
			B Officially cut for use in other brands		£25.00	—
A	BW	25	Military Portraits (1914)	H.201	£5.00	£125.00
A	C	25	Modern Statesmen (1906):			
			A 'Butterfly' back		£5.00	£125.00
			B 'Pioneer' back		£5.00	£125.00
A	C	20	*Music Hall Artistes (c1900)	H.202	£60.00	—
—	C	1	Oracle Butterfly (shaped) (c1898)		—	£125.00
A	C	25	Panama Canal (1914)		£6.00	£150.00
A2	C	12	*Pretty Girl Series — 'RASH' (c1900)	H.8	£50.00	—
—	C	6	*Story of a Boy Who Robs a Stork's Nest (118 × 88mm) (c1890)	H.742	£500.00	—
—	BW	25	*V.C. Heroes (35 × 72mm) (1901)	H.203	£50.00	—
A	C	20	*Yachts (c1902):	H.204		
			A Gold on black back		£65.00	—
			B Black on white back		£65.00	—

B POST-1920 ISSUES

Size	Printing	Number in set	Title	Handbook reference	Price per card	Complete set
A	C	50	Actors — Natural and Character Studies (1938)	H.571-1	£1.60	£80.00
A	C	50	A.F.C. Nicknames (1933)	H.571-2	£6.00	—
A	C	50	Air-Raid Precautions (1939)	H.544	£1.20	£60.00
A	C	50	Arms and Armour (1924)	H.273	£3.00	£150.00
A	C	50	British Birds and Their Eggs (1938)	H.571-3	£2.80	—
A	U	50	Broadcasting (1935)	H.571-4	£2.80	—
A	U	50	Celebrated Old Inns (1925)		£3.00	£150.00
A	C	50	Champions of 1936 (1937)	H.571-5	£2.80	£140.00
A	C	25	Common Objects of the Sea-Shore (1924)		£2.40	£60.00
A	C	50	Coronation Procession (sectional) (1937)	H.571-6	£2.50	—
A	C	50	Dogs (1936)	H.571-7	£2.20	£110.00
A	C	50	Football Caricatures (1935)	H.571-8	£3.40	£170.00
A	C	50	Football Club Captains (1935)	H.571-9	£3.40	£170.00
A	U	25	Historical London (1926)		£2.60	£65.00
A	C	50	How to Swim (1935)	H.571-10	£1.20	£60.00
A	C	25	International Caps and Badges (1924)		£4.00	£100.00
A	C	25	Life in Pond & Stream (1925)		£3.00	£75.00
A	C	50	Modern Railways (1936)	H.571-11	£2.50	£125.00
A	C	50	Ocean Greyhounds (1938)	H.571-12	£1.60	£80.00
A	U	25	*The Prince of Wales' Empire Tour (1924)		£2.40	£60.00
A	U	50	Prominent Cricketers of 1938 (1938)	H.571-13	£3.50	£175.00

Size	Print-ing	Number in set		Handbook reference	Price per card	Complete set

HIGNETT BROS. & CO., Liverpool *(continued)*

Size	Print	Num	Title	Handbook	Price	Set
A	C	50	Prominent Racehorses of 1933 (1934)	H.571-14	£2.60	£130.00
A	C	50	Sea Adventure (1939)	H.571-15	50p	£25.00
A	C	25	Ships Flags & Cap Badges (1926)		£4.40	£110.00
A	C	25	Ships Flags & Cap Badges, 2nd Series (1927)		£4.40	£110.00
A	C	50	Shots from the Films (1936)	H.571-16	£3.50	—
A	C	50	Trick Billiards (1934)	H.571-17	£6.00	—
A	U	25	Turnpikes (1927)		£2.60	£65.00
A	C	50	Zoo Studies (1937)	H.571-18	£1.00	£50.00

R. & J. HILL LTD, London

28 page reference book — £4.00

A PRE-1919 ISSUES

Size	Print	Num	Title	Handbook	Price	Set
A	C	26	*Actresses — 'FROGA A' (c1900)	H.20	£60.00	—
D	BW	30	*Actresses, Continental (c1905):	H.205		
			A 'The Seven Wonders' back		£18.00	—
			B 'Black and White Whisky' back		£25.00	—
			C Plain back		£18.00	—
D	BW	16	*Actresses — 'HAGG B' (c1900):	H.24		
			A 'Smoke Hill's Stockrider ...'		£35.00	—
			B 'Issued with Hill's High Class'		£35.00	—
—	BW	25	*Actresses (Belle of New York Series) (1899):	H206		
			A White back (41 × 75mm)		£25.00	—
			B Toned back, thick card (39 × 74mm)		£25.00	—
D1	U	20	*Actresses, chocolate tinted (1917):	H.207		
			A 'Hill's Tobaccos' etc back		£18.00	—
			B 'Issued with Hill's ...' back		£20.00	—
			C Plain back		£18.00	—
C	C	20	*Animal Series (1909):	H.743		
			A 'R. & J. Hill Ltd.' back		£25.00	—
			B 'Crowfoot Cigarettes' back		£25.00	—
			C 'The Cigarettes with which ...' back		£30.00	—
			D Space at back		£25.00	—
			E Plain Back		£25.00	—
A	BW	? 17	*Battleships (c1908):	H.208		
			A 'For the Pipe Smoke Oceanic ...' back		£300.00	—
			B Plain back		£50.00	—
A	C	25	*Battleships and Crests (1901)		£20.00	£500.00
D2	C	12	*Boer War Generals ('Campaigners') (c1901)	H.209	£32.00	£385.00
A1	C	20	Breeds of Dogs (1914):	H.211		
			A 'Archer's M.F.H.' back		£22.00	—
			B 'Hill's Badminton' back		£22.00	—
			C 'Hill's Verbena Mixture' back		£22.00	—
			D 'Spinet Tobacco' back		£22.00	—
D1	BW	? 48	*British Navy Series (c1902)	H.210	£25.00	—
A	BW	? 1	*Celebrated Pictures (c1905)	H.744	£600.00	—
C	C		*Colonial Troops (c1900):	H.40		
		30	A i 'Hill's Leading Lines ...' back		£22.00	—
		30	A ii 'Perfection vide Dress ...' back		£22.00	—
		50	B 1-50. 'Sweet American' back		£22.00	—
D1	U	28	Famous Cricketers Series (1912):			
			A Red back, blue picture		£65.00	—
			B Deep blue back, brown picture		£65.00	—
			C Blue back, black picture		£65.00	—
D1	BW	20	Famous Footballers Series (1912)		£25.00	£500.00

Size	Print-ing	Number in set		Handbook reference	Price per card	Complete set

R. & J. HILL LTD, London *(continued)*

Size	Print-ing	Number in set	Description	Handbook reference	Price per card	Complete set
—	U	25	Famous Pictures: (41 × 70mm) (c1912):	H.468		
			A 'Prize Coupon' back		£4.00	£100.00
			B Without 'Prize Coupon' back		£4.00	£100.00
C	C	30	*Flags and Flags with Soldiers (c1902)	H.41	£24.00	—
—	C	24	*Flags, Arms and Types of Nations, 'Black & White' Whisky advert back (41 × 68mm) (c1910)	H.115	£12.50	£300.00
D	BW	20	Football Captain Series. Nd. 41-60 (1906):			
			A Small title		£40.00	—
			B Larger title, back re-drawn		£50.00	—
—		10	Fragments from France (38 × 67mm) (1916):	H.212		
	C		A Coloured, caption in script		£24.00	£240.00
	U		B Sepia-brown on buff, caption in block		£27.00	£270.00
	U		C As B, but black and white		£85.00	—
—	C	10	Fragments from France, different subjects, caption in block (38 × 67mm) (1916)	H.212	£24.00	£240.00
A1	U	25	Hill's War Series (c1916)	H.35	£12.00	£300.00
C2	C	20	Inventors and Their Inventions Series, Nd. 1-20, (1907):	H.213		
			A Black back, white card		£4.50	£90.00
			B Black back, toned card (shorter)		£6.00	—
C2	C	20	Inventors and Their Inventions Series, Nd. 21-40, (1907)		£7.00	£140.00
—		15	*Japanese Series (40 × 66mm) (1904):	H.214		
	C		A 'Hills' on red tablet		£65.00	—
	BW		B 'Hills' on black tablet		£45.00	—
—	C	20	Lighthouse Series — without frame lines to picture (42 × 68mm) (c1903)		£35.00	—
—	C	30	Lighthouse Series — with frame line. Nos. 1-20 re-touched and 10 cards added (c1903)		£35.00	—
D	C	20	National Flag Series (1914)	H.473	£8.00	£160.00
			Plain back		£7.00	—
—	BW	25	*Naval Series unnumbered (42 × 64mm) (1901)	H.215	£45.00	—
D1	BW	30	Naval Series Nd. 21-50 (1902):	H.215		
			A Numbered 21-40		£12.00	—
			B Numbered 41-50		£60.00	—
C	C	20	Prince of Wales Series (1911)	H.22	£12.00	£240.00
—	BW	20	Rhymes — black and white sketches (c1905)	H.217	£26.00	—
A1	BW	30	*Statuary — Set 1 (c1900):	H.218-1		
			A Black and white front, matt		£35.00	—
	BW		B Black and white front, varnished		£11.00	—
A	BW	30	*Statuary — Set 2 (c1900)	H.218-2	£8.00	£240.00
C1	BW		*Statuary — Set 3 (c1900):	H.218-3		
		? 26	A Name panel white lettering on black background		£25.00	—
		? 4	B Name panel black lettering on grey background		£50.00	—
		? 26	C Name panel black lettering on white background		£50.00	—
D	C	20	*Types of the British Army (1914):			
			A 'Badminton' back		£30.00	—
			B 'Verbena' back		£30.00	—
A	U	25	World's Masterpieces — 'Second Series' (c1915)		£2.00	£50.00

B   POST-1920 ISSUES

Size	Print-ing	Number in set	Description	Handbook reference	Price per card	Complete set
C	U	30	The All Blacks (1924)		£6.00	£180.00
A	BW	25	Aviation Series (1934):			
			A 'Issued by R. & J. Hill …'		£3.40	£85.00
			B 'Issued with "Gold Flake Honeydew" …'		£3.60	£90.00
	U	50	Caricatures of Famous Cricketers (1926):			
C			A Small size		£3.00	£150.00
B1			B Large size		£2.00	£100.00

47

Size	Print-ing	Number in set		Handbook reference	Price per card	Complete set

R. & J. HILL LTD, London (continued)

Size	Print-ing	Number in set	Description	Handbook reference	Price per card	Complete set
D1	C	50	Celebrities of Sport (1939):			
			A 'Issued by R. & J. Hill ...'		£2.20	£110.00
			B 'Issued with "Gold Flake Honeydew" ...'		£3.80	—
A2	C	35	Cinema Celebrities (1936):	H.572		
			A Inscribed 'These Cigarettes are guaranteed'		£1.15	£40.00
			B Inscribed 'The Spinet House'		£1.30	£45.00
D1	BW	40	Crystal Palace Souvenir:			
			A Front matt (1936)		£2.50	£100.00
			B Front varnished (1937)		£2.00	£80.00
D1	C	48	Decorations and Medals (1940):			
			A 'Issued by R. & J. Hill ...'		£1.50	£75.00
			B 'Issued with Gold Flake Cigarettes'		£3.00	—
	P		Famous Cinema Celebrities (1931):	Ha.573		
		? 48	Set 1:			
—			A Medium size (74 × 56mm) inscribed 'Series A':			
			1 'Kadi Cigarettes' at base of back		£5.00	—
			2 Space at base of back blank		£4.00	—
A			B1 Small size, inscribed 'Spinet Cigarettes'		£4.50	—
A			B2 Small size, without 'Spinet Cigarettes'		£4.50	—
		50	Set 2:			
—			C Small size (66 × 41mm) inscribed 'Series C':			
			1 'Devon Cigarettes' at base of back		£7.00	—
			2 'Toucan Cigarettes' at base of back		£7.00	—
			3 Space at base of back blank		£4.00	—
			D Medium size (74 × 56mm) inscribed 'Series D':			
			1 'Kadi Cigarettes' at base of back		£4.00	—
			2 Space at base of back blank		£4.00	—
C	U	40	Famous Cricketers (1923)	H.633	£5.00	£200.00
	U	50	Famous Cricketers, including the S. Africa Test Team — 'Sunripe Cigarettes' (1924):			
C			A Small size		£5.00	£250.00
B1			B Large size		£5.50	£275.00
—	C	30	Famous Engravings — Series XI (80 × 61mm) (c1920)		£4.50	—
A2	BW	40	Famous Film Stars (1938):	H.634-1		
			A Text in English		£1.25	£50.00
			B *Text in Arabic, caption in English (see also Modern Beauties)*		£1.00	£40.00
C	U	50	Famous Footballers (1923)		£3.50	£175.00
D	C	50	Famous Footballers (1939):	H.574		
			A Shoreditch address		£2.40	£120.00
			B 'Proprietors of Hy. Archer ...'		£2.50	£125.00
D	C	25	Famous Footballers, Nd. 51-75 (1939)		£3.00	£75.00
D	C	50	Famous Ships:			
			A Front matt (1939)		£1.10	£55.00
			B Front varnished (1940)		90p	£45.00
D	C	48	Film Stars and Celebrity Dancers (1935)		£1.50	£75.00
	C		Historic Places from Dickens' Classics (1926):			
D		50	A Small size		60p	£30.00
B1			B Large size:			
			1 Nos. 2-26, small numerals		70p	£17.50
			2 Nos. 1-50, large numerals		60p	£30.00
	U	50	Holiday Resorts (1925):			
C			A Small size:			
			1 Back in grey		90p	£45.00
			2 Back in brown		£1.50	—
B1			B Large size:			
			1 Back in grey		80p	£40.00
			2 Back in brown		£1.50	—

Size	Print- ing	Number in set			Handbook reference	Price per card	Complete set

R. & J. HILL LTD, London *(continued)*

Size	Print- ing	Number in set	Description		Handbook ref.	Price per card	Complete set
A	BW	20	*Inventors and Their Inventions (plain back)* (1934)		H.213	£1.50	£30.00
			Magical Puzzles — see 'Puzzle Series'				
A2	BW		Modern Beauties (1939):		H.634-2		
		50	A Titled 'Modern Beauties'. Text in English			£1.00	£50.00
		40	B Titled 'Famous Film Stars' (selection):				
			i) Text in Arabic, No Captions, Numbered			£2.00	—
			ii) Text in Arabic, No Captions, Unnumbered			£12.00	—
	C	30	Music Hall Celebrities — Past and Present (1930):				
D1			A Small size			£2.50	£75.00
B1			B Large size			£2.50	£75.00
D	C	30	Nature Pictures — 'The Spotlight Tobaccos' (c1930)			£1.20	£36.00
C2	C	30	Nautical Songs (1937)			£1.35	£40.00
	U	30	'Our Empire' (1929):				
D1			A Small size			40p	£12.00
B1			B Large size			70p	£21.00
—	BW		Popular Footballers — Season 1934-5 (68 × 49mm):				
		30	'Series A' — Nd. 1-30			£3.20	£95.00
		20	'Series B' — Nd. 31-50			£3.50	£70.00
	U		Public Schools and Colleges (1923):		H.575		
		50	A 'A Series of 50':				
C			1 Small size			70p	£35.00
B1			2 Large size			70p	£35.00
		75	B 'A Series of 75':				
C			1 Small size			90p	£70.00
B1			2 Large size			90p	£70.00
A1	C	50	Puzzle Series:		H.660		
			A Titled 'Puzzle Series' (1937)			£1.20	£60.00
			B Titled 'Magical Puzzles' (1938)			£2.00	£100.00
	U	50	The Railway Centenary — 'A Series of 50' (1925):				
C			A Small size			£1.30	£65.00
B1			B Large size:				
			1 Back in brown			£1.30	£65.00
			2 Back in grey			£3.30	—
	U	25	The Railway Centenary — '2nd Series — 51 to 75' (1925):				
C			A Small size			£1.80	£45.00
B1			B Large size			£1.80	£45.00
C2	P	42	Real Photographs — Set 1 (Bathing Beauties) (c1930):		H.576-1		
			A 'London Idol Cigarettes' at base of back:				
			1 Front black and white, glossy			£2.50	—
			2 Front brown, matt			£2.50	—
			B Space at base of back blank:				
			1 Front black and white, glossy			£2.50	—
			2 Front brown, matt			£2.50	—
C2	P	42	Real Photographs — Set 2 (Beauties) (c1930)		H.576-2	£3.00	—
			The River Thames — see 'Views of the River Thames'				
D1	P	50	Scenes from the Films (1932):				
			A Front black and white			£3.30	—
			B Front sepia			£3.30	—
A2	BW	40	Scenes from the Films (1938)			80p	£32.00
D1		35	Scientific Inventions and Discoveries (1929):		H.213		
	C		A Small size, 'The Spinet House …' back			£1.20	£42.00
	BW		B Small size, 'The Spotlight Tobaccos …' back			£1.20	£42.00
B1	C		C Large size			£1.20	£42.00
Dl	P	50	Sports (1934):				
			A Titled 'Sports', numbered front and back			£5.00	—
			B Titled 'Sports Series', numbered front only			£12.00	—
		*C	Untitled, numbered front only			£15.00	—

Size	Printing	Number in set		Handbook reference	Price per card	Complete set

R. & J. HILL LTD, London *(continued)*

Size	Print	Num	Description	Ref	Price	Set
D1	C	100	*Transfers (c1935)	Ha.596-2	£6.00	—
B2	CP		Views of Interest:			
		48	'A First Series ...' Nd. 1-48 (1938):			
			A 'The Spinet House ...' back		30p	£15.00
			B 'Sunripe & Spinet Ovals ...' back		25p	£12.50
		48	'Second Series ...' Nd. 49-96 (1938)		25p	£12.50
		48	'Third Series ...' Nd. 97-144 (1939)		25p	£12.50
		48	'Fourth Series ...' Nd. 145-192 (1939)		50p	£25.00
		48	'Fifth Series ...' Nd. 193-240 (1939)		50p	£25.00
B2	CP		Views of Interest — British Empire Series ...:			
		48	'1st Issue — Canada — Nos. 1-48' (1940)		35p	£17.50
		48	'2nd Issue — India — Nos. 49-96' (1940)		£2.50	£120.00
	U	50	Views of London (1925):	H.577		
C			A Small size		80p	£40.00
B1			B Large size		90p	£45.00
	C	50	Views of the River Thames (1924):			
D			A Small size:			
			Nos. 1-25		£1.80	£45.00
			Nos. 26-50		£1.40	£35.00
B1			B Large size:			
			1 Back in green (thin card)		£1.50	£75.00
			2 Back in green and black (thick card)		£1.50	£75.00
	U	50	Who's Who in British Films (Nov. 1927):			
A2			A Small size		£1.60	£80.00
B2			B Large size		£1.60	£80.00
C	C	84	Wireless Telephony (1923)		£1.50	£125.00
B1	U	20	Wireless Telephony — Broadcasting Series (1923)		£2.50	£50.00
	U	50	Zoological Series (1924):	H.578		
C			A Small size:			
			1 Back in light brown		80p	£40.00
			2 Back in grey		90p	£45.00
B1			B Large size:			
			1 Back in light brown		90p	£45.00
			2 Back in dark brown		90p	£45.00

C POST-1940 ISSUE

A	U	50	Famous Dog Breeds 1954 (Airmail Cigarettes Slides)	H.889	£8.00	—

D CANVASES. Unbacked canvases. The material is a linen fabric, glazed to give the appearance of canvas. Specimens are found rubber stamped in red on back 'The Pipe Tobacco de Luxe Spinet Mixture'.

—	C	30	'Britain's Stately Homes' (78 × 61mm) (c1915)		£3.70	—
—	C		*Canvas Masterpieces — Series 1 (73 × 61mm) (c1915):			
			A 'Badminton Tobacco Factories ...' back:			
		40	1 'H.T. & Co., Ltd., Leeds' at right base		£1.50	—
		20	2 Cardigan Press, Leeds' at right base (Nos. 21-40)		£1.50	—
		10	3 Without printers' credit (Nos. 21-30)		£1.50	—
		3	4 As 3, but size 73 × 53mm (Nos. 23-25)		£1.50	—
		40	B 'The Spinet House ...' back		£2.00	£80.00
—	C	40	*Canvas Masterpieces — Series 2, Nd. 41-80 (73 × 61mm) (c1915)	H.509	£2.50	£100.00
—	C	10	*Canvas Masterpieces — Series 2, Nd. 1-10 (c1915):			
			Nos. 1 to 5		£2.00	£10.00
			Nos. 6 to 10		£3.00	£15.00
—	C	5	Chinese Pottery and Porcelain — Series 1 (132 × 108mm) (c1915)		—	£40.00
			4 Different (minus No. 5)		60p	£2.50

Size	Print-ing	Number in set		Handbook reference	Price per card	Complete set

R. & J. HILL LTD, London (continued)
| | C | 11 | Chinese Pottery and Porcelain — Series 2 (107 × 62mm) (c1915) | | £5.50 | — |
| | C | 23 | *Great War Leaders — Series 10 (73 × 60mm) (1919) | | £5.50 | — |

L. HIRST & SON, Leeds
PRE-1919 ISSUE
| | C | ?5 | *Soldiers and their Uniforms (cutouts) (c1915) | H.138 | £200.00 | — |

J. W. HOBSON, Huddersfield
PRE-1919 ISSUE
| C2 | C | 18 | Motor Cycle Series (c1914) | H.469 | £90.00 | |

J. & T. HODGE, Glasgow
PRE-1919 ISSUES
	C	?4	*British Naval Crests (70 × 38mm) (c1896)	H.219	£450.00	—
A	BW	16	British Royal Family (c1901)	H.28	£200.00	—
	U		*Scottish Views (c1898):	H.220		
		?11	A Thick card (74 × 39mm)		£160.00	—
		?10	B Thin card (80 × 45mm)		£160.00	—

HOOK OF HOLLAND CIGARETTES
PRE-1919 ISSUE
| A | U | ?5 | *Footballers (c1905) | H.745 | £500.00 | — |

HUDDEN & CO. LTD, Bristol
A PRE-1919 ISSUES
C	C	26	*Actresses — 'FROGA A' (c1900)	H.20	£60.00	—
C	C	25	*Beauties — 'CHOAB' (c1900)	H.21	£50.00	—
A2	U	20	*Beauties — 'Crown Seal Cigarettes' (c1898)	H.221	£120.00	—
A	U	24	*Beauties — 'HUMPS' (c1898):	H.222		
			A Blue scroll back		£70.00	—
			B Orange scroll back		£60.00	—
			C Typeset back in brown		£300.00	—
D1	C	?12	Comic Phrases (c1900)	H.223	£100.00	—
A	C	25	*Flags of All Nations (c1905)	H.37	£24.00	£600.00
	C	48	*Flowers and Designs (55 × 34mm) (c1900):	H.224		
			A 'Hudden Cigarettes' back		£85.00	—
			B 'Hudden's — Dandy Dot' back		£150.00	—
A	C	18	*Pretty Girl Series — 'RASH' (c1900)	H.8	£80.00	—
A	C	25	Soldiers of the Century, Nd. 26-50 (1901)		£50.00	—
A	C	25	*Star Girls (c1900)	H.30	£100.00	—
A	C	25	Types of Smokers (c1903)		£45.00	—

B POST-1920 ISSUES. All export
D	U	25	Famous Boxers (1927)	H.721	£32.00	—
C	U	50	Public Schools and Colleges (c1925)	H.575	£2.00	£100.00
A	C	25	Sports and Pastimes Series 1 (c1925)	H.225	£55.00	—

HUDSON
PRE-1919 ISSUES
| D | U | ?1 | *Actresses — 'ANGOOD' (c1900) | H.187 | £450.00 | — |
| C | C | 25 | *Beauties — selections from 'BOCCA' (c1900) | H.39 | £400.00 | — |

Size	Print-ing	Number in set		Handbook reference	Price per card	Complete set

HUNTER, Airdrie

PRE-1919 ISSUE
| A | BW | ? 11 | *Footballers (c1910) | H.227 | £1250.00 | — |

J. T. ILLINGWORTH & SONS, Kendal

A PRE-1919 ISSUE
| A | BW | 25 | Views from the English Lakes (c1895) | H.228 | £200.00 | — |

B POST-1920 ISSUES
—	P	48	Beautiful Scotland (77 × 52mm) (1939)	H.564-1	£2.00	—
C1	C	25	*Cavalry (1924)		£5.00	£125.00
—	P	48	Coastwise (77 × 52mm) (1938)	H.564-2	£1.00	£50.00
A	C	25	'Comicartoons' of sport (1927)		£6.00	£150.00
—	P	48	Flying (77 × 52mm) (1938)	H.564-3	£1.80	£90.00
A	C	25	*Motor Car Bonnets (1925)		£7.20	£180.00
A	C	25	*Old Hostels (1926)		£6.00	£150.00
—	P	48	Our Countryside (77 × 52mm) (1938)	H.564-4	£2.00	£100.00
—	P	24	Shots from the Films (1937)	H.566	£4.50	—

THE IMPERIAL TOBACCO CO. (of Great Britain & Ireland) Ltd, Bristol—

A PRE-1919 ISSUES
| A | C | 50 | British Birds (c1910) | H.229 | £5.00 | — |
| C | C | 1 | Folder — Coronation of His Majesty King Edward VII (1902) | | — | £90.00 |

B POST-1940 ISSUES
—	C	10	Out of the Blue — Richmond Adverts (2002):			
			A Size 75 × 32mm		£2.00	—
			B Size 80 × 47mm		£2.00	—
			C Size 90 × 47mm		£1.50	—

INGRAM'S, 1A, 27 & 33 Leigh Road, Eastleigh

PRE-1919 ISSUE
| D | C | 30 | *Army Pictures, Cartoons, etc (1916) | H.12 | £110.00 | — |

INTERNATIONAL TOBACCO CO. LTD, London

POST-1920 ISSUES

A HOME ISSUES
—	C	28	Domino cards (69 × 35mm) (1938)		25p	£7.00
	U		Famous Buildings and Monuments of Britain (1934) (bronze metal plaques)	H.580		
		50	'Series A':			
A1			1 Nos. 1-30, small size		£1.00	£30.00
B2			2 Nos. 31-50, large size		£1.00	£20.00
		50	'Series B':			
A1			1 Nos. 51-80, small size		£1.80	£55.00
B2			2 Nos. 81-100, large size		£1.80	£36.00
A	C	50	International Code of Signals (1934)		80p	£40.00
D	C	48	Screen Lovers — 'Summit' (unissued) (c1940)		£3.20	—

B EXPORT ISSUES. Inscribed 'International Tobacco (Overseas), Ltd.'
A2	C	100	Film Favourites (c1937):	H.581		
			A Back in grey		£2.20	—
			B Back in black		£2.20	—
—	C	100	'Gentlemen! The King!' — (60 small, 40 large) (1937):	H.582		
			A Back in blue		50p	£50.00
			B Back in black		20p	£20.00

*The same plaques were also used for an export issue, with envelopes inscribed 'International Tobacco (Overseas), Ltd.'

Size	Print-ing	Number in set		Handbook reference	Price per card	Complete set

J.L.S. TOBACCO CO., London

PRE-1919 ISSUES

('Star of the World' Cigarettes)

Size	Printing	Number	Title	Handbook	Price	Set
D	BW	20	*Boer War Cartoons (1901)	H.42	£100.00	—
B2	BW	? 29	*Boer War Celebrities — 'JASAS' (c1901)	H.133	£175.00	—
A2	C	30	*Colonial Troops (c1901)	H.40	£80.00	—

PETER JACKSON, London

POST-1920 ISSUES

A HOME ISSUES

Size	Printing	Number	Title	Handbook	Price	Set
	P		Beautiful Scotland (1939):	H.564-1		
D		28	A Small size		£1.25	£35.00
—		48	B Medium size, 77 × 52mm		£1.00	£50.00
	P		Coastwise (1938):	H.564-2		
D		28	A Small size		£1.25	£35.00
—		48	B Medium size, 77 × 52mm		£1.25	£60.00
D	P	28	Famous Film Stars (1935)		£3.50	£100.00
D	P	27	Famous Films (1934)		£3.50	£100.00
D	P	28	Film Scenes (1936)		£3.50	£100.00
B	P	28	Film Scenes (1936)		£4.50	£125.00
	P		Flying (1938):	H.564-3		
D		28	A Small size		£3.00	—
—		48	B Medium size (77 × 52mm)		£3.50	—
D	P	28	Life in the Navy (1937)		£1.75	£50.00
B	P	28	Life in the Navy (1937)		£2.50	£70.00
	P		Our Countryside (1938):	H.564-4		
D		28	A Small size		£1.00	£28.00
—		48	B Medium size (77 × 52mm)		£1.25	£60.00
	P		Shots from the Films (1937):	H.566		
D		28	A Small size		£3.00	£85.00
—		24	B Medium size (77 × 52mm)		£3.25	£80.00
D	P	28	Stars in Famous Films (1935)		£3.40	£90.00

B EXPORT ISSUES. Inscribed 'Peter Jackson (Overseas), Ltd.'

Size	Printing	Number	Title	Handbook	Price	Set
—	C	100	'Gentlemen! The King!' (60 small, 40 large) (1937):	H.582		
			A Overprinted on International black back		£1.00	£100.00
			B Overprinted on International blue back		£1.00	—
			C Reprinted with Jackson's name at base:			
			i Back in black		£1.00	—
			ii Back in blue		£2.00	—
—	C	150	The Pageant of Kingship — 90 small, 60 large (1937):			
			A Inscribed 'Issued by Peter Jackson'		50p	£75.00
			B Inscribed 'Issued by Peter Jackson (Overseas), Ltd.':			
			1 Printed on board		50p	£75.00
			2 Printed on paper		33p	£50.00
—	C	250	Speed — Through the Ages (170 small, 80 large) (1937)	H.583	30p	£75.00

JACOBI BROS. & CO. LTD, London

PRE-1919 ISSUE

Size	Printing	Number	Title	Handbook	Price	Set
A	BW	? 29	*Boer War Celebrities — 'JASAS' (c1901):	H.133		
			A Black and white front		£200.00	—
			B As A, but mauve tinted		£200.00	—

Size	Print-ing	Number in set		Handbook reference	Price per card	Complete set

JAMES & CO. (Birmingham) LTD

PRE-1919 ISSUE
— C 20 Arms of Countries (c1915):
    A Size 70 × 40mm .... £150.00 —
    B Size 70 × 49mm .... £150.00 —

JAMES'S (GOLD LEAF NAVY CUT)

PRE-1919 ISSUE
A U ? 11 Pretty Girl Series — 'BAGG' (c1898) .... H.45 £350.00 —

J.B. JOHNSON & CO., London

PRE-1919 ISSUE
A C 25 *National Flags and Flowers — Girls (c1900) .... H.123 £300.00 —

JOHNSTON'S CIGARETTES

PRE-1919 ISSUE
A U ? 1 *British Views (c1910) .... H.746 £600.00 —

JONES BROS., Tottenham

PRE-1919 ISSUES
A BW 20 *Spurs Footballers: H.230
    A 12 small titles (1911) .... From £12.00 —
    B 6 large titles (1912) .... From £12.00 —
    C 1 Team Group of 36 (1910-11) .... £800.00 —
    D 1 Team Group of 34 (1911-12) .... £800.00 —

A.I. JONES & CO. Ltd, London

PRE-1919 ISSUE
— C 1 *Advertisement Card — Alexia Mixture (80 × 46mm)
    (c1900) .... H.748 — £600.00
D C 12 Nautical Terms (c1905) .... H.231 £45.00 —

A.S. JONES, Grantham

PRE-1919 ISSUE
D C 30 Army Pictures, Cartoons, etc (c1916) .... H.12 £110.00 —

ALEX. JONES & CO., London

PRE-1919 ISSUES
D2 U ? 9 *Actresses — 'ANGOOD' (c1898) .... H.187 £200.00 —
A BW 1 Portrait of Queen Victoria 1897 .... — £150.00

T. E. JONES & CO., Aberavon

PRE-1919 ISSUES
D C ? 2 *Conundrums (c1900) .... H.232 £200.00 —
A2 C 48 *Flags of All Nations (c1899) .... H.233 £85.00 —
D C 12 Well-known Proverbs (c1900) .... H.235 £175.00 —
— BW 50 Welsh Rugby Players (64 × 34mm) (1899) .... H.234 £200.00 —

C.H. JORDEN LTD, London

PRE-1919 ISSUE
— P ? 12 *Celebrities of the Great War (c1915) (35 × 64mm) ... H.236 £85.00 —

Size	Print-ing	Number in set		Handbook reference	Price per card	Complete set

J. & E. KENNEDY, Dublin

PRE-1919 ISSUE

| A | U | 25 | *Beauties — 'FECKSA' (c1900) | H.58 | £50.00 | — |

RICHARD KENNEDY, Dundee

PRE-1919 ISSUE

| — | C | ? 24 | *Naval & Military Cartoons (130 × 90mm) (c1905) | H.701 | £200.00 | — |
| A | U | 50 | War Portraits (1916) | H.86 | £90.00 | — |

KINNEAR LTD, Liverpool

PRE-1919 ISSUES

A	C	? 13	*Actresses (c1898)	H.237	£110.00	—
D1	BW	? 15	*Australian Cricketers (1897)	H.238	£225.00	—
—	BW	? 1	Cricket Fixture Folder (89 × 69mm) (1903)	H.750	£1200.00	—
A	C	? 17	*Cricketers (c1895)	H.269	£400.00	—
A2	C	25	*Footballers and Club Colours (c1898)	H.239	£200.00	—
—	U	1	The Four Generations (Royal Family) (65 × 70mm) (1897)	H.749	—	£400.00
—	BW	1	'A Gentleman in Kharki' (44 × 64mm) (1900)		—	£70.00
A	C		*Jockeys (1896):	H.240		
		12	— see H.240–I-1		£60.00	—
		1	— see H.240–I-2		£100.00	—
		25	— see H.240–II-A		£100.00	—
		4	— see H.240–II-B		£100.00	—
A	C	? 2	*Prominent Personages (c1902)	H.479	£700.00	—
D1	U	13	*Royalty (1897)	H.241	£45.00	—
—	U	? 32	Views (49 × 35mm) (c1899)	H.751	£400.00	—

B. KRIEGSFELD & CO., Manchester

PRE-1919 ISSUES

—	C	1	*Advertisement Card— Apple Blossom (c1900)	H.752	—	£1400.00
A2	U		*Beauties — 'KEWA' (c1900):	H.139		
		? 61	A Matt surface		£80.00	—
		? 6	B Glossy surface		£150.00	—
A	C	? 10	Celebrities (c1900):	H.242		
			A Backs Horizontal Format		£175.00	—
			B Backs Vertical Format		£175.00	—
A	C	50	*Flags of All Nations (c1900)	H.233	£65.00	—
A	C	50	*Phrases and Advertisements (c1900)	H.243	£80.00	—

A. KUIT LTD, Manchester

PRE-1919 ISSUES

—	C	? 12	Arms of Cambridge Colleges (17 × 25mm) (c1914)	H.458	£100.00	—
—	C	? 12	Arms of Companies (30 × 33mm) (c1914)	H.459	£100.00	—
—	C	30	British Beauties — oval card (36 × 60mm) (c1914)	H.244	£50.00	—
—	P	? 43	*'Crosmedo'Bijoucards (55 × 37mm) (c1915)	H.245	£110.00	—
A	U	25	Principal Streets of British Cities and Towns (1916)		£100.00	—
A	CP	50	Types of Beauty (c1914)	H.246	£100.00	—

LAMBERT & BUTLER, London

32 page reference book — £4.00

A **PRE-1919 ISSUES**

A1	BW	20	*Actresses — 'BLARM' (c1900)	H.23	£30.00	£600.00
—	C	10	*Actresses and Their Autographs (c1898):	H.247		
			A Wide card (70 × 38mm): 'Tobacco' back		£150.00	—
			B Narrow card (70 × 34mm): 'Cigarettes' back		£125.00	—

Size	Print-ing	Number in set		Handbook reference	Price per card	Complete set

LAMBERT & BUTLER, London *(continued)*

Size	Print-ing	Number in set	Description	Handbook reference	Price per card	Complete set
A2	BW	50	*Admirals (1900):	H.248		
			A 'Flaked Gold Leaf Honeydew' back		£18.00	—
			B 'May Blossom' back		£18.00	—
			C 'Prize Medal Bird's Eye' back		£18.00	—
			D 'Viking' back		£24.00	—
C	C	1	*Advertisement Card — Spanish Dancer (1898)	H.249	—	£450.00
A	C	40	Arms of Kings and Queens of England (1906)		£4.50	£180.00
A	C	25	Aviation(1915)		£4.00	£100.00
A2	C	26	*Beauties — 'HOL' (c1900):	H.192		
			A 'Flaked Gold Leaf Honey Dew' back		£32.00	—
			B 'Log Cabin' back		£32.00	—
			C 'May Blossom' back		£32.00	—
			D 'Viking Navy Cut' back		£32.00	—
A	C	50	Birds and Eggs (1906)	H.60	£3.20	£160.00
C	BW	25	*Boer War and Boxer Rebellion — Sketches (1904) ..	H.46	£30.00	—
C	B	10	*Boer War Generals — 'FLAC' (1901)	H.47	£37.00	—
C	U	20	*Boer War Generals 'CLAM' (1900):	H.61		
			I 10. No frame lines to back:			
			A Brown back		£32.00	—
			B Black back		£32.00	—
			II 10. With frame lines to back:			
			A Brown back		£32.00	—
			B Black back		£32.00	—
C	U	1	*Boer War Series — 'The King of Scouts' (Col. R.S.S. Baden-Powell) (1901)	H.753	—	£400.00
—	C	50	*Conundrums (38 × 57mm) (1901):	H.250		
			A Blue back — thick card		£22.00	—
			B Green back		£16.00	—
A2	C	12	Coronation Robes (1902)	H.251	£18.00	£220.00
A	C	20	International Yachts (1902)		£60.00	—
A	C	25	Japanese Series (1904):			
			A Thick toned card		£7.00	£175.00
			B Thin white card		£7.00	£175.00
—	C	4	*Jockeys, no frame lines (35 × 70mm) (c1903)	H.252	£55.00	£220.00
—	C	10	*Jockeys with frame lines (35 × 70mm) (c1903)	H.252	£55.00	£550.00
A	C	1	*Mayblossom Calendar, 1900		—	£700.00
A	C	25	Motors (1908):	H.703		
			A Green back		£27.00	—
			B Plain back		£27.00	—
A	BW	25	Naval Portraits (1914)	H.253	£4.00	£100.00
A	BW	50	Naval Portraits, incl. above 25 (1915)	H.253	£4.00	£200.00
A	C	50	The Thames from Lechlade to London:	H.754		
			A Small numerals (1907)		£6.00	£300.00
			B Large numerals (1908)		£6.00	£300.00
			C Plain back		£6.00	—
—	C	4	*Types of the British Army & Navy (35 × 70mm) (c1897):	H.254		
			A 'Specialities' back in brown		£70.00	—
			B 'Specialities' back in black		£70.00	—
			C 'Viking' back in black		£70.00	—
A	C	25	*Waverley series (1904)	H.255	£12.00	£300.00
A	C	25	Winter Sports (1914)		£4.40	£110.00
A	C	25	Wireless Telegraphy (1909)		£5.00	£125.00
A	C	25	World's Locomotives, Nd. 1-25 (1912)		£4.00	£100.00
A	C	50	World's Locomotives Nd. 1-50 (1912)		£5.00	£250.00
A	C	25	World's Locomotives, Nd. 1A-25A (c1913)		£4.60	£115.00

Size	Printing	Number in set		Handbook reference	Price per card	Complete set

LAMBERT & BUTLER, London *(continued)*

B POST-1920 ISSUES

Size	Printing	Number in set	Title	Handbook reference	Price per card	Complete set
A	C	50	Aeroplane Markings (1937)		£1.70	£85.00
A	C	25	British Trees and Their Uses (1927)	H.654	£2.00	£50.00
A	C	25	Common Fallacies (1928)		£2.00	£50.00
A	C	25	Dance Band Leaders (1936)		£4.00	£100.00
A	C	50	Empire Air Routes (1936)		£2.00	£100.00
A	BW	25	Famous British Airmen and Airwomen (1935)		£1.80	£45.00
A	U	25	Fauna of Rhodesia (1929)		£1.20	£30.00
A	C	50	Find Your Way:			
			A Address 'Box No. 152, London' (1932)		£1.50	£75.00
			B Address 'Box No. 152, Drury Lane, London' (1932)		£1.50	£75.00
			C Overprinted in red (1933)		£1.50	£75.00
A	BW	1	D Joker Card:			
			i Without overprint (1932)		—	£12.00
			ii With overprint (1933)		—	£12.00
A	C	50	Footballers 1930-1 (1931)		£4.00	—
A	C	25	Garden Life (1930)	H.449	£1.00	£25.00
A	C	25	Hints and Tips for Motorists (1929)		£4.00	£100.00
A	U	25	A History of Aviation:			
			A Front in green (1932)		£2.00	£50.00
			B Front in brown (1933)		£2.60	£65.00
A	C	50	Horsemanship (1938)		£2.50	£125.00
A	C	25	How Motor Cars Work (1931)		£2.20	£55.00
A	C	50	Interesting Customs and Traditions of the Navy, Army and Air Force (1939)		£1.00	£50.00
A	C	25	Interesting Musical Instruments (1929)		£2.60	£65.00
A	C	50	Interesting Sidelights on the Work of the GPO (1939)		£1.00	£50.00
A	C	50	Keep Fit (1937)		80p	£40.00
A	C	25	London Characters (1934):			
			A With Album Clause		£2.40	£60.00
			B Without Album Clause		£20.00	—
A	C	25	Motor Car Radiators (1928)		£6.00	£150.00
A	C	25	Motor Cars — 'A Series of 25', green back (1922)		£2.60	£65.00
A	C	25	Motor Cars — '2nd Series of 25' (1923)		£2.60	£65.00
A	C	50	Motor Cars — '3rd Series of 50' (1926)		£4.00	£200.00
A	C	25	Motor Cars — 'A Series of 25', grey back (1934)		£3.60	£90.00
A	C	50	Motor Cycles (1923)		£3.50	£175.00
A	C	50	Motor Index Marks (1926)		£2.60	£130.00
A	C	25	Pirates and Highwaymen (1926)	Ha.584	£1.40	£35.00
A	U	25	Rhodesian Series (1928)		£1.40	£35.00
A	U	25	Third Rhodesian Series (1930)		60p	£15.00
A	C	25	Wonders of Nature (1924)		70p	£17.50

C POST-1940 ISSUES

Size	Printing	Number in set	Title	Handbook reference	Price per card	Complete set
—	C	12	Advertisement Cards — Facts about Lambert & Butler (2002):			
			A Size 75 × 32mm		£2.00	—
			B Size 80 × 47mm		£1.50	—

LAMBKIN BROS., Cork

POST-1920 ISSUES

Size	Printing	Number in set	Title	Handbook reference	Price per card	Complete set
A	C	36	*Country Scenes — Small size (1924) (6 sets of 6):			
			Series 1 — Yachting		£6.00	—
			Series 2 — Country		£6.00	—
			Series 3 — Far East		£6.00	—
			Series 4 — Sailing		£6.00	—

Size	Printing	Number in set		Handbook reference	Price per card	Complete set
			LAMBKIN BROS., Cork (*continued*)			
			Series 5 — Country		£6.00	—
			Series 6 — Country		£6.00	—
C	C	36	*Country Scenes — Large size (1924) (6 sets of 6):			
			Series 7 — Yachting		£6.00	—
			Series 8 — Country		£6.00	—
			Series 9 — Far East		£6.00	—
			Series 10 — Sailing		£6.00	—
			Series 11 — Country		£6.00	—
			Series 12 — Windmill Scenes		£6.00	—
—	C	? 9	*Irish Views, anonymous. inscribed 'Eagle, Cork' (68 × 67mm) (c1925)	H.585	£40.00	—
—	C	? 5	*'Lily of Killarney' Views (73 × 68mm) (c1925)	H.586	£150.00	—

LANCS & YORKS TOBACCO MANUFACTURING CO. LTD, Burnley (L. & Y. Tob. Mfg. Co.)

PRE-1919 ISSUE

C	C	26	*Actresses — 'FROGA A' (c1900)	H.20	£350.00	—

C. & J. LAW, Hertford

PRE-1919 ISSUES

A	C	25	*Types of British Soldiers (c1914)	H.144	£26.00	—
A	U	50	War Portraits (1916)	H.86	£100.00	—

R.J. LEA LTD, Manchester

A PRE-1919 ISSUES

A	C	1	*Advertisement Card — Swashbuckler (c1913)		—	£1000.00
A1	C	50	Chairman Miniatures 1-50 (1912):			
			A No border		£3.00	£150.00
			B Gilt border		£3.00	£150.00
A1	C	50	Chairman and Vice Chair Miniatures, 51-100 (1912)		£3.00	£150.00
A1	BW	25	Chairman War Portraits (marked 'War Series' on front) (1915)		£5.00	£125.00
A	C	70	Cigarette Transfers (Locomotives) (1916)		£8.00	—
A	BW	25	Civilians of Countries Fighting with the Allies (1914)		£12.00	£300.00
A1	C	50	Flowers to Grow (The Best Perennials) (1913)		£4.00	£200.00
A1	C	50	Modern Miniatures (1913)	H.756	—	£355.00
			46 different, less 1, 8, 12, 32		£1.50	£70.00
A1	C	12	More Lea's Smokers (1906):	H.256		
			A Green borders		£80.00	—
			B Red borders		£100.00	—
A1	C	50	Old English Pottery and Porcelain, 1-50 (1912)		£2.00	£100.00
A1	C	50	Old Pottery and Porcelain, 51-100 (1912):			
			A 'Chairman Cigarettes'		£1.60	£80.00
			B 'Recorder Cigarettes'		£6.00	—
A1	C	50	Old Pottery and Porcelain, 101-150 (1912):			
			A 'Chairman Cigarettes'		£1.60	£80.00
			B 'Recorder Cigarettes'		£6.00	—
A1	C	50	Old Pottery and Porcelain, 151-200 (1913)		£1.60	£80.00
A1	C	50	Old Pottery and Porcelain, 201-250 (1913)		£1.60	£80.00
A	BW	25	War Pictures (1915)		£4.40	£110.00

B POST-1920 ISSUES

		48	Coronation Souvenir (1937):			
A2	P		A Small size, glossy:			
			1 Lea's name		60p	£30.00
			2 'Successors to ...'		40p	£20.00

Size	Print-ing	Number in set			Handbook reference	Price per card	Complete set

R. J. LEA LTD, Manchester *(continued)*

Size	Print-ing	Number in set	Description		Handbook reference	Price per card	Complete set
A2	BW		B Small size, matt:				
				1 Lea's name		£1.00	£50.00
				2 Successors to		50p	£25.00
—	P		C Medium size (77 × 51mm)			60p	£30.00
A2	C	50	Dogs (1923):				
				1 Nos. 1-25 — A White card		£4.00	—
				B Cream card		£4.00	—
				2 Nos. 26-50		£6.00	—
A2	C	25	English Birds (1922):				
				A Glossy front		£3.00	£75.00
				B Matt front		£6.00	
A2	C	25	The Evolution of the Royal Navy (1925)			£2.40	£60.00
A2	P	54	Famous Film Stars (1939)			£1.30	£70.00
	CP	48	Famous Racehorses of 1926 (1927):				
A2			A Small size			£2.80	£140.00
			B Medium size (75 × 50mm)			£6.00	—
		48	Famous Views (1936):				
A2	P		A Small size — 1 Glossy			25p	£12.50
	BW		2 Matt			£1.00	£50.00
—	P		B Medium size (76 × 51mm)			50p	£25.00
A2	P	36	Film Stars — 'A First Series ...' (1934)			£3.00	£110.00
A2	P	36	Film Stars — 'A Second Series ...' (1934)			£2.75	£100.00
A2	C	25	Fish (1926)			£2.40	£60.00
A2		48	Girls from the Shows (1935):				
	P		A Glossy front			£2.20	£110.00
	BW		B Matt front			£2.50	£125.00
A2		54	Radio Stars (1935):				
	P		A Glossy front			£2.00	£110.00
	BW		B Matt front			£2.50	£135.00
A2	C	50	Roses (1924)			£1.60	£80.00
A2	C	50	Ships of the World (1925)			£1.80	£90.00
		48	Wonders of the World (1938):				
A2	P		A Small size — 1 Glossy			60p	£30.00
	BW		2 Matt			£1.40	£65.00
	P		B Medium size (76 × 50mm)			60p	£30.00

C SILKS. All paper-backed.

—	C		*Butterflies and Moths III (c1925):		H.505-7		
		12	1 Small size (70 × 44mm)			£4.50	£55.00
		12	2 Large size (70 × 88mm)			£4.00	£50.00
		6	3 Extra-large size (143 × 70mm)			£4.50	£27.00
—	C	54	*Old Pottery — Set 1 (68 × 38mm) (c1915)		H.505-14	£1.00	£55.00
—	C	72	*Old Pottery — Set 2 (61 × 37mm) (c1915)		H.505-14	£1.00	£75.00
—	C	50	Regimental Crests and Badges — Series I (48mm sq.) (c1920)		H.502-4	£1.50	—
—	C	50	Regimental Crests and Badges — Series II (48 mm sq.) (c1920)		H.502-4	£1.80	—

D MISCELLANEOUS

—	C	24	Old English Pottery and Porcelain (Post Card Size) (Inscribed Chairman Cigarette Series or other firms' names) (c1910)		H.257	£6.00	

ALFRED L. LEAVER, London

POST-1920 ISSUE

—	U	12	Manikin Cards (79 × 51mm) (c1925)		H.481	£100.00	—

Size	Print-ing	Number in set		Handbook reference	Price per card	Complete set

J. LEES, Northampton

PRE-1919 ISSUE
| A | C | ?21 | Northampton Town Football Club (No. 301-321) (c1912) | | £120.00 | — |

A. LEWIS & CO. (WESTMINSTER) LTD, London

POST-1920 ISSUE
| A2 | C | 52 | Horoscopes (1938) | H.587 | 80p | £42.00 |

H. C. LLOYD & SON, Exeter

PRE-1919 ISSUES
A	U	28	Academy Gems (c1900):	H.258		
			A Red-brown tint		£50.00	—
			B Purple tint		£50.00	—
			C Green tint		£50.00	—
D	BW	?26	*Actresses and Boer War Celebrities (c1900)	H.260	£40.00	—
—	BW		*Devon Footballers and Boer War Celebrities (c1901):	H.259		
		?42	Set 1 — Without framelines (70 × 41mm)		£45.00	—
		?6	Set 2 — With framelines (70 × 45mm)		£200.00	—
A1	C	25	*Star Girls — 'Tipsy Loo Cigarettes' (c1898)	H.30	£250.00	—
—	BW	36	War Pictures (73 × 69mm) (c1914)		£250.00	—

RICHARD LLOYD & SONS, London

A   PRE-1919 ISSUES
—	BW	25	*Boer War Celebrities (35 × 61mm) (1899)	H.261	£35.00	—
—	U	?23	*General Interest — Actresses, Celebrities and Yachts (62 × 39mm) (c1900)	H.262	£100.00	—
A1	C	96	*National Types, Costumes and Flags (c1900)	H.263	£35.00	—
A	C	10	Scenes from San Toy (c1905)	H.462	£9.00	£90.00

B   POST-1920 ISSUES. Most cards inscribed 'Branch of Cope Bros. & Co., Ltd.' See also under 'Cope Bros'.
A	C	25	Atlantic Records (1936)		£3.00	£75.00
A2	P	27	Cinema Stars, glossy — 'A Series of 27', Nd. 1-27 (c1934)		£7.00	—
A2	P	27	Cinema Stars, glossy — 'A Series of 27', Nd. 28-54 (c1934)		£2.50	£70.00
A2	P	27	Cinema Stars, glossy — 'Third Series of 27', Nd. 55-81 (1935)		£7.00	—
A2	U	25	Cinema Stars, matt — 'A Series of 25' (c1937)		£2.00	£50.00
A	BW	25	*Famous Cricketers (Puzzle Series) (1930)	H.661	£6.50	—
D	C		Old Inns:			
		25	A1 Titled 'Old English Inns' (1923)		£1.60	£40.00
		25	A2 Titled 'Old Inns — Series 2' (1924)		£3.00	£75.00
		50	B Titled 'Old Inns' (1925)		£1.60	£80.00
A	BW	25	Tricks and Puzzles (1935)		£1.00	£25.00
A2	U	25	Types of Horses (1926):			
			A Back in light brown		£4.00	£100.00
			B Back in dark brown		£4.00	£100.00
A2	U	25	'Zoo' Series (1926)	H.588	£1.00	£25.00

A. LOWNIE, Abroath

PRE-1919 ISSUE
| A | C | 30 | *Army Pictures, Cartoons, etc. (c1916) | H.12 | £110.00 | — |

LUSBY LTD, London

PRE-1919 ISSUE
| D | C | 25 | Scenes from Circus Life (c1900) | H.264 | £120.00 | — |

60

Size	Printing	Number in set		Handbook reference	Price per card	Complete set

HUGH McCALL, Edinburgh, Glasgow and Aberdeen

POST-1920 ISSUE
| C | C | ?1 | *RAF Advertisement Card (c1924) | H.594 | £350.00 | — |

D. & J. MACDONALD, Glasgow

PRE-1919 ISSUES
A	C	?10	*Actresses — 'MUTA' (c1891)	H.265	£110.00	—
A	BW	25	*Cricketers (c1902)	H.266	£400.00	—
—	BW	?24	*Cricket and Football Teams (71 × 69mm) (c1902):	H.267		
			A 'Winning Team' Cigarettes		£450.00	—
			B 'Tontine' Cigarettes		£450.00	—
—	C	?1	County Cricket Team (71 × 69mm) (1900)	H.267	£1800.00	—

MACKENZIE & CO., Glasgow

PRE-1919 ISSUES
—	P	50	*Actors and Actresses (32 × 58mm) (c1902)	H.268	£20.00	—
—	U	50	Victorian Art Pictures — Photogravure (32 × 58mm) (c1908)		£22.00	—
A	BW	50	The Zoo (c1910)		£26.00	—

WM. M'KINNELL, Edinburgh

PRE-1919 ISSUE
| A | C | 12 | European War Series (1915) | H.129 | £75.00 | — |
| A | U | 50 | War Portraits (1916) | H.86 | £95.00 | — |

MACNAUGHTON, JENKINS & CO. LTD, Dublin

POST-1920 ISSUES
—	C	50	Castles of Ireland (1924):	H.662		
			A Size 76 × 45mm		£3.20	£160.00
			B Size 74 × 44mm		£3.60	—
D	C	50	Various Uses of Rubber (1924)		£2.60	£130.00

A. McTAVISH, Elgin

PRE-1919 ISSUE
| D | C | 30 | *Army Pictures, Cartoons etc (c1916) | H12 | £110.00 | — |

McWATTIE & SONS, Arbroath

PRE-1919 ISSUE
| D | C | 30 | *Army Pictures, Cartoons etc (c1916) | H12 | £110.00 | — |

THE MANXLAND TOBACCO CO., Isle of Man

PRE-1919 ISSUES
| D | BW | ?6 | *Views in the Isle of Man (c1900) | H.491 | £400.00 | — |

MARCOVITCH & CO., London

A POST-1920 ISSUE
| A2 | P | 18 | *Beauties (anonymous with plain backs, numbered left base of front) (1932) | Ha.627 | £1.00 | £18.00 |

B POST-1940 ISSUE
| — | U | 7 | The Story in Red and White (75 × 66mm) (1955) | | £2.00 | £14.00 |

Size	Print-ing	Number in set		Handbook reference	Price per card	Complete set

MARCUS & CO., Manchester

PRE-1919 ISSUES
A	C	?17	*Cricketers, 'Marcus Handicap Cigarettes' (1895)	H.269	£400.00	—
A	C	25	*Footballers and Club Colours (1896)	H.239	£200.00	—
—	BW	1	The Four Generations (Royal Family) (65 × 70mm) (1897)	H.749	—	£300.00

T.W. MARKHAM, Bridgwater

PRE-1919 ISSUE
| — | BW | ?27 | Views of Bridgwater (68 × 42mm) (c1906) .... | H.709 | £120.00 | — |

MARSUMA LTD, Congleton

PRE-1919 ISSUE
| A | BW | 50 | *Famous Golfers and Their Strokes (c1914) .... | | £45.00 | — |

C. MARTIN, Moseley

PRE-1919 ISSUE
| D | C | 30 | *Army Pictures, Cartoons etc. (c1916) .... | H12 | £110.00 | — |

MARTINS LTD, London

PRE-1919 ISSUES
A	C	1	''Arf a Mo', Kaiser!' (c1915)		—	£75.00
—	U	?14	Carlyle Series — folding card (c1918)	H.270	£100.00	—
D	U	25	*VC Heroes (c1916)		£26.00	£650.00

R. MASON & CO., London

PRE-1919 ISSUES
C	C	30	*Colonial Troops (c1902)	H.40	£50.00	—
D2	C	40	*Naval and Military Phrases (c1904):	H.14		
			A White Border		£45.00	—
			B No Border		£45.00	—

JUSTUS VAN MAURIK

POST-1920 ISSUE
| — | C | 12 | *Dutch Scenes (108 × 70mm) (c1920) .... | H.622 | £125.00 | — |

MAY QUEEN CIGARETTES

POST-1940 ISSUE
| — | C | 12 | Interesting Pictures (68 × 48mm) (c1960) .... | | £1.00 | — |

MENTORS LTD, London

PRE-1919 ISSUE
| — | C | 32 | Views of Ireland (42 × 67mm) (c1912) .... | H.271 | £11.00 | — |

J. MILLHOFF & CO. LTD, London

A ***PRE-1919 ISSUE***
			Theatre Advertisement Cards (c1905):			
—	BW	?9	A Medium size (83 × 56mm)		£160.00	—
—	BW	?2	B Large size (108 × 83mm)		£200.00	—

Size	Print-ing	Number in set		Handbook reference	Price per card	Complete set

J. MILLHOFF & CO. LTD, London *(continued)*

B POST-1920 ISSUES

Size	Print-ing	Number in set	Description	Handbook reference	Price per card	Complete set
	CP		Antique Pottery (1927):			
A2		54	A Small size		90p	£50.00
—		56	B Medium size (74 × 50mm)		80p	£45.00
	C		Art Treasures:			
D		30	A Small size (1927)		£1.00	£30.00
B		50	B Large size (1926)		70p	£35.00
B	C	25	Art Treasures — '2nd Series of 50', Nd. 51-75 (1928)		£1.00	£25.00
B	C	25	England, Historic and Picturesque — 'Series of 25' (1928)		£1.20	£30.00
B	C	25	England, Historic and Picturesque — 'Second Series ...' (1928)		£1.00	£25.00
A2	P	27	Famous Golfers (1928)		£13.00	—
	P	27	Famous 'Test' Cricketers (1928):			
A2			A Small size		£5.00	—
			B Medium size (76 × 51mm)		£5.00	—
—	C	25	Gallery Pictures (76 × 51mm) (1928)		£1.20	£30.00
A2	C	50	'Geographia' Map Series (sectional) (1931)		£1.80	£90.00
	CP		The Homeland Series (1933):	Ha.539		
A2		54	A Small size		28p	£15.00
—		56	B Medium size (76 × 51mm)		40p	£22.00
A2	P	36	In the Public Eye (1930)		£1.50	£55.00
D	C	25	Men of Genius (1924)		£5.00	£125.00
B	C	25	Picturesque Old England (1931)		£1.20	£30.00
A2	P		Real Photographs:	Ha.538		
		27	'A Series of 27' —			
			A Matt front (c1931)		80p	£22.00
			B Glossy front (c1931)		40p	£11.00
		27	'2nd Series of 27' (c1931)		80p	£22.00
		27	'3rd Series of 27' (c1932)		40p	£11.00
		27	'4th Series of 27' (c1932)		80p	£22.00
		27	'5th Series of 27' (c1933)		£1.10	£30.00
		27	'6th Series of 27' (c1933)		£1.10	£30.00
C	C	25	Reproductions of Celebrated Oil Paintings (1928)	Ha.542	£1.40	£35.00
B	C	25	Roses (1927)		£2.80	£70.00
A2	C	50	Things to Make — 'De Reszke Cigarettes' (1935)		60p	£30.00
A2	C	50	What the Stars Say — 'De Reszke Cigarettes' (1934)		80p	£40.00
A2	P	36	Zoological Studies (1929)		30p	£11.00

C MISCELLANEOUS

Size	Print-ing	Number in set	Description	Handbook reference	Price per card	Complete set
—	U		'RILETTE' Miniature Pictures (60 × 45mm) (c1925):			
		20	A Inscribed Series of 20		£3.50	—
		25	B Inscribed Series of 25		£3.50	—
		30	C Inscribed Series of 30		£3.50	—
		42	D Inscribed Series of 42		£3.50	—
		43	E Inscribed Series of 43		£3.50	—
		56	F Inscribed Series of 56		£3.50	—
		74	G Inscribed Series of 74		£3.50	—

MIRANDA LTD, London

POST-1920 ISSUES

Size	Print-ing	Number in set	Description	Handbook reference	Price per card	Complete set
A	C	20	Dogs (c1925)	H.211	£8.00	—
A	C	25	Sports and Pastimes — Series I (c1925)	H.225	£6.00	£150.00

Size	Print-ing	Number in set		Handbook reference	Price per card	Complete set

STEPHEN MITCHELL & SON, Glasgow

A PRE-1919 ISSUES

Size	Print	Number	Title	Handbook	Price	Complete
C	C	51	*Actors and Actresses — Selection from 'FROGA B and C' (c1900)	H.20	£22.00	—
C	U	25	*Actors and Actresses — 'FROGA C' (c1900)	H.20	£22.00	—
C	U	50	*Actors and Actresses — 'FROGA D' (c1900)	H.20	£22.00	—
C	U	26	*Actresses — 'FROGA B' (c1900)	H.20	£22.00	—
A	U	1	Advertisement Card 'Maid of Honour' (c1900)		—	£700.00
A	C	50	Arms and Armour (1916)	H.273	£3.80	£190.00
A	C	25	Army Ribbons and Buttons (1916)		£4.00	£100.00
C	BW	25	*Boxer Rebellion — Sketches (c1904)	H.46	£28.00	—
D1	BW	25	British Warships, 1-25 (1915)		£7.00	£175.00
D1	BW	25	British Warships, Second series 26-50 (1915)		£7.00	£175.00
A	C	50	Interesting Buildings (1905)	H.70	£8.00	£400.00
A	C	25	Medals (1916)	H.71	£5.00	£125.00
A	C	25	Money (1913)		£5.00	£125.00
A	C	25	*Regimental Crests, Nicknames and Collar Badges (1900)	H.274	£14.00	£350.00
A	C	25	Scottish Clan Series No. 1 (1903)	H.33	£14.00	£350.00
A	C	25	Seals (1911)		£5.00	£125.00
A	C	25	Sports (1907)	H.275	£13.00	£325.00
A	C	25	Statues and Monuments (1914)		£4.60	£115.00

B POST-1920 ISSUES

Size	Print	Number	Title	Handbook	Price	Complete
A	C	50	Air Raid Precautions (1938)	H.544	£1.00	£50.00
A	C	25	Angling (1928)	H.655	£7.00	£175.00
A	C	50	Clan Tartans — 'A Series of 50' (1927)	H.663	£1.90	£95.00
A	C	25	Clan Tartans — '2nd Series, 25' (1927)		£1.00	£25.00
A	C	25	Empire Exhibition, Scotland, 1938 (1938)		£1.00	£25.00
A2	C	25	Famous Crosses (1923)		70p	£17.50
A	C	50	Famous Scots (1933)		£1.60	£80.00
A	U	50	First Aid (1938)		£1.10	£55.00
A	U	50	A Gallery of 1934 (1935)		£2.80	£140.00
A	U	50	A Gallery of 1935 (1936)		£1.90	£95.00
A	C	50	Humorous Drawings (1924)	H.590	£2.50	£125.00
A	C	40	London Ceremonials (1928)		£1.50	£60.00
A	C	30	A Model Army (cut-outs) (1932)		£1.20	£36.00
A	C	25	Old Sporting Prints (1930)	H.563	£1.40	£35.00
A	U	50	Our Empire (1937)	H.522	50p	£25.00
A	C	70	River and Coastal Steamers (1925)		£3.50	—
A	C		A Road Map of Scotland (1933):			
		50	A Small numerals		£3.50	£175.00
		50	B Large numerals in circles		£3.50	£175.00
		50	C Overprinted in red		£4.50	£225.00
		1	D Substitute card (Blue)		—	£16.00
A	C	50	Scotland's Story (1929)		£2.60	£130.00
A	U	50	Scottish Footballers (1934)		£3.00	£150.00
A	U	50	Scottish Football Snaps (1935)		£3.00	£150.00
A	C	25	Stars of Screen and History (1939)		£2.60	£65.00
—	C	25	Village Models Series (1925):	Ha.591		
A			A Small size		£2.20	£55.00
			B Medium size (68 × 62mm)		£5.00	£125.00
—	C	25	Village Models Series — 'Second' (1925):	H.664		
A			A Small size:			
			1 Inscribed 'Second Series'		£2.20	£55.00
			2 Not inscribed 'Second Series'		£5.00	—
			B Medium size (68 × 62mm)		£5.00	£125.00
A	U	50	Wonderful Century (1937)		70p	£35.00
A	U	50	The World of Tomorrow (1936)		£1.60	£80.00

Size	Printing	Number in set		Handbook reference	Price per card	Complete set

MOORGATE TOBACCO CO., London

POST-1940 ISSUE
	BW	30	The New Elizabethan Age (20 small, 10 large) (1953):			
			A Matt front		£3.00	—
			B Varnished front		£1.80	£55.00

B. MORRIS & SONS LTD, London

A PRE-1919 ISSUES
	BW	30	*Actresses (41 × 68mm) (1898)	H.276	£2.00	£60.00
C	U	26	*Actresses — 'FROGA A (c1900):	H.20		
			A 'Borneo Queen' back		£30.00	—
			B 'Gold Seals' back		£30.00	—
			C 'Morris's Cigarettes' back		£30.00	—
			D 'Tommy Atkins' back		£80.00	—
—	C	? 4	*Actresses — selection from 'FROGA B' — 'Morris's High Class Cigarettes' on front (76 × 66mm) (c1900)	H.20	£900.00	—
A1	P	1	*Advertisement Card (Soldier and Girl) (c1900)	H.758	—	£1500.00
A	U	21	*Beauties — 'MOM' (c1900):	H.277		
			A 'Borneo Queen' back		£30.00	—
			B 'Gold Seals' back		£30.00	—
			C 'Morris's Cigarettes' back		£30.00	—
			D 'Tommy Atkins' back		£80.00	—
A	C	50	*Beauties — 'CHOAB' (c1900):	H.21		
			A 'Gold Flake Honeydew' back		£45.00	—
			B 'Golden Virginia' back		£45.00	—
			C 'Levant Favourites' back		£45.00	—
			D 'Reina Regenta' back		£45.00	—
A	U	? 53	*Beauties — Collotype (c1897)	H.278	£150.00	—
A	C	20	Boer War, 1900 (VC Heroes)	H.279	£35.00	—
A	BW	25	*Boer War Celebrities — 'PAM' (c1901)	H.140	£30.00	—
A	C	30	*General Interest — six cards each entitled (c1910):	H.280		
			i Agriculture in the Orient		£6.50	£40.00
			ii Architectural Monuments		£6.50	£40.00
			iii The Ice Breaker		£6.50	£40.00
			iv Schools in Foreign Countries		£6.50	£40.00
			v Strange Vessels		£6.50	£40.00
D	BW	20	London Views (c1905):	H.34		
			A 'American Gold' back		£32.00	—
			B 'Morris's Gold Flake' back		£32.00	—
			C 'Smoke Borneo Queen' back		£32.00	—
			D 'Smoke Reina Regenta' back		£32.00	—
A	C	25	Marvels of the Universe Series (c1912)	H.281	£4.00	£100.00
D	C	50	National and Colonial Arms (1917)	H.704	£6.00	£300.00
C	U	25	War Celebrities (1915)		£5.00	£125.00
D	C	25	War Pictures (1916)	H.51	£7.00	£175.00

B POST-1920 ISSUES
A1	C	50	Animals at the Zoo (1924):	H.520		
			A Back in blue		70p	£35.00
			B Back in grey		80p	£40.00
A1	C	35	At the London Zoo Aquarium (1928)		50p	£17.50
A1	BW	25	Australian Cricketers (1925)		£3.60	£90.00
A2	C	25	Captain Blood (1937)		£1.10	£27.50
D	U	50	Film Star Series (1923)		£3.40	—
D	U	25	Golf Strokes Series (1923)		£6.00	£150.00
A1	—	12	Horoscopes (wording only) (1936):			
			A White card		£1.00	—
			B Cream card		70p	£8.50

Size	Printing	Number in set		Handbook reference	Price per card	Complete set

B. MORRIS & SONS LTD, London *(continued)*

Size	Print	Num	Title	Handbook	Price	Set
A2	C	25	How Films are Made (1934):			
			A White card		£1.20	£30.00
			B Cream Card		£1.40	£35.00
A1	BW	50	How to Sketch (1929)		£1.20	£60.00
A1	C	25	Measurement of Time (1924)		£1.40	£35.00
D	U	25	Motor Series (Motor parts) (1922)		£4.40	£110.00
A1	C	25	The Queen's Dolls' House (1925)		£3.00	£75.00
D	U	25	Racing Greyhounds — 'Issued by Forecasta' (1939) ..		£1.60	£40.00
A1	BW	24	Shadowgraphs (1925)		£2.60	£65.00
A1	C	13	Treasure Island (1924)		£1.50	£20.00
A1	C	50	Victory Signs (1928)		70p	£35.00
A	C	25	Wax Art Series (1931)		50p	£12.50
A	C	25	Whipsnade Zoo (1932)		60p	£15.00
D	C	25	Wireless Series (1923)		£4.40	£110.00

C *SILKS*

—	C	24	Battleship Crests (70 × 50mm) (paper backed) (c1915)	H.504-3	£35.00	—
—	C		English Flowers (78 × 56mm) (paper backed) (c1915):	H.505-4		
		25	A Series of 25		£4.00	£100.00
		50	B Series of 50		£4.50	—
—	C	25	English and Foreign Birds (78 × 56mm) (paper backed) (c1915)	H.505-1	£4.60	£115.00
—	C	25	*Regimental Colours IV* (75 × 55m) (unbacked and anonymous (c1915))	H.502-9	£3.60	£85.00
—	C	4	*Regimental Colours* (210 × 190mm) (c1915)	H.502-13	£60.00	—

PHILIP MORRIS & CO. LTD, London

POST-1920 ISSUES

	U	50	British Views (1924):			
C			A Small size		£3.00	—
—			B Large size (79 × 67mm)		£3.00	—

P. MOUAT & CO., Newcastle-on-Tyne

PRE-1919 ISSUE

C	C	30	*Colonial Troops (c1902)	H.40	£200.00	—

MOUSTAFA LTD, London

POST-1920 ISSUES

D2	CP	50	Camera Studies (1923):			
			A Front with number and caption, back in black ..		£3.00	—
			* B *Front without letterpress, plain back*		£3.00	—
D2	C	25	*Cinema Stars — Set 8* (1924)	Ha.515-8	£5.00	—
A2	C	40	Leo Chambers Dogs Heads (1924)		£3.20	£130.00
D2	C	25	*Pictures of World Interest* (1923)		£3.00	—
A2	P	25	Real Photos (Views) (1925)		44p	£11.00

MUNRO, Glasgow

PRE-1919 ISSUE

C	C	30	Colonial Troops (c1900)		£350.00	—

B. MURATTI, SONS & CO. LTD, Manchester and London

A PRE-1919 ISSUES

—	U	? 24	*Actresses, cabinet size, collotype (106 × 69mm) (c1898)	H.282	£125.00	

Size	Print-ing	Number in set		Handbook reference	Price per card	Complete set

B. MURATTI, SONS & CO. LTD, Manchester and London *(continued)*

Size	Print-ing	Number in set	Description	Handbook reference	Price per card	Complete set
C	C	26	*Actresses — 'FROGA A' (c1900):	H.20		
			A 'To the Cigarette Connoisseur' back		£25.00	—
			B 'Muratti's Zinnia Cigarettes' back		£30.00	—
—	C		*Actresses and Beauties — Green Corinthian column framework — 'Neb-Ka' vertical backs (117 × 67mm) (c1900):			
		? 18	Actresses — selection from 'FROGA C'	H.20	£150.00	—
		? 3	Beauties — selection from 'MOM'	H.277	£200.00	—
—	C		*Actresses and Beauties — brown and yellow ornamental framework (117 × 67mm) (c1900): I 'Neb-Ka' horizontal backs:			
		26	i Actresses — selection from 'FROGA A' ..	H.20	£140.00	—
		50	ii Beauties — selection from 'CHOAB'	H.21	£140.00	—
		25	II Rubber stamped back. Beauties — selection from 'CHOAB'	H.21	£140.00	—
		25	III Plain back — Beauties — selection from 'CHOAB'	H.21	£140.00	—
—	C		*Advertisement Cards, Globe design back (88 × 66mm) (c1900):	H.283		
		? 10	i Brown borders to front		£400.00	—
		? 19	ii White borders to front		£400.00	—
C	C	50	*Beauties — 'CHOAB' (Zinnia back) (c1900):	H.21		
			A Black printing on back		£40.00	—
			B Olive green printing on back		£45.00	—
—	C	? 66	*Beautiful Women, Globe design back (54 × 75mm) (c1900)	H.284	£90.00	—
—	BW	20	*Boer War Generals — 'CLAM' (35 × 61mm) (c1901)	H.61	£35.00	—
—	C	15	*Caricatures (42 × 62mm) (c1903):	H.285		
			A 'Sole Manufacturers of ...' brown back		£25.00	—
			B 'Muratti's Zinnia Cigarettes' brown back		£30.00	—
			C 'Muratti's Zinnia Cigarettes' black back		£25.00	—
			D 'Muratti's Vassos Cigarettes' (not seen)		—	—
			E As D, but 'Vassos' blocked out, brown back ...		£45.00	—
—	C	35	Crowned Heads (53 × 83mm) (c1913)		£13.00	—
C	C	52	*Japanese Series, Playing Card inset (c1904)		£15.00	—
			Plain back		£14.00	—
—	P		Midget Post Card Series (1902):	H.286		
		? 99	A Matt Front (90 × 70mm)		£11.00	—
		? 5	B Matt Front (80 × 65mm)		£11.00	—
			C Glossy front (85 × 65mm few 75-80 × 65mm):			
		? 136	i With serial numbers		£11.00	—
		? 76	ii Without serial numbers		£11.00	—
—	P	? 99	'Queens' Post Card Series (90 × 70mm) (c1902):	H.287		
			A Front in black/sepia		£15.00	—
			B Front in reddish brown		£15.00	—
A1	BW	19	*Russo-Japanese Series (1904)	H.184	£14.00	£265.00
A1	C	25	*Star Girls (c1898)	H.30	£200.00	—
A	U	? 51	*Views of Jersey (c1912):	H.288		
			A Plain back		£16.00	—
			B 'Opera House, Jersey' back		£18.00	—
A	U	25	*War Series — 'MURATTI I', white card (1916)	H.289	£22.00	—
A	U	50	*War Series — 'MURATTI II', toned card (1917) Nos. 1-25 (and alternative cards)	H.290	£13.00	—

B POST-1920 ISSUES

A2	P	24	Australian Race Horses (export) (c1930)		80p	£20.00

67

Size	Print- ing	Number in set		Handbook reference	Price per card	Complete set

B. MURATTI, SONS & CO. LTD, Manchester and London *(continued)*

C SILKS. For summary of paper-backed issues, see Ha.497.

—	C		*Flags — Set 3 (70 × 52mm) (paper backed) (c1915):	Ha.501-3		
		25	1st Series — Series C, Nd. 20-44		£3.50	—
		24	2nd Series:			
			Series A, Nd. 26-49		£3.50	—
			Series E, Nd. 48-72, paper backing in grey (No. 52 unissued)		£3.50	—
			Series E, Nd. 48-72, paper backing in green (No. 52 unissued)		£3.50	—
—	C		*Flags — Set 8 (paper backed) (c1915):	Ha.501-8		
		3	Series A, Nd. 1-3 (89 × 115mm)		£9.00	—
		1	Series B, Nd. 19 (70 × 76mm)		—	£12.00
		18	Series C, Nd. 1-18 (89 × 115mm)		£9.00	—
		3	Series D, Nd. 45-47 (89 × 115mm)		£9.00	—
		6	Series F, Nd. 73-78 (89 × 115mm)		£9.00	—
—	C	18	*Great War Leaders — Series P (89 × 115mm) (paper backed) (c1916)	Ha.504	£13.00	—
—	C		*Regimental Badges I (paper backed) (c1915):	H.502-1		
		25	Series A, Nd. 1-25 (70 × 52mm)		£4.50	—
		48	Series B, Nd. 1-48 (76 × 70mm)		£5.50	—
		15	Series B, Nd. 4-18 (76 × 70mm)		£5.50	—
		16	Series G, Nd. 79-94 (76 × 70mm)		£8.00	—
—	C	25	*Regimental Colours I — Series CB (76 × 70mm) (paper backed) (c1915)	Ha.502-6	£9.00	—
—	C	72	*Regimental Colours V — Series RB (70 × 52 mm) (paper backed) (c1915)	Ha.502-10	£5.50	—

D CANVASES. Unbacked canvases. The material is not strictly canvas, but a linen fabric glazed to give the appearance of canvas.

—	C	40	Canvas Masterpieces — Series M (71 × 60mm) (c1915):	H.509		
			A Shaded back design, globe 12mm diam		£5.50	—
			B Unshaded back design, globe 6mm diam		£2.50	£100.00
—	C	16	Canvas Masterpieces — Series P (114 × 90mm) (c1915)		£12.00	—

MURRAY, SONS & CO. LTD, Belfast

A PRE-1919 ISSUES

A	BW	20	*Actresses — 'BLARM' (c1900):	H.23		
			A 'Pineapple Cigarettes' back		£90.00	—
			B 'Special Crown Cigarettes' back		£100.00	—
C	C	15	Chess and Draughts Problems — Series F (1912)	H.291	£75.00	—
A	BW	54	*Cricketers and Footballers — Series H (c1912):	H.292		
			20 Cricketers. A Thick card		£70.00	—
			B Thin card		£70.00	—
			C Brown Printing		£150.00	—
			34 Footballers. A Thick card		£45.00	—
			B Thin card		£45.00	—
—	C	28	Football Flags (shaped) (60 × 32mm) (c1905):	H.759		
			A Maple Cigarettes		£70.00	—
			B Murray's Cigarettes		£70.00	—
C	C	25	*Football Rules (c1911)		£27.00	—
A	BW	104	*Footballers — Series J (c1910)	H.293	£45.00	—
C	U	25	*Irish Scenery Nd. 101-125 (1905):			
			A 'Hall Mark Cigarettes'		£22.00	—
			B 'Pine Apple Cigarettes'		£22.00	—
			C 'Special Crown Cigarettes'		£22.00	—
			D 'Straight Cut Cigarettes'		£22.00	—
			E 'Yachtsman Cigarettes'		£22.00	—

Size	Printing	Number in set		Handbook reference	Price per card	Complete set

MURRAY, SONS & CO. LTD, Belfast *(continued)*

Size	Print	No.	Description	Handbook	Price	Complete
C	BW	25	Polo Pictures — E Series (1911)	H.294	£24.00	—
—	U	50	Prominent Politicians — B Series (41 × 70mm) (1909):	H.295		
			A Without '... in two strengths' in centre of back ..		£18.00	—
			B With '... in two strengths' in centre of back		£2.50	£125.00
C	U	25	Reproduction of Famous Works of Art — D Series (1910)	H.296	£22.00	£550.00
C	U	24	Reproductions of High Class Works of Art — C Series (1910)	H.297	£22.00	£550.00
A1	C	35	*War Series — Series K (1915)	H.298	£25.00	—
C2	U	25	*War Series — Series L, Nd. 100-124 (c1916):			
			A Sepia		£3.00	£75.00
			B Grey-brown		£3.00	—
			C Purple-brown		£3.00	—

B POST-1920 ISSUES

Size	Print	No.	Description	Handbook	Price	Complete
D1	P	22	Bathing Beauties (1929)		£5.50	—
A1	BW	40	Bathing Belles (1939)	H.592	40p	£16.00
D1	P	22	Cinema Scenes (1929)		£6.00	—
A1	BW	25	Crossword Puzzles (c1925)		£100.00	—
D1	P	26	Dancers (1929)		£5.00	—
D	P		Dancing Girls (1929):			
		25	A 'Belfast-Ireland' at base		£3.20	£80.00
		25	B 'London & Belfast' at base		£3.20	£80.00
		26	C Inscribed 'Series of 26'		£3.40	—
A	C	20	Holidays by the LMS (1927)	H.593	£10.00	—
A1	C	20	Inventors Series (1924)	H.213	£4.50	£90.00
—	C	50	Puzzle Series (1925):	H.660		
A1			A With coupon attached at top		£18.00	—
			B Without coupon		£7.00	—
D2	C	50	Stage and Film Stars — 'Erinmore Cigarettes' (c1926)		£4.00	£200.00
A1	BW	25	Steam Ships (1939)		£1.40	£35.00
A1	C	50	The Story of Ships (1940)		40p	£20.00
A2	C	25	Types of Aeroplanes (1929)		£1.40	£35.00
C	C	20	Types of Dogs (1924):	H.211		
			A Normal back		£6.50	—
			B Normal back, with firm's name rubber-stamped in red		£6.50	—

C SILKS

Size	Print	No.	Description	Handbook	Price	Complete
—	C	? 16	*Flags, small (70 × 42mm) — 'Polo Mild Cigarettes' (plain paper backing) (c1915)	H.498-1	£20.00	
—	C	? 3	*Flags and Arms, large (102 × 71mm) — 'Polo Mild Cigarettes' (plain paper backing) (c1915)	H.498-2	£65.00	
—	C	? 31	*Orders of Chivalry II, 'Series M' (70 × 42mm) (paper backed, Nd. 35-65) (c1915)	H.504-15	£18.00	
—	C	? 25	*Regimental Badges (70 × 42mm) — 'Polo Mild Cigarettes' (plain paper backing) (c1915)	H.498-3	£18.00	

H.J. NATHAN, London

PRE-1919 ISSUE

Size	Print	No.	Description	Handbook	Price	Complete
D	C	40	Comical Military and Naval Pictures (c1905):	H.14		
			A White Border		£60.00	
			B No Border		£60.00	

JAMES NELSON, London

PRE-1919 ISSUE

Size	Print	No.	Description	Handbook	Price	Complete
A	P	? 23	*Beauties — 'FENA' (c1899)	H.148	£600.00	

Size	Printing	Number in set		Handbook reference	Price per card	Complete set

NETTLETON AND MITCHELL, Ossett

PRE-1919 ISSUE
| A | C | 30 | *Army Pictures, Cartoons, etc. (c1916) .... | H.12 | £135.00 | — |

THE NEW MOSLEM CIGARETTE CO., London

PRE-1919 ISSUE
| D | C | 30 | *Proverbs (c1902) .... | H.15 | £100.00 | — |

E.J. NEWBEGIN, Sunderland

PRE-1919 ISSUES
—	P	50	*Actors and Actresses (39 x 60mm) (c1902)	H.299	£45.00	—
A	BW	10	*Actresses — 'HAGG A' (c1900)	H.24	£150.00	—
D	C	? 4	Advertisement Cards (c1900)	H.761	£750.00	—
A	BW	20	Cricketers Series (1901)	H.29	£450.00	—
A	BW	19	*Russo-Japanese Series (1904)	H.184	£150.00	—
D	C	12	Well-Known Proverbs (c1905)	H.235	£140.00	—
D	C	25	Well-Known Songs (c1905)	H.300	£140.00	—

W.H. NEWMAN, Birmingham

PRE-1919 ISSUES
| C | C | 18 | Motor Cycle Series (c1914) .... | H.469 | £90.00 | — |

THOS. NICHOLLS & CO., Chester

PRE-1919 ISSUE
| A | C | 50 | Orders of Chivalry (1916) .... | H.301 | £7.00 | £350.00 |

THE NILMA TOBACCO COY., London

PRE-1919 ISSUES
| A | C | 40 | *Home and Colonial Regiments (c1903) .... | H.69 | £90.00 | — |
| D | C | 30 | *Proverbs (c1903) .... | H.15 | £85.00 | — |

M.E. NOTARAS LTD, London

POST-1920 ISSUES
| A2 | P | 36 | National Types of Beauty (c1925) .... | Ha.558 | 90p | £32.00 |
| — | U | 24 | *Views of China (68 x 43mm) (1925) .... | | 80p | £20.00 |

A. NOTON, Sheffield

POST-1920 ISSUE
| — | U | 12 | 'Manikin' Cards (79 x 51mm) (c1920) .... | H.481 | £100.00 | — |

OGDENS LTD, Liverpool

A PRE-1919 ISSUES
Home Issues *(excluding 'Guinea Gold' and 'Tabs', but including some early issued abroad).*
C	C	25	*Actresses — coloured, 'Ogden's Cigarettes contain no glycerine' back (c1895):	H.302		
			A Titled in black		£90.00	—
			B Titled in brown		£90.00	—
D2	U	? 1	*Actresses — green, green borders (c1900)	H.303	£700.00	—
D1	U	50	*Actresses — green photogravure (c1900)	H.304	£11.00	—
D	P	? 589	*Actresses — 'Ogden's Cigarettes' at foot (c1900) ...	H.305	£3.00	—
D	P		*Actresses and Beauties — collotype (c1895):	H.306		
		? 83	i named:			
			A *Plain back*		£80.00	—
			B 'Midnight Flake' back		£60.00	—

Size	Print-ing	Number in set		Handbook reference	Price per card	Complete set

OGDENS LTD, Liverpool (continued)

Size	Print-ing	Number in set	Description	Handbook reference	Price per card	Complete set
		? 21	ii unnamed:			
			A Plain back		£80.00	—
			B 'Midnight Flake' back:			
			(blue)		£60.00	—
			(red)		£90.00	—
D	P		*Actresses and Beauties — collotype, 'Ogden's Cigarettes' back (1895):	H.306		
		? 54	i named		£60.00	—
		? 45	ii unnamed		£60.00	—
A	P	? 205	*Actresses and Beauties — woodbury-type (c1894) ...	H.307	£35.00	—
—	C	192	Army Crests and Mottoes (39 × 59mm) (c1902)		£5.00	—
A	C	28	*Beauties — 'BOCCA' (c1900)	H.39	£26.00	—
—	C	50	*Beauties — 'CHOAB' (c1900):	H.21		
			Nos 1-25 (size 65 × 36mm)		£28.00	—
			Nos 26-50 (size 67 × 37mm)		£28.00	—
A	C	26	*Beauties — 'HOL' (c1900):	H.192		
			A 'Guinea Gold' red rubber stamp back		£225.00	—
			B Blue Castle Design back		£20.00	£520.00
A2	C	52	*Beauties — 'Playing Card' series (c1900):	H.308		
			A 52 with playing card inset		£28.00	—
			B 26 without playing card inset		£35.00	—
A2	C	52	*Beauties and Military — PC inset (c1898)		£28.00	—
—	P	50	Beauty Series, numbered, 'St. Julien Tobacco' (36 × 54mm) (c1900)		£3.00	£150.00
D	P	? 83	Beauty Series, unnumbered, issued Australia (c1900) ..	H.309	£65.00	—
A	C	50	Birds' Eggs (1904):			
			A White back		£2.00	£100.00
			B Toned back		£1.80	£90.00
D	P	? 142	*Boer War and General Interest — 'Ogden's Cigarettes' at foot (c1900)	H.310	£3.20	—
H2	P	? 68	*Boer War and General Interest — 'Ogden's Cigarettes' at foot (c1900)		£40.00	—
—	P	? 3	*Boer War & General Interest (Liners) 'Ogdens Cigarettes' at foot (72 × 55mm) (c1900)	H.310	£150.00	—
A	C	50	Boxers (1915)		£7.00	£350.00
A	C	25	Boxing (1914)	H.311	£6.00	£150.00
—	C	? 6	*Boxing Girls (165 × 94mm) (c1895)	Ha.482	£500.00	—
A	C	50	Boy Scouts (1911):	H.62		
			A Blue back		£3.20	£160.00
			B Green back		£4.50	£225.00
A	C	50	Boy Scouts, 2nd series (1912):	H.62		
			A Blue back		£3.20	£160.00
			B Green back		£4.50	£225.00
A	C	50	Boy Scouts, 3rd series (1912):	H.62		
			A Blue back		£3.20	£160.00
			B Green back		£4.50	£225.00
A	C	50	Boy Scouts, 4th series, green back (1913)		£3.20	£160.00
A	C	25	Boy Scouts, 5th series, green back (1914)		£3.20	£80.00
A	C	50	British Birds:	H.229		
			A White back (1905)		£2.00	£100.00
			B Toned back (1906)		£1.80	£90.00
A	C	50	British Birds, Second Series (1908)		£2.20	£110.00
A	C	50	British Costumes from 100 BC to 1904 (1905)	H.312	£6.00	£300.00
A	C	50	Club Badges (1914)		£5.00	£250.00
—	C	? 27	*Comic Pictures (1890-95) (size varies)	H.313	£325.00	—
A2	C	12	*Cricket and Football Terms — Women (c1896)	H.314	£350.00	—
D2	U	50	*Cricketers and Sportsmen (c1898)	H.315	£90.00	—

Size	Print-ing	Number in set		Handbook reference	Price per card	Complete set

OGDENS LTD, Liverpool (continued)

Size	Print-ing	Number in set	Description	Handbook reference	Price per card	Complete set
A	U	28	*Dominoes — Actresses — 'FROGA A' back (c1900):	H.20		
			A Mitred corners (7 backs)		£25.00	—
			B Unmitred corners (7 backs)		£25.00	—
A	U	56	*Dominoes — Beauties — 'MOM' back (c1900)	H.277	£25.00	—
A2	BW	55	*Dominoes — black back (1909)		£1.40	£75.00
A	C	50	Famous Footballers (1908)		£4.00	£200.00
A	C	50	Flags and Funnels of Leading Steamship Lines (1906)	H.67	£4.00	£200.00
—	C	43	*Football Club Badges (shaped for buttonhole) (c1910)	H.316	£7.00	—
A	C	51	Football Club Colours (1906):	H.68		
			Nos. 1-50		£3.80	£190.00
			No. 51		—	£5.00
A	C	50	Fowls, Pigeons and Dogs (1904)	H.64	£3.20	£160.00
—	C	1	*History of the Union Jack (threefold card) (51 × 37mm closed) (1901)		—	£225.00
A	BW	50	Infantry Training (1915)	H.317	£2.50	£125.00
K2	C	52	*Miniature Playing Cards — Actresses and Beauties back (c1900):	H.319		
			I Unnamed, no numeral (76 backs known)		£4.00	—
			II Unnamed, 'numeral 40' (26 backs known)		£4.00	—
			III Named, 'numeral 46' (26 backs known)	H.20	£4.00	—
			IV Named, no numeral (26 backs known)	H.20	£4.00	—
K2	C	52	*Miniature Playing Cards, blue Tabs 'Shield and Flower' design back (1909)		£3.00	—
K2	C	52	*Miniature Playing Cards, yellow 'Coolie Plug' design back:			
			A Yellow back (1904)		£3.00	—
			B Yellow back with white border (1904)		£4.00	—
A	BW	50	Modern War Weapons (1915):	H.320		
			A Original numbering		£3.20	£160.00
			B Numbering re-arranged		£11.00	—
A	C	50	Orders of Chivalry (1907)		£3.50	£175.00
A	C	25	Owners, Racing Colours and Jockeys (1914)		£4.00	£100.00
A	C	50	Owners, Racing Colours and Jockeys (1906)		£3.20	£160.00
A	C	25	Poultry (1915):			
			A 'Ogden's Cigarettes' on front		£4.80	£120.00
			B Without 'Ogden's Cigarettes' on front		£5.40	£135.00
A	C	25	Poultry, 2nd series, as 'B' above (1916)		£5.40	£135.00
A	C	25	Pugilists and Wrestlers, Nd. 1-25 (1908)		£5.00	£125.00
A	C	25	Pugilists and Wrestlers, Nd.26-50:			
			A White back (1909)		£5.00	£125.00
			B Toned back (1908)		£5.00	£125.00
A	C	25	Pugilists and Wrestlers, 2nd series, Nd. 51-75 (1909) ...		£5.60	£140.00
A	C	50	Racehorses (1907)		£3.50	£175.00
A	C	25	Records of the World (1908)		£3.00	£75.00
A	C	50	Royal Mail (1909)	H.82	£4.20	£210.00
A	C	50	Sectional Cycling Map (1910)	H.74	£3.20	£160.00
A	C	50	*Shakespeare Series (c1903):	H.321		
			A Unnumbered		£13.00	£650.00
			B Numbered		£13.00	£650.00
A	C		Soldiers of the King (1909):			
		50	A Grey printing on front		£5.00	£250.00
		25	B Brown printing on front		£6.00	—
D	C	25	*Swiss Views, Nd. 1-25 (c1905)		£4.00	£100.00
D	C	25	*Swiss Views, Nd. 26-50 (c1905)		£5.00	£125.00
D	C	48	Victoria Cross Heroes (1901)	H.322	£15.00	£750.00

Size	Print-ing	Number in set		Handbook reference	Price per card	Complete set

OGDENS LTD, Liverpool *(continued)*

B 'Guinea Gold' Series (The S and X numbers represent the reference numbers quoted in the Ogden's Reference Book).

Size	Print-ing	Number in set	Description	Handbook reference	Price per card	Complete set
D	P	1148	1-1148 Series (c1901):			
			Nos. 1-200		60p	£120.00
			Nos. 201-500		£1.25	—
			Nos. 501-900, excl. 523 and 765		£1.00	—
			Nos. 901-1000, excl. 940, 943, 947 and 1000		£1.75	—
			Nos. 1001-1148, excl. 1003, 1006-8, 1024, 1030, 1033, 1034, 1037, 1040, 1042, 1048, 1066, 1081, 1082, 1088		£1.75	—
			Scarce Nos: 523, 940, 943, 947, 1000, 1003, 1007, 1008, 1024, 1030, 1033, 1034, 1037, 1040, 1042, 1048, 1066, 1088		£60.00	—
			Very scarce Nos. 765, 1006, 1081, 1082		—	—
D	CP	?	Selected numbers from 1-1148 Series (c1900)		£5.00	—
D	P		400 New Series I (c1902)		£1.20	£480.00
D	P		400 New Series B (c1902)		£1.50	£600.00
D	P		300 New Series C (c1902)		£1.20	£360.00
D	P	? 323	Set 73S Base B Actresses (c1900)		£3.00	—
			Set 75S Base D (c1900):			
D	P	? 318	List DA — White Panel Group		£1.00	—
D	P	? 58	List DB — The Denumbered Group		£2.50	—
D	P	? 62	List DC — The Political Group		£1.00	—
D	P	? 193	List DD — Boer War etc		£1.00	—
D	P	? 46	List DE — Pantomime and Theatre Group		£4.00	—
D	P	? 376	List DF — Actors and Actresses		£1.30	—
D	P	? 40	Set 76S Base E Actors and Actresses (c1900)		£3.50	—
D	P	? 59	Set 77S Base F Boer War etc (c1901)		£1.00	—
			Set 78S Base I (c1900):			
			List IA — The small Machette Group:			
D	P	83	I Actors and Actresses		£1.30	—
D	P	14	II London Street Scenes		£3.20	—
D	P	32	III Turner Pictures		£1.80	—
D	P	11	IV Cricketers		£13.00	—
D	P	18	V Golf		£22.00	—
D	P	10	VI Views and Scenes Abroad		£1.60	—
D	P	30	VII Miscellaneous		£1.30	—
D	P	639	List IB — The Large Machette Group		£1.20	—
D	P	5	List IC — The White Panel Group		£5.00	—
D	P	30	Set 79S Base J Actresses (c1900)		£4.00	—
D	P	238	Set 80S Base K Actors and Actresses (c1900)		£3.00	—
D	P	216	Set 81S Base L Actors and Actresses (c1900)		£2.40	—
			Set 82S Base M (c1901):			
D	P	3	List Ma Royalty		£3.00	£9.00
D	P	77	List Mb Cricketers		£25.00	—
D	P	50	List Mc Cyclists		£6.00	—
D	P	150	List Md Footballers		£20.00	—
D	P	50	List Me Pantomime and Theatre Group		£6.00	—
D	P	33	List Mf Footballers and Cyclists		£15.00	—
D	P	27	List Mg Boer War and Miscellaneous		£1.10	—
D	P	? 2951	List Mh Actors and Actresses		£1.20	—
Ba			Guinea Gold Series, Large and Medium			
	P	77	Set 73X Actresses Base B (c1900)		£18.00	—
	P	1	Set 74X Actress Base C (c1900)		—	£50.00
	P	575	Set 75X Actors, Actresses, Boer War Etc Base D (c1901)		From £2.00	—
	P	24	Set 78X Actresses Base I (c1900)		£40.00	—

73

Size	Printing	Number in set		Handbook reference	Price per card	Complete set

OGDENS LTD, Liverpool *(continued)*

| | P | 406 | Set 82X Actors, Actresses, Boer War Etc Base M (c1901). | | £1.70 | — |

C 'TABS' SERIES
(Numbers in parentheses following word 'item' represent the reference numbers quoted in Ogden's Reference Book. The listing includes both home and overseas 'Tabs' issues.)

Size	Print	Number	Description	Ref	Price	Complete
D	BW	200	*Actresses (item 7) (c1900)		£2.50	—
D	BW	200	*Actresses and Foreign Views (item 14) (c1900)		£2.20	—
D	BW ?	331	*Composite Tabs Series, with 'Labour Clause' (item 63) (1901):			
		1	General de Wet		—	£5.00
		1	General Interest		—	£6.00
		17	Heroes of the Ring		£7.50	—
		1	HM the Queen		—	£5.00
		2	HRH the Prince of Wales		£4.00	£8.00
		14	Imperial Interest		£1.00	£14.00
		106	Imperial or International Interest		£1.00	—
		3	International Interest		£2.00	£6.00
		14	International Interest or a Prominent British Officer		£1.00	£14.00
		22	Leading Athletes		£2.50	—
		15	Leading Favourites of the Turf		£4.00	—
		54	Leading Generals at the War		£1.00	£54.00
		2	Members of Parliament		£3.50	£7.00
		11	Notable Coursing Dogs		£7.50	—
		12	Our Leading Cricketers		£14.00	—
		17	Our Leading Footballers		£8.00	—
		37	Prominent British Officers		£1.00	£37.00
		1	The Yacht 'Columbia'		—	£6.00
		1	The Yacht 'Shamrock'		—	£6.00
D	BW ?	71	*Composite Tabs Series, without 'Labour Clause' (item 64) (c1900):			
		40	General Interest		£26.00	—
		31	Leading Artists of the Day		£22.00	—
D	BW ?	114	*Composite Tabs Series, Sydney issue (item 65) (c1900):			
		1	Christian de Wet		£10.00	—
		1	Corporal G. E. Nurse, VC		£10.00	—
		15	English Cricketer Series		£60.00	—
		1	Imperial Interest		£10.00	—
		29	Imperial or International Interest		£8.00	—
		6	International Interest		£8.00	—
		1	Lady Sarah Wilson		£10.00	—
		41	Leading Generals at the War		£8.00	—
		13	Prominent British Officers		£8.00	—
D	BW	150	General Interest, Series 'A' (1901)		£1.10	—
D	BW	200	General Interest, Series 'B' (1902)		90p	£180.00
D	BW	470	General Interest, Series 'C' (1902):			
			C.1-200		90p	£180.00
			C.201-300		£2.20	—
			C.301-350		£1.10	£55.00
			No Letter, Nd 1-120		£1.20	—
D	BW	200	General Interest, Series 'D' (1902)		80p	£160.00
D	BW	120	General Interest, Series 'E' (1902)		£1.10	—
D	BW	420	General Interest, Series 'F' (1902):			
			F.1-200		£1.20	—
			F.201-320		£1.20	—
			F.321-420		£2.70	—

Size	Print-ing	Number in set		Handbook reference	Price per card	Complete set

OGDENS LTD, Liverpool *(continued)*

Size	Print	Num	Description	Ref	Price	Set
D	BW	? 500	General Interest, Sydney issue (c1902):			
			Nd 1-100 on front		£2.75	—
			Nd 101-400 on back		£2.75	—
			Unnumbered, mostly similar numbered cards 101-200 (item 99-a)		£5.00	—
D	BW	196	*General Interest, unnumbered, similar style C.201-300 (item 95) (1902):			
			76 Stage Artistes		80p	—
			41 Celebrities		80p	—
			56 Footballers		£2.50	—
			23 Miscellaneous		80p	—
D	BW	100	*General Interest, unnumbered, similar style C.301-350 (item 96) (1902):			
			28 Actresses		£1.00	—
			40 Castles		£1.00	—
			12 Dogs		£1.25	—
			20 Miscellaneous		£2.00	—
D	BW	300	*General Interest, unnumbered, similar style F.321-420 (item 97) (1903):			
			A 100 with full stop after caption		£1.30	£130.00
			B Without full stop after caption:			
			79 I Stage Artistes		90p	£70.00
			21 II Cricketers		£10.00	—
			25 III Football		£5.00	—
			15 IV Golf		£20.00	—
			10 V Cyclists		£5.00	—
			9 VI Fire Brigades		£5.00	—
			5 VII Aldershot Gymnasium		£3.00	£15.00
			36 VIII Miscellaneous		90p	—
D	BW	? 111	*General Interest, 'oblong' back (item 98) (c1900)		£15.00	—
D	BW	? 75	*Leading Artistes of the Day, numbered 126-200, plain backs (item 109) (see H.1) (c1900)		£12.00	—
D	BW	? 71	Leading Artistes of the Day with 'Labour Clause' (item 110) (c1900):			
			A Type-set back		£1.20	—
			B Plain back		£20.00	—
D	BW	? 25	Leading Artistes of the Day, without 'Labour Clause' (item 111-1) (c1900):			
			A With caption, type-set back		£15.00	—
			B With caption, plain back		£15.00	—
			C Without caption, type-set back		£15.00	—
D	BW	? 91	Leading Artistes of the Day, without 'Labour Clause' (item 111-2) (c1900):			
			A Type-set back		£11.00	—
			B Plain back		£11.00	—
D	BW	25	Leading Generals at the War, with descriptive text (item 112) (c1900):			
			A 'Ogden's Cigarettes' back		£2.00	—
			B 'Ogden's Tab Cigarettes' back		£1.40	£35.00
D	BW		Leading Generals at the War, without descriptive text (item 113) (c1900):			
		? 47	A 'Ogden's Tab Cigarettes' back (47 known)		£1.00	—
		? 25	B 'Ogden's Lucky Star' back (25 known)		£5.00	—
D	BW	50	*Stage Artistes and Celebrities (item 157) (c1900)		£2.50	£125.00
D	***POST-1920 ISSUES***					
A	C	25	ABC of Sport (1927)		£3.00	£75.00
A	C	50	Actors — Natural and Character Studies (1938)	H.571-1	£1.00	£50.00

Size	Printing	Number in set		Handbook reference	Price per card	Complete set

OGDENS LTD, Liverpool *(continued)*

Size	Printing	Number in set		Handbook reference	Price per card	Complete set
A	C	50	AFC Nicknames (1933)	H.571-2	£4.50	£225.00
A	C	50	Air-Raid Precautions (1938)	H.544	90p	£45.00
A	C	50	Applied Electricity (1928)		£1.10	£55.00
A	U	36	Australian Test Cricketers, 1928-29		£3.60	£130.00
A	C	50	Billiards, by Tom Newman (1928)		£2.20	£110.00
A	C	50	Bird's Eggs (cut-outs) (1923)		£1.10	£55.00
A	C	50	The Blue Riband of the Atlantic (1929)		£2.50	£125.00
A	C	50	Boy Scouts (1929)		£2.50	£125.00
A	C	50	British Birds (Cut-Outs) (1923)		£1.00	£50.00
A	C	50	British Birds and Their Eggs (1939)	H.571-3	£2.60	£130.00
A	U	50	Broadcasting (1935)	H.571-4	£1.70	£85.00
A	C	50	By the Roadside (1932)		£1.10	£55.00
A	C	44	Captains of Association Football Clubs and Colours (1926)		£3.00	£130.00
A	U	50	Cathedrals and Abbeys (1936):			
			A Cream card		£1.10	£55.00
			B White card		£1.10	£55.00
A	C	50	Champions of 1936 (1937)	H.571-5	£1.80	£90.00
A	C	50	Children of All Nations (cut-outs) (1923)	H.656	£1.00	£50.00
A	C	50	Colour in Nature (1932)		£1.00	£50.00
A	C	50	Construction of Railway Trains (1930)		£2.50	£125.00
A	C	50	Coronation Procession (sectional) (1937)	H.571-6	£1.60	£80.00
A	U	50	Cricket, 1926		£2.60	£130.00
A	C	25	Derby Entrants, 1926		£2.60	£65.00
A	C	50	Derby Entrants, 1928		£2.00	£100.00
A	U	50	Derby Entrants, 1929		£2.40	£120.00
A	C	50	Dogs (1936)	H.571-7	£2.20	£110.00
A	C	25	Famous Dirt-Track Riders (1929)		£5.00	£125.00
A	U	50	Famous Rugby Players (1926-27)		£2.40	£120.00
A	C	50	Football Caricatures (1935)	H.571-8	£2.60	£130.00
A	C	50	Football Club Captains (1935)	H.571-9	£2.40	£120.00
A	C	50	Foreign Birds (1924)		90p	£45.00
A	U	25	Greyhound Racing — '1st Series ...' (1927)		£4.00	£100.00
A	U	25	Greyhound Racing — '2nd Series ...' (1928)		£4.00	£100.00
A	C	50	How to Swim (1935)	H.571-10	90p	£45.00
A	C	50	Jockeys, and Owners' Colours (1927)		£2.40	£120.00
A	C	50	Jockeys, 1930		£2.40	£120.00
A	C	50	Leaders of Men (1924)		£1.80	£90.00
A	C	25	Marvels of Motion (1928)		£2.00	£50.00
A	C	50	Modern British Pottery (1925)		£1.00	£50.00
A	C	50	Modern Railways (1936)	H.571-11	£2.00	£100.00
A	C	25	Modes of Conveyance (1927)		£2.40	£60.00
A	C	50	Motor Races 1931 (1931)		£2.60	£130.00
A	C	50	Ocean Greyhounds (1938)	H.571-12	£1.00	£50.00
A	C	25	Optical Illusions (1923)	H.560	£3.00	£75.00
A	C	25	Picturesque People of the Empire (1927)		£1.40	£35.00
A	U	50	Picturesque Villages (1936)		£1.20	£60.00
A	C	25	Poultry Alphabet (1924)		£4.00	£100.00
A	C	25	Poultry Rearing and Management — '1st Series ...' (1922)		£2.80	£70.00
A	C	25	Poultry Rearing and Management — '2nd Series ...' (1923)		£2.80	£70.00
A	U	50	Prominent Cricketers of 1938 (1938)	H.571-13	£2.20	£110.00
A	C	50	Prominent Racehorses of 1933 (1934)	H.571-l4	£2.00	£100.00
A	U	50	Pugilists in Action (1928)		£3.50	£175.00
A	C	50	Racing Pigeons (1931)		£3.50	£175.00
A	C	50	Sea Adventure (1939)	H.571-15	50p	£25.00

Size	Print-ing	Number in set		Handbook reference	Price per card	Complete set

OGDENS LTD, Liverpool (continued)

Size	Print	Num	Title	Handbook	Price	Complete
A	C	50	Shots from the Films (1936)	H.571-16	£2.00	£100.00
A	U	25	Sights of London (1923)		£1.60	£40.00
A	C	50	Smugglers and Smuggling (1932)		£2.20	£110.00
A	U	50	Steeplechase Celebrities (1931)		£2.00	£100.00
A	C	50	Steeplechase Trainers, and Owners' Colours (1927)		£2.00	£100.00
A	C	50	The Story of Sand (1934)		90p	£45.00
A	C	50	Swimming, Diving and Life-Saving (1931)	H.523	£1.20	£60.00
A	C	25	Trainers, and Owners' Colours — '1st Series ...' (1925)		£2.40	£60.00
A	C	25	Trainers, and Owners' Colours — '2nd Series ...' (1926)		£3.00	£75.00
A	C	50	Trick Billiards (1934)	H.571-17	£1.50	£75.00
A	C	50	Turf personalities (1929)		£2.40	£120.00
A	C	25	Whaling (1927)		£2.60	£65.00
A	C	50	Yachts and Motor Boats (1930)		£2.50	£125.00
A	C	50	Zoo Studies (1937)	H.571-18	50p	£25.00

THE ORLANDO CIGARETTE & CIGAR CO., London

PRE-1919 ISSUE

A	C	40	*Home & Colonial Regiments (c1901)	H.69	£500.00	—

OSBORNE TOBACCO CO. LTD, Portsmouth & London

POST-1940 ISSUES

A	U	50	Modern Aircraft (1953):	H.895		
			A Dark Blue back:			
			i Firm's name in one line		50p	£25.00
			ii Firm's name in two lines		£2.00	—
			B Light Blue back		£1.00	£50.00
			C Brown back		50p	£25.00

W.T. OSBORNE & CO., London

PRE-1919 ISSUE

D	C	40	*Naval and Military Phrases (c1904):	H.14		
			A White Border		£40.00	—
			B No Border		£40.00	—

PALMER & CO., Bedford

POST-1920 ISSUE

—	U	12	'Manikin' Cards (79 × 51mm) (c1920)	H.481	£100.00	—

J.A. PATTREIOUEX, Manchester

A 1920s PHOTOGRAPHIC SERIES. Listed in order of letters and/or numbers quoted on cards. References after word 'back' refer to the nine backs illustrated in Handbook Part II under Ha.595.

H2	P	50	*Animals and Scenes — unnumbered ('Junior Member'). Back 4 (c1925)	H.595-1	£1.20	—
H2	P	50	Animals and Scenes, Nd 1-50. Back 1 (c1925)		£1.20	—
H2	P	50	*Scenes, Nd 201-250 ('Junior Member'). Back 4 (c1925)		£1.20	—
C	P	96	Animals and Scenes, Nd 250-345 (c1925):	H.595-2B		
			A Back in style 2 in (i) grey		£1.20	—
			(ii) brown		£1.20	—
			* B 'Junior Member' back 9		£1.20	—
C	P	96	Animals and Scenes, Nd 346-441 (c1925):			
			A Back 2		£1.20	—
			B Back style 1 and back 3		£1.20	—
			* C 'Junior Member' back 9		£1.20	—

Size	Printing	Number in set		Handbook reference	Price per card	Complete set

J.A. PATTREIOUEX, Manchester (continued)

Size	Printing	Number in set	Description	Handbook reference	Price per card	Complete set
H	P	50	*Animal Studies, Nd A42-A91 ('Junior Member'). Back 4 (c1925)		£1.20	—
H	P	50	*Animal Studies, Nd A92-A141 ('Junior Member'). Back 4 (c1925)		£1.20	—
H	P	50	*Animal Studies, Nd A151-A200 ('Junior Member'). Back 4 (c1925)		£1.20	—
C	P		*Natives and Scenes (c1925):	H.595-2G		
		36	A 'Series 1/36 B' on front, Nd 1-36 ('Junior Member'). Back 9		£1.50	—
		96	B 'Series 1/96 B' on front, Nd 1-96. Back 6		£1.20	—
C	P	96	*Foreign Scenes, Nd 1/96C-96/96C. Back 6 (c1925) ..		£1.20	—
C	P	96	Cricketers, Nd C1-C96, 'Casket Cigarettes' on front (c1925):	H.595-2C		
			A Back 5		£40.00	—
	*		B Plain back		£40.00	—
C	P	96	*Animals — 'Series Nos CA1 to 96'. Back 7 (c1925) ..	H.595-2A	£1.20	—
C	P	96	*Natives and Scenes (c1925):			
			A 'C.B.1 to 96' on front. Back 7:			
			1 Nd 1-96		£1.20	—
			2 Nd C.B.1-C.B.96		£1.20	—
			B 'J.S. 1 to 96' on front. 'Junior Member'. Back 9		£1.20	—
C	P	96	*Animals and Scenes — 'CC1 to 96' on front. Back 7 (c1925)		£1.20	—
H2	P	50	*British Scenes — 'Series C.M.1-50.A' on front. Back style 7 (c1925)		£1.20	—
H2	P	50	*Foreign Scenes (c1925):			
			A 'Series CM. 1/50 B' on front. Back style 7		£1.20	—
			B 'J.M. Series 1/50' on front. 'Junior Member' back 9		£1.20	—
H2	P	50	*Foreign Scenes (c1925):	H.595-2H		
			A 'Series C.M. 101-150.S' on front. Back style 7 ..		£1.20	—
			B Nd S.101-S.150 on front. Back 4		£1.20	—
C	P	96	*Foreign Scenes, Nd 1/96D-96/96D. Back 6 (c1925) ...		£1.50	—
H2	P	50	*Foreign Scenes, Nd 1/50E-50/50E. Back 6 (c1925) ..		£1.20	—
H2	P	50	*Foreign Scenes, Nd 1/50F-50/50F. Back 6 (c1925) ..		£1.20	—
C	P	96	Footballers, Nd F.1-F.96. 'Casket' and 'Critic' back style 5 (c1925)		£10.00	—
C	P	95	Footballers, Nd F.97-F.191. 'Casket' and 'Critic' back styles (c1925)		£10.00	—
H	P	50	Football Teams, Nd F.192-F.241. ('Casket' and 'Critic') (c1925)	H.595-2F	£45.00	—
C	P	96	*Footballers — 'Series F.A. 1/96' on front. Back 8 (c1925)		£7.00	—
C	P	96	*Footballers — 'Series F.B. 1/96' on front. Back 8 (c1925)	H.595-2D	£7.00	—
C	P	96	*Footballers — 'Series F.C. 1/96' on front. Back 8 (c1925)	H.595-2E	£7.00	—
H2	P	50	*Scenes — 'G. 1/50' on front. 'Junior Member'. Back 9 (c1925)		£1.50	—
H2	P	50	*Scenes — '1/50. H' on front. 'Junior Member'. Back 9 (c1925)	H.595-2J	£1.20	—
H2	P	50	*Animals and Scenes, Nd I.1-I.50. Back style 6 (c1925)		£1.20	—
H2	P	50	Famous Statues — 'J.C.M. 1 to 50 C' on front. Back style 6 (c1925)		£2.00	—
H2	P	50	*Scenes, Nd JCM 1/50D-JCM 50/50D (c1925):			
			A Back style 6		£1.30	—
			B Back style 9 ('Junior Member')		£1.30	—

Size	Print-ing	Number in set		Handbook reference	Price per card	Complete set

J.A. PATTREIOUEX, Manchester *(continued)*

Size	Print-ing	Number in set	Description	Handbook reference	Price per card	Complete set
B1	P	30	Child Studies, Nd J.M. No. 1-J.M. No. 30. 'Junior Member', back style 9 (c1925)		£4.00	—
B1	P	30	*Beauties, Nd J.M.1-J.M.30. 'Junior Member', back style 9 (c1925)		£3.00	—
H2	P	50	*Foreign Scenes — 'J.M. 1 to 50 A' on front. 'Junior Member', back style 9 (c1925)	H.595-2I	£1.20	—
H2	P	50	British Empire Exhibition 'J.M. 1 to 50 B' on front (c1925)		£2.00	—
C	P	96	*Animals and Scenes — 'J.S. 1/96A'on front. 'Junior Member', back style 9 (c1925)		£1.00	—
H2	P	50	*Scenes, Nd S.1-S.50.' Junior Member', back 4 (c1925)		£1.20	—
H2	P	50	*Scenes, Nd S.51-S.100.' Junior Member', back 4 (c1925)		£1.20	—
B1	P	50	*Cathedrals and Abbeys, Nd S.J. 1-S.J. 50. Plain back (c1925)	Ha.595-3	£2.50	—
B1	P	50	*British Castles. Nd S.J. 51-S.J. 100. Plain back (c1925)	Ha.595-3	£2.50	—
H2	P	4	*Scenes, Nd V.1-V.4. 'Junior Member', back 4 (c1925)	H.595-1	£5.00	—

B   COLOURED AND LETTERPRESS SERIES

Size	Print-ing	Number in set	Description	Handbook reference	Price per card	Complete set
A	C	50	British Empire Exhibition Series (c1928)		£2.50	£125.00
A	C	50	Builders of the British Empire (c1929)		£3.00	£150.00
A	C	50	Celebrities in Sport (c1930)		£5.00	£250.00
A	C	75	Cricketers Series (1926)	H.665	£10.00	—
A	C	50	Dirt Track Riders (1929)		£10.00	—
A	C	30	Drawing Made Easy (c1930)		£2.50	£75.00
A	C	52	The English and Welsh Counties (c1928)		£2.00	£105.00
A	C		Footballers Series (c1928):			
		50	A Captions in blue		£8.00	—
		100	B Captions in brown		£8.00	—
A	C	25	'King Lud' Problems (c1935)	H.638	£18.00	—
A	C	26	Maritime Flags (c1932)		£10.00	—
A	U	25	Photos of Football Stars (c1930)	H.666	£30.00	—
D	C	50	Railway Posters by Famous Artists (c1930)		£8.00	—
A	C	50	Sports Trophies (c1931)		£2.80	£140.00
A2	CP	51	*Views (c1930)	H.597	£1.10	£55.00

C   1930s PHOTOGRAPHIC SERIES

Size	Print-ing	Number in set	Description	Handbook reference	Price per card	Complete set
	P		Beautiful Scotland (1939):	H.564-1		
D		28	A Small size		£1.10	£30.00
—		48	B Medium size (77 × 52mm)		30p	£15.00
—	P	48	The Bridges of Britain (77 × 52mm) (1938)		30p	£15.00
—	P	48	Britain from the Air (77 × 52mm) (1939)		30p	£15.00
—	P	48	British Railways (77 × 52mm) (1938)		70p	£35.00
	P		Coastwise (1939):	H.564-2		
D		28	A Small size		£1.25	£35.00
—		48	B Medium size (77 × 52mm)		30p	£15.00
D	P	54	Dirt Track Riders (1930):			
			A Descriptive back		£12.00	—
			* B Non-descriptive back		£25.00	—
—	P	48	Dogs (76 × 51mm) (1939)		50p	£25.00
	P		Flying (1938):	H.564-3		
D		28	A Small size		£1.80	—
		48	B Medium size (77 × 52mm)		50p	£24.00
A2	P	78	Footballers in Action (1934)		£3.50	—
—	P	48	Holiday Haunts by the Sea (77 × 52mm) (1937)		30p	£15.00

79

Size	Print-ing	Number in set		Handbook reference	Price per card	Complete set
			J.A. PATTREIOUEX, Manchester (continued)			
—	P	48	The Navy (1937):			
			A Large captions		60p	£30.00
			B Smaller captions		60p	£30.00
	P		Our Countryside (1938):	H.564-4		
D		28	A Small size		£1.50	£42.00
		48	B Medium size (77 × 52mm)		25p	£12.00
A2	P	54	Real Photographs of London (1936)		£2.20	—
D	P	28	Shots from the Films (1938)	H.566	£2.75	—
—	P	48	Sights of Britain — 'Series of 48' (76 × 51 mm) (1936)		50p	£25.00
—	P	48	Sights of Britain — 'Second Series ...' (76 × 51mm) (1936):			
			A Large captions		25p	£12.00
			B Smaller captions		30p	£15.00
—	P	48	Sights of Britain — 'Third Series ...' (76 × 51mm) (1937)		40p	£20.00
—	P	48	Sights of London — 'First Series ...' (76 × 51mm) (1935)		£1.25	£60.00
—	P	12	Sights of London — 'Supplementary Series of 12 Jubilee Pictures' (76 × 51mm) (1935)		£1.00	£12.00
A2	P	54	Sporting Celebrities (1935)		£4.00	—
—	P	96	Sporting Events and Stars (76 × 50mm) (1935)		£1.75	£175.00
A2	P	54	Views of Britain (1937)		£1.60	—
—	P	48	Winter Scenes (76 × 52mm) (1937)		30p	£15.00
D	***POST-1940 ISSUES***					
—	C	24	Cadet's Jackpot Jigsaws (90 × 65mm) (1969)		£1.50	—
—	C	24	Treasure Island (65 × 45mm) (1968)		£1.50	—

W. PEPPERDY

PRE-1919 ISSUES
A	C	30	*Army Pictures, Cartoons, etc (c1916)	H.12	£110.00	—

M. PEZARO & SON, London

PRE-1919 ISSUES
D	C	25	*Armies of the World (c1900):	H.43		
			A Cake Walk Cigarettes		£130.00	—
			B Nestor Virginia Cigarettes		£130.00	—
D	C	? 17	Song Titles Illustrated (c1900)	H.323	£300.00	—

GODFREY PHILLIPS LTD, London

40 page reference book — £4.00

A ***PRE-1919 ISSUES***
D1	C	25	*Actresses 'C' Series, Nd 101-125 (c1900):			
			A Blue Horseshoe design back		£30.00	—
			B Green back, 'Carriage' Cigarettes		£30.00	—
			C Blue back, 'Teapot' Cigarettes		£85.00	—
			D Blue back, 'Volunteer' Cigarettes		£85.00	—
			E Blue back, 'Derby' Cigarettes		£85.00	—
			F Blue back 'Ball of Beauty' Cigarettes		£85.00	—
—	C	50	*Actresses — oval card (38 × 62mm) (1916):	H.324		
			A With name		£7.00	—
			B *Without Maker's and Actress's Name*		£5.00	£250.00
D	C	40	Animal Series (c1905)		£6.50	£260.00
D1	C	25	*Beauties, Nd B.801-825 (c1902)	H.325	£12.00	£300.00

Size	Print-ing	Number in set		Handbook reference	Price per card	Complete set

GODFREY PHILLIPS LTD, London *(continued)*

Size	Print-ing	Number in set	Description	Handbook reference	Price per card	Complete set
A1	U	24	*Beauties, collotype — 'HUMPS' (c1895):	H.222		
			A 'Awarded 7 Gold Medals 1895' on front		£80.00	—
			B 'PLUMS' on front		£400.00	—
A	C	30	*Beauties, 'Nymphs' (c1896)	H.326	£80.00	—
D			*Beauties — 'Plums' (1897):	H.186		
	BW	? 60	A Front in black and white		£150.00	—
	C	50	B Plum-coloured background		£65.00	—
	C	50	C Green background		£65.00	—
A1	C	50	Beautiful Women (c1905):	H.284		
			A Inscribed 'W.I. Series'		£11.00	—
			B Inscribed 'I.F. Series'		£11.00	—
—	C	50	Beautiful Women, Nd W.501-550 (55 × 75mm) (c1905)	H.284	£22.00	—
D1	C	25	*Boxer Rebellion — Sketches (1904)	H.46	£30.00	—
—	C	30	*British Beauties — Oval Card (36 × 60mm) Plain back (c1910)	H.244	£3.00	£90.00
D	U	50	'British Beauties' photogravure (c1916)	H.327	£8.00	£400.00
—	PC	76	British Beauties (37 × 55mm) (c1916)		£3.00	£230.00
A	C	54	British Beauties Nd 1-54 (1914):	H.328		
			(a) Blue back, grey-black, glossy front		£2.50	£135.00
			(b) *Plain back, grey-black, glossy front*		£3.50	—
			(c) *Plain back, sepia, matt front*		£3.50	—
A	C	54	British Beauties Nd 55-108 (1914):	H.328		
			A Blue back, grey-black, semi-glossy front		£2.50	£135.00
			B Blue back, grey-black matt front		£2.50	£135.00
			C *Plain back, grey-black matt front*		£3.50	—
D1	C	30	British Butterflies, No. 1 issue (1911)		£4.50	£135.00
D1	U	25	British Warships, green photo style (1915)		£8.00	£200.00
L	U	25	British Warships, green photo style (1915)		£35.00	—
A1	P	80	British Warships, 'real photographic' (c1916)	H.329	£15.00	—
D1	C	50	*Busts of Famous People (1906):			
			A Pale green back, caption in black		£25.00	—
			B Brown back, caption in black		£40.00	—
			C Green back, caption in white		£7.00	£350.00
D1	C	25	*Chinese Series (c1910):	H.330		
			A Back in English		£7.00	£175.00
			B 'Volunteer' Cigarettes back		£8.00	£200.00
A	C	50	*Colonial Troops (1904)	H.40	£25.00	—
D1	C	30	Eggs, Nests and Birds, No. 1 issue (1912):			
			A Unnumbered	H.331	£6.00	£180.00
			B Numbered		£6.00	£180.00
D	C	25	First Aid Series, green back (1914)		£6.00	£150.00
A	C	13	*General Interest (c1895)	H.332	£45.00	£600.00
—	BW	100	*Guinea Gold Series, unnumbered (64 × 38mm) Inscribed 'Phillips' Guinea Gold', matt (1899)	H.333	£6.00	
—	BW	90	*Guinea Gold Series, numbered 101-190 (68 × 41mm). Inscribed 'Smoke Phillips …' (1902):			
			A Glossy		£4.50	—
			B Matt		£4.50	—
			*Guinea Gold Series, unnumbered (63 × 41mm) (c1900) Actresses:	H.333		
	BW	135	A Black front		£4.50	—
	U	100	B Brown front		£9.00	—
	BW	26	Celebrities, Boer War		£4.50	—
D1	C	25	How To Do It Series (1913)		£7.00	£175.00
D	C	25	Indian Series (1908)		£14.00	£350.00
K1	C	52	*Miniature Playing Cards (c1905)	H.334	£120.00	—

81

Size	Print-ing	Number in set		Handbook reference	Price per card	Complete set

GODFREY PHILLIPS LTD, London *(continued)*

Size	Print-ing	Number in set	Description	Handbook reference	Price per card	Complete set
D1	C	30	Morse and Semaphore Signalling (1916):	H.335		
			'Morse Signalling' back		£9.00	£270.00
			'Semaphore Signalling' back		£9.00	£270.00
—	P	27	Real Photo Series — Admirals and Generals of the Great War. Cut-outs for buttonhole — 20 × 40mm (c1915)		£7.50	—
A	C	20	Russo-Japanese War Series (1904)	H.100	£250.00	—
		30	Semaphore Signalling — See 'Morse and Semaphore Signalling'			
D1	C	25	Sporting Series (c1910)		£18.00	—
D1	C	25	*Statues and Monuments (cut-outs) (1907):			
			A Provisional Patent No. 20736		£8.00	£200.00
			B Patent No. 20736		£8.00	£200.00
D	C	25	*Territorial Series (Nd 51-75) (1908)		£24.00	—
A1	C	25	*Types of British and Colonial Troops (1899)	H.76	£45.00	—
D1	C	25	*Types of British Soldiers (Nd M.651-75) (1900)	H.144	£24.00	£600.00
A	C	63	*War Photos (1916)	H.336	£8.00	—

B POST-1920 ISSUES

Size	Print-ing	Number in set	Description	Handbook reference	Price per card	Complete set
A2	C	1	*Advertisement Card — 'Grand Cut' (1934)		—	£15.00
A2	C	1	*Advertisement Card — 'La Galbana Fours' (1934) ..		—	£15.00
A	C	50	Aircraft (1938)	Ha.598	£1.80	£90.00
A2	C	54	Aircraft — Series No. 1 (1938):			
			A Millhoff and Philips names at base		£4.00	
			B Phillips and Associated Companies at base:			
			1 Front varnished		£3.00	£160.00
			2 Front matt		50p	£27.00
A2	U	50	*Animal Studies (Australia) (c1930)	Ha.538	£2.00	—
—	C	30	Animal Studies (61 × 53mm) (1936)		30p	£9.00
A2	C	50	Annuals (1939):			
			A Home issue		25p	£12.50
			B New Zealand issue (dates for planting 4-6 months later)		£1.20	£60.00
B	C	25	Arms of the English Sees (1924)		£4.40	£110.00
D	BW	50	Australian Sporting Celebrities (Australia) (1932)		£3.00	—
A	C	44	Beauties of Today, small — 'A Series of 44 ...' (1937)		£1.50	—
A	C	50	Beauties of Today, small — 'A Series of 50 ...' (1938)	Ha.514	£1.00	£50.00
A2	P	54	Beauties of Today, small — 'A Series of Real Photographs ...' (1939)		£1.30	£70.00
A	C	36	Beauties of Today, small — 'A Series of 36 ... Second Series' (1940)		£1.10	£40.00
—	P		Beauties of Today, large (83 × 66mm) (c1938)			
		36	First arrangement, known as 'Series A'		£3.50	—
		36	Second arrangement, known as 'Series B'		£5.00	—
J2	P	36	Beauties of Today, extra-large, unnumbered (1937) ...		£1.50	£55.00
J2	P	36	Beauties of Today, extra-large — 'Second Series' (1938)		£1.25	£45.00
J2	P	36	Beauties of Today, extra-large — 'Third Series' (1938)		£1.10	£40.00
J2	P	36	Beauties of Today, extra-large — 'Fourth Series' (1938)		£1.10	£40.00
J2	P	36	Beauties of Today, extra-large — 'Fifth Series' (1938) .		£1.00	£36.00
J2	P	36	Beauties of Today, extra-large — 'Sixth Series' (1939)		£1.00	£36.00
J2	P	36	Beauties of Today, extra-large — Unmarked (1939):			
			A Back 'Godfrey Phillips Ltd'		£1.00	£36.00
			B Back 'Issued with B.D.V. Medium Cigarettes ...'		35p	£12.00
A2	BW	36	Beauties of the World — Stage, Cinema, Dancing Celebrities (1931)		£1.50	£55.00

Size	Printing	Number in set		Handbook reference	Price per card	Complete set

GODFREY PHILLIPS LTD, London (continued)

Size	Printing	Number in set	Description	Handbook reference	Price per card	Complete set
A2	C	36	Beauties of the World — Series No. 2 — Stars of Stage and Screen (1933)		£1.65	£60.00
—	C	30	Beauty Spots of the Homeland (126 × 89mm) (1938)		50p	£15.00
A	C	50	Bird Painting (1938)		90p	£45.00
A	C	50	British Birds and Their Eggs (1936)		£1.10	£55.00
A	C	25	British Butterflies:	Ha.517-1		
			A Back in pale blue (1923)		£1.40	£35.00
			B Back in dark blue (1927)		£1.00	£25.00
			C 'Permacal' transfers (1936)		80p	£20.00
A2	C	25	British Orders of Chivalry and Valour (1939):	Ha.599		
			A Back 'Godfrey Phillips Ltd'		£2.80	£70.00
			B Back 'De Reszke Cigarettes' (no maker's name)		£2.80	£70.00
—	C	36	Characters Come to Life (61 × 53mm) (1938)		£1.00	£36.00
—	P	25	*Cinema Stars — Circular (57mm diam.) (1924)		£3.20	—
A	P	52	Cinema Stars — Set 1 (1929)	Ha.515-1A	£2.75	—
A2	U	30	Cinema Stars — Set 2 (1924)	Ha.515-2	£2.75	—
A2	BW	30	Cinema Stars — Set 3 (1931)	Ha.515-3	£1.50	£45.00
A2	C	32	Cinema Stars — Set 4 (1934)	Ha.515-4	£1.50	£48.00
A2	BW	32	Cinema Stars — Set 5 (1934)	Ha.515-5	£1.75	£55.00
	C		Come to Life Series — see 'Zoo Studies' Coronation of Their Majesties (1937):			
A2		50	A Small size		25p	£12.50
—		36	B Medium size (61 × 53mm)		25p	£9.00
—		24	C Postcard size (127 × 89mm)		£1.40	£35.00
	P		Cricketers (1924):			
K2		198	*A Miniature size, 'Pinnace' photos (Nd 16c-225c)		£8.00	—
D		192	B Small size, brown back (selected Nos)		£8.00	—
B1		? 58	*C Large size, 'Pinnace' photos		£40.00	—
B1		25	D Large size, brown back (selected Nos)		£22.00	—
—		? 165	*E Cabinet size		£40.00	—
D	C	25	Derby Winners and Jockeys (1923)		£4.00	£100.00
D1	C	25	Empire Industries (1927)	Ha.600	£1.20	£30.00
A2	C	50	*Evolution of the British Navy* (1930)		—	£90.00
			49 different (minus No 40)		£1.00	£50.00
D	C	25	Famous Boys (1924)		£2.60	£65.00
D	C	32	Famous Cricketers (1926)		£5.00	—
A	C	25	Famous Crowns (1938)		32p	£8.00
A2	C	50	Famous Footballers (1936)		£2.00	£100.00
—	C	36	Famous Love Scenes (60 × 53mm) (1939)		70p	£25.00
A2	C	50	Famous Minors (1936)		30p	£15.00
—	C	26	Famous Paintings (128 × 89mm) (1938)		£1.30	£35.00
D	C	25	Feathered Friends (1928)	Ha.516	£1.60	£40.00
A2	C	50	Film Favourites (1934)	Ha.517-2	70p	£35.00
D	BW	50	Film Stars (Australia) (1934)		£2.00	—
A2	C	50	Film Stars (1934)		80p	£40.00
—	C	24	*Film Stars — '... No. ... of a series of 24 cards ...' (128 × 89mm) (1934):			
			A Postcard format back		£3.00	£75.00
			B Back without postcard format		£4.00	£100.00
—	C	24	*Film Stars — '... No. ... of a series of cards', Nd 25-48 (128 × 89mm) (1935):			
			A Postcard format back		£3.00	—
			B Back without postcard format		£6.00	—
—	C	24	*Film Stars '... No. ... of a series of cards', vivid backgrounds (128 × 89mm) (1936):			
			A Postcard format back	Ha.517-3	£2.00	—
			B Back without postcard format		£3.00	—

Size	Print-ing	Number in set		Handbook reference	Price per card	Complete set

GODFREY PHILLIPS LTD, London *(continued)*

Size	Print-ing	Number in set	Title	Handbook reference	Price per card	Complete set
D	C	50	First Aid (1923)		£1.50	£75.00
D	C	25	*Fish (1924)		£2.60	£65.00
	C	30	Flower Studies (1937):			
			A Medium size (61 × 53mm)		25p	£7.50
—			*B Postcard size (128 × 89mm)		70p	£21.00
	P		Footballers — 'Pinnace' photos (1922-24):			
K2			A Miniature size: (Prices shown apply to numbers 1 to 940, for numbers above 940 prices are doubled)			
		112	1a 'Oval' design back, in brown		£3.50	—
		400	1b 'Oval' design back, in black		£2.00	—
		517	2 Double-lined oblong back		£2.00	—
		1109	3 Single-lined oblong back, address 'Photo'		£1.30	—
			4 Single-lined oblong back, address 'Pinnace' photos:			
		2462	a Name at head, team at base		£1.30	—
		? 1651	b Name at base, no team shown		£1.30	—
		? 217	c Team at head, name at base		£1.30	—
—			B Large size (83 × 59mm):			
		? 400	1 'Oval' design back		£3.50	—
		? 2000	2 Double-lined oblong back:			
			a Address 'Photo'		£7.50	—
			b Address 'Pinnace' photos		£3.50	—
		? 2462	3 Single-lined oblong back:			
			a Name at head, team at base		£3.50	—
			b Name at base, no team shown		£3.50	—
			c Team and name at base		£3.50	—
—		? 2462	C Cabinet size		£10.00	—
—	C	30	Garden Studies (128 × 89mm) (1938)		40p	£12.00
A2	C	25	Home Pets (1924)	Ha.540	£2.20	£55.00
A2	U	25	How to Build a Two Valve Set (1929)		£2.60	£65.00
D	C	25	How to Make a Valve Amplifier ..., Nd 26-50 (1924)		£3.20	£80.00
A	C	25	How to Make Your Own Wireless Set (1923)		£2.60	£65.00
A2	C	54	In the Public Eye (1935)		50p	£27.00
A2	C	50	International Caps (1936)		£1.80	£90.00
A2	C	37	Kings and Queens of England (1925):			
			Nos 1 and 4		£30.00	—
			Other numbers		£2.00	£70.00
A2	U	25	Lawn Tennis (1930)		£3.00	£75.00
K2	C	53	*Miniature Playing Cards (1932-34):			
			A Back with exchange scheme:			
			1 Buff. Offer for 'pack of playing cards'		60p	—
			2 Buff. Offer for 'playing cards, dominoes or chess'		60p	£30.00
			3 Buff. Offer for 'playing cards, dominoes or draughts'		60p	£30.00
			4 Lemon		60p	—
			5 White, with red over-printing		60p	—
			B *Blue scroll back, see Fig. 30, Plate 5, RB13*		60p	£30.00
A2	C	25	Model Railways (1927)		£3.00	£75.00
D	C	50	Motor Cars at a Glance (1924)		£4.00	£200.00
D	C	20	Novelty Series (1924)		£11.00	—
A2	C	48	The 'Old Country' (1935)		70p	£35.00
A	C	25	Old Favourites (1924)	Ha.517-4	£1.80	£45.00
—	C	36	Old Masters (60 × 53mm) (1939)		30p	£11.00
A	U	36	Olympic Champions Amsterdam, 1928		£2.50	£90.00
A	C	25	Optical Illusions (1927)		£2.60	£65.00

Size	Print-ing	Number in set		Handbook reference	Price per card	Complete set

GODFREY PHILLIPS LTD, London *(continued)*

Size	Print-ing	Number in set	Description	Handbook reference	Price per card	Complete set
	C		'Our Dogs' (1939):			
A2		36	A Small size (export)		£1.60	£60.00
—		30	B Medium size (60 × 53mm)		60p	£18.00
—		30	*C Postcard size (128 × 89mm)		£3.40	—
—	BW	48	'Our Favourites' (60 × 53mm) (1935)		25p	£12.50
—	C	30	Our Glorious Empire (128 × 89mm) (1939)		70p	£21.00
	C	30	'Our Puppies' (1936):			
—			A Medium size (60 × 53mm)		£1.65	£50.00
—			*B Postcard size (128 × 89mm)		£1.80	£55.00
A2	C	25	Personalities of Today (Caricatures) (1932)		£2.00	£50.00
A2	C	25	Popular Superstitions (1930)		£1.60	£40.00
A	C	25	Prizes for Needlework (1925)		£2.20	£55.00
D	C	25	Railway Engines (1924)		£3.20	£80.00
D	C	25	Red Indians (1927)	Ha.601	£3.40	£85.00
A	C	25	School Badges (1927)	Ha.543	£1.10	£27.50
A	C		Screen Stars (1936):			
		48	First arrangement, known as 'Series A':			
			i Frame embossed		£1.20	£60.00
			ii Frame not embossed		£1.60	£80.00
		48	Second arrangement, known as 'Series B'		£1.00	£50.00
A2	C		A Selection of B.D.V. Wonderful Gifts:			
		48	'... based on 1930 Budget' (1930)		£1.20	—
		48	'... based on 1931 Budget' (1931)		£1.20	—
		48	'... based on 1932 Budget' (1932)		£1.00	£50.00
D	C	25	Ships and Their Flags (1924)	Ha.602	£3.00	£75.00
—	C	36	Ships that have Made History (60 × 53mm) (1938)		60p	£22.00
—	C	48	Shots from the Films (60 × 53mm) (1934)		80p	£40.00
A2	C	50	Soccer Stars (1936)		£1.80	£90.00
A2	C	36	Soldiers of the King (1939):	Ha.603		
			A Inscribed 'This surface is adhesive'		£1.60	—
			B Without the above:			
			1 Thin card		70p	£25.00
			2 Thick card		70p	£25.00
	C		Special Jubilee Year Series (1935):			
—		20	A Medium size (60 × 53mm)		40p	£8.00
—		12	B Postcard size (128 × 89mm)		£2.00	£24.00
A2	U	30	Speed Champions (1930)		£2.00	£60.00
A2	U	36	Sporting Champions (1929)		£2.50	£90.00
D	C	25	Sports (1923):			
			A White card		£4.00	—
			B Grey card		£4.00	—
A2	C	50	*Sportsmen — 'Spot the Winner' (1937):			
			A Inverted back		£1.10	£55.00
			B Normal back		£1.50	£75.00
A2	C		Stage and Cinema Beauties (1933):	H.572		
		35	First arrangement — known as 'Series A'		£1.15	£40.00
		35	Second arrangement — known as 'Series B'		£1.15	£40.00
A2	C	50	Stage and Cinema Beauties (1935)	Ha.517-5	£1.20	£60.00
D	C	50	Stars of British Films (Australia) (1934):			
			A Back 'B.D.V. Cigarettes'		£1.80	—
			B Back 'Grey's Cigarettes ...'		£1.80	—
			C Back 'De Reszke Cigarettes'		£1.80	—
			D Back 'Godfrey Phillips (Aust)'		£1.80	—
A2	CP	54	Stars of the Screen — 'A Series of 54' (1934)		£1.20	£65.00
A2	C	48	Stars of the Screen — 'A Series of 48' (1936):			
			A Frame not embossed		90p	£45.00
			B Frame embossed		90p	£45.00
			C In strips of three, per strip		£2.50	£40.00

Size	Print-ing	Number in set		Handbook reference	Price per card	Complete set

GODFREY PHILLIPS LTD, London *(continued)*

Size	Print-ing	Number in set	Description	Handbook reference	Price per card	Complete set
D	BW	38	Test Cricketers, 1932-1933 (Australia):			
			A 'Issued with Grey's Cigarettes'		£3.30	—
			B 'Issued with B.D.V. Cigarettes'		£3.30	—
			C Back 'Godfrey Phillips (Aust.)'		£3.30	—
A	U	25	The 1924 Cabinet (1924)		£2.00	£50.00
A	C	50	This Mechanized Age — First Series (1936):			
			A Inscribed 'This surface is adhesive'		30p	£15.00
			B Without the above		36p	£18.00
A	C	50	This Mechanized Age — Second Series (1937)		30p	£15.00
D2	C		Victorian Footballers (Australia) (1933):			
		50	1 'Series of 50':			
			A 'Godfrey Phillips (Aust.)'		£3.50	—
			B 'B.D.V. Cigarettes ...'		£3.50	—
			C 'Grey's Cigarettes'		£3.50	—
		75	2 'Series of 75':			
			D 'B.D.V. Cigarettes ...'		£4.00	—
D	BW	50	Victorian League and Association Footballers (Australia) (1934)............................		£4.00	—
A2	C	100	*Who's Who in Australian Sport (Australia) (1933) ...		£3.50	—
—	C	30	Zoo Studies — Come to Life Series (101 × 76mm) (1939)		£1.30	£40.00
			Spectacles for use with the above		—	£8.00

C SILKS. Known as 'the B.D.V. Silks'. All unbacked. Inscribed 'B.D.V. Cigarettes' or 'G.P.' (Godfrey Phillips), or anonymous. Issued about 1910-25.

Size	Print-ing	Number in set	Description	Handbook reference	Price per card	Complete set
—	C	62	*Arms of Countries and Territories (73 × 50mm) — Anonymous	Ha.504-12	£3.75	—
—	C	32	*Beauties — Modern Paintings (B.D.V.):	Ha.505-13		
			A Small size (70 × 46mm)		£12.00	—
			B Extra-large size (143 × 100mm)		£40.00	—
—	C	100	*Birds II (68 × 42mm) — B.D.V	Ha.505-2	£2.50	—
—	C	12	*Birds of the Tropics III — B.D.V.:	Ha.505-3		
			A Small size (71 × 47mm)		£11.00	—
			B Medium size (71 × 63mm)		£13.00	—
			C Extra-large size (150 × 100mm)		£17.00	—
—	U	24	*British Admirals (83 × 76mm) — Anonymous	Ha.504-5	£6.00	—
—	C		*British Butterflies and Moths II — Anonymous:	Ha.505-6		
		40	Nos 1-40. Large size, 76 × 61mm		£6.00	—
		10	Nos 41-50. Medium size. 70 × 51mm		£6.00	—
—	C	108	*British Naval Crests II:	Ha.504-4		
			A B.D.V., size 70 × 47mm		£2.00	—
			B Anonymous, size 70 × 51mm		£2.00	—
—	C	25	*Butterflies I (70 × 48mm) — Anonymous	Ha.505-5	£9.00	—
—	C	47	Ceramic Art — B.D.V.:	Ha.505-16		
			A Small size (70 × 43mm)		£1.00	£47.00
			B Small size (70 × 48mm)		£1.00	—
			C Medium size (70 × 61mm)		£1.75	—
—	C		*Clan Tartans:			
			A Small size (71 × 48mm):	Ha505-15		
		49	1 Anonymous		£1.00	£50.00
		65	2 B.D.V		£1.10	£70.00
		56	B Medium size (70 × 60mm) — B.D.V		£2.75	—
		12	C Extra-large size (150 × 100mm) B.D.V. (selected Nos.)		£5.00	—
—	C	108	*Colonial Army Badges (71 × 50mm) — Anonymous ...	Ha.502-3	£2.50	—
—	C	17	County Cricket Badges (69 × 48mm):	Ha.505-8		
			A Anonymous		£18.00	—
			B B.D.V		£18.00	—

Size	Print- ing	Number in set		Handbook reference	Price per card	Complete set

GODFREY PHILLIPS LTD, London *(continued)*

Size	Print- ing	Number in set	Description	Handbook reference	Price per card	Complete set
—	C	108	*Crests and Badges of the British Army II:	H.502-2		
			A1 *Small size (70 × 48mm) Anonymous:*			
			(a) *Numbered*		£1.30	£140.00
			(b) *Unnumbered*		£1.30	£140.00
			A2 Small size (70 × 48mm) — B.D.V.		£1.30	£140.00
			A3 Medium size (70 × 60mm):			
			(a) *Anonymous*		£1.50	—
			(b) B.D.V.		£1.50	—
—	C		*Flags — Set 4 — Anonymous:*	Ha.501-4		
		? 143	A *'Long' size (82 × 53mm)*		£1.70	—
			B *'Short' size (70 × 48mm):*			
		? 143	*1 First numbering arrangement (as A)*		£1.40	—
		? 108	*2 Second numbering arrangement*		90p	—
		? 113	*3 Third numbering arrangement*		90p	—
—	C		*Flags — Set 5 — Anonymous:*	Ha.501-5		
			A *Small size (70 × 50mm):*			
		20	*1 With caption*		£1.00	—
		6	*2 Without caption, flag 40 × 29mm*		£1.20	—
		? 6	*3 Without caption, flag 60 × 41mm*		£1.20	—
		? 8	B *Extra-large size (155 × 108mm)*		£14.00	—
—	C	18	*Flags — Set 6 — Anonymous:*	Ha.501-6		
			A Size 69 × 47mm		£1.00	£18.00
			B Size 71 × 51mm		£1.00	£18.00
—	C	20	*Flags — Set 7 (70 × 50mm) — Anonymous*	Ha.501-7	£1.00	—
—	C	50	*Flags — Set 9 — ('5th Series') (70 × 48mm) — Anonymous*	Ha.501-9	£1.60	£80.00
—	C		*Flags — Set 10:	Ha.501-10		
		120	'7th Series' (70 × 48mm) — Anonymous		80p	—
		120	'10th Series' (70 × 62mm) — Anonymous		£1.00	—
		120	'12th Series' (70 × 48mm) — Anonymous		90p	—
		65	'15th Series' (70 × 62mm) (selected Nos.) — B.D.V.		£1.10	—
		65	'16th Series' (70 × 62mm) (selected Nos.) — B.D.V.		£1.10	—
		132	'20th Series' (70 × 48 mm) — B.D.V. in brown or red		90p	—
		126	'25th Series' (70 × 48mm) — B.D.V. in brown or black		80p	—
		62	'25th Series' (70 × 62mm) (selected Nos.) — B.D.V.		£2.75	—
		112	'26th Series' (70 × 48mm) — B.D.V. in brown or blue		80p	—
		70	'28th Series' (70 × 48mm) (selected Nos.) — B.D.V.		£1.00	—
—	C		*Flags — Set 12:	Ha.501-12		
		1	A *'Let 'em all come' (70 × 46mm) — Anonymous*		—	£11.00
			B Allied Flags (grouped):			
		1	*Four Flags — Anonymous:*			
			1 Small size (70 × 46mm)		—	£9.00
			2 Extra-large size (163 × 120mm)		—	£35.00
		1	Seven Flags (165 × 116mm):			
			1 Anonymous		—	£9.00
			2 B.D.V. in brown or orange		—	£9.00
		1	Eight Flags (165 × 116mm) — B.D.V.		—	£35.00
—	C		*Flags — Set 13:	Ha.501-13		
		? 23	A *Size 163 × 114mm — Anonymous*		£2.00	—
		? 27	B Size 163 × 114mm — B.D.V. in brown, orange, blue, green or black		£2.25	—
		? 23	C Size 150 × 100mm — B.D.V.		£2.00	—
—	C	26	*Flags — Set 14 ('House Flags') (68 × 47mm) — Anonymous*	Ha.501-14	£8.50	—

Size	Printing	Number in set			Handbook reference	Price per card	Complete set

GODFREY PHILLIPS LTD, London *(continued)*

Size	Print.	No.		Description	Handbook ref.	Price	Set
—	C	25		*Flags — Set 15 (Pilot and Signal Flags) (70 × 50mm):	Ha.501-15		
			A	Numbered 601-625 — Anonymous		£3.60	£85.00
			B	Inscribed 'Series II' — B.D.V.		£2.40	£60.00
—	C			*Football Colours:	Ha.505-9		
		? 21	A	Anonymous. size 68 × 49mm		£7.00	—
		? 86	B	B.D.V., size 68 × 49mm		£6.00	—
		? 78	C	B.D.V., size 150 × 100mm		£6.00	—
—	C	126		G.P. Territorial Badges (70 × 48mm)	Ha.502-12	£2.00	—
—	U	25		*Great War Leaders II (81 × 68mm) — Anonymous	Ha.504-7	£6.00	—
—	U	? 53		*Great War Leaders III and Warships, sepia, black or blue on white or pink material (70 × 50mm) — Anonymous	Ha.504-10	£6.00	—
—	C			*Great War Leaders IV and Celebrities:	Ha.504-11		
		3	A	Small size (70 × 48mm) — Anonymous		£6.00	—
		4	B	Small size (70 × 48mm) — B.D.V.		£6.50	—
		3	C	Medium size (70 × 63mm) — Anonymous		£6.00	—
		2	D	Medium size (70 × 63mm) — B. D.V.		£6.00	—
		? 18	E	Extra-large size (150 × 100mm) — B.D.V.		£6.00	—
		? 4	F	Extra-large size (150 × 110mm) — Anonymous		£6.00	£24.00
		? 1	G	Extra-large size (150 × 110mm) — B.D.V.		—	£12.00
		? 26	H	Extra-large size (163 × 117mm) — Anonymous		£6.00	—
		? 46	I	Extra-large size (163 × 117mm) — B.D.V.		£6.00	—
—	C			Heraldic Series — B.D.V.:	Ha.504-17		
		25	A	Small size (68 × 47mm)		£1.20	£30.00
		25	B	Small size (68 × 43mm)		£1.20	£30.00
		25	C	Medium size (68 × 60mm)		£3.00	—
		12	D	Extra-large size (150 × 100mm) (selected Nos)		£5.00	£60.00
—	C	10		*Irish Patriots — Anonymous:	Ha.505-11		
			A	Small size (67 × 50mm)		£12.00	—
			B	Large size (83 × 76mm)		£12.00	—
			C	Extra-large size (152 × 110mm)		£17.00	—
—	C	1		*Irish Republican Stamp (70 × 50mm)	Ha.505-12	—	£1.75
—	C	54		*Naval Badges of Rank and Military Headdress (70 × 47mm) — Anonymous	Ha.504-9	£6.00	—
—	C	40		*Old Masters — Set 1 (155 × 115mm) — B.D.V.	Ha.503-1	£30.00	—
—	C	20		*Old Masters — Set 2 (150 × 105mm):	Ha.503-2		
			A	Anonymous		£4.00	—
			B	B.D.V. wording above picture		£4.00	—
			C	B.D.V. wording below picture		£6.00	—
—	C			*Old Masters — Set 3A (70 × 50mm):	Ha.503-3A		
		40	A	B.D.V.		£2.75	—
		55	B	Anonymous		£2.50	—
—	C	30		*Old Masters — Set 3B (70 × 50mm) — Anonymous	Ha.503-3B	£2.50	—
—	C	120		*Old Masters — Set 4 (70 × 50mm) — Anonymous	Ha.503-4	£2.00	—
—	C			*Old Masters — Set 5 (70 × 50mm):	Ha.503-5		
		20	A	Unnumbered — Anonymous		£3.00	—
		60	B	Nd. 1-60 — B.D.V		£1.20	£72.00
		20	C	Nd. 101-120 — Anonymous:			
			1	Numerals normal size		£1.60	—
			2	Numerals very small size		£1.60	£32.00
		20	D	Nd. 101-120 — B.D.V.		£1.60	£32.00
—	C	50		*Old Masters — Set 6 (67 × 42mm) — B.D.V.	Ha.503-6	£1.20	£60.00
—	C	50		*Old Masters — Set 7, Nd. 301-350 (67 × 47mm) — Anonymous	Ha.503-7	£2.50	—
—	C	50		*Orders of Chivalry I (70 × 48mm) — Anonymous	Ha.504-14	£2.20	—
—	C	24		*Orders of Chivalry — Series 10 (70 × 50mm):	Ha.504-16		
			A	Nd. 1-24 — B.D.V.		£1.60	£40.00
			B	Nd. 401-424 — G.P		£1.80	£45.00

Size	Print-ing	Number in set		Handbook reference	Price per card	Complete set

GODFREY PHILLIPS LTD, London *(continued)*

Size	Print.	Number	Description	Handbook ref.	Price per card	Complete set
—	C	72	*Regimental Colours II (76 × 70mm) — Anonymous	Ha.502-7	£4.50	—
—	C		*Regimental Colours and Crests III:	Ha.502-8		
			A Small size (70 × 51mm):			
		40	1 Colours with faint backgrounds — Anonymous		£1.50	—
		120	2 Colours without backgrounds — Anonymous		£1.60	—
		120	3 Colours without backgrounds — B.D.V.		£1.60	—
		120	B Extra-large size (165 × 120mm):			
			1 Anonymous — unnumbered		£6.50	—
			2 B.D.V. — numbered		£6.00	—
—	C	50	*Regimental Colours — Series 12 (70 × 50mm) — B.D.V.	Ha.502-11	£2.00	£100.00
—	C	10	*Religious Pictures — Anonymous:	Ha.505-10		
			A Small size (67 × 50mm)		£18.00	—
			B Large size (83 × 76 mm)		£20.00	—
			C Extra-large size (155 × 110mm)		£27.00	—
—	C	75	*Town and City Arms — Series 30 (48 unnumbered, 27 numbered 49-75) — B.D.V.:	Ha.504-13		
			A Small size (70 × 50mm)		£1.80	—
			B Medium size (70 × 65mm)		£2.70	—
—	C	25	*Victoria Cross Heroes I (70 × 50mm) — Anonymous	Ha.504-1	£11.00	—
—	C	? 25	*Victoria Cross Heroes II (70 × 50mm) — Anonymous	Ha.504-2	£12.00	—
—	C	90	*War Pictures (70 × 48mm) — Anonymous	Ha.504-8	£5.50	—

D MISCELLANEOUS

A	BW		B.D.V. Package Issues (1932-34):			
		17	Boxers		£7.00	—
		54	Cricketers		£8.00	—
		67	Film Stars		£2.50	—
		132	Footballers		£6.00	—
		19	Jockeys		£4.00	—
		21	Speedway Riders		£9.00	—
		27	Sportsmen		£4.00	—
A	BW		Sports Package Issues:			
		25	Cricketers (1948)		£9.00	—
		25	Cricketers (1951)		£9.00	—
		25	Footballers (1948)		£8.00	—
		50	Footballers (1950)		£8.00	—
		25	Footballers (1951)		£8.00	—
		25	Football & Rugby Players (1952)		£6.50	—
		25	Jockeys (1952)		£5.00	—
		25	Radio Stars (1949)		£3.00	—
		50	Sportsmen (1948)		£4.50	—
		25	Sportsmen (1949)		£4.50	—
		25	Sportsmen (1953)		£4.50	—
		25	Sportsmen (1954)		£4.50	—
D	BW	1	Cricket Fixture Card (Radio Luxembourg) (1936)		—	£7.00
J2		20	'Private Seal' Wrestling Holds (export) (c1920)		£30.00	—
			Rugs (miscellaneous designs) (c1920)		£9.00	—
A	U	?	Stamp Cards (four colours, several wordings) (c1930)		£2.25	—

JOHN PLAYER & SONS, Nottingham———————————————

44 page reference book — £4.00

A PRE-1919 ISSUES

A	C	25	*Actors and Actresses (1898)	H.337	£24.00	£600.00
A1	BW	50	*Actresses (c1897)	H.339	£24.00	—

Size	Print-ing	Number in set		Handbook reference	Price per card	Complete set

JOHN PLAYER & SONS, Nottingham *(continued)*

Size	Print-ing	Number in set	Description	Handbook reference	Price per card	Complete set
A	C	8	*Advertisement Cards (1893-94)	H.338	From £300.00	—
J	C	10	Allied Cavalry or Regimental Uniforms:	H.340		
			Allied Cavalry (1914)		£9.00	£90.00
			Regimental Uniforms (1914)		£9.00	£90.00
A	C	50	Arms and Armour (1909)	H.273	£2.50	£125.00
A	C	25	Army Life (1910)	H.78	£2.00	£50.00
J	C	12	Artillery in Action (1917)		£5.00	£60.00
A	C	50	Badges and Flags of British Regiments (1904):	H.341		
			A Brown back, unnumbered		£2.50	£125.00
			B Brown back, numbered		£2.50	£125.00
A	C	50	Badges and Flags of British Regiments (1903):			
			A Green back, thick card		£2.50	£125.00
			B Green back, thin card		£2.50	£125.00
—	P	10	*Bookmarks — Authors (148 × 51mm) (1905)	H.342	£60.00	—
A	C	50	British Empire Series (1904):	H.343		
			A Grey-white card, matt		£1.30	£65.00
			B White card, semi-glossy		£1.50	£75.00
	C	25	British Livestock:	H.344		
A			A Small card (1915)		£2.80	£70.00
J			B Extra-large card, brown back (May 1916)		£3.60	£90.00
A	C	50	Butterflies and Moths (1904)	H.80	£1.90	£95.00
	C		Bygone Beauties:			
A		25	A Small card (1914)		£1.60	£40.00
J		10	B Extra-large card (1916)		£4.50	£45.00
—	U	? 32	*Cabinet Size Pictures, 1898-1900 (220 × 140mm):	H.476		
			A Plain back		£90.00	—
			B Printed back		£90.00	—
A	C	20	Castles, Abbeys etc (c1894):	H.345		
			A Without border		£28.00	£560.00
			B White border		£28.00	£560.00
A	C	50	Celebrated Bridges (1903)	H.346	£3.00	£150.00
A	C		Celebrated Gateways (1909):	H.347		
		50	A Thick card		£1.50	£75.00
		25	B Thinner card (26-50 only)		£1.80	—
A	C	25	Ceremonial and Court Dress (1911)	H.145	£1.80	£45.00
	C		Characters from Dickens:	H.348		
A		25	Small card, 1st series (1912)		£2.40	£60.00
J		10	Extra-large card (1912)..		£6.00	£60.00
A	C	25	Characters from Dickens, 2nd series (1914)	H.348	£2.40	£60.00
A	C	25	Characters from Thackeray (1913)		£1.60	£40.00
A	C	50	Cities of the World (1900):			
			A Grey-mauve on white back		£4.00	—
			B Grey-mauve on toned back		£4.00	—
			C Bright mauve on white back		£4.00	—
A	C	25	Colonial and Indian Army Badges (1916)		£1.40	£35.00
A	C	25	*Counties and Their Industries:	H.349		
			A Unnumbered (c1910)		£2.40	£60.00
			B Numbered (1914)		£2.40	£60.00
A	C	50	*Countries — Arms and Flags:			
			A Thick card (1905)		90p	£45.00
			B Thin Card (1912)		£1.10	£55.00
A	C	50	*Country Seats and Arms (1906)		90p	£45.00
A	C		*Country Seats and Arms, 2nd series (1907):			
		25	A Nd. 51-75 First printing		£1.60	£40.00
		50	B Nd. 51-100 Second printing		90p	£45.00
A	C	50	*Country Seats and Arms, 3rd series (1907)		90p	£45.00

Size	Print-ing	Number in set		Handbook reference	Price per card	Complete set

JOHN PLAYER & SONS, Nottingham *(continued)*

Size	Print-ing	Number in set	Description	Handbook reference	Price per card	Complete set
	C		Cries of London:	H.350		
A		25	Small cards, 1st series (1913)		£2.00	£50.00
J		10	Extra-large cards, 1st series (1912)		£4.50	£45.00
J		10	Extra-large cards, 2nd series (1914)		£4.00	£40.00
A	C	25	Cries of London, 2nd series (1916)		£1.00	£25.00
A	C	25	Egyptian Kings and Queens, and Classical Deities (1911)		£2.00	£50.00
J	C	10	Egyptian Sketches (1915)	H.351	£4.00	£40.00
A	C	25	*England's Military Heroes (1898):	H.352		
			A Wide card		£40.00	—
			A1 Wide card plain back		£40.00	—
			B Narrow card		£32.00	—
			B2 Narrow card, plain back		£30.00	—
A	C	25	England's Naval Heroes (1897):	H.353		
			A Wide card		£40.00	—
			B Narrow card		£26.00	£650.00
A	C	25	England's Naval Heroes (1898), descriptions on back:	H.353		
			A Wide card		£40.00	—
			A2 Wide card, plain back		£40.00	—
			B Narrow card		£26.00	£650.00
			B2 Narrow card, plain back		£26.00	—
A	C	25	Everyday Phrases by Tom Browne (1901):	H.354		
			A Thickcard		£16.00	£400.00
			B Thin card		£16.00	£400.00
	C	20	Famous Authors and Poets (1902):			
A			A Wide card		£28.00	£560.00
			B Narrow card		£20.00	£400.00
J	C	10	Famous Paintings (1913)	H.355	£3.50	£35.00
A	C	50	Fishes of the World (1903)	H.66	£2.40	£120.00
A	C	50	Gallery of Beauty (1896):	H.356		
			A Wide Card:			
			I Set of 50		£22.00	—
			II 5 Alternative Pictures		£60.00	—
			B Narrow Card:			
			I Set of 50		£20.00	—
			II 5 Alternative Pictures		£60.00	—
A	C	25	Gems of British Scenery (1914)		£1.20	£30.00
A	C	25	Highland Clans (1908)		£4.40	£110.00
J	C	10	Historic Ships (1910):			
			A Thick card		£4.50	£45.00
			B Thin card		£4.50	£45.00
A	C	50	Life on Board a Man of War in 1805 and 1905 (1905)	H.38	£2.20	£110.00
A	C	50	Military Series (1900)		£20.00	—
A	C	25	Miniatures (1916)		44p	£11.00
A	C	25	Napoleon (1915)	H.364	£2.00	£50.00
	C		Nature Series:			
A		50	Small card (1908)		£1.40	£70.00
J		10	Extra-large card (Birds) (1908)		£12.00	—
J		10	Extra-large card (Animals) (1913)		£5.00	£50.00
A	C	50	Old England's Defenders (1898)		£18.00	£900.00
A	C	25	Players — Past and Present (1916)		90p	£22.50
A	C	25	Polar Exploration (1915)		£2.60	£65.00
A	C	25	Polar Exploration, 2nd series (1916)		£2.20	£55.00
A	C	25	Products of the World:			
			A Thick card (1909)		80p	£20.00
			B Thin card (1908)		£1.20	£30.00

Size	Print-ing	Number in set		Handbook reference	Price per card	Complete set

JOHN PLAYER & SONS, Nottingham *(continued)*

Size	Print-ing	Number in set	Description	Handbook reference	Price per card	Complete set
A	C	50	*Regimental Colours and Cap Badges (1907)	H.73	£1.30	£65.00
A	C	50	*Regimental Colours and Cap Badges — Territorial Regiments (1910):			
			A Blue back		£1.30	£65.00
			B Brown back		£1.30	£65.00
J	C	10	Regimental Uniforms — See 'Allied Cavalry'			
A	C	50	Regimental Uniforms (1-50):			
			A Blue back (Jul. 1912)		£2.20	£110.00
			B Brown back (Jul. 1914)		£2.40	£120.00
A	C	50	Regimental Uniforms (51-100) (1914)		£1.40	£70.00
A	C	50	Riders of the World:	H.358		
			A Thick grey card (1905)		£1.60	£80.00
			B Thinner white card (1914)		£1.60	£80.00
—	P	6	The Royal Family (101 × 154mm) (1902)	H.359	—	£270.00
—	P	? 30	Rulers and Views (101 × 154mm) (1902)	H.363	£90.00	—
A	C	25	Shakespearean Series (1914)		£1.40	£35.00
A	C	25	Ships' Figureheads (1912):			
			A Numerals 'sans serif'		£2.80	£70.00
			B Numerals with serif		£2.60	£65.00
A	BW	? 148	Stereoscopic Series (c1900)	H.357	£110.00	—
A	C	25	Those Pearls of Heaven (1914)		£1.40	£35.00
A	BW	66	Transvaal Series (1902):	H.360		
			A Black front		£5.00	—
			B Violet-black front		£5.00	—
A	C	50	Useful Plants and Fruits (1904)	H.361	£2.40	£120.00
A	C	25	Victoria Cross (1914)		£2.60	£65.00
A	C	50	Wild Animals of the World (1902):	H.77		
			A 'John Player & Sons Ltd.'		£3.00	£150.00
			B 'John Player & Sons, Branch, Nottingham'		£4.50	—
			C1 As B, 'Branch' omitted but showing traces of some or all of the letters		£4.50	—
			C2 As B. New printing with 'Branch' omitted		£3.00	£150.00
A2	C	45	Wild Animals of the World, narrow card (1902):	H.77		
			A 'John Player & Sons Ltd.'		£5.00	£225.00
			B 'John Player & Sons, Branch, Nottingham'		£7.00	—
			C1 As B, 'Branch' omitted but showing traces of some or all of the letters		£5.00	—
			C2 As B. New printing with 'Branch' omitted		£5.00	£225.00
A	C	50	Wonders of the Deep (1904)	H.365	£1.80	£90.00
A	C	25	Wonders of the World, blue back (1913)	H.362	80p	£20.00
J	C	10	Wooden Walls (1909):			
			A Thick card		£6.00	£60.00
			B Thin card		£6.00	£60.00
A	C	25	Wrestling and Ju-Jitsu (blue back) (1911)	H.467	£2.20	£55.00

B POST-1920 ISSUES. Series with I.T.C. Clause.

Size	Print-ing	Number in set	Description	Handbook reference	Price per card	Complete set
	C	1	*Advertisement Card (Sailor) (c1930):			
A			A Small size		—	£5.00
B			B Large size		—	£20.00
A	C	50	Aeroplanes (1935):			
			A Home issue — titled 'Aeroplanes (Civil)'		£1.10	£55.00
			B Irish issue — titled 'Aeroplanes'		£1.40	£70.00
A	C	50	Aircraft of the Royal Air Force (1938)		£1.00	£50.00
A	C	50	Animals of the Countryside (1939):			
			A Home issue — adhesive		22p	£11.00
			B Irish issue — non-adhesive, green numerals overprinted		£1.00	—

Size	Printing	Number in set		Handbook reference	Price per card	Complete set

JOHN PLAYER & SONS, Nottingham *(continued)*

Size	Printing	Number in set	Description	Handbook reference	Price per card	Complete set
B	C	25	Aquarium Studies (1932)		£1.80	£45.00
B	C	25	Architectural Beauties (1927)		£2.20	£55.00
A	C	50	Army Corps and Divisional Signs, 1914-1918 (1924) ..		60p	£30.00
A	C	100	Army Corps and Divisional Signs, 1914-1918, '2nd Series' (1925):			
			Nos. 51-100		60p	£30.00
			Nos. 101-150		60p	£30.00
A	U	50	Association Cup Winners (1930)	H.667	£1.80	£90.00
	C		Aviary and Cage Birds:			
A		50	A Small size (1933):			
			1 Cards		£1.00	£50.00
			2 Transfers		40p	£20.00
B		25	B Large size (1935)		£3.60	£90.00
A	C	50	Birds and Their Young (1937):			
			A Home issue — adhesive		22p	£11.00
			B Irish issue — 1 Adhesive		£1.00	—
			2 Non-adhesive		£1.00	—
A	C	25	Boxing (1934)		£6.00	—
A	C	50	Boy Scout and Girl Guide Patrol Signs and Emblems (1933):			
			A Cards		40p	£20.00
			B Transfers		40p	£20.00
B	C	25	British Butterflies (1934)		£4.40	£110.00
J	C	25	British Live Stock (blue back) (1923)	H.344	£3.60	£90.00
B	C	25	British Naval Craft (1939)		£1.00	£25.00
J	C	20	British Pedigree Stock (1925)		£4.00	£80.00
B	C	25	British Regalia (1937)		£1.20	£30.00
A	C	50	Butterflies (1932):			
			A Cards		£1.30	£65.00
			B Transfers		40p	£20.00
B	C	24	Cats (1936)		£7.00	—
B	C	25	Championship Golf Courses (1936)		£7.00	£175.00
A	C	50	Characters from Dickens (1923)	H.348	£1.40	£70.00
B	C	25	Characters from Fiction (1933)		£3.80	£95.00
B	C	20	Clocks — Old and New (1928)		£5.00	£100.00
A	C	50	Coronation Series Ceremonial Dress (1937)		28p	£14.00
B	C	25	Country Sports (1930)		£5.60	£140.00
A	C	50	Cricketers, 1930 (1930)		£1.50	£75.00
A	C	50	Cricketers, 1934 (1934)		£1.20	£60.00
A	C	50	Cricketers, 1938 (1938)		£1.00	£50.00
A	C	50	Cricketers, Caricatures by 'Rip' (1926)		£1.80	£90.00
A	C	50	Curious Beaks (1929)		80p	£40.00
A	C	50	Cycling (1939):			
			A Home issue — adhesive		90p	£45.00
			B Irish issue — 1 Adhesive		£1.50	—
			2 Non-adhesive		£1.50	—
	C		Dandies (1932):			
A		50	A Small size		40p	£20.00
B		25	B Large size		£1.80	£45.00
A	C	50	Derby and Grand National Winners (1933):			
			A Cards		£1.70	£85.00
			B Transfers		50p	£25.00
	C		Dogs (1924) — Scenic backgrounds:			
A		50	A Small size		£1.00	£50.00
J		12	B Extra-large size		£3.25	£40.00

Size	Print-ing	Number in set			Handbook reference	Price per card	Complete set

JOHN PLAYER & SONS, Nottingham *(continued)*

Size	Print-ing	Number in set	Description		Handbook reference	Price per card	Complete set
	C		Dogs — Heads:				
A		50	A Small size — Home issue (1929)			£1.00	£50.00
A		25	B Small size — Irish issue, 'A Series of 25' (1927)			£2.00	£50.00
A		25	C Small size — Irish issue, '2nd Series of 25' (1929)			£2.00	£50.00
B		20	D Large size — Home issue, 'A Series of 20' (1926)			£2.75	£55.00
B		20	E Large size — Home issue, '2nd Series of 20' (1928)			£2.75	£55.00
	C		Dogs — Full length:		H.668		
A		50	A Small size (1931):				
				1 Cards		90p	£45.00
				2 Transfers		50p	£25.00
B		25	B Large size (1933)			£2.60	£65.00
A	C	50	Dogs' Heads (silver-grey backgrounds) (1940)			£3.00	—
A	C	50	Drum Banners and Cap Badges (1924):				
			A Base panel joining vertical framelines			90p	£45.00
			B Fractional space between the above			80p	£40.00
B	BW	25	Fables of Aesop (1927)			£2.40	£60.00
B	C	25	Famous Beauties (1937)			£1.80	£45.00
A	C	50	Famous Irish-Bred Horses (1936)			£3.50	£175.00
A	C	50	Famous Irish Greyhounds (1935)			£5.50	—
A	C	50	Film Stars — 'Series of 50' (1934)			£1.20	£60.00
A	C	50	Film Stars — 'Second Series …':				
			A Home issue — Album 'price one penny' (1934)			90p	£45.00
			B Irish issue — Album offer without price (1935)			£1.60	£80.00
A	C	50	Film Stars:				
			A Home issue — titled 'Film Stars — Third Series …' (1938)			80p	£40.00
			B Irish issue — titled 'Screen Celebrities' (1939)			£2.00	—
B	BW	25	Film Stars — Large size (1934):				
			A Home issue — with album offer			£3.00	£75.00
			B Irish issue — without album offer			£6.00	—
A	C	50	Fire-Fighting Appliances (1930)			£1.60	£80.00
A	C	50	Flags of the League of Nations (1928)			50p	£25.00
A	C	50	Football Caricatures by 'Mac' (1927)			£1.30	£65.00
A	C	50	Football Caricatures by 'Rip' (1926)			£1.30	£65.00
A	C	50	Footballers, 1928 (1928)			£1.80	£90.00
A	C	25	Footballers, 1928-9 — '2nd Series' (1929)			£1.80	£45.00
	C		Fresh-Water Fishes:				
A		50	A Small size, Home issue:				
				1 Pink card (1933)		£1.40	£70.00
				2 White card (1934)		£1.60	£80.00
B		25	B Large size, Home issue — adhesive (1935)			£2.60	£65.00
B		25	C Large size, Irish issue — non-adhesive (1935)			£5.00	£125.00
A	C	25	From Plantation to Smoker (1926)			32p	£8.00
	C		Game Birds and Wild Fowl:				
A		50	A Small size (1927)			£1.50	£75.00
B		25	B Large size (1928)			£5.00	£125.00
	C		Gilbert and Sullivan — 'A Series of …':				
A		50	A Small size (1925)			£1.10	£55.00
J		25	B Extra-large size (1926)			£3.40	£85.00
	C		Gilbert and Sullivan — '2nd Series of …':				
A		50	A Small size (1927)			£1.10	£55.00
B		25	B Large size (1928)			£3.60	£90.00
B	C	25	Golf (1939)			£7.50	£190.00

Size	Printing	Number in set		Handbook reference	Price per card	Complete set

JOHN PLAYER & SONS, Nottingham *(continued)*

Size	Printing	Number in set	Description	Handbook reference	Price per card	Complete set
A	C	25	Hidden Beauties (1929)		30p	£7.50
A	C	50	Hints on Association Football (1934)	H.669	90p	£45.00
	C		History of Naval Dress:			
A		50	A Small size (1930)		£1.20	£60.00
B		25	B Large size (1929)		£2.00	£50.00
A	C	50	International Air Liners:			
			A Home issue — Album 'price one penny' (1936)		50p	£25.00
			B Irish issue — Album offer without price (1937)		£1.00	£50.00
A	C	25	Irish Place Names — 'A Series of 25' (1927)		£2.40	£60.00
A	C	25	Irish Place Names — '2nd Series of 25' (1929)		£2.40	£60.00
	C	50	Kings and Queens of England (1935):	H.670		
A			A Small size		£1.50	£75.00
B			B Large size		£2.60	£130.00
A	C	25	Live Stock (1925)		£3.60	£90.00
A	C	50	Military Head-Dress (1931)		£1.10	£55.00
A	C	50	Military Uniforms of the British Empire Overseas (1938)		80p	£40.00
A	C	50	Modern Naval Craft (1939):			
			A Home issue — adhesive		50p	£25.00
			B Irish issue — non-adhesive		£1.00	—
A	C	50	Motor Cars — 'A Series of 50' (1936):			
			A Home issue — Album 'price one penny'		£1.40	£70.00
			B Irish issue — Album offer without price		£2.20	—
A	C	50	Motor Cars — 'Second Series ...' (1937)		£1.00	£50.00
B	U	20	Mount Everest (1925)		£4.00	£80.00
A	C	50	National Flags and Arms:			
			A Home issue — Album 'price one penny' (1936)		40p	£20.00
			B Irish issue — Album offer without price (1937) .		£1.00	£50.00
B	C	25	The Nation's Shrines (1929)		£2.00	£50.00
	C		Natural History:			
A		50	A Small size (1924)		32p	£16.00
J		12	B Extra-large size — 'A Series of 12' (1923)		£1.25	£15.00
J		12	C Extra-large size — '2nd Series of 12' (1924) ...		£1.25	£15.00
B	C	24	A Nature Calendar (1930)		£4.00	£100.00
B	C	25	'Old Hunting Prints' (1938)		£2.60	£65.00
B	C	25	Old Naval Prints (1936)		£2.40	£60.00
J	BW	25	Old Sporting Prints (1924)		£4.40	£110.00
B	C	25	Picturesque Bridges (1929)		£2.80	£70.00
B	C	25	Picturesque Cottages (1929)		£3.40	£85.00
B	C	25	Picturesque London (1931)		£4.40	£110.00
B	C	25	Portals of the Past (1930)		£2.20	£55.00
A	C	50	Poultry (1931):	H.671		
			A Cards		£1.80	£90.00
			B Transfers		50p	£25.00
A	C	50	Products of the World — Scenes only (1928)		30p	£15.00
A	C	25	Racehorses (1926)		£5.00	£125.00
A	U	40	Racing Caricatures (1925)		80p	£32.00
B	C	25	Racing Yachts (1938)		£3.80	£95.00
A	C	50	RAF Badges (1937):			
			A Without motto		60p	£30.00
			B With motto		60p	£30.00
A	C	50	Regimental Standards and Cap Badges (1930)		80p	£40.00
—	C	1	The Royal Family (55 × 66mm) (1937)		—	£2.50
			Screen Celebrities — see Film Stars			
A	C	50	Sea Fishes:			
			A Home issue — Album 'price one penny' (1935)		40p	£20.00
			B Irish issue — Album offer without price (1937) .		£1.00	—

Size	Print-ing	Number in set		Handbook reference	Price per card	Complete set

JOHN PLAYER & SONS, Nottingham *(continued)*

Size	Print.	No.	Title	Ref	Price	Set
A	C	50	A Sectional Map of Ireland (1937)		£2.50	—
A	U	1	A Sectional Map of Ireland Joker (1937)		—	£15.00
B	C	20	Ship-Models (1926)		£2.50	£50.00
B	C	25	Ships' Figure-Heads (1931)		£1.80	£45.00
A	C	50	Speedway Riders (1937)		£1.80	£90.00
A	C	50	Straight Line Caricatures (1926)		60p	£30.00
A	C	25	Struggle for Existence (1923)		32p	£8.00
A	C	50	Tennis (1936)	H.524	90p	£45.00
B	C	25	Treasures of Britain (1931)		£1.60	£40.00
A	C	25	Treasures of Ireland (1930)		£2.00	£50.00
B	C	25	Types of Horses (1939)		£3.80	£95.00
A	C	50	Uniforms of the Territorial Army (Oct. 1939)		90p	£45.00
A	C	90	War Decorations and Medals (1927)		80p	£70.00
	C		Wild Animals:	H.673		
A		50	A Small size — 'Wild Animals' Heads' (1931)		70p	£35.00
A		25	B Small transfers, number in series not stated (1931)		£1.50	—
A		50	C Small transfers — 'A Series of 50' (1931)		50p	£25.00
B		25	D Large size — 'Wild Animals — A Series of ...' (1927)		£1.80	£45.00
B		25	E Large size — 'Wild Animals — 2nd Series ...' (1932)		£1.80	£45.00
	C		Wild Birds:			
A		50	A Small size (1932):			
			1 Cards		50p	£25.00
			2 Transfers		40p	£20.00
B		25	B Large size (1934)		£2.80	£70.00
B	C	25	Wild Fowl (1937)		£3.20	£80.00
A	C	25	Wonders of the World (grey back) (1926)	H.362	£1.40	£35.00
A	C	25	Wrestling and Ju-Jitsu (grey back) (1925)	H.467	£1.60	£40.00
A	C	26	Your Initials (transfers) (1932)		70p	£18.00
B	C	25	Zoo Babies (1938)		60p	£15.00

C POST-1940 ISSUES

Size	Print.	No.	Title	Price	Set
G	C	30	African Wildlife (1990)	50p	£15.00
—	BW	9	Basket Ball Fixtures (114 × 71mm) (1972)	£6.00	—
G	C	32	Britain's Endangered Wildlife:		
			A Grandee Issue (1984)	25p	£8.00
			B Doncella Issue (1984)	30p	£9.00
H2	C	30	Britain's Maritime History (1989)	40p	£12.00
G	C	30	Britain's Nocturnal Wildlife:		
			A Grandee Issue (1987)	27p	£8.00
			B Doncella Issue (1987)	£1.00	£30.00
G	C	30	Britain's Wayside Wildlife (1988)	30p	£9.00
G	C	30	Britain's Wild Flowers:		
			A Grandee Issue (1986)	25p	£7.50
			B Doncella Issue (1986)	60p	£18.00
G	C	32	British Birds (1980)	50p	£16.00
G	C	32	British Butterflies:		
			A Grandee Issue (1983)	40p	£13.00
			B Doncella Issue (1984)	60p	£19.00
G	C	30	British Mammals:		
			A Grandee Issue (1982):		
			1 Imperial Tobacco Ltd	27p	£8.00
			2 Imperial Group PLC	33p	£10.00
			B Doncella Issue (1983)	50p	£15.00
G	C	32	Country Houses and Castles (1981)	25p	£8.00

Size	Print-ing	Number in set		Handbook reference	Price per card	Complete set

JOHN PLAYER & SONS, Nottingham *(continued)*

Size	Print	Num	Title	Ref	Price	Set
—	U	116	Corsair Game (63 × 38mm) (1965)	H.897	£1.00	—
H2	C	32	Exploration of Space (1983)		20p	£6.50
G	C	28	Famous MG Marques (1981)		90p	£25.00
G	C	24	The Golden Age of Flying (1977)	H.898	25p	£6.00
G	C	1	The Golden Age of Flying Completion Offer (1977)	H.898	—	£3.50
G	C	24	The Golden Age of Motoring (1975):	H.899		
			A With set completion offer		£3.50	—
			B Without set completion offer		27p	£6.50
G	C	24	The Golden Age of Sail (1978)		25p	£6.00
G	C	1	The Golden Age of Sail Completion Offer (1978)		—	£3.50
G	C	24	The Golden Age of Steam (1976)	H.900	27p	£6.50
G	C	1	The Golden Age of Steam Completion Offer (1976)	H.900	—	£3.50
G	U	7	Grandee Limericks (1977)		£10.00	—
H2	C	30	History of Britain's Railways (1987)		60p	£18.00
H2	C	30	History of British Aviation (1988)		80p	£24.00
H2	C	30	History of Motor Racing (1986):			
			A Imperial Tobacco Ltd		90p	£27.00
			B Imperial Group PLC		£1.20	£36.00
G	C	24	History of the VC (1980)		£1.00	£24.00
G	C	1	History of the VC completion offer (1980)		—	£5.00
—	BW	5	Jubilee Issue (70 × 55mm) (1960)	H.901	£1.50	£7.50
G	C	30	The Living Ocean:			
			A Grandee Issue (1985)		25p	£7.50
			B Doncella Issue (1985)		40p	£12.00
H2	C	32	Myths and Legends (1982)		£1.00	£32.00
G	C	24	Napoleonic Uniforms (1979)		25p	£6.00
G	C	1	Napoleonic Uniforms Completion Offer (1979)		—	£4.00
G	C	7	Panama Puzzles (1975)		£6.00	—
G	BW	6	Play Ladbroke Spot-Ball (1975)		£6.00	—
—	U	4	Tom Thumb Record Breakers (82 × 65mm) (1976)	H.909	£6.00	—
G	C	25	Top Dogs (1979)		£1.20	£30.00
H2	C	32	Wonders of the Ancient World (1984)		40p	£12.50
H2	C	30	Wonders of the Modern World (1985)		30p	£9.00
G	C	6	World of Gardening (1976)		£10.00	—

D UNISSUED SERIES

Size	Print	Num	Title	Price	Set
A	C	25	Birds and Their Young, 1st series (1955)	24p	£6.00
A	C	25	Birds and Their Young, 2nd series (1955)	20p	£4.00
A	C	25	Cries of London, '2nd Series ...' (black back) (1916)	£5.00	—
A	C	50	Decorations and Medals (c1940)	£2.00	£100.00
A	C	50	Dogs' Heads by Biegel (c1955)	90p	£45.00
B	C	25	Dogs — Pairs and Groups (c1955)	£1.40	£35.00
A	C	50	Shipping (c1960)	£1.50	£75.00

E MISCELLANEOUS

Size	Print	Num	Title	Ref	Price	Set
B	BW	1	Advertisement Card — Wants List (1936)		—	£1.00
A	C	1	Card Scheme — Joker Card (c1935)		—	£5.00
—	C	?	Football Fixture Folders (1946-61)		£12.00	—
—	C	8	Snap Cards (93 × 65mm) (c1930)	H.672	£7.00	—

JAS. PLAYFAIR & CO., London

PRE-1919 ISSUE

Size	Print	Num	Title	Ref	Price	Set
A	C	25	How to Keep Fit — Sandow Exercises (c1912)	H.136	£32.00	—

THE PREMIER TOBACCO MANUFACTURERS LTD, London

POST-1920 ISSUES

Size	Print	Num	Title	Ref	Price	Set
D	U	48	Eminent Stage and Screen Personalities (1936)	H.569	£1.80	—
K2	C	52	*Miniature Playing Cards (c1935)		£7.50	—

Size	Print-ing	Number in set		Handbook reference	Price per card	Complete set

THE PREMIER TOBACCO MANUFACTURERS LTD, London *(continued)*

	BW		Stage and Screen Personalities (57 × 35mm) (1937):	H.674		
		100	A Back in grey		£1.50	—
		50	B Back in brown (Nos. 51-100)		£2.20	—

PRITCHARD & BURTON LTD, London

PRE-1919 ISSUES

A2	C	51	*Actors and Actresses — 'FROGA B and C' (c1900):	H.20		
			A Blue back		£22.00	—
			B Grey-black back		£70.00	—
A	C	15	*Beauties 'PAC' (c1900)	H.2	£55.00	—
D	BW	20	*Boer War Cartoons (1900)	H.42	£100.00	—
A1	C		*Flags and Flags with Soldiers (c1902):	H.41		
			A Flagstaff Draped:			
		30	1st printing		£16.00	£480.00
		15	2nd printing		£20.00	—
		15	B Flagstaff not Draped (Flags only)		£20.00	—
D	U	25	*Holiday Resorts and Views (c1902)	H.366	£18.00	—
A	C	40	*Home Colonial Regiments (c1901)	H.69	£50.00	—
D	U	25	*Royalty series (1902)	H.367	£20.00	—
D	U	25	*South African Series (1901)	H.368	£20.00	—
A2	C	25	*Star Girls (c1900)	H.30	£175.00	—

G. PRUDHOE, Darlington

PRE-1919 ISSUES

C	C	30	*Army Pictures, Cartoons, etc (c1916)	H.12	£110.00	—

JAMES QUINTON LTD, London

PRE-1919 ISSUE

A	C	26	*Actresses — 'FROGA A' (c1900)	H.20	£175.00	—

RAY & CO. LTD, London

PRE-1919 ISSUES

—	C		*Flags of The Allies (Shaped) (c1915):	H.49		
		1	A Grouped Flag 'All Arms' Cigarettes		£80.00	—
		5	B Allies Flags 'Life Ray' Cigarettes		£80.00	—
A	BW	25	War Series — 1-25 — Battleships (c1915)	H.472	£13.00	—
A	C	75	War Series — 26-100 — British and Foreign Uniforms (c1915)	H.472	£10.00	—
A	C	24	War Series — 101-124 — British and Dominion Uniforms (c1915)	H.472	£23.00	—

RAYMOND REVUEBAR, London

POST-1940 ISSUE

—	P	25	Revuebar Striptease Artists (72 × 46mm) (1960)		£16.00	—

RECORD CIGARETTE & TOBACCO CO., London

POST-1920 ISSUE

—	U	? 2	Gramophone Records (100mm Diameter) (c1935)	H.675	£100.00	—
—	U	? 34	The 'Talkie' Cigarette Card — (gramophone record on reverse) (70mm square) (c1935):			
			A Back 'Record Tobacco Company'		£45.00	—
			B Back 'Record Cigarette Company'		£45.00	—

Size	Print-ing	Number in set		Handbook reference	Price per card	Complete set

J. REDFORD & CO., London

PRE-1919 ISSUES

Size	Print	Num	Description	Ref	Price	Set
A	BW	20	*Actresses — 'BLARM' (c1900)	H.23	£70.00	—
A2	C	25	*Armies of the World (c1901)	H.43	£55.00	—
A2	C	25	*Beauties — 'GRACC' (c1899)	H.59	£120.00	—
A2	C	30	*Colonial Troops (c1902)	H.40	£50.00	—
D	C	24	*Nautical Expressions (c1900)	H.174	£80.00	—
D2	C	40	*Naval and Military Phrases (c1904)	H.14	£60.00	—
A	C	25	Picture Series (c1905)	H.369	£65.00	—
A	C	25	Sports and Pastimes Series 1 (c1905)	H.225	£75.00	—
D1	BW	50	Stage Artistes of the Day (c1908)	H.370	£18.00	£900.00

RELIANCE TOBACCO MFG. CO. LTD

POST-1920 ISSUES

Size	Print	Num	Description	Ref	Price	Set
A2	C	24	British Birds (c1935)	H.604	£5.00	—
A2	C	35	*Famous Stars* (c1935)	H.572	£5.00	—

RICHARDS & WARD

PRE-1919 ISSUE

Size	Print	Num	Description	Ref	Price	Set
A1	P	? 11	*Beauties — 'Topsy Cigarettes' (c1900)	H.371	£600.00	—

A. S. RICHARDSON, Luton

POST-1920 ISSUE

Size	Print	Num	Description	Ref	Price	Set
—	U	12	*Manikin Cards (82 × 51mm) (c1920)	H.481	£100.00	—

THE RICHMOND CAVENDISH CO. LTD, London

PRE-1919 ISSUES

Size	Print	Num	Description	Ref	Price	Set
A2	C	26	*Actresses — 'FROGA A' (c1900)	H.20	£30.00	—
D2	BW	28	*Actresses — 'PILPI I' (c1902)	H.195	£14.00	—
D	P	50	*Actresses 'PILPI II' (c1902)	H.196	£10.00	—
A	U		*Actresses Photogravure, 'Smoke Pioneer Cigarettes' back (c1905):	H.372		
		50	I Reading bottom to top		£7.00	£350.00
		? 179	IIA Reading top to bottom. Different subjects		£6.50	—
		? 13	B Plain back		£10.00	—
A	C	14	*Beauties 'AMBS' (1899):	H.373		
			A Verses 'The Absent-minded Beggar' back (4 verses and 4 choruses)		£45.00	
			B Verses 'Soldiers of the Queen' back (3 verses and 1 chorus)		£45.00	
A	C	52	*Beauties — 'ROBRI' playing card inset (c1898)	H.374	£45.00	—
—	C	40	*Medals (34 × 72mm) (c1900)	H.200	£18.00	£720.00
A2	C	20	Music Hall Artistes (c1902)	H.202	£45.00	—
A	C	12	*Pretty Girl Series — 'RASH' (c1900)	H.8	£40.00	—
A	C	20	*Yachts (c1900):	H.204		
			A Gold on black back		£65.00	
			B Black on white back		£65.00	

RIDGWAYS, Manchester

PRE-1919 ISSUE

Size	Print	Num	Description	Ref	Price	Set
—	C	? 2	*Play Up' Sporting Shields (c1895)	H.718	£150.00	—

Size	Print-ing	Number in set		Handbook reference	Price per card	Complete set

R. ROBERTS & SONS, London

PRE-1919 ISSUES

Size	Print	Num	Description	Ref	Price	Set
A2	C	26	*Actresses — 'FROGA A' (c1900)	H.20	£70.00	—
A	C	25	*Armies of the World (c1900):	H.43		
			A 'Fine Old Virginia' back		£50.00	—
			B Plain back		£50.00	—
A2	C	50	*Beauties — 'CHOAB' (c1900):	H.21		
			1-25 without borders to back		£70.00	—
			26-50 with borders to back		£85.00	—
—	C	50	*Beautiful Women (60 × 43mm) (c1900)	H.284	£225.00	—
A2	C	50	*Colonial Troops (c1902)	H.40	£40.00	—
A	BW	28	*Dominoes (c1905)		£80.00	—
K1	C	52	*Miniature Playing Cards (c1905)	H.334	£65.00	—
D2	C	24	*Nautical Expressions (c1900):	H.174		
			A 'Navy Cut Cigarettes' on front		£60.00	—
			B Firm's name only on front		£60.00	—
A2	C	70	Stories without words (c1905)		£60.00	—
A2	C	25	*Types of British and Colonial Troops (c1900)	H.76	£50.00	—

ROBINSON & BARNSDALE LTD, London

PRE-1919 ISSUES

Size	Print	Num	Description	Ref	Price	Set
—	C	1	*Advertisement Card — Soldier, 'Colin Campbell Cigars' (29 × 75mm) (c1897)	H.764	—	£120.00
—	BW	?24	*Actresses, 'Colin Campbell Cigars' (c1898):	H.375		
			A Size 43 × 70mm		£140.00	—
			B Officially cut narrow — 32 × 70mm		£140.00	—
A	P	?29	*Actresses, 'Cupola' Cigarettes (c1898)	H.376	£225.00	—
A1	P		*Beauties — collotype (c1895):	H.377		
		?9	A 'Our Golden Beauties' back in black		£250.00	—
		?17	B 'Nana' back in red on white		£250.00	—
		?1	C 'Nana' back in vermillion on cream		£250.00	—
A	C	?1	*Beauties — 'Blush of Day' (c1898)	H.378	£250.00	—
—	C	?15	*Beauties — 'Highest Honors' (44 × 73mm) (c1895)	H.379	£350.00	—
A2	U	?3	Beauties 'KEWA II' (c1895)	H.139	£250.00	—

E. ROBINSON & SONS LTD, Stockport

A PRE-1919 ISSUES

Size	Print	Num	Description	Ref	Price	Set
A1	C	10	*Beauties 'ROBRI' (c1900)	H.374	£60.00	—
A	BW	?43	Derbyshire and the Peak (c1905)	H.380	£200.00	—
A2	C	25	Egyptian Studies (c1914)		£25.00	—
A	C	6	Medals and Decorations of Great Britain (c1905)	H.484	£225.00	—
A2	C	40	Nature Studies (c1912)		£22.00	—
A2	C	25	Regimental Mascots (1916)		£70.00	—
A	C	25	Types of British Soldiers (1900)	H.144	£350.00	—
A2	C	25	Wild Flowers (c1915)		£20.00	£500.00

B POST-1920 ISSUE

Size	Print	Num	Description	Ref	Price	Set
A	C	25	King Lud Problems (c1934)	H.638	£20.00	—

ROMAN STAR CIGARS

PRE-1919 ISSUES

Size	Print	Num	Description	Ref	Price	Set
C	C	26	*Actresses 'FROGA A' (c1900)	H.20	£150.00	—
A	C	25	*Beauties 'BOCCA' (c1900)	H.39	£150.00	—

Size	Print-ing	Number in set		Handbook reference	Price per card	Complete set

ROTHMAN'S LTD, London

A POST-1920 ISSUES

	C		Beauties of the Cinema (1936):	H.605		
D1		40	A Small size		£1.60	£65.00
—		24	B Circular cards, 64mm diam:			
			1 Varnished		£4.00	£100.00
			2 Unvarnished		£4.00	£100.00
A2	P	24	Cinema Stars — Small size (c1925)		£1.60	£40.00
B	P	25	Cinema Stars — Large size (c1925)		£1.00	£25.00
C	U	36	Landmarks in Empire History (c1936)		£1.25	£45.00
D1	U	50	Modern Inventions (1935)		£1.10	£55.00
B2	P	54	New Zealand (c1930)		£1.00	£55.00
D1	U	24	Prominent Screen Favourites (1934)	H.568	£1.00	£25.00
A2	BW	50	'Punch Jokes' (c1935)		55p	£27.50

B POST-1940 ISSUES

—	C	30	Country Living (Consulate) (112 × 102mm) (1973) ...		—	£15.00
A1	C	5	Rare Banknotes (1970)		£4.00	—

C MISCELLANEOUS

—	C	6	Diamond Jubilee Folders (127 × 95mm) (1950)		£12.00	—
C2	C	50	International Football Stars (unissued) (1984)	H.912	—	£20.00
		?	Metal Charms (c1930)		£4.00	—

WM. RUDDELL LTD, Dublin and Liverpool

POST-1920 ISSUES

K	U	? 3	*Couplet Cards (c1925)	H.676	£30.00	—
D	C	25	Grand Opera Series (1924)		£7.40	£185.00
A2	C	25	Rod and Gun (1924)		£7.00	£175.00
D	C	50	Songs that will Live for Ever (c1925)		£4.00	£200.00

RUTHERFORD

PRE-1919 ISSUE

A	BW	? 1	Footballers (c1900)	H.765	£1800.00	—

I. RUTTER & CO., Mitcham

PRE-1919 ISSUES

D	BW	15	*Actresses — 'RUTAN' (c1900):	H.381		
			A Rubber-stamped on plain back		£80.00	—
			B Red printed back		£55.00	—
			C *Plain back*		£35.00	—
A	BW	1	Advertisement Card 'Tobacco Bloom' (1899)	H.485	—	£900.00
A	BW	7	*Boer War Celebrities (c1901)	H.382	£50.00	—
D1	C	54	*Comic Phrases (c1905)	H.223	£18.00	—
A	BW	20	Cricketers Series (1901)	H.29	£300.00	—
C	C		*Flags and Flags with Soldiers (c1902):	H.41		
		15	A Flagstaff Draped, 2nd printing		£24.00	—
		15	B Flagstaff not Draped (Flags only)			
			(a) white back		£24.00	—
			(b) cream back		£24.00	—
C	C	24	*Girls, Flags and Arms of Countries (c1900):	H.383		
			A Blue back		£35.00	—
			B *Plain back*		£25.00	—
A	C	25	Proverbs (c1905):	H.384		
			A Green Seal on front		£45.00	—
			B Red Seal on front		£45.00	—
A	C	25	*Shadowgraphs (c1905)	H.44	£40.00	—

Size	Print-ing	Number in set		Handbook reference	Price per card	Complete set

S.D.V. TOBACCO CO. LTD, Liverpool

PRE-1919 ISSUES

| A | BW | 16 | British Royal Family (c1901) | H.28 | £600.00 | — |

ST. PETERSBURG CIGARETTE CO. LTD, Portsmouth

PRE-1919 ISSUES

| A | BW | ? 11 | Footballers (c1900) | H.410 | £1000.00 | — |

SALMON & GLUCKSTEIN LTD, London

A PRE-1919 ISSUES

—	C	1	*Advertisement Card ('Snake Charmer' Cigarettes) (73 × 107mm) (c1897)	H.767	—	£450.00
C	C	15	*Billiard Terms (c1905):			
			A Small numerals		£70.00	—
			B Larger numerals		£70.00	—
A	C	12	British Queens (c1897)	H.480	£45.00	—
—	C	30	*Castles, Abbeys and Houses (76 × 73mm) (c1906):			
			A Brown back		£17.00	—
			B Red back		£24.00	—
C	C	32	*Characters from Dickens (c1903)	H.385	£28.00	—
A	C	25	Coronation Series (1911)		£12.00	£300.00
—	U	25	*Famous Pictures — Brown photogravure (57 × 76mm) (c1910)	H.386	£10.00	£250.00
—	U	25	*Famous Pictures — Green photogravure (58 × 76mm) (c1910)	H.387	£8.00	£200.00
A2	C	6	Her Most Gracious Majesty Queen Victoria (1897):	H.388		
			A Thin card		£50.00	£300.00
			B Thick card		£50.00	£300.00
A	C	50	The Great White City (c1908)		£12.00	£600.00
C	C	40	Heroes of the Transvaal War (1901)	H.389	£15.00	£600.00
C	C	30	*Music Hall Celebrities (c1902)		£50.00	—
—	C	25	*Occupations (64 × 18mm) (c1898)	H.390	£500.00	—
C	C	20	'Owners and Jockeys' Series (c1900)	H.392	£80.00	—
—	C	48	*The Post in Various Countries (41 × 66mm) (c1900)	H.391	£25.00	—
A2	C	6	*Pretty Girl Series — 'RASH' (c1900)	H.8	£65.00	—
—	C	22	Shakespearian Series (c1902):	H.393		
			A Large format, frame line back (38 × 69mm)		£32.00	—
			B Re-drawn, small format, no frame line back (37 × 66mm)		£32.00	—
A	C	25	*Star Girls (c1900):	H.30		
			A Red back		£120.00	—
			B Brown back, different setting		£120.00	—
A	C	25	Traditions of the Army and Navy (c1917):			
			A Large numerals		£14.00	£350.00
			B Smaller numerals, back redrawn		£14.00	£350.00

B POST-1920 ISSUES

| D2 | C | 25 | Magical Series (1923) | | £7.00 | £175.00 |
| A2 | C | 25 | Wireless Explained (1923) | | £6.00 | £150.00 |

C SILKS

—	C	50	*Pottery Types (paper-backed) (83 × 55mm) (c1915):	H.505-17		
			A Numbered on front and back		£4.00	—
			B Numbered on back only		£4.00	—

Size	Print-ing	Number in set		Handbook reference	Price per card	Complete set

W. SANDORIDES & CO. LTD, London

POST-1920 ISSUES

	U	25	Aquarium Studies from the London Zoo (1925):	H.607		
C2			A Small size:			
			1 Small lettering on back		£3.60	£90.00
			2 Larger lettering on back		£3.60	£90.00
B1			B Large size		£3.60	£90.00
	C	25	Cinema Celebrities (1924):	H.530		
C2			A Small size		£2.60	£65.00
—			B Extra-large size (109 × 67mm)		£4.00	£100.00
	C	25	Cinema Stars (export) (c1924):	H.530		
C2			A Small size, with firm's name at base of back ...		£6.00	—
C2			B Small size, 'Issued with Lucana Cigarettes		£6.00	—
C2			C Small size, 'Issued with Big Gun Cigarettes ...'		£8.00	—
—			D Extra-large size (109 × 67mm) 'Issued with Big Gun Cigarettes		£2.60	£65.00
—			E Extra-large size (109 × 67mm) issued with Lucana 66		£7.50	—
	U	50	Famous Racecourses (1926) — 'Lucana':	H.608		
C2			A Small size		£4.00	£200.00
B1			B Large size		£4.50	£225.00
C2	U	50	Famous Racehorses (1923):	H.609		
			1A Back in light brown		£3.00	£150.00
			1B Back in dark brown		£3.00	£150.00
			2 As 1A, with blue label added, inscribed 'Issued with Sandorides Big Gun Cigarettes ...'		£12.00	—
A	C	25	Sports & Pastimes — Series 1 — 'Big Gun Cigarettes (c1924)	H.225	£12.00	

SANSOM'S CIGAR STORES, London

PRE-1919 ISSUE

—	P	? 2	*London Views (52 × 37mm) (c1915)	H.768	£400.00	—

NICHOLAS SARONY & CO., London

A PRE-1919 ISSUE

—	U	? 2	Boer War Scenes (67 × 45mm) (c1901)	H.394	£600.00	—

B POST-1920 ISSUES

	C	50	Around the Mediterranean (1926):	Ha.610		
C2			A Small size		£1.00	£50.00
B1			B Large size		£1.00	£50.00
	U	25	Celebrities and Their Autographs, Nd 1-25 (1923):			
C1			A Small size		80p	£20.00
B1			B Large size		80p	£20.00
	U	25	Celebrities and Their Autographs, Nd 26-50 (1924):			
C1			A Small size:			
			1 Small numerals		80p	£20.00
			2 Large numerals		80p	£20.00
B1			B Large size:			
			1 Small numerals		80p	£20.00
			2 Large numerals		80p	£20.00
	U	25	Celebrities and Their Autographs. Nd 51-75 (1924):			
C1			A Small size		80p	£20.00
B1			B Large size		80p	£20.00

Size	Print-ing	Number in set			Handbook reference	Price per card	Complete set

NICHOLAS SARONY & CO., London *(continued)*

Size	Print-ing	Number in set	Title		Handbook reference	Price per card	Complete set
	U	25	Celebrities and Their Autographs, Nd 76-100 (1925):				
C1			A Small size			80p	£20.00
B1			B Large size			80p	£20.00
A2	U	50	Cinema Stars — Set 7 (1933)		Ha.515-7	£1.20	£60.00
—	U		Cinema Stars — Postcard size (137 × 85mm):				
		38	'of a Series of 38 Cinema Stars' (1929)			£9.00	—
		42	'of a second Series of 42 Cinema Stars' (c1930)			£5.00	£210.00
		50	'of a third Series of 50 Cinema Stars' (c1930)			£5.00	£250.00
		42	'of a fourth Series of 42 Cinema Stars' (c1931)			£5.00	£210.00
		25	'of a fifth Series of 25 Cinema Stars' (c1931)			£5.00	£125.00
D	U	25	Cinema Studies (1929)			£1.10	£27.50
	C	25	A Day on the Airway (1928):				
C2			A Small size			£1.20	£30.00
B2			B Large size			£1.20	£30.00
A2	P	54	Life at Whipsnade Zoo (1934)		Ha.556	55p	£30.00
	BW	25	Links with the Past — First 25 subjects, Nd 1-25 (1925):				
C1			A Small size			36p	£9.00
B			B Large size			50p	—
	BW	25	Links with the Past — Second 25 subjects (1926):				
C			A Home issue, Nd 26-50:				
B				1 Small size		30p	£7.50
B				2 Large size, descriptive back		30p	£7.50
				3 Large size, advertisement back		£1.80	—
			B Sydney issue, Nd 1-25:				
C				1 Small size		£1.00	£25.00
B				2 Large size		£1.00	£25.00
			C Christchurch issue, Nd 1-25:				
C				1 Small size		80p	£20.00
B				2 Large size		40p	£10.00
	BW	25	Museum Series (1927):				
			A Home issue:				
C2				1 Small size		30p	£7.50
B				2 Large size, descriptive back		30p	£7.50
B				3 Large size, advertisement back		£1.00	£25.00
B			B Sydney issue, large size			70p	£17.50
			C Christchurch issue:				
C2				1 Small size		60p	£15.00
B				2 Large size		70p	£17.50
	P	36	National Types of Beauty (1928):		Ha.558		
A2			A Small size			40p	£14.00
—			B Medium size (76 × 51mm)			40p	£14.00
	C	15	Origin of Games (1923):				
A			A Small size			£4.60	£70.00
B2			B Large size			£5.00	£75.00
	C	50	'Saronicks' (1929):		Ha.557		
D2			A Small size			40p	£20.00
—			B Medium size (76 × 51 mm)			40p	£20.00
	C	50	Ships of All Ages (1929):				
D			A Small size			80p	£40.00
—			B Medium size (76 × 52mm)			£1.00	£50.00
D	C	25	Tennis Strokes (1923)			£3.40	£85.00

T. S. SAUNT, Leicester

PRE-1919 ISSUE

Size	Print-ing	Number in set	Title	Handbook reference	Price per card	Complete set
D	C	30	*Army Pictures, Cartoons etc (c1916)	H.12	£110.00	—

Size	Print-ing	Number in set		Handbook reference	Price per card	Complete set

SCOTTISH CO-OPERATIVE WHOLESALE SOCIETY LTD, Glasgow ('S.C.W.S.')

POST-1920 ISSUES

A2	C	25	Burns (1924):	H.611		
			A Printed back:			
			1 White card		£2.60	—
			2 Cream card		£1.60	£40.00
			*B Plain back		£7.00	—
C	C	20	Dogs (1925)	H.211	£10.00	—
A2	C	25	Dwellings of All Nations (1924):	H.612		
			A Printed back:			
			1 White card		£3.50	—
			2 Cream card		£2.20	£55.00
			*B Plain back		£7.00	—
B	C	25	Famous Pictures (1924)		£7.50	—
H2	C	25	Famous Pictures — Glasgow Gallery (1927):			
			A Non-adhesive back		£2.20	£55.00
			B Adhesive back		£1.40	£35.00
H2	C	25	Famous Pictures — London Galleries (1927):			
			A Non-adhesive back		£2.20	£55.00
			B Adhesive back		£1.40	£35.00
A2	C	50	Feathered Favourites (1926):			
			A Grey borders		£2.40	£120.00
			B White borders:			
			1 Non-adhesive back		£2.40	£120.00
			2 Adhesive back		£1.80	£90.00
A	C	25	Racial Types (1925)		£8.00	£200.00
A2	C	50	Triumphs of Engineering (1926):			
			A Brown border		£2.20	£110.00
			B White border		£2.50	—
A2	C	50	Wireless (1924)		£4.00	£200.00

SELBY'S TOBACCO STORES, Cirencester

POST-1920 ISSUE

—	U	12	'Manikin' Cards (79 × 51mm) (c1920)	H.481	£100.00	—

SHARPE & SNOWDEN, London

PRE-1919 ISSUES

A	U	? 1	*Views of England (c1905)	H.769	£500.00	—
A	U	? 23	*Views of London (c1905)	H.395	£250.00	—

W.J. SHEPHERD, London

PRE-1919 ISSUES

A	U	25	*Beauties — 'FECKSA' (c1900)	H.58	£100.00	—

SHORT'S, London

POST-1920 ISSUE

—	BW		*Short's House Views (c1925):	H.562		
		? 13	1 Numbered (75 × 60mm)		£60.00	—
		? 6	2 Unnumbered (77 × 69mm)		£40.00	—

Size	Print-ing	Number in set		Handbook reference	Price per card	Complete set

JOHN SINCLAIR LTD, Newcastle-on-Tyne

A PRE-1919 ISSUES

Size	Print	Number	Description	Handbook	Price	Set
D2	U	? 89	*Actresses (42 × 63 mm) (c1900)	H.396	£80.00	—
D	P	? 52	Football Favourites (c1910)		£150.00	—
A	BW	4	*North Country Celebrities (c1905)	H.397	£65.00	£260.00
D	P	? 55	Northern Gems (c1902)		£65.00	—
A	C	50	Picture Puzzles and Riddles (c1910)		£25.00	—
A	C	50	Trick Series (c1910)		£25.00	—
D2	C	50	World's Coinage (c1915)	H.398	£18.00	£900.00

B POST-1920 ISSUES

Size	Print	Number	Description	Handbook	Price	Set
—	P		*Birds (1924):	H.613		
C		? 41	A Small size, back 'Specimen Cigarette Card'		£7.50	—
C		48	B Small size, descriptive back:			
			1 White front		£2.80	—
			2 Pinkish front		£2.80	—
—		50	C Large size (78 × 58mm)		£6.50	—
A	C	50	British Sea Dogs (1926)		£5.50	£275.00
	P		Champion Dogs — 'A Series of ...' (1938):			
A2		54	A Small size		75p	£40.00
B2		52	B Large size		75p	£40.00
	P		Champion Dogs — '2nd Series ...' (1939):			
A2		54	A Small size		£3.25	£175.00
B2		52	B Large size		£3.50	—
A2	P	50	English and Scottish Football Stars (1935)		£1.50	£75.00
A	P	54	Film Stars — 'A Series of 54 Real Photos' (1934)		£2.20	£120.00
A	P	54	Film Stars — 'A Series of Real Photos', Nd 1-54 (1937)		£1.70	£90.00
A	P	54	Film Stars — 'A Series of Real Photos', Nd 55-108 (1937)		£1.30	£70.00
	P		*Flowers and Plants (1924):	H.614		
C		? 37	A Small size, back 'Specimen Cigarette Card'		£7.00	—
C		96	B Small size, descriptive back:			
			1 White front		£2.30	—
			2 Pinkish front		£2.30	—
A	P	54	Radio Favourites (1935)		£1.50	£80.00
K2	C	53	Rubicon Cards (miniature playing cards) (c1935)		£6.00	—
A	BW	50	Well-Known Footballers — North Eastern Counties (1938)		£1.20	£60.00
A	BW	50	Well-Known Footballers — Scottish (1938)		£1.20	£60.00

C SILKS

Size	Print	Number	Description	Handbook	Price	Set
—	C		*Flags — Set 2 (70 × 52mm) (unbacked and anonymous) (c1915):	H.501-2		
		? 12	A Numbered Nos 25-36		£14.00	—
			B Unnumbered:			
		? 24	1 Caption in red		£8.00	—
		? 24	2 Caption in myrtle-green		£7.00	—
		? 24	3 Caption in bright green		£7.00	—
		? 24	4 Caption in blue		£8.00	—
		? 25	5 Caption in black		£12.00	—
—	C		*Flags — Set 11 (unbacked and anonymous) (c1915):	H.501-11		
		50	'Fourth Series' (49 × 70mm)		£6.00	—
		50	'Fifth Series' (49 × 70mm)		£6.00	—
		50	'Sixth Series':			
			1 Nos 1-25 (49 × 70mm)		£7.00	—
			2 Nos 26-50 (68 × 80mm)		£7.00	—
		? 10	'Seventh Series' (115 × 145mm)		£50.00	—
—	C	? 1	The Allies (140 × 100mm) (numbered 37) (c1915)		—	£35.00

Size	Print-ing	Number in set		Handbook reference	Price per card	Complete set

JOHN SINCLAIR LTD, Newcastle-on-Tyne *(continued)*

Size	Print-ing	Number in set	Description	Handbook ref	Price per card	Complete set
—	C	50	*Regimental Badges I (paper backed) (70 × 52mm) (c1915)	H.502-1	£6.00	—
—	C	? 24	*Regimental Colours II (unbacked and anonymous) (c1915):	H.502-7		
			1 Nos 38-49 (No. 49 not seen) (76 × 70mm) ...		£13.00	—
			2 Nos 50-61 (65 × 51mm)		£13.00	—

ROBERT SINCLAIR TOBACCO CO. LTD, Newcastle-on-Tyne

A PRE-1919 ISSUE

Size	Print-ing	Number in set	Description	Handbook ref	Price per card	Complete set
A2	U	28	Dominoes (c1900)		£60.00	—
A	BW	? 9	*Footballers (c1900)	H.399	£800.00	—
D	C	12	*Policemen of the World (c1899)	H.164	£180.00	—

B POST-1920 ISSUES

Size	Print-ing	Number in set	Description	Handbook ref	Price per card	Complete set
C2	C		Billiards by Willie Smith (1928):			
		10	1 First set of 10		£9.00	£90.00
		15	2 Second Set of 15		£11.00	£165.00
		3	3 Third Set of 25 (Nos 26-28 only issued)		£16.00	£48.00
	C	12	The 'Smiler' Series (1924):			
A			A Small size (inscribed '... 24 cards'), ...		£7.00	—
H			B Large size		£12.00	—

C SILKS. *Unbacked silks, inscribed with initials 'R.S.' in circle.*

Size	Print-ing	Number in set	Description	Handbook ref	Price per card	Complete set
—	C	4	*Battleships and Crests (73 × 102mm) (c1915)	H.499-1	£50.00	—
—	C	10	*Flags (70 × 51 mm) (c1915)	H.499-2	£26.00	—
—	C	6	*Great War Area — Cathedrals and Churches (140 × 102mm) (c1915)	H.499-3	£40.00	—
—	C	10	*Great War Heroes (70 × 51 mm) (c1915)	H.499-4	£35.00	—
—	C	1	*Red Cross Nurse (73 × 102mm) (c1915)	H.499-5	—	£50.00
—	C	5	*Regimental Badges (70 × 51 mm) (c1915)	H.499-6	£30.00	—

J. SINFIELD, Scarborough

PRE-1919 ISSUE

Size	Print-ing	Number in set	Description	Handbook ref	Price per card	Complete set
A	U	24	*Beauties — 'HUMPS' (c1900)	H.222	£600.00	—

SINGLETON & COLE LTD, Shrewsbury

A PRE-1919 ISSUES

Size	Print-ing	Number in set	Description	Handbook ref	Price per card	Complete set
A	C	50	*Atlantic Liners (1910)		£22.00	—
D1	BW	50	*Celebrities — Boer War Period (c1901):	H.400		
		25	Actresses		£18.00	£450.00
		25	Boer War Celebrities		£18.00	£450.00
A	BW	35	Famous Officers — Hero Series (1915):			
			A1 'Famous Officers' on back toned card		£14.00	£490.00
			A2 'Famous Officers' thin white card		£35.00	—
			B 'Hero Series' on back		£300.00	—
D1	BW	50	*Footballers (c1905)		£140.00	—
C	C	40	*Kings and Queens (1902)	H.157	£20.00	—
A	C	25	Maxims of Success (c1905):	H.401		
			A Orange border		£27.00	—
			B Lemon yellow border		£150.00	—
A	BW		Orient Royal Mail Line (c1905):	H.402		
		8	A 'Orient-Pacific Line' Manager's back		£60.00	—
		8	B 'Orient Royal Mail Line' Singleton and Cole back		£45.00	—
		10	C 'Orient Line' Manager's back (5 ports)		£45.00	—
		10	D 'Orient Line' Managers back (11 ports)		£45.00	—

Size	Print-ing	Number in set		Handbook reference	Price per card	Complete set

SINGLETON & COLE LTD, Shrewsbury *(continued)*

Size	Print	Number	Description	Handbook	Price	Set
A	C	25	Wallace Jones — Keep Fit System (c1910)		£26.00	—
B	**POST-1920 ISSUES**					
A	C	25	Bonzo Series (1928)	H.678	£8.00	£200.00
A2	BW	35	Famous Boxers (1930):			
			A Numbered		£15.00	—
			B Unnumbered		£40.00	—
A2	BW	25	Famous Film Stars (1930)		£10.00	—
—	U	12	'Manikin' Cards (77 × 49mm) (c1920)	H.481	£100.00	—
C	**SILKS**					
—	C	110	Crests and Badges of the British Army (paper-backed) (66 × 40mm) (c1915)	H.502-2	£4.00	—

F. & J. SMITH, Glasgow

36 page reference book — £4.00

A PRE-1919 ISSUES

Size	Print	Number	Description	Handbook	Price	Set
A	C	25	*Advertisement Cards (1899)	H.403	£200.00	—
A	C	50	Battlefields of Great Britain (1913)	Ha.475	£14.00	£700.00
A1	BW	25	*Boer War Series 'Studio' Cigarettes back (1900)		£65.00	—
A	C	50	*Boer War Series (1900)		£28.00	—
D	BW		*Champions of Sport (1902):	H.404		
		50	Red back. Numbered		£80.00	—
		50	Blue back. Unnumbered		£90.00	—
A	U	50	Cricketers (1912)		£15.00	£750.00
A	U	20	Cricketers, 2nd Series, Nd 51-70 (1912)		£30.00	£600.00
A	U	50	Derby Winners (1913)		£14.00	£700.00
A	C	50	Famous Explorers (1911)		£15.00	£750.00
D	U	120	*Footballers, brown back (1902)		£40.00	—
A	U	50	*Footballers, blue back Nd 1-52 (Nos 1 and 13 not issued) (1910):			
			A Black portrait		£13.00	—
			B Brown portrait		£13.00	—
A	U	50	*Footballers, blue back. Nd 55-104 (Nos 53 and 54 not issued) (1910):			
			A Black portrait		£13.00	—
			B Brown portrait		£13.00	—
A	U	150	*Footballers, yellow frame line (1914):			
			A Pale blue back		£13.00	—
			B Deep blue back		£13.00	—
A	C	50	Football Club Records, 1913 to 1917 (1918)		£17.00	£850.00
A	C	50	Fowls, Pigeons and Dogs (1908)	H.64	£10.00	£500.00
A	C		*Medals:	H.71		
		20	A Unnumbered — thick card (1902)		£15.00	£300.00
		50	B Numbered. 'F. & J. Smith' thick card (1902)		£10.00	£500.00
		50	C Numbered. 'The Imperial Tobacco Co.' very thin card (1903)		£32.00	—
		50	D Numbered. 'The Imperial Tobacco Company' thin card (1906)		£10.00	£500.00
A	C	50	Naval Dress and Badges:	H.172		
			A Descriptive back (1911)		£9.00	£450.00
			B Non-descriptive back (1914)		£9.00	£450.00
A	C	50	*Phil May Sketches, blue-grey back (1908)	H.72	£9.00	£450.00
A	C	40	Races of Mankind (1900):	H.483		
			A Series title on front		£45.00	—
			*B Without series title		£65.00	—
A	C	25	Shadowgraphs (1915)	H.466	£7.00	£175.00

Size	Print-ing	Number in set		Handbook reference	Price per card	Complete set

F. & J. SMITH, Glasgow (continued)

Size	Print	Number	Description	Handbook	Price	Complete
A	C	50	*A Tour Round the World:			
			A Script Advertisement back (1904)		£22.00	—
			B Post-card format back (1905)		£40.00	—
A	C	50	A Tour Round the World (titled series) (1906)	H.75	£10.00	£500.00
A	BW	25	War Incidents (1914):	H.405		
			A White back		£7.00	£175.00
			B Toned back		£7.00	£175.00
A	BW	25	War Incidents, 2nd series (1915):	H.405		
			A White back		£7.00	£175.00
			B Toned back		£7.00	£175.00

B POST-1920 ISSUES

A	C	25	'Cinema Stars' (1920)	H.615	£11.00	£275.00
A	C	50	Football Club Records, 1921-22 (1922)		£17.00	£850.00
A	C	25	Holiday Resorts (1925)		£7.00	£175.00
A	C	50	Nations of the World (1923)	H.454	£6.00	£300.00
A	C	50	Phil May Sketches (brown back) (1924)	H.72	£6.00	£300.00
A	C	25	Prominent Rugby Players (1924)		£12.00	£300.00

SNELL & CO., Plymouth and Devonport

PRE-1919 ISSUE

A	BW	25	*Boer War Celebrities — 'STEW' (c1901)	H.105	£200.00	—

SOCIETE JOB, London (and Paris)

A PRE-1919 ISSUES

D	BW	25	*Dogs (1911)	H.406	£26.00	£650.00
D	BW	25	*Liners (1912)	H.407	£30.00	—
D	BW	25	*Racehorses — 1908-09 Winners (1909)	H.408	£26.00	£650.00

B POST-1920 ISSUES

A	C	25	British Lighthouses (c1925)		£7.00	£175.00
—	U		*Cinema Stars (c1926):	H.616		
		48	A Unnumbered size (58 × 45mm):			
			1 Complete Set		—	£75.00
			2 46 different (minus Love, Milovanoff) ...		£1.00	£46.00
		43	B Unnumbered size (58 × 36mm)		£3.00	—
		?	C Numbered 100-192 (56 × 45mm) (sepia)		£4.00	—
		? 1	D Numbered 39 (57 × 45mm) (reddish brown) ...		£10.00	—
D1	C	52	*Miniature Playing Cards (c1925)		£7.00	—
A2	C	25	Orders of Chivalry (1924)		£3.60	£90.00
A2	C	25	Orders of Chivalry (Second series) (1927)		£3.60	£90.00
A2	C	3	Orders of Chivalry (unnumbered) (1927)		£8.00	£24.00

LEON SOROKO, London

POST-1920 ISSUE

—	U	6	Jubilee series (1935):			
			A Small size (75 × 41mm)		£75.00	—
			B Large size (83 × 73mm)		£75.00	—

SOUTH WALES TOB. MFG CO. LTD, Newport and London

PRE-1919 ISSUES

A	BW	? 91	Game of Numbers (c1910)		£80.00	—
A	U	25	*Views of London (c1910)	H.409	£24.00	£600.00

Size	Print-ing	Number in set		Handbook reference	Price per card	Complete set

SOUTH WALES TOBACCO CO. (1913) LTD, Newport

PRE-1919 ISSUE
D C 30 *Army Pictures, Cartoons, etc. (c1916) .... H.12 £110.00 —

S.E. SOUTHGATE & SON, London

PRE-1919 ISSUE
A1 C 25 *Types of British and Colonial Troops (c1900) ...... H.76 £130.00 —

T. SPALTON, Macclesfield

PRE-1919 ISSUE
D C 30 *Army Pictures, cartoons etc (c1916) .... H.12 £110.00 —

SPIRO VALLERI & CO.

PRE-1919 ISSUE
A BW ? 10 Noted Footballers (c1905) .... H.772 £1200.00 —

G. STANDLEY, Newbury

POST-1920 ISSUE
— U 12 'Manikin' Cards (77 × 49mm) (c1920) .... H.481 £100.00 —

A. & A.E. STAPLETON, Hastings

POST-1920 ISSUE
— U 12 *'Manikin' Cards (79 × 51mm) (c1920) .... H.481 £100.00 —

H. STEVENS & CO., Salisbury

POST-1920 ISSUES
A1 C 20 *Dogs (1923) .... H.211 £10.00 —
A1 U 25 *Zoo series (1926) .... H.588 £6.00 —

A. STEVENSON, Middleton

PRE-1919 ISSUE
A U 50 War Portraits (1916) .... H.86 £95.00 —

ALBERT STOCKWELL, Porthcawl

PRE-1919 ISSUE
D C 30 *Army Pictures, Cartoons, etc (c1916)............ H.12 £110.00 —

STRATHMORE TOBACCO CO. LTD, London

POST-1920 ISSUE
— U 25 British Aircraft (76 × 50mm) (1938) £2.80 £70.00

TADDY & CO., London

32 page reference book — £4.00

PRE-1919 ISSUES
— U ? 72 *Actresses — collotype (40 × 70mm) (c1897) .... H.411 £110.00 —
A C 25 *Actresses — with flowers (c1900) .... £80.00 —
A BW 37 Admirals and Generals — The War (c1915):
            A 25 Commoner Cards .... H.412 £18.00 —
            B 12 Scarce Cards (Nos 8, 9, 10, 13, 14, 17, 18, 21,
               22, 23, 24, 25) .... £40.00 —

110

Size	Print-ing	Number in set		Handbook reference	Price per card	Complete set
TADDY & CO., London *(continued)*						
A	BW	25	Admirals and Generals — The War (South African printing) (c1915)	H.412	£35.00	—
A	C	25	Autographs (c1910)	H.413	£20.00	£500.00
A	C	20	Boer Leaders: (c1901)			
			A White back		£22.50	£450.00
			B Cream back		£22.50	—
A	C	50	British Medals and Decorations — Series 2 (c1905)		£13.00	£650.00
A	C	50	British Medals and Ribbons (c1903)		£13.00	£650.00
A	C	20	*Clowns and Circus Artistes (c1915)	H.414	£750.00	—
C2	C	30	Coronation series (1902):			
			A Grained card		£23.00	£700.00
			B Smooth card		£23.00	£700.00
A	BW	238	County Cricketers (c1907)	H.415	£40.00	—
A	C	50	Dogs (c1900)	H.487	£30.00	—
C	U	5	*English Royalty — collotype (c1898)	H.416	£750.00	—
A	C	25	Famous Actors — Famous Actresses (c1903)		£20.00	£500.00
A	BW	50	Famous Horses and Cattle (c1912)		£100.00	—
A2	C	25	Famous Jockeys (c1905):	H.417		
			A Without frame line — blue title		£34.00	—
			B With frame line — brown title		£30.00	—
A	BW	50	Footballers (export issue) (c1906)	H.418	£90.00	—
A	C	25	'Heraldry' series (c1910)		£20.00	£500.00
A	C	25	Honours and Ribbons (c1910)		£24.00	£600.00
C	C	10	Klondyke series (c1900)		£65.00	£650.00
C	BW	60	Leading Members of the Legislative Assembly (export issue) (c1900)		£800.00	—
A	C	25	*Natives of the World (c1900)	H.419	£65.00	—
A	C	25	Orders of Chivalry (c1911)	H.301	£20.00	£500.00
A	C	25	Orders of Chivalry, second series (c1912)	H.301	£24.00	£600.00
A	BW		Prominent Footballers — Grapnel and/or Imperial back:	H.420		
		? 595	A without 'Myrtle Grove' footnote (1907)		£25.00	—
		? 403	B with 'Myrtle Grove' footnote (1908-9)		£25.00	—
A	BW	? 406	Prominent Footballers — London Mixture back (1913-14)	H.420	£45.00	—
—	C	20	*Royalty, Actresses, Soldiers (39 × 72mm) (c1898)	H.421	£225.00	—
A	C	25	'Royalty' series (c1908)		£18.00	£450.00
A	C	25	*Russo-Japanese War (1-25) (1904)		£20.00	£500.00
A	C	25	*Russo-Japanese War (26-50) (1904)		£24.00	£600.00
A	BW	16	South African Cricket Team 1907	H.422	£60.00	—
A	BW	26	South African Football Team 1906-07	H.423	£25.00	—
A	C	25	Sports and Pastimes — Series 1 (c1912)		£22.00	£550.00
A	C	25	Territorial Regiments — Series 1 (1908)		£24.00	£600.00
A	C	25	Thames series (c1903)		£34.00	£850.00
C	C	20	Victoria Cross Heroes (1-20) (c1900)		£70.00	—
C	C	20	Victoria Cross Heroes (21-40) (c1900)		£70.00	—
A	C	20	VC Heroes — Boer War (41-60) (1901):			
			A White back		£20.00	—
			B Toned back		£20.00	£400.00
A	C	20	VC Heroes — Boer War (61-80) (1901):			
			A White back		£20.00	—
			B Toned back		£20.00	£400.00
A	C	20	VC Heroes — Boer War (81-100) (1902):			
			A White back		£22.00	—
			B Toned back		£22.00	£440.00
A	C	25	Victoria Cross Heroes (101-125) (1905)		£60.00	—
A2	BW	2	*Wrestlers (c1910)	H.424	£300.00	—

ILLUSTRATIONS

1. Rothmans. Landmarks in Empire History
2. Wills. Alpine Flowers
3. Lewis. Horoscopes
4. Ardath. Silver Jubilee
5. Wills. Ships (1895)
6. Players. Motor Cars 2nd Series
7. Morris. At The London Zoo Aquarium
8. Mackenzie. The Zoo
9. Ogdens. Steeplechase Celebrities
10. Players. Dogs' Heads (unissued)
11. Players. Characters From Dickens
12. C.W.S. Wayside Flowers
13. Ardath. Film Stage and Radio Stars
14. Sinclair. Picture Puzzles & Riddles
15. Wills. Lucky Charms
16. Ogdens. Trick Billiards
17. G. Phillips. Beauties of Today 6th Series
18. Players. Ships Figure-Heads
19. Millhoff. Art Treasures 2nd Series
20. Players. Egyptian Sketches
21. Gallaher. Film Episodes
22. Ogdens. By The Roadside
23. Gallaher. Famous Film Scenes
24. Wills. Ships Badges
25. Churchman. World Wonders Old and New
26. Lambert & Butler. Motor Cars 1st Series
27. Players. Life On Board A Man of War in 1805 and 1905
28. Wills. Historical Events
29. Ogdens. Picturesque People of The Empire
30. C.W.S. Boy Scout Badges
31. F & J Smith. Boer War Series (Series of 50)
32. Wills. Physical Culture
33. Mitchell. Seals
34. Pattreieouex. Builders of the British Empire
35. G. Phillips. Beauties of Today (Series of 44)
36. Lambert & Butler. London Characters
37. Ogdens. British Birds 2nd Series
38. Drapkin. Optical Illusions
39. Players. British Empire Series
40. Sarony. Origin of Games
41. Wills. Mining
42. American Tobacco Co. Beauties Playing Cards
43. Cope. The World's Police
44. Morris. Shadowgraphs
45. Wills Overseas. Safety First
46. G. Phillips. Kings & Queens of England
47. Jones. Spurs Footballers
48. Duke. Musical Instruments
49. Adkin. Wild Animals of The World
50. Hignett. Dogs
51. G. Phillips. Our Favourites
52. Players. Historic Ships
53. Bucktrout. Football Teams
54. Cope. Golf Strokes
55. Carreras. Military Uniforms
56. Taddy. Famous Jockeys
57. Players. Military Series
58. Wills. Actresses grey scroll back
59. Fairweather. Historic Buildings of Scotland
60. Players. Cities of The World
61. Carreras. Famous British Fliers
62. C.W.S. How To Do It
63. Faulkner. Nautical Terms 2nd Series
64. Players. Gilbert and Sullivan 2nd Series
65. British American Tobacco. Indian Chiefs
66. Players. Actresses
67. Hill. Sports
68. Hignett. Animal Pictures
69. Wills. Roses 1926
70. Players. Players Past & Present
71. British American Tobacco. Keep Fit
72. Ardath. Football Clubs of Midlands
73. Cope. Household Hints
74. Gallaher. Art Treasures of The World
75. Players. Old Sporting Prints
76. Wills. Old English Garden Flowers 1st Series
77. R. Lloyd. Cinema Stars (Nos. 28 to 54)
78. Bucktrout. Inventors Series
79. United Kingdom Tobacco. British Orders of Chivalry and Valour
80. Players. International Air Liners
81. Wills. Household Hints 1st Series
82. Gallaher. Dogs (Series of 24)
83. Gallaher. Sports Series
84. G. Phillips. Personalities of Today
85. Carreras. School Emblems
86. Lambert & Butler. Wonders of Nature
87. Wills. The Reign of H.M. King George V

1. The Battle of Alexandria.
2. Californian Gum Plant. (Wills's Cigarettes)
3. Capricorn — Lucky Number 9, Lucky Stone White Onyx, December 21–January 20.
4. H.R.H. The Princess Royal in V.A.D. Uniform.
5. First Class Torpedo Boat.
6. Delage D8. 100 Mouette Saloon. (Player's Cigarettes)
7. Brown Trout.
8. The Rhinoceros. (Mackenzie's Cigarettes)
9. P. Powell. (Ogden's Cigarettes)
10. Smooth Fox Terrier. (Player's Cigarettes)
11. Mr Pickwick. (Player's Cigarettes)
12. The Dog Rose.

13
14
15
16
17
18
19
20

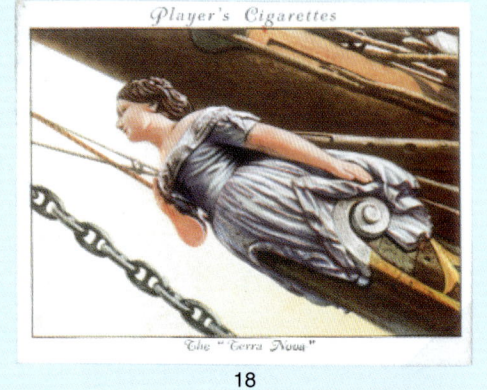

21
22
23
24
25
26
27
28
29
30
31
32

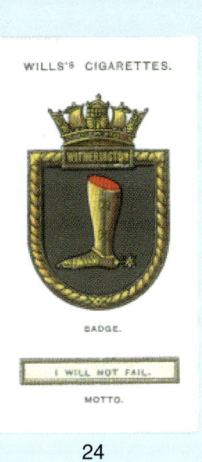

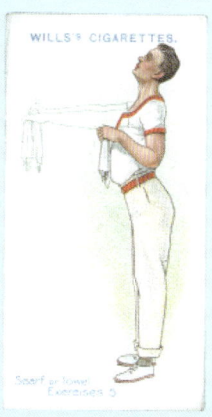

33. MITCHELL'S CIGARETTES — SEAL OF THE BOROUGH OF NEWPORT

34. DUKE OF WELLINGTON

35. MARY CARLISLE

36. LAMBERT & BUTLER'S CIGARETTES — "London Characters" THE QUACK MEDICINE MAN

37. BRITISH BIRDS. HAWFINCH. OGDEN'S CIGARETTES

38. OPTICAL ILLUSIONS — THE CUBE ILLUSION

39. BRITISH EMPIRE SERIES No. 24 — NAUTCH DANCE, INDIA — Player's Cigarettes

40. ROMAN SOLDIERS PLAYING HOCKEY

41. WILLS'S CIGARETTES

42. 10 (of Hearts)

43. COPE'S CIGARETTES — IRAQ

44.

45
46
47
48
49
50
51
52
53
54

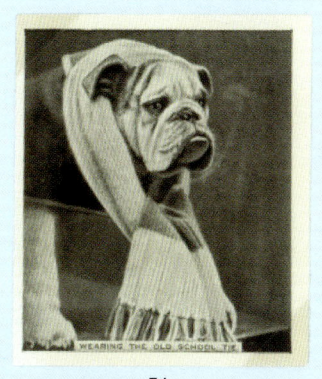

55

56 FAMOUS JOCKEYS. H. WATTS

57 Player's Cigarettes GRENADIER GUARDS.

58 WILL'S Cigarettes Miss Ethel Matthews.

59 FAIRWEATHER'S CIGARETTES

60 PARIS

61 TURF CIGARETTES — C. W. A. SCOTT & T. CAMPBELL BLACK — 1934 Flew from England to Australia in 2 days, 22 hrs. 54 mins. D.H. 88 Comet — 50 FAMOUS BRITISH FLIERS No. 31

62 C.W.S. TOBACCO FACTORY MANCHESTER

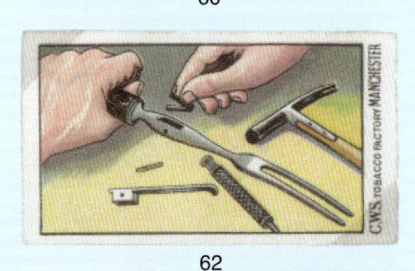

63 "CROSSING THE BAR" UNION JACK CIGARETTES. W. & F. Faulkner Ltd. London, S.E.

64 PLAYER'S CIGARETTES, MABEL "THE PIRATES OF PENZANCE"

65 KING OF THE CROWS. CROW.

66 L. Brayton — Player's High Class Cigarettes

67

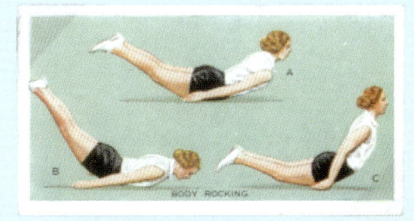

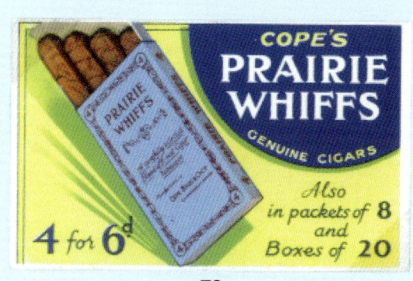

69

70

68

71

72

73

74

75

76  77  78  79

80 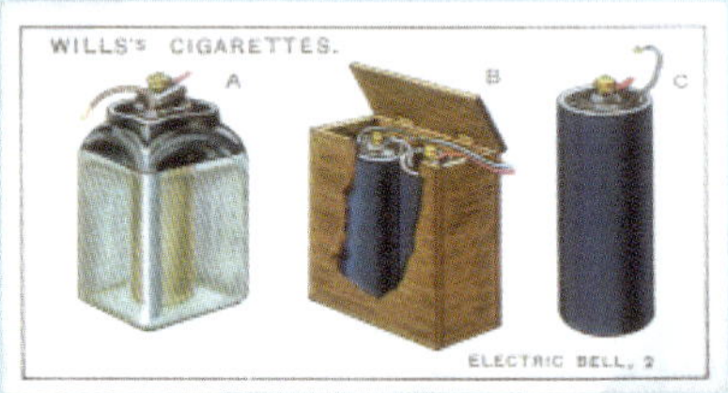 81

82  83

84  85  86  87

Size Print- Number   Handbook   Price   Complete

TADDY & CO., London and Grimsby

POST-1940 ISSUES

—	C	8	Advertisement Cards, three sizes (1980)	60p	£5.00
A	C	26	Motor Cars, including checklist (1980):		
			A 'Clown Cigarettes' back	40p	£10.00
			B 'Myrtle Grove Cigarettes' back	40p	£10.00
A	C	26	Railway Locomotives including checklist (1980):		
			A 'Clown Cigarettes' back	40p	£10.00
			B 'Myrtle Grove Cigarettes' back	40p	£10.00

W. & M. TAYLOR, Dublin

PRE-1919 ISSUES

A	C	8	European War series (c1915):	H.129		
			A 'Bendigo Cigarettes' back		£45.00	—
			B 'Tipperary Cigarettes' back		£45.00	
A	U	25	*War series — 'Muratti II' (c1915):	H.290		
			A 'Bendigo Cigarettes' back		£60.00	—
			B 'Tipperary Cigarettes' back		£16.00	£400.00

TAYLOR WOOD, Newcastle

PRE-1919 ISSUE

C	C	18	Motor Cycle series (c1914)	H.469	£90.00	—

TEOFANI & CO. LTD, London

***A* POST-1920 HOME ISSUES**

Cards inscribed with Teofani's name.

A2	C	24	Past and Present — Series A — The Army (1938):			
			A With framelines		£2.00	£50.00
			B Without framelines		£1.70	£40.00
A2	C	24	Past and Present — Series B — Weapons of War (1938)		£1.00	£25.00
A2	C	4	Past and Present — Series C — Transport (1940)	H.679	£5.00	—

***B* POST-1920 EXPORT ISSUES**

(Cards mostly without Teofani's name.)

C2	U	25	Aquarium Studies from the London Zoo ('Lucana' cards with green label added, inscribed 'Issued with Teofani Windsor Cigarettes') (c1925)	H.607	£12.00	—
D1	U	50	Cinema Celebrities (c1928):	Ha.617		
			A 'Presented with Broadway Novelties'		£5.00	—
			B 'Presented with these well-known ...'		£3.50	—
	C	25	Cinema Stars (c1928):	H.530		
			1 *Anonymous printings:*			
C2			A *Small size*		£7.00	—
			B *Extra-large size (109 × 67mm)*		£7.00	—
			2 Teofani printings:			
C2			A Small size — 'Issued with Blue Band Cigarettes'		£7.00	—
C2			B Small size — 'Three Star Cigarettes'		£7.00	—
C2			C Small size — 'Three Star Magnums'		£7.00	—
C2			D Small Size — 'The Favourite Cigarettes'		£7.00	—
—			E Extra-large size (109 × 67mm) — 'Three Star Magnums'		£7.00	—
D	U	25	*Famous Boxers — 'Issued with The 'Favourite Magnums ...' (c1925)	H.721	£10.00	—

Size	Print-ing	Number in set		Handbook reference	Price per card	Complete set

TEOFANI & CO. LTD, London *(continued)*

Size	Print-ing	Number in set	Description	Handbook reference	Price per card	Complete set
C2	P	32	Famous British Ships and Officers — 'Issued with these High Grade Cigarettes' (1934)		£3.50	£115.00
B1	U	50	Famous Racecourses ('Lucana' cards with mauve label added, inscribed 'Issued with The Favourite Cigarettes' (c1926)	H.608	£17.00	—
A	U	?24	Famous Racehorses (c1925)	H.609	£12.00	—
—	BW	12	*Film Actors and Actresses (56 × 31mm) (plain back) (1936)	H.618	£1.25	£15.00
C2	C	20	Great Inventors (c1924)	H.213	£4.50	—
A	C	20	*Head Dresses of Various Nations (plain back) (c1925)	H.619-1	£15.00	—
—	BW	12	*London Views (57 × 31mm) (plain back) (c1936)	H.620	50p	£6.00
D2	U	48	Modern Movie Stars and Cinema Celebrities (1934)	H.569	£1.00	£50.00
A	C	50	*Natives in Costume (plain back) (c1925)	Ha.619-2	£16.00	—
C	U	50	Public Schools and Colleges — 'Issued with these Fine Cigarettes' (c1924)	H.575	£3.60	—
D	C	50	Ships and Their Flags — 'Issued with these well-known cigarettes' (c1925)	Ha.602	£3.40	£170.00
A	C	25	Sports and Pastimes Series I — 'Smoke these cigarettes always' (c1925)	H.225	£14.00	—
—	P	22	*Teofani Gems I — Series of 22 (53 × 35mm) (plain back) (c1925)	Ha.621-1	£3.00	—
—	P	28	*Teofani Gems II — Series of 28 (53 × 35mm) (plain back) (c1925)	Ha.621-2	£1.00	—
—	P	36	*Teofani Gems III — Series of 36 (53 × 35mm) (plain back) (c1925)	Ha.621-3	£3.00	—
—	P	2	Teofani Gems — unnumbered (53 × 35mm) (plain back) (c1925)		£3.00	£6.00
A2	P	36	Views of the British Empire — 'Issued with these Famous Cigarettes' (c1928):			
			A Front in black and white		£1.25	£45.00
			B Front in light brown		£1.25	£45.00
C	U	50	Views of London — 'Issued with these World Famous Cigarettes' (c1925)	H.577	£3.00	—
C2	U	24	Well-Known Racehorses (c1924)	H.609	£9.00	—
A	C	50	*World's Smokers (plain back) (c1925)	Ha.619-3	£15.00	—
	U	50	Zoological Studies (c1924):	H.578		
C			A Standard Size		£3.50	—
B1			B Large Size		£7.00	—

TETLEY & SONS LTD, Leeds

PRE-1919 ISSUES

Size	Print-ing	Number in set	Description	Handbook reference	Price per card	Complete set
A2	C	1	*'The Allies' (grouped flags) (c1915)	H.425	—	£900.00
A	U	50	War Portraits (c1916)	H.86	£85.00	—
D	C	25	World's Coinage (1914)	H.398	£65.00	—

THEMANS & CO., Manchester

A PRE-1919 ISSUES

Size	Print-ing	Number in set	Description	Handbook reference	Price per card	Complete set
A	—	55	Dominoes (Sunspot brand issue) (c1914)		£80.00	—
C	C	18	Motor Cycle series (c1914)	H.469	£75.00	—
A	C	?2	Riddles and Anecdotes (c1913)	H.426	£600.00	—
A	U	50	*War Portraits (1916)	H.86	£50.00	—
—	C	14	War Posters (63 × 41 mm) (c1916)	H.486	£300.00	—

Size	Print-ing	Number in set		Handbook reference	Price per card	Complete set

THEMANS & CO., Manchester *(continued)*

B SILKS

Anonymous silks with blue border, plain board backing. Reported also to have been issued with firm's name rubber stamped on backing.

—	C		*Miscellaneous Subjects (c1915):*	H.500		
		? 8	Series B1 — *Flags (50 × 66mm)*		£10.00	—
		? 3	Series B2 — *Flags (50 × 66mm)*		£10.00	—
		? 12	Series B3 — *Regimental Badges (50 × 66mm)*		£7.00	—
		? 12	Series B4 — *Ship's Badges (50 × 66mm)*		£20.00	—
		? 7	Series B5 — *British Views and Scenes (50 × 66mm)*		£20.00	—
		? 48	Series B6 — *Film Stars (50 × 66mm)*		£10.00	—
		? 2	Series C1 — *Flags (65 × 55mm)*		£10.00	—
		? 3	Series C2 — *Flags (70 × 65mm)*		£10.00	—
		? 4	Series C3 — *Regimental Badges (64 × 77mm)*		£10.00	—
		? 2	Series C4 — *Crests of Warships (64 × 77mm)*		£10.00	—
		? 1	Series D1 — *Royal Standard (138 × 89mm)*		£15.00	—
		? 1	Series D2 — *Shield of Flags (138 × 89mm)*		£15.00	—
		? 1	Series D3 — *Regimental Badge (138 × 89mm)*		£15.00	—
		? 1	Series D5 — *British Views and Scenes (138 × 89mm)*		£20.00	—
		? 14	Series D6 — *Film Stars (138 × 89mm)*		£10.00	—

THOMSON & PORTEOUS, Edinburgh

PRE-1919 ISSUES

D2	C	50	Arms of British Towns (c1905)		£16.00	£800.00
A	BW	25	*Boer War Celebrities — 'STEW' (c1901)	H.105	£50.00	—
A	C	20	European War series (c1915)	H.129	£14.00	£280.00
A	C	25	*Shadowgraphs (c1905)	H.44	£40.00	—
A	C	41	VC Heroes (c1915):	H.427		
			Ai Name on back — Luntin Cigarettes		£13.00	£575.00
			Aii As above, but No. 6 Type B		—	£530.00
			B Without Maker's Name		£13.00	£530.00

TOBACCO SUPPLY SYNDICATE, London (T.S.S.)

PRE-1919 ISSUE

D	C	24	*Nautical Expressions (c1900)	H.174	£100.00	—

TURKISH MONOPOLY CIGARETTE CO. LTD

PRE-1919 ISSUE

—	C	? 16	*Scenes from the Boer War (113 × 68mm, folded in three) (c1901)	H.478	£400.00	—

UNITED KINGDOM TOBACCO CO., London

POST-1920 ISSUES

A	C	50	Aircraft — 'The Greys Cigarettes' (1938)	Ha.598	£1.60	£80.00
—	U	48	Beautiful Britain — 'The Greys Cigarettes' (140 × 90mm) (1929)		£1.70	£85.00
—	U	48	Beautiful Britain — Second series 'The Greys Cigarettes' (140 × 90mm) (1929)		£1.50	£75.00
A2	C	25	British Orders of Chivalry and Valour — 'The Greys Cigarettes' (1936)	Ha.599	£1.40	£35.00
A	U	24	Chinese Scenes (1933)		75p	£18.00
A2	U	32	Cinema Stars — Set 4 (1933)	Ha.515-4	£1.70	£55.00

Size	Print-ing	Number in set		Handbook reference	Price per card	Complete set

UNITED KINGDOM TOBACCO CO. LTD, London *(continued)*

A2	U	50	Cinema Stars — Set 7 (1934):	Ha.515-7		
			A *Anonymous back*		£2.50	£125.00
			B Back with firm's name		£1.70	£85.00
A2	C	36	Officers Full Dress (1936)		£2.00	£70.00
A2	C	36	Soldiers of the King — 'The Greys Cigarettes' (1937)	Ha.603	£2.00	£70.00

UNITED SERVICES MANUFACTURING CO. LTD, London

A POST-1920 ISSUES

A1	C	50	Ancient Warriors (1938)		£2.00	£100.00
A1	BW	50	Bathing Belles (1939)	H.592	70p	£35.00
D	U	100	Interesting Personalities (1935)		£2.75	—
D	U	50	Popular Footballers (1936)		£4.50	—
D	U	50	Popular Screen Stars (1937)		£3.80	—

B POST-1940 ISSUE

A	C	25	Ancient Warriors (1954)		£4.00	—

UNITED TOBACCONISTS' ASSOCIATION LTD

PRE-1919 ISSUES

A	C	10	*Actresses — 'MUTA' (c1900)	H.265	£150.00	—
A2	C	12	*Pretty Girl Series 'RASH' (c1900)	H.8	£350.00	—

WALKER'S TOBACCO CO. LTD, Liverpool

PRE-1919 ISSUE

A	BW	28	*Dominoes 'Old Monk' issue (1908)		£65.00	—

POST-1920 ISSUES

C	P	60	*British Beauty Spots (c1925)	H.553	£18.00	—
D2	U	28	*Dominoes 'W.T.C.' Monogram back (c1925)	H.535-2	£5.00	—
A2	P	32	Film Stars — 'Tatley's Cigarettes' (1936)	H.623	—	£70.00
			31 Different (minus Lombard)		£1.50	£46.00
A2	P	48	*Film Stars — Walker's name at base (1937)	H.623	£4.50	—

WALTERS TOBACCO CO. LTD, London

POST-1920 ISSUE

B	U	6	Angling Information (wording only) (1939)	H.624	£1.50	£9.00

E.T. WATERMAN, Coventry

PRE-1919 ISSUE

D	C	30	*Army Pictures, Cartoons, etc. (1916)	H.12	£110.00	—

WEBB & RASSELL, Reigate

PRE-1919 ISSUE

A	U	50	War Portraits (1916)	H.86	£95.00	—

H.C. WEBSTER (Q.V. Cigars)

PRE-1919 ISSUE

—	BW	?7	*Barnum and Bailey's Circus (60 × 42mm) (c1900)	H.428	£250.00	—

HENRY WELFARE & CO., London

PRE-1919 ISSUE

D	P	?22	Prominent Politicians (c1911)	H.429	£70.00	—

Size	Print-ing	Number in set		Handbook reference	Price per card	Complete set

WESTMINSTER TOBACCO CO. LTD, London

POST-1920 ISSUES

Inscribed 'Issued by the Successors in the United Kingdom to the Westminster Tobacco Co., Ltd. ...'. For other issues see Section II Foreign Cards.

Size	Print	Num	Title	Ref	Price	Set
A2	P	36	Australia — 'First Series' (1932)		25p	£9.00
A2	P	48	British Royal and Ancient Buildings (1925):			
			A Unnumbered, without descriptive text		80p	£40.00
			B Numbered, with descriptive text		£1.00	£50.00
A2	P	48	British Royal and Ancient Buildings — 'A Second Series ...' (1926)		35p	£17.50
A2	P	36	Canada — 'First Series' (1927)		70p	£25.00
A2	P	36	Canada — 'Second Series' (1928)		70p	£25.00
A2	P	48	Indian Empire — 'First Series' (1926)		35p	£17.50
A2	P	48	Indian Empire — 'Second Series' (1927)		35p	£17.50
A2	P	36	New Zealand — 'First Series' (1929)		40p	£15.00
A2	P	36	New Zealand — 'Second Series' (1930)		25p	£9.00
A2	P	36	South Africa — 'First Series' (1930)		70p	£25.00
A2	P	36	South Africa — 'Second Series' (1931)		70p	£25.00

NOT ISSUED

A2	P	36	Australia, Second Series, plain back (1933)	H.680	25p	£9.00

WHALE & CO.

PRE-1919 ISSUE

A	C	? 11	Conundrums (c1900)	H.232	£250.00	—

M. WHITE & CO., London

PRE-1919 ISSUE

—	BW	20	*Actresses — 'BLARM' (c1900)	H.23	£175.00	—

WHITFIELD'S, Walsall

PRE-1919 ISSUE

D	C	30	*Army Pictures, Cartoons etc. (c1916)	H.12	£110.00	—

WHITFORD & SONS, Evesham

POST-1920 ISSUE

C2	C	20	*Inventors series (c1924)	H.213	£45.00	—

WHOLESALE TOBACCO SUPPLY CO., London ('Hawser' Cigarettes)

PRE-1919 ISSUES

A	C	25	Armies of the World (c1902)	H.43	£70.00	—
A	C	40	Army Pictures (c1902)	H.69	£90.00	—

P. WHYTE, England

PRE-1919 ISSUE

D	C	30	*Army Pictures, Cartoons, etc. (1916)	H.12	£110.00	—

W. WILLIAMS & CO., Chester

A **PRE-1919 ISSUES**

A	BW	25	*Boer War Celebrities 'STEW' (c1901)	H.105	£70.00	—
A	C	50	Interesting Buildings (c1910)	H.70	£13.00	£650.00
A	BW	12	Views of Chester (c1910)	H.430	£30.00	£360.00
A	BW	12	Views of Chester — As It Was (c1910):	H.430		
			A Toned card		£30.00	£360.00
			B Bleuté card		£30.00	—

Size	Print-ing	Number in set		Handbook reference	Price per card	Complete set

W. WILLIAMS & CO., Chester (continued)

B POST-1920 ISSUES

Size	Print.	No.	Title	H. ref	Price	Set
A	U	30	Aristocrats of the Turf (c1925)	H.554	£7.00	£210.00
A	U	36	Aristocrats of the Turf 2nd series (c1925)	H.554	£14.00	—
A	C	25	Boxing (c1924)	H.311	£9.00	£225.00

W.D. & H.O. WILLS, Bristol

402 page reference book The Card Issues of Wills and British American Tobacco Co. combined — £20.00

A PERIOD TO 1902 — INCLUDING SERIES ISSUED ABROAD.

Size	Print.	No.	Title	H. ref	Price	Set
A	U		*Actresses — collotype (c1894):	H.431		
		25	A 'Wills' Cigarettes'		£90.00	—
		43	B 'Wills's Cigarettes'		£90.00	—
A	C	? 9	*Actresses, brown type-set back (c1895)	H.432	£1000.00	—
A	C	52	*Actresses, brown scroll back, with PC inset (c1898)		£17.00	£900.00
A	C	52	*Actresses, grey scroll back (c1897):	H.433		
			A Without PC inset		£17.00	£900.00
			B With PC inset		£17.00	£900.00
A	U		*Actresses and Beauties — collotype, 'Three Castles' and 'Firefly' front (c1895):	H.434		
		? 86	Actresses		£100.00	—
		? 32	Beauties		£100.00	—
A	C		*Advertisement Cards:	H.435		
		?4	1888 issue (cigarette packets)		£2000.00	—
		? 1	1889-90 issue (serving maid)		£800.00	—
		? 11	1890-93 issues (tobacco packings)		£1000.00	—
		? 3	1893 issue (various backs) (showcards)		£300.00	—
		? 6	1893-94 issue (posters)		£300.00	—
A	C	50	*Animals and Birds in Fancy Costumes (c1896)	H.436	£45.00	—
A	U	? 17	*Beauties — collotype (c1894):	H.437		
			A 'W.D. & H.O. Wills' Cigarettes'		£150.00	—
			B 'Firefly' Cigarettes		£150.00	—
A1	C	? 9	*Beauties ('Girl Studies'), type-set back (c1895)	H.438	£1000.00	—
A	C		*Beauties, brown backs (c1897):	H.439		
		52	A With PC inset — scroll back		£18.00	£925.00
		10	B As A, 10 additional pictures		£65.00	—
		? 48	C 'Wills' Cigarettes' front, scroll back		£175.00	—
		? 35	D 'Wills' Cigarettes' front, type-set back		£250.00	—
K	C	52	*Beauties, miniature cards, PC inset, grey scroll back (c1896)		£26.00	
A	C	50	Builders of the Empire (1898):			
			A White card		£7.50	£375.00
			B Cream card		£7.50	£375.00
A	C	60	Coronation Series (1902):			
			A 'Wide arrow' type back		£6.00	£360.00
			B 'Narrow arrow' type back		£6.00	£360.00
A	C	50	*Cricketers (1896)	H.440	£80.00	—
A	C		Cricketer series, 1901:			
		50	A With Vignette		£24.00	
		25	B Without Vignette		£24.00	
A	C		*Double Meaning (1898):			
		50	A Without PC inset		£9.00	£450.00
		52	B With PC inset		£9.00	£470.00
A	C	50	Japanese series (c1900)	H.441	£35.00	—
	C		*Kings and Queens:	H.442		
A1		50	A Short card (1897):			
			a Grey back, thin card		£6.00	£300.00
			b Grey back, thick card		£6.00	£300.00
			c Brown back		£10.00	—

Size	Print-ing	Number in set			Handbook reference	Price per card	Complete set

W.D. & H.O. WILLS, Bristol *(continued)*

Size	Print-ing	Number in set	Description	Handbook ref	Price per card	Complete set
A			B Standard size card (1902):			
		51	a Blue-grey back with 5 substitute titles:			
			i 50 different		£6.00	£300.00
			ii Edward The Martyr		—	£50.00
		50	b Grey back, different design, thinner card		£13.00	—
A	C		*Locomotive Engines and Rolling Stock:	H.443		
		50	A Without ITC Clause (1901)		£8.00	£400.00
		7	B As A, 7 additional cards (1901)		£30.00	—
			C With ITC Clause — See B Period			
A	C	50	*Medals (1902):	H.71		
			A White card		£2.70	£135.00
			B Toned card		£2.70	£135.00
A	C	25	*National Costumes (c1895)		£200.00	—
A	C	?8	*National Types (c1893)		£1000.00	—
A	C	20	Our Gallant Grenadiers (c1901):	H.163		
			A Deep grey on toned card		£32.00	—
			B Blue-grey on bluish card		£32.00	—
A	C	50	Seaside Resorts (1899)		£11.00	£550.00
A	C		*Ships:	H.444		
		25	A Without 'Wills' on front (1895):			
			a 'Three Castles' back		£28.00	£700.00
			b Grey scroll back		£28.00	£700.00
		50	B With 'Wills' on front, dark grey back (1896)		£18.00	—
		100	C Green scroll back on brown card (1898-1902):			
			i 1898-25 subjects as A		£18.00	—
			ii 1898-50 subjects as B		£18.00	—
			iii 1902-25 additional subjects		£18.00	—
A	C		*Soldiers of the World (1895-7):	H.445		
			A Without PC inset:			
		100	a With 'Ld.' back, thick card		£7.50	£750.00
		100	b With 'Ld.' back, thin card		£7.50	—
		100	c Without 'Ld.' back, thin card		£7.50	£750.00
		1	Additional card (as c) 'England, Drummer'		—	£125.00
		52	B With PC inset		£22.00	£1150.00
A	C	50	*Soldiers and Sailors (c1894):	H.446		
			A Grey back		£40.00	—
			B Blue back		£40.00	—
A	C	50	Sports of All Nations (1900)		£11.00	£550.00
A	BW		Transvaal series:	H.360		
		50	A With black border (1899)		£9.00	—
		66	Bi Without black border (1900-01)		£1.75	£115.00
		258	Bii Intermediate cards — additions and alternatives (1900-01)		£1.75	
		66	C Final 66 subjects, as issued with 'Capstan' back (*see B Period*) (1902).			
A	C		'Vanity Fair' series (1902):	H.447		
		50	1st series		£6.50	£325.00
		50	2nd series		£6.50	£325.00
		50	Unnumbered — 43 subjects as in 1st and 2nd, 7 new subjects		£6.50	£325.00
A	C		Wild Animals of the World (c1900):	H.77		
		50	A Green scroll back		£6.00	£300.00
		52	B Grey back, PC inset		£11.00	£570.00
		?7	C Text back		£30.00	—

B PERIOD 1902-1919 — HOME ISSUES I.E. SERIES BEARING IMPERIAL TOBACCO CO. ('I.T.C.') CLAUSE

Size	Print-ing	Number in set	Description	Handbook ref	Price per card	Complete set
A	C	50	Allied Army Leaders (1917)		£1.70	£85.00

Size	Printing	Number in set		Handbook reference	Price per card	Complete set

W.D. & H.O. WILLS, Bristol *(continued)*

Size	Printing	Number in set	Title	Handbook reference	Price per card	Complete set
A	C	50	Alpine Flowers (1913)		90p	£45.00
A	C	50	Arms of the Bishopric (1907)		£1.00	£50.00
A	C	50	Arms of the British Empire (1910)		80p	£40.00
A	C	50	Arms of Companies (1913)		80p	£40.00
A	C	50	Arms of Foreign Cities (1912):			
			A White card		80p	£40.00
			B Cream card		90p	—
			C As A, with 'Mark'		£1.00	—
A	C	50	Aviation (1910)		£2.50	£125.00
A	C	50	Billiards (1909)		£2.00	£100.00
A	C	50	*Borough Arms (1-50):			
			A Scroll back, unnumbered (1904)	H.448	£1.00	£50.00
			B Scroll back, numbered on front (1904)		£10.00	—
			C Descriptive back, numbered on back (1905)		£1.00	£50.00
			D 2nd Edition — 1-50 (1906)		80p	£40.00
A	C	50	*Borough Arms (51-100):			
			A 2nd Series (1905)		70p	£35.00
			B 2nd Edition, 51-100 (1906)		70p	£35.00
A	C	50	*Borough Arms (101-150):			
			A 3rd Series, Album clause in grey (1905)		90p	£45.00
			B 3rd Series, Album clause in red (1905)		70p	£35.00
			C 2nd Edition, 101-150 (1906)		70p	£35.00
A	C	50	*Borough Arms (151-200), 4th series (1905)		70p	£35.00
A	C	24	*Britain's Part in the War (1917)		£1.00	£25.00
A	C	50	British Birds (1917)		£1.20	£60.00
A	C	1	*Calendar for 1911 (1910)		—	£15.00
A	C	1	*Calendar for 1912 (1911)		—	£10.00
B	U	25	Celebrated Pictures (1916):			
			A Deep brown back		£2.00	£50.00
			B Yellow-brown back		£1.80	£45.00
B	U	25	Celebrated Pictures, 2nd Series (1916)		£2.20	£55.00
A	C	50	Celebrated Ships (1911)		£1.20	£60.00
A	C	50	The Coronation Series (1911)		£1.00	£50.00
A	C	50	Cricketers (1908):			
			A 1-25 'Wills' S' at top front		£9.00	£225.00
			B 1-50 'Wills's' at top front		£7.50	£375.00
B	C	25	Dogs (1914)		£3.60	£90.00
B	C	25	Dogs, 2nd Series (1915)		£3.60	£90.00
A	C	50	Famous Inventions (1915)		£1.00	£50.00
A	C	50	First Aid:			
			A Without Album Clause (1913)		£1.50	£75.00
			B With Album Clause (1915)		£1.50	£75.00
A	C	50	Fish & Bait (1910)	H.65	£2.50	£125.00
A	U	66	*Football Series (1902)	H.81	£9.00	—
A	C	50	Garden Life (1914)	H.449	70p	£35.00
A	C	50	Gems of Belgian Architecture (1915)		60p	£30.00
A	C	50	Gems of French Architecture (1917):			
			A White card		£1.40	£70.00
			B Bleuté card		£1.60	—
			C Rough brown card		£1.60	—
A	C	50	Gems of Russian Architecture (1916)		70p	£35.00
A	C	50	Historic Events (1912)	H.464	£1.20	£60.00
A	C	50	*Locomotive Engines and Rolling Stock, with I.T.C. Clause (1902)		£8.00	£400.00
			For issue without I T. C. Clause see Period A.			
A	C	50	Military Motors (1916):			
			A Without 'Passed by Censor'		£1.80	£90.00
			B With 'Passed by Censor'		£1.80	£90.00

Size	Print-ing	Number in set		Handbook reference	Price per card	Complete set

W.D. & H.O. WILLS, Bristol *(continued)*

Size	Print	Num	Title	Ref	Price	Set
A	C	50	Mining (1916)	H.450	£1.50	£75.00
A	C	50	Musical Celebrities (1911)		£2.50	£125.00
A	C	50	Musical Celebrities — Second Series (1916):	H.465		
			Set of 50 with 8 substituted cards		£3.50	£175.00
			8 original cards (later substituted)		£250.00	—
A	C	50	Naval Dress & Badges (1909)	H.172	£3.20	£160.00
A	C	50	Nelson Series (1905)		£5.00	£250.00
A	C	50	Old English Garden Flowers (1910)		£1.50	£75.00
A	C	50	Old English Garden Flowers, 2nd Series (1913)		£1.00	£50.00
A	C	50	Overseas Dominions (Australia) (1915)	H.451	80p	£40.00
A	C	50	Overseas Dominions (Canada) (1914)		60p	£30.00
A	C	50	Physical Culture (1914)		£1.00	£50.00
A	U	100	*Portraits of European Royalty (1908):			
			Nos. 1-50		£1.50	£75.00
			Nos. 51-100		£1.50	£75.00
B	U	25	Punch Cartoons (1916):			
			A Toned card		£3.60	£90.00
			B Glossy white card		£6.00	—
B	U	25	Punch Cartoons — Second Series (1917)		£18.00	—
A	C	12	Recruiting Posters (1915)	H.452	£7.50	£90.00
A	C	50	Roses (1912)		£1.60	£80.00
A	C	50	Roses, 2nd Series (1914)		£1.60	£80.00
A	C	50	School Arms (1906)		80p	£40.00
A	C	50	Signalling Series (1911)	H.453	£1.80	£90.00
A	C	50	Time and Money in Different Countries (1906)	H.454	£1.80	£90.00
A	BW	66	Transvaal Series, 'Capstan' back (1902)	H.360	£5.50	£365.00
			For other 'Transvaal Series' see A Period.			
A	C	25	The World's Dreadnoughts (1910)		£3.00	£75.00

C POST-1920 ISSUES

Home issues, i.e. series with I.T.C. Clause.

Size	Print	Num	Title	Ref	Price	Set
A	C		Air Raid Precautions (1938):	H.544		
		50	A Home issue — adhesive back		90p	£45.00
		40	B Irish issue — non-adhesive back		£1.50	—
A	C	48	Animalloys (sectional) (1934)		40p	£20.00
B	C	25	Animals and Their Furs (1929)		£1.80	£45.00
B	C	25	Arms of the British Empire — 'First Series' (1931)		£1.80	£45.00
B	C	25	Arms of the British Empire — 'Second Series' (1932)		£1.80	£45.00
B	C	42	Arms of Oxford and Cambridge Colleges (1922)		£1.30	£55.00
B	C	25	Arms of Public Schools — '1st Series' (1933)		£2.00	£50.00
B	C	25	Arms of Public Schools — '2nd Series' (1934)		£2.00	£50.00
B	C	25	Arms of Universities (1923)		£1.60	£40.00
A	C	50	Association Footballers 'Frameline' back (1935)		£1.30	£65.00
A	C	50	Association Footballers — 'No frameline' back (1939):			
			A Home issue — adhesive back		£1.30	£65.00
			B Irish issue — non-adhesive back		£2.40	£120.00
B	C	25	Auction Bridge (1926)		£2.20	£55.00
B	C	25	Beautiful Homes (1930)		£2.60	£65.00
A	C	50	British Butterflies (1927)		£1.10	£55.00
B	C	25	British Castles (1925)		£2.60	£65.00
B	C	25	British School of Painting (1927)		£1.40	£35.00
—	BW	48	British Sporting Personalities (66 × 52mm) (1937)		£1.00	£50.00
B	C	40	Butterflies and Moths (1938)		90p	£36.00
B	C	25	Cathedrals (1933)		£4.40	£110.00
A	C	25	Cinema Stars — 'First Series' (1928)		£1.60	£40.00
A	C	25	Cinema Stars — 'Second Series' (1928)		£1.60	£40.00
A	U	50	Cinema Stars — 'Third Series' (1931)		£1.80	£90.00

Size	Printing	Number in set		Handbook reference	Price per card	Complete set

W.D. & H.O. WILLS, Bristol *(continued)*

Size	Print	Num	Title	Ref	Price	Set
A	C	50	Cricketers, 1928 (1928)		£1.80	£90.00
A	C	50	Cricketers — '2nd Series' (1929)		£1.80	£90.00
A	C	50	Dogs — Light backgrounds (1937):			
			A Home issue — adhesive back		60p	£30.00
			B Irish issue — non-adhesive back		£1.50	£75.00
A	C		Do You Know:			
		50	'A Series of 50' (1922)		50p	£25.00
		50	'2nd Series of 50' (1924)		50p	£25.00
		50	'3rd Series of 50' (1926)		50p	£25.00
		50	'4th Series of 50' (1933)		60p	£30.00
A	C	50	Engineering Wonders (1927)		£1.00	£50.00
A	C	50	English Period Costumes (1929)		£1.00	£50.00
B	C	25	English Period Costumes (1927)		£2.60	£65.00
B	C	40	Famous British Authors (1937)		£1.75	£70.00
B	C	30	Famous British Liners — 'First Series' (1934)		£5.50	—
B	C	30	Famous British Liners — 'Second Series' (1935)		£3.60	£110.00
B	C	25	Famous Golfers (1930)		£16.00	—
A	C		A Famous Picture — (sectional):			
		48	Series No. 1 — 'Between Two Fires' (1930)		30p	£15.00
		48	Series No. 2 — 'The Boyhood of Raleigh' (1930)		30p	£15.00
		48	Series No. 3 — 'Mother and Son' (1931)		30p	£15.00
		48	'The Toast' (1931):			
			A Home issue — Series No. 4		50p	£24.00
			B Irish issue — Series No. 1		£2.00	—
		48	'The Laughing Cavalier' (1931):			
			A Home issue — Series No. 5:			
			1 No stop after numeral		40p	£20.00
			2 Full stop after numeral		40p	£20.00
			B Irish issue — Series No. 2		£2.00	—
		49	Series No. 6 — 'And When did you Last See Your Father?' (1932)		£1.00	£50.00
A	C	25	Flags of the Empire (1926)		£1.40	£35.00
A	C	25	Flags of the Empire — '2nd Series' (1929)		£1.00	£25.00
A	C	50	Flower Culture in Pots (1925)		45p	£22.50
B	C	30	Flowering Shrubs (1935)		£1.00	£30.00
A	C	50	Flowering Trees and Shrubs (1924)		70p	£35.00
A	C	50	Garden Flowers (1933)		70p	£35.00
A	C	50	Garden Flowers by Richard Sudell (1939):			
			A Home issue — four brands quoted at base		25p	£12.50
			B Irish issue — no brands at base		50p	£25.00
B	C	40	Garden Flowers — New Varieties — 'A Series' (1938)		60p	£24.00
B	C	40	Garden Flowers — New Varieties — '2nd Series' (1939)		50p	£20.00
A	C	50	Garden Hints (1938):			
			A Home issue — Albums 'one penny each'		25p	£12.50
			B Irish issue — Album offer without price		40p	£20.00
A	C	50	Gardening Hints (1923)		35p	£17.50
B	C	25	Golfing (1924)		£8.40	
B	C	25	Heraldic Signs and Their Origin (1925)		£1.80	£45.00
A2	P	54	Homeland Events (1932)		60p	£32.00
A	C	50	Household Hints (1927)		50p	£25.00
A	C	50	Household Hints — '2nd Series' (1930)		50p	£25.00
A	C	50	Household Hints (1936):			
			A Home issue — Albums 'one penny each'		25p	£12.50
			B Irish issue — Album offer without price		50p	£25.00
A	BW	50	Hurlers (1927)		£1.80	£90.00
A	C	25	Irish Beauty Spots (1929)		£4.40	—
A	C	25	Irish Holiday Resorts (1930)		£4.40	—

Size	Print-ing	Number in set		Handbook reference	Price per card	Complete set

W.D. & H.O. WILLS, Bristol *(continued)*

Size	Printing	Number in set	Title	Handbook ref	Price per card	Complete set
A	C	50	Irish Industries (1937):			
			A Back 'This surface is adhesive …'		£3.00	—
			B Back 'Ask your retailer …'		£1.20	£60.00
A	U	25	Irish Rugby Internationals (1928)		£11.00	—
A	C	50	Irish Sportsmen (1935)		£4.00	—
B	C	40	The King's Art Treasures (1938)		30p	£12.00
B	C	25	Lawn Tennis, 1931 (1931)		£9.00	—
A	C	50	Life in the Royal Navy (1939)		30p	£15.00
A	C	50	Life in the Tree Tops (1925)		40p	£20.00
A	C	50	Lucky Charms (1923)		60p	£30.00
A	C	50	Merchant Ships of the World (1924)		£1.40	£70.00
K2	C	53	*Miniature Playing Cards (1932-34):			
			A Home issue, blue back — 'narrow 52' (2 printings)		50p	£25.00
			B Home issue, blue back — 'wide 52' (4 printings)		50p	£25.00
			C Home issue, pink back (3 printings)		60p	—
			D Irish issue, blue back (7 printings)		£1.00	—
B	C	25	Modern Architecture (1931)		£1.60	£40.00
B	U	30	Modern British Sculpture (1928)		£1.30	£40.00
B	C	25	Old Furniture — '1st Series' (1923)		£2.80	£70.00
B	C	25	Old Furniture — '2nd Series' (1924)		£2.80	£70.00
B	C	40	Old Inns — 'A Series of 40' (1936)		£3.00	£120.00
B	C	40	Old Inns — 'Second Series of 40' (1939)		£1.75	£70.00
B	C	25	Old London (1929)		£3.60	£90.00
B	C	30	Old Pottery and Porcelain (1934)		£1.20	£36.00
B	C	25	Old Silver (1924)		£2.40	£60.00
B	C	25	Old Sundials (1928)		£2.80	£70.00
A	BW	50	Our King and Queen (1937)		25p	£12.50
B	C	25	Public Schools (1927)		£2.40	£60.00
B	C	40	Racehorses and Jockeys, 1938 (1939)		£2.25	£90.00
A	C	50	Radio Celebrities — 'A Series …' (1934):			
			A Home issue — back 'This surface …'		80p	£40.00
			B Irish issue — back 'Note. This surface …'		£1.50	—
A	C	50	Radio Celebrities — 'Second Series — (1935):			
			A Home issue — back 'This surface …'		50p	£25.00
			B Irish issue — back 'Note. This surface …'		£1.30	—
A	C	50	Railway Engines (1924)		£1.20	£60.00
A	C	50	Railway Engines (1936):			
			A Home issue — back 'This surface …'		£1.00	£50.00
			B Irish issue — back 'Note. This surface …'		£1.50	£75.00
A	C	50	Railway Equipment (1939)		40p	£20.00
A	C	50	Railway Locomotives (1930)		£1.60	£80.00
A	C	50	The Reign of H. M. King George V (1935)		70p	£35.00
B	C	25	Rigs of Ships (1929)		£3.60	£90.00
A	C	50	Romance of the Heavens (1928):			
			A Thin card		£1.10	£55.00
			B Thick card		£1.10	£55.00
A	C	50	Roses (1926)		90p	£45.00
B	C	40	Roses (1936)		£1.60	£65.00
—	BW	48	Round Europe (66 × 52mm) (1937)		40p	£20.00
A	C	50	Rugby Internationals (1929)		£2.00	£100.00
A	C	50	Safety First (1934):			
			A Home issue — 'This surface …'		£1.20	£60.00
			B Irish issue — 'Note. This surface …'		£2.00	—
A	C	50	The Sea-Shore (1938):			
			A Home issue — special album offer		25p	£12.50
			B Irish issue — general album offer		70p	£35.00

Size	Print-ing	Number in set		Handbook reference	Price per card	Complete set

W.D. & H.O. WILLS, Bristol (continued)

Size	Print-ing	Number in set	Description		Price per card	Complete set
A	U	40	Shannon Electric Power Scheme (1931)		£1.50	£60.00
A	U	50	Ships' Badges (1925)		80p	£40.00
A	C	50	Speed (1930)		£1.50	£75.00
A	C	50	Speed (1938):			
			A	Home issue — four brands quoted at base	35p	£17.50
			B	Irish issue — no brands at base	70p	£35.00
A	C	50	Strange Craft (1931)		£1.00	£50.00
B	C	40	Trees (1937)		£1.60	£65.00
B	C	25	University Hoods and Gowns (1926)		£3.00	£75.00
A	C	50	Wild Flowers (1923):			
			A	With dots in side panels	70p	£35.00
			B	Without dots in side panels	70p	£35.00
A	C	50	Wild Flowers — 'Series of 50' (1936):			
			A	Home issue — back 'This surface ...'	40p	£20.00
			B	Irish issue — back 'Note. This surface ...'	70p	—
A	C	50	Wild Flowers — '2nd Series.' (1937):			
			A	Home issue — adhesive back	20p	£10.00
			B	Irish issue — non-adhesive back	60p	£30.00
A	C	50	Wonders of the Past (1926)		60p	£30.00
A	C	50	Wonders of the Sea (1928)		50p	£25.00

D POST-1940 ISSUES

Size	Print-ing	Number in set	Description	Price per card	Complete set
H2	C	30	Britain's Motoring History (1991)	£1.40	£42.00
—	C	6	Britain's Motoring History (149 × 104mm) (1991)	£1.25	—
H2	C	30	Britain's Steam Railways (1998)	£1.20	£36.00
G2	C	30	British Aviation (1994)	£1.20	£36.00
—	C	6	British Aviation (1994) Beer Mats	50p	£3.00
G2	C	30	Classic Sports Cars (1996)	£1.20	£36.00
G2	C	30	Donington Collection (1993)	£1.20	£36.00
—	C	6	Donington Collection (1993) Beer Mats	£1.25	—
G2	BW	48	Familiar Phrases (1986)	£1.20	£60.00
G2	C	10	Golden Era (1999)	£2.00	£20.00
H2	C	30	History of Britain's Railways (1987)	£1.20	£36.00
H2	C	30	History of Motor Racing (1987)	£1.50	—
G2	C	30	In Search of Steam (1992)	£1.20	£36.00
—	C	6	In Search of Steam (1992) Beer Mats	£1.25	—
G2	BW	5	Pica Punchline (1984)	£1.20	£6.00
H2	U	144	Punch Lines (1983)	70p	—
G2	U	288	Punch Lines (1983)	70p	—
G2	U	48	Ring the Changes (1985):		
			A With 'Wills' name	£1.20	—
			B Without 'Wills' Name	£1.20	—
—	C	12	Russ Abbot Advertising Cards (80 × 47mm) (1993)	£1.50	£18.00
G2	C	30	Soldiers of Waterloo (1995)	£1.20	£36.00
G2	BW	10	Spot the Shot (1986)	£2.50	—
G2	C	30	The Tank Story (1997)	£1.20	£36.00
—	C	56	Wonders of the World (1986):		
			A Size 90 × 47mm	50p	£28.00
			B Size 80 × 47mm	70p	£40.00
			C Size 80 × 35mm	90p	—
C1	C	36	World of Firearms (1982)	25p	£9.00
C1	C	36	World of Speed (1981)	25p	£9.00

E UNISSUED SERIES

Size	Print-ing	Number in set	Description	Price per card	Complete set
A	P	50	Gems of Italian Architecture (1960) (reprint)	70p	£35.00
A	C	50	Life in the Hedgerow (c1950)	50p	£25.00
A	C	50	Life of King Edward VIII (1936)	—	£900.00
A	C	25	Pond and Aquarium 1st Series (c1950)	32p	£8.00

Size	Printing	Number in set		Handbook reference	Price per card	Complete set

W.D. & H.O. WILLS, Bristol *(continued)*

Size	Print	Num	Description	Ref	Price	Set
A	C	25	Pond and Aquarium 2nd Series (c1950)		32p	£8.00
B	C	40	Puppies (c1950)		—	—
A	C	50	Waterloo (c1916)		£120.00	—

F MISCELLANEOUS

Size	Print	Num	Description	Ref	Price	Set
B	BW	1	Advertisement Card — Wants List (1935)		—	75p
—	—	? 8	Boer War Medallions (c1901)		£90.00	—
—	C	12	The British Empire (133 × 101mm) (c1930)		£9.00	—
—	C	12	Cities of Britain (133 × 101mm) (c1930)		£9.00	—
—	C	6	Flags of the Allies (shaped) (c1915)		£12.00	—
—	C	32	Happy Families (non-insert) (91 × 63mm) (c1935)		£5.00	—
—	C	12	Industries of Britain (133 × 101mm) (c1930)		£9.00	—
—	—	1	Pinchbeck Medallion (1897)		£100.00	—
			Three Castles Sailing Ship Model advertisement cards (1965):			
A	C	1	A View from Stern: Three Castles Filter:			
			I. Three Castles Cigarettes		—	£4.00
			II. In the eighteenth century		—	£1.50
A	C	1	B Views from Bows:			
			I. Three Castles Filter		—	£1.50
			II. Three Castles Filter magnum		—	£1.50
A	BW	1	C Sailing Ship Black Line Drawing		—	£5.00
A	BW	1	D Three Castles Shield Black Line Drawing		—	£5.00
—	C		200th Anniversary Presentation Packs (2 sets of Playing Cards) (1986)		—	£90.00

WILSON & CO., Ely

PRE-1919 ISSUE

Size	Print	Num	Description	Ref	Price	Set
A	U	50	War Portraits (1916)	H.86	£95.00	—

W. WILSON, Birmingham

PRE-1919 ISSUES

Size	Print	Num	Description	Ref	Price	Set
D	C	30	*Army Pictures. Cartoons, etc (1916)	H.12	£110.00	—
A	U	50	War Portraits (1916)	H.86	£95.00	—

HENRI WINTERMANS (UK) LTD

POST-1940 ISSUES

Size	Print	Num	Description	Ref	Price	Set
G	C	30	Disappearing Rain Forest (1991)		40p	£12.00
G	C	30	Wonders of Nature (1992)		40p	£12.00

A. & M. WIX, London and Johannesburg

POST-1920 ISSUES

Size	Print	Num	Description	Ref	Price	Set
—	—		Cinema Cavalcade (50 coloured, 200 black and white; sizes — 70 small, 110 large, 70 extra-large):			
		250	'A Series of 250 …' ('Max Cigarettes') (1939)		£1.20	—
		250	'2nd Series of 250 …' ('Max Cigarettes') (1940)		£1.40	—
A2	C	100	Film Favourites — 'Series of 100 …' (c1937)	H.581-1	£2.50	—
A2	C	100	Film Favourites — '2nd Series of 100 …' (1939)	H.581-2	£2.50	—
A2	C	100	Film Favourites — '3rd Series of 100 …' (c1939)	H.581-3	£1.25	£125.00
J1	C	100	*Men of Destiny (folders) (P.O. Box 5764, Johannesburg) (c1935)		£2.00	—
—	C	250	Speed Through the Ages (171 small, 79 large) (1938):	H.583		
			A Back in English and Afrikaans		32p	£80.00
			B Back in English		40p	£100.00

Size	Print-ing	Number in set		Handbook reference	Price per card	Complete set

A. & M. WIX, London and Johannesburg *(continued)*

| | C | 250 | This Age of Power and Wonder (170 small, 80 large) ('Max Cigarettes') (c1935) .... | | 30p | £75.00 |

J. WIX & SONS LTD, London

A POST-1920 ISSUES

Size	Print-ing	Number in set		Handbook reference	Price per card	Complete set
C	C	50	Builders of Empire — 'Kensitas' (1937)		60p	£30.00
A2	C	50	Coronation (1937):			
			A J. Wix back:			
			1. Linen finish		25p	£12.50
			2. Varnished		60p	£30.00
			B 'Kensitas' back		25p	£12.50
	C		Henry:	H.625		
			'A Series of ...' (1935):			
B1		50	A Large size		80p	£40.00
—		25	B Extra-large size		£3.00	£75.00
			'2nd Series ...' (1935):			
B1		50	A Large size		£1.00	£50.00
—		25	B Extra-large size		£3.00	£75.00
B1		50	3rd Series (1936)		80p	£40.00
B1		50	4th Series (1936)		70p	£35.00
B1		50	5th Series (1936)		60p	£30.00
	U	25	Love Scenes from Famous Films — 'First Series' (1932):			
C2			A Small size		£3.00	£75.00
B1			B Large size		£3.00	£75.00
—			C Extra-large size (127 × 88mm)		£6.00	—
	U	19	Love Scenes from Famous Films — 'Second Series' (1932) (Nos. 5, 9, 13, 20, 23, 24 withdrawn):			
C2			A Small size		£2.50	£50.00
B1			B Large size		£3.00	£60.00
			C Extra-large size (127 × 88mm)		£7.50	—
K2	C	53	*Miniature Playing Cards (anonymous)* (c1935):	H.535-3		
			A Scroll design:			
			1 Red back		20p	£9.00
			2 Blue back		25p	£12.50
			B Ship design:			
			1 Red border — Nelson's 'Victory'		35p	£17.50
			2 Black border — Drake's 'Revenge'		35p	£17.50
	U	25	Scenes from Famous Films — 'Third Series' (1933):			
C2			A Small size		£2.60	£65.00
—			B Extra-large size (127 × 88mm)		£7.00	—

B SILKS

Size	Print-ing	Number in set		Handbook reference	Price per card	Complete set
—	C	48	British Empire Flags — 'Kensitas' (78 × 54mm) (1933)	H.496-4		
			A Inscribed 'Printed in U.S.A.'		90p	£45.00
			B Without the above		90p	£45.00
—	C	60	Kensitas Flowers — 'First Series', small (68 × 40mm) (1934):	H.496-1		
			1 Back of folder plain		£3.00	—
			2 Back of folder printed in green:			
			(a) Centre oval, 19mm deep		£3.00	—
			(b) Centre oval, 22mm deep		£3.00	—
			(c) As (b), inscribed 'washable ...'		£3.00	—
—	C	60	Kensitas Flowers — 'First Series', medium (76 × 55mm) (1934):	H.496-1		
			A Back of folder plain		£4.50	—
			B Back of folder printed in green		£4.50	—

Size	Printing	Number in set		Handbook reference	Price per card	Complete set

J. WIX & SONS LTD, London *(continued)*

	C	30	Kensitas Flowers — 'First Series' Extra-large (138 × 96mm) (1934):	H.496-1		
			A Back of folder plain		£40.00	—
			B Back of folder printed in green		£40.00	—
—	C	40	Kensitas Flowers — 'Second Series' (1935):	H.496-2		
			A Small size, 68 × 40mm			
			1. Nos 1-30		£6.00	—
			2. Nos. 31 to 40		£25.00	—
			B Medium size, 76 × 55mm			
			1. Nos 1-30		£6.00	—
			2. Nos. 31 to 40		£26.00	—
	C	60	National Flags — 'Kensitas' (78 × 54mm) (1934)	H.496-3	£1.15	£70.00

C POST-1940 ISSUES

			Ken-cards (102 × 118mm):			
		12	Series 1. Starters/Snacks (1969)		—	£5.00
		12	Series 2. Main Courses (1969)		—	£5.00
		12	Series 3. Desserts (1969)		—	£5.00
		12	Series 4. Motoring (1969)		—	£5.00
		12	Series 5. Gardening (1969)		—	£5.00
		12	Series 6. Do It Yourself (1969)		—	£5.00
		12	Series 7. Home Hints (1969)		—	£5.00
		12	Series 8. Fishing (1969)		—	£5.00

D MISCELLANEOUS

—	C	80	Bridge Favours and Place Cards (diecut) (1937)	H.681	£14.00	—
—	C	50	Bridge Hands (140 × 105mm) (1930)	H.682	£18.00	—
		42	Card Tricks by Jasper Maskelyne (c1935):	H.535-3		
			A Size 70 × 34mm		£6.00	—
			B Size 70 × 47mm		£6.00	—
	U		Jenkynisms:			
			A 'The K4's' Series (75-78 × 65mm) (c1932):			
		102	I. Known as 1st Series	H.636-1	80p	—
		50	II. Known as 2nd Series	H.636-2	80p	£40.00
		30	III. Known as 3rd Series	H.636-3	80p	—
		1	IV. Known as 4th Series	H.636-4	—	£2.50
			B The Red Bordered series (2 sizes each) (c1932):			
		21	I. Series of Quotations	H.637-1	£4.00	—
		? 44	II. 'Today's Jenkynisms'	H.637-2	£4.00	—

WOOD BROS., England

PRE-1919 ISSUE

—	BW	28	Dominoes (63 × 29mm) (c1910)		£70.00	—

T. WOOD, Cleckheaton

PRE-1919 ISSUE

D	C	30	*Army Pictures, Cartoons, etc (1916)	H.12	£110.00	—

JOHN J. WOODS, London

PRE-1919 ISSUE

A	BW	? 23	*Views of London (c1905)	H.395	£200.00	—

W. H. & J. WOODS LTD, Preston

A PRE-1919 ISSUE

—	C	1	Advertisement Card 'Perfection Flake' (86 × 35mm) (c1900)	H.773	—	£900.00
A	C	25	*Types of Volunteers and Yeomanry (c1902)	H.455	£32.00	£800.00

Size	Printing	Number in set		Handbook reference	Price per card	Complete set
W. H. & J. WOODS LTD, Preston *(continued)*						
B	**POST-1920 ISSUES**					
A2	U	25	Aesop's Fables (c1932)	H.518	£1.60	£40.00
A2	P	50	Modern Motor Cars (c1936)		£5.00	£250.00
D	C	25	Romance of the Royal Mail (c1933)		£1.20	£30.00

J. & E. WOOLF

PRE-1919 ISSUE

A	U	? 4	*Beauties 'KEWA' (c1900)	H.139	£600.00	—

M. H. WOOLLER, London

PRE-1919 ISSUE

A	—	25	Beauties 'BOCCA' (c1900)		£900.00	—

T. E. YEOMANS & SONS LTD, Derby

PRE-1919 ISSUES

—	C	72	Beautiful Women (75 × 55mm) (c1900)	H.284	£200.00	—
A	U	50	War Portraits (1916)	H.86	£95.00	—

JOHN YOUNG & SONS LTD, Bolton

PRE-1919 ISSUES

A2	C	12	Naval Skits (c1904)	H.457	£140.00	—
A2	C	12	*Russo-Japanese Series (1904)	H.456	£90.00	—

A. ZICALIOTTI

PRE-1919 ISSUE

A	C	1	Advertisement Card 'Milly Totty' (c1900)	H.774	—	£1250.00

LONDON CIGARETTE CARD CO LTD WEBSITE

www.londoncigcard.co.uk

Our website is a secure site so there are no worries about using your credit/debit card to place an order. The website now has over 100 pages for you to browse through.

New Issues and additions to stock from September 1999.
Sample card from each of more than 4000 series shown in colour.

36 Thematic Lists containing thousands of sets covering many subjects such as Football, Cricket, Motoring, Royalty, Military, Sci Fi & Films, etc.

Full range of storage albums illustrated.

Details of around 50 books on the subject of card collecting.

Sets of the month from September 2000 onwards with description of each set.

Article on the auction with a taster of what's up for sale each month.

Details on Card Collectors News Magazine, Our Shop in West Street, Somerton, Framing Kits, Who's Who at the LCCC etc. Plus special offers pages changed each month.

Size	Print-ing	Number in set		Handbook reference	Price per card	Complete set

ANONYMOUS SERIES

A   PRE-1919 ISSUES. WITH LETTERPRESS ON BACK OF CARD

Size	Print-ing	Number in set	Description	Handbook reference	Price per card	Complete set
A2	C	20	Animal Series: See Hill			
			A 'The cigarettes with which ...' back			
			B Space at back			
A	U	? 40	*Beauties — 'KEW A' England Expects ...' back	H.139	£125.00	—
D	BW	25	*Boxers, green back See Cohen Weenen			
A1	C	? 2	*Celebrities — Coloured. 1902 Calendar back. See Cohen Weenen			
D	C	? 2	*Celebrities — 'GAINSBOROUGH I', 1902 Calendar back, gilt border to front. See Cohen Weenen	H.90		
A2	C	20	*Interesting Buildings and Views, 1902 Calendar back. See Cohen Weenen	H.96		
D2	C	? 1	*Nations, 1902 Calendar back. See Cohen Weenen ...	H.97		
A	C	25	*Types of British Soldiers, 'General Favourite Onyx' back	H.144	—	—
D	C	25	V.C. Heroes (Nos. 51-75 — See Cohen Weenen)			
A	C	41	V.C. Heroes — 'Pure Virginia Cigarettes' — Dobson Molle & Co. Ltd. — Printers	H.427	£8.00	—
A	C	41	V.C. Heroes — See Thomson and Porteous	H.427		
D	U	50	*War Series (Cohen Weenen — Nos. 1-50)	H.103		

B   PRE-1919 ISSUES. WITH PLAIN BACK

Size	Print-ing	Number in set	Description	Handbook reference	Price per card	Complete set
A	U	25	*Actors and Actresses — 'FROGA C'	H.20	£12.00	—
D2	U	? 9	*Actresses — 'ANGLO'	H.185	£80.00	—
	U		*Actresses — 'ANGOOD':	H.187		
			A Brown tinted —			
		? 2	i. Thick board		—	—
		? 12	ii. Thin board		—	—
		? 9	B Green tinted		—	—
		? 25	C Black tinted		£30.00	—
A1	BW	20	*Actresses — 'BLARM'	H.23	£10.00	—
D	U	20	*Actresses — Chocolate tinted. See Hill	H.207		
A	C	? 50	*Actresses — 'DAVAN':	H.124		
			A Portrait in red only		—	—
			B Portrait in colour		£40.00	—
D	BW	12	*Actresses — 'FRAN'. See Drapkin	H.175		
A		26	*Actresses — 'FROGA A':	H.20		
	C		i. Coloured		£12.00	—
	U		ii. Unicoloured		£12.00	—
A1	BW	10	*Actresses — 'HAGG A'	H.24	£10.00	—
A1	BW	? 9	*Actresses — 'HAGG B'	H.24	£10.00	—
A	BW	15	*Actresses — 'RUTAN' See Rutter	H.381		
—	C	50	*Actresses Oval Card (as Phillips)	H.324		
A1	U		*Actresses and Beauties — Collotype (See Ogden) ...	H.306		
C	C	20	*Animal Series. See Hill			
—	C	? 12	*Arms of Cambridge Colleges (17 × 25mm). See Kuit .	H.458		
—	C	? 12	*Arms of Companies (30 × 33mm). See Kuit	H.459		
A2	BW	? 13	*Battleships. See Hill	H.208		
A	C	25	*Beauties — 'BOCCA'	H.39	£15.00	—
A		50	*Beauties — 'CHOAB':	H.21		
	U		A Unicoloured		£12.00	—
	C		B Coloured		£10.00	—
A			*Beauties — 'FECKSA':	H.58		
	U	50	A Plum-coloured front		£9.00	—
	C	? 6	B Coloured front		£45.00	—
D2	U	? 23	*Beauties — 'FENA'	H.148	£45.00	—

Size	Print-ing	Number in set		Handbook reference	Price per card	Complete set

ANONYMOUS SERIES (continued)

Size	Print-ing	Number in set	Title	Handbook reference	Price per card	Complete set
A2	C	25	*Beauties — 'GRACC'	H.59	£16.00	—
A	C	26	*Beauties — 'HOL'	H.192	£11.00	—
A	U	? 41	*Beauties 'KEWA'	H.139	—	—
D	BW	50	*Beauties — 'PLUMS' (c1900)	H.186	—	—
—	C	30	*Beauties — Oval card (36 × 60mm.) (See Phillips)	H.244		
A	U	? 17	*Beauties — Collotype	H.278	—	—
D1	U		*Bewlay's War Series:	H.477		
		12	1. Front without captions		—	—
		? 1	2. Front with captions		—	—
A2	BW	20	*Boer War Cartoons	H.42	£20.00	—
A	C		*Boer War and General Interest:	H.13		
		? 17	A Plain cream back		£40.00	—
		? 22	B Brown Leaf Design back		£40.00	—
		? 12	C Green Leaf Design back		£40.00	—
		? 6	D Green Daisy Design back		—	—
A2	BW	? 16	*Boer War Celebrities — 'CAG'	H.79	£25.00	—
A		? 7	Boer War Celebrities 'RUTTER':	H.382		
	BW		A Front in Black and White		£25.00	—
	U		B Front in light orange brown		£25.00	—
D2	BW	20	*Boer War Generals — 'CLAM'	H.61	£16.00	—
A1	BW	? 10	*Boer War Generals — 'FLAC'	H.47	£16.00	—
D	C	25	*Boxer Rebellion — Sketches (1904)	H.46	£12.00	—
A	C	54	*British Beauties (Phillips) (1-54)	H.328		
A	C	54	*British Beauties (Phillips) (55-108) Matt	H.328		
A	C	12	British Queens	H.480	£20.00	—
A	BW	16	*British Royal Family	H.28	£10.00	—
A	C	45	*Celebrities — Coloured (Cohen Weenen)	H.89		
D	C	39	*Celebrities — 'GAINSBOROUGH I'. See Cohen Weenen	H.90		
D	BW	? 147	*Celebrities — 'GAINSBOROUGH II'. See Cohen Weenen	H.91		
A1	P	36	*Celebrities of the Great War (1916). See Major Drapkin & Co			
A	BW	? 12	Celebrities of the Great War	H.236	—	—
A	C		*Colonial Troops:	H.40		
		30	A Cream card		—	—
		50	B White card		£15.00	—
A	BW	20	Cricketers Series	H.29	£225.00	—
A	C	50	Dogs (as Taddy) (c1900):	H.487		
			A Borders in green		£25.00	—
			B Borders in white		£25.00	—
A	C	25	*England's Military Heroes. See Player:	H.352		
			A Wide card			
			B Narrow card			
A	C	25	*England's Naval Heroes. See Player:	H.353		
			A Wide card			
			B Narrow card			
A	C	20	*The European War Series	H.129	£7.00	—
A	C		*Flags, Arms and Types of Nations:	H.115		
		24	A Numbered		£8.00	—
		? 2	B Unnumbered		—	—
A	C		*Flags and Flags with Soldiers:	H.41		
		30	A Flagstaff Draped		£8.00	—
		15	B Flagstaff not Draped (Flags only)		£8.00	—
A1	C	30	*Flags of Nations. See Cope	H.114		
A1	C	24	*Girls, Flags and Arms of Countries. See Rutter	H.383		
A	C	40	*Home and Colonial Regiments	H.69	£9.00	—

Size	Print-ing	Number in set		Handbook reference	Price per card	Complete set

ANONYMOUS SERIES (continued)

Size	Print-ing	Number in set		Handbook reference	Price per card	Complete set
A	C	52	*Japanese Series, P.C. Inset. See Muratti			
A1	P	? 2	*King Edward and Queen Alexandra	H.460	£18.00	—
C	C	20	*National Flag Series. See Hill			
D	C	20	*Nations, gilt border. See Cohen Weenen	H.97		
D	C	40	*Naval and Military Phrases:	H.14		
			A Plain front (no border)		£9.00	
			B Front with gilt border		—	—
—	U	? 1	*Portraits. See Drapkin & Millhoff (48 × 36mm)	H.461		
A	U	? 47	*Pretty Girl Series — 'BAGG'	H.45	£16.00	—
A2	C	12	*Pretty Girl Series 'RASH' (c1897)	H.8	£16.00	—
A1	C	20	*Prince of Wales Series. See Hill	H.22	£12.00	—
D	C	30	*Proverbs	H.15	£10.00	—
A	BW	19	Russo-Japanese Series	H.184	£20.00	—
A	C	20	Russo-Japanese War Series	H.100	£20.00	—
A	C	10	Scenes from San Toy. See Richard Lloyd	H.462		
A	C	25	Sports and Pastimes Series No.1	H.225	£8.00	—
A	C	25	*Star Girls	H.30	£12.00	—
A1	BW	? 28	*Statuary (Hill A-D).............................	H.218		
A	C	25	*Types of British and Colonial Troops	H.76		
A2	C	25	*Types of British Soldiers	H.144	£10.00	—
—	U	? 22	Views and Yachts (narrow, abt. 63 × 30mm)	H.262-2	£50.00	—
D	BW	12	*Views of the World. See Drapkin	H.176		
D	BW	8	*Warships. See Drapkin	H.463		
D			*War Series:	H.103		
	U	? 1	A Front in brown		—	—
	BW	? 3	B Front in black and white		—	—

C POST-1920 ISSUES. WITH LETTERPRESS ON BACK

Size	Print-ing	Number in set		Handbook reference	Price per card	Complete set
	C	25	Cinema Stars — see Teofani:	H.530		
C2			A Small size			
—			B Extra-large size (109 × 67mm)			
A2	U	50	Cinema Stars — Set 7 — see United Kingdom Tobacco Co...............................	Ha.515-7		
D2	C	25	Cinema Stars — Set 8 — see Moustafa	Ha.515-8		
A2	C	50	Evolution of the British Navy — see Godfrey Phillips .			
A2	BW	40	Famous Film Stars, text in Arabic (two series) — see Hill			
A2	C	50	Famous Footballers — see Godfrey Phillips			
A2	C	35	Famous Stars — see Reliance Tobacco Mfg. Co.	H.572		
C2	C	20	Great Inventors — see Teofani	H.213		
D2	U	48	Modern Movie Stars and Cinema Celebrities — see Teofani	H.569		
D2	C	25	Pictures of World Interest — see Moustafa			
C2	U	24	Well-Known Racehorses — see Teofani	H.609		

D POST-1920 ISSUES. WITH DESIGNS ON BACK

Size	Print-ing	Number in set		Handbook reference	Price per card	Complete set
A	BW	25	Careless Moments (1922)		80p	£20.00
D2	U	28	*Dominoes ("W.T.C." monogram back) — see Walker's Tobacco Co........................	H.535-2		
—	C	53	*Miniature Playing Cards (68 × 42mm) (red back, black cat trade mark in centre) — see Carreras	H.535-1		
K2	C	53	*Miniature Playing Cards (blue scroll back) — see Godfrey Phillips			
K2	C	53	*Miniature Playing Cards — see J. Wix:	H.535-3		
			A Scroll design:			
			1 Red back			
			2 Blue back			
			B Ship design:			
			2 Black border — Drake's "Revenge"			

Size	Printing	Number in set		Handbook reference	Price per card	Complete set

ANONYMOUS SERIES *(continued)*

Size	Printing	Number in set	Description	Handbook reference	Price per card	Complete set
C			*Playing Cards and Dominoes — see Carreras:	H.535-1		
C		52	A Small size:			
			1 Numbered			
			2 Unnumbered			
—		26	B Large size (77 × 69mm):			
			1 Numbered			
			2 Unnumbered			

E POST-1920 ISSUES. WITH PLAIN BACK

Size	Printing	Number in set	Description	Handbook reference	Price per card	Complete set
A2	P	36	Australia. Second Series — see Westminster			
A2	P	18	*Beauties — see Marcovitch	Ha.627		
A1	P	60	*British Beauty Spots — see Coudens	H.553		
B1	P	50	*British Castles, Nd. S.J.51-S.J.100 — see Pattreiouex	Ha.595-3		
—	C	108	*British Naval Crests (74 × 52mm)	Ha.504-4	—	—
D2	CP	50	*Camera Studies — see Moustafa			
B1	P	50	*Cathedrals and Abbeys. Nd. S.J.1-S.J.50 — see Pattreiouex	Ha.595-3		
A	C	25	*Charming Portraits — see Continental Cigarette Factory	H.549		
A2	U	30	*Cinema Stars — Set 3	Ha.515-3	—	—
A2	U	30	*Cinema Stars — Set 6 (1935)	Ha.515-6	90p	£27.00
—	C	110	*Crests and Badges of the British Army (74 × 52mm):	H.502-2		
			(a) Numbered		—	—
			(b) Unnumbered		£3.00	—
—	BW	12	*Film Actors and Actresses (56 × 31mm) — see Teofani	H.618		
A	C	20	*Head Dresses of Various Nations — see Teofani	Ha.619-1		
A	—	20	*Inventors and Their Inventions — see Hill	H.213		
—	C	? 9	*Irish Views (68 × 67mm) — see Lambkin	H.585		
—	BW	12	*London Views (57 × 31mm) — see Teofani	H.620		
A	C	50	*Natives in Costume — see Teofani	Ha.619-2		
—	P	30	*Photographs (Animal Studies) (64 × 41mm)	Ha.541	£1.70	—
—	C	? 48	*Regimental Colours II (76 × 70mm)	H.502-7	£12.00	—
—	P	22	*Teofani Gems I — Series of 22 (53 × 35mm) — see Teofani	Ha.621-1		
—	P	28	*Teofani Gems II — Series of 28 (53 × 35mm) see Teofani	Ha.621-2		
—	P	36	*Teofani Gems III — Series of 36 (53 × 35mm) — see Teofani	Ha.621-3		
A	C	50	*World's Smokers — see Teofani	Ha.619-3		

F POST-1920 ISSUES. ANONYMOUS SERIES — Silks and Other Novelty Issues

For Anonymous Metal Plaques — see International Tobacco Co.
For Anonymous Metal Charms — see Rothman's.
For Anonymous Miniature Rugs — see Godfrey Phillips.
For Anonymous Lace Motifs — see Carreras.
For Anonymous Woven Silks — see Anstie and J. Wix.
For Anonymous Printed Silks with Blue Borders — see Themans.

SECTION II

FOREIGN CIGARETTE CARDS

INDEX OF BRANDS

Admiral Cigarettes — see National Cigarette & Tobacco Co.
Albert Cigarettes — see British American Tobacco Co.
S. Anargyros — see American Tobacco Co.
Between the Acts — see American Tobacco Co.
Big Run Cigarettes — see American Tobacco Co.
Black Spot Cigarettes — see Scerri
British Consuls — see Macdonald
Broadleaf Cigarettes — see American Tobacco Co.
Cairo Monopol Cigarettes — see American Tobacco Co.
Carolina Brights — see American Tobacco Co.
Copain Cigarettes — see British American Tobacco Co.
Coronet Cigarettes — see Sniders & Abrahams
Cycle Cigarettes — see American Tobacco Co.
Derby Little Cigars — see American Tobacco Co.
Domino Cigarettes — see British American Tobacco Co.
Egyptienne Luxury — see American Tobacco Co.
Emblem Cigarettes — see American Tobacco Co.
Fez Cigarettes — see American Tobacco Co.
Fume Emblem — see Westminster Tobacco Co.
Gold Coin Tobacco — see Buchner
Hassan Cigarettes — see American Tobacco Co.

Havelock Cigarettes — see Wills
Helmar Cigarettes — see American Tobacco Co.
Herbert Tareyton Cigarettes — see American Tobacco Co.
Hindu Cigarettes — see American Tobacco Co.
Hoffman House Magnums — see American Tobacco Co.
Honest Long Cut — see Duke or American Tobacco Co.
Hustler Little Cigars — see American Tobacco Co.
Islander, Fags, Specials, Cubs — see Bucktrout
Jack Rose Little Cigars — see American Tobacco Co.
Just Suits Cut Plug — see American Tobacco Co.
Kopec Cigarettes — see American Tobacco Co.
Lennox Cigarettes — see American Tobacco Co.
Le Roy Cigars — see Miller
Lifeboat Cigarettes — see United Tobacco Co.
Lotus Cigarettes — see United Tobacco Co.
Lucky Strike Cigarettes — see American Tobacco Co.
Luxury Cigarettes — see American Tobacco Co.
Magpie Cigarettes — see Schuh
Mascot Cigarettes — see British American Tobacco Co.
Mecca Cigarettes — see American Tobacco Co.
Milo Cigarettes — see Sniders & Abrahams

Miners Extra Smoking Tobacco — see American Tobacco Co.
Mogul Cigarettes — see American Tobacco Co.
Murad Cigarettes — see American Tobacco Co.
Nebo Cigarettes — see American Tobacco Co.
OK Cigarettes — see African Tobacco Mfrs.
Obak Cigarettes — see American Tobacco Co.
Officers Mess Cigarettes — see African Tobacco Mfrs.
Old Gold Cigarettes — see American Tobacco Co.
Old Judge Cigarettes — see Goodwin
Old Mills Cigarettes — see American Tobacco Co.
One of the Finest — see Buchner
Our Little Beauties — see Allen & Ginter
Oxford Cigarettes — see American Tobacco Co.

Pan Handle — see American Tobacco Co.
Perfection Cigarettes — see American Tobacco Co.
Peter Pan Cigarettes — see Sniders & Abrahams
Picadilly Little Cigars — see American Tobacco Co.
Piedmont Cigarettes — see American Tobacco Co.
Pinhead Cigarettes — see British American Tobacco Co.
Pirate Cigarettes — see Wills
Polo Bear Cigarettes — see American Tobacco Co.
Puritan Little Cigars — see American Tobacco Co.
Purple Mountain Cigarettes — see Wills

Recruit Little Cigars — see American Tobacco Co.
Red Cross — see Lorillard or American Tobacco Co.
Richmond Gem Cigarettes — see Allen & Ginter
Richmond Straight Cut Cigarettes — see American Tobacco Co.
Royal Bengal Little Cigars — see American Tobacco Co.

St. Leger Little Cigars — see American Tobacco Co.
Scots Cigarettes — see African Tobacco Mfrs
Scrap Iron Scrap — see American Tobacco Co.
Senator Cigarettes — see Scerri
Sensation Cut Plug — see Lorillard
Silko Cigarettes — see American Tobacco Co.
Sovereign Cigarettes — see American Tobacco Co.
Sportsman — see Carreras
Springbok Cigarettes — see United Tobacco Co.
Standard Cigarettes — see Carreras or Sniders & Abrahams
Sub Rosa Cigarros — see American Tobacco Co.
Sultan Cigarettes — see American Tobacco Co.
Sweet Caporal — see Kinney or American Tobacco Co. or ITC Canada
Sweet Lavender — see Kimball

Teal Cigarettes — see British American Tobacco Co.
Three Bells Cigarettes — see Bell
Tiger Cigarettes — see British American Tobacco Co.
Tokio Cigarettes — see American Tobacco Co.
Tolstoy Cigarettes — see American Tobacco Co.
Trumps Long Cut — see Moore & Calvi
Turf Cigarettes — see Carreras
Turkey Red Cigarettes — see American Tobacco Co.
Turkish Trophy Cigarettes — see American Tobacco Co.
Twelfth Night Cigarettes — see American Tobacco Co.

U.S. Marine — see American Tobacco Co.
Uzit Cigarettes — see American Tobacco Co.

Vanity Fair Cigarettes — see Kimball
Vice Regal Cigarettes — see Wills
Virginia Brights Cigarettes — see Allen & Ginter

Wings Cigarettes — see Brown & Williamson

Size	Number in set		Price per card	Complete set
AFRICAN CIGARETTE CO. LTD, Egypt				
	50	Actresses ALWICS (c1905)	£9.00	—
L	25	Auction Bridge (c1925)	£7.00	—
AFRICAN TOBACCO MANUFACTURERS, South Africa				
A CARD ISSUES				
L	29	All Blacks South African Tour (1928)	£16.00	—
	60	Animals (c1920):		
		A Cut Outs	£3.50	—
		B Not Cut Out	£3.25	—
	25	The Arcadia Fair (1924)	£10.00	—
MP	48	British Aircraft (1932)	£4.50	—
	50	Chinese Transport (1930)	£4.00	—
MP	48	Cinema Artistes (1930)	£3.50	—
	50	Cinema Stars "OMBI" Officers Mess Issue 1st Series (1921)	£1.80	£90.00
	50	Cinema Stars "OMBI" Officers Mess Issue 2nd Series (1921)	£2.00	£100.00
M	50	Famous and Beautiful Women (1938)	£2.50	—
L	50	Famous and Beautiful Women (1938)	£3.00	—
	33	Houses of Parliament (c1920)	£6.00	—
	58	Miniatures (c1925)	£6.00	—
MP	48	National Costume (1930)	£3.25	—
K	53	Playing Cards MP-SA Virginia Cigarettes (c1930)	£3.00	—
K	53	Playing Cards, OK Cigarettes (c1930)	£1.80	—
K	53	Playing Cards, Scotts Cigarettes (c1930)	£1.80	—
MP	48	Popular Dogs (1930)	£5.00	—
M	100	Postage Stamps, Rarest Varieties (1929)	£1.50	£150.00
M	80	Prominent NZ and Australian Rugby Players and Springbok 1937 Touring Team (1937)	£5.00	—
L	80	Prominent NZ and Australian Rugby Players and Springbok 1937 Touring Team (1937)	£3.00	—
	25	The Racecourse (1924)	£10.00	—
M	132	S. African Members of the Legislative Assembly (1921)	£35.00	—
M	100	The World of Sport (1938)	£4.00	—
L	100	The World of Sport (1938)	£3.50	—
B SILK ISSUES				
M	30	Some Beautiful Roses (c1925)	£9.00	—
M	25	Types of British Birds (c1925)	£9.00	—
M	20	Types of British Butterflies (c1925)	£11.00	—
M	25	Types of Railway Engines (c1925)	£26.00	—
M	25	Types of Sea Shells (c1925)	£13.00	—
ALLEN & GINTER, USA				
ALL SERIES ISSUED 1885-95				
	?	Actors and Actresses (sepia photographic)	£6.00	—
	?	Actresses and Beauties (coloured)	£8.00	—
	50	American Editors	£28.00	—
L	50	American Editors	£35.00	—
	50	Arms of All Nations	£22.00	—
	50	Birds of America	£13.00	£650.00
L	50	Birds of America	£25.00	—
	50	Birds of the Tropics	£14.00	£700.00
L	50	Birds of the Tropics	£26.00	—
	50	Celebrated American Indian Chiefs	£35.00	—
	50	City Flags	£12.00	—
	50	Fans of the Period	£25.00	—
	50	Fish from American Waters	£14.00	—

Size	Number in set		Price per card	Complete set
		ALLEN & GINTER, USA *(continued)*		
L	50	Fish from American Waters	£25.00	—
	50	Flags of All Nations (series title curved)	£8.00	£400.00
	48	Flags of All Nations (series title in straight line)	£8.00	£400.00
	50	Flags of All Nations, 2nd series	£10.00	£500.00
	47	Flags of the States and Territories	£12.00	—
	50	Fruits	£20.00	—
	50	Game Birds	£12.00	£600.00
L	50	Game Birds	£24.00	—
	50	General Government and State Capitol Buildings	£12.00	—
	50	Great Generals	£32.00	—
	50	Natives in Costume	£30.00	—
	50	Naval Flags	£14.00	£700.00
	50	Parasol Drill	£22.00	—
	50	Pirates of the Spanish Main	£35.00	—
	50	Prize and Game Chickens	£22.00	—
	50	Quadrupeds	£15.00	—
L	50	Quadrupeds	£27.00	—
	50	Racing Colors of the World:		
		A Front with white frame	£20.00	—
		B Front without white frame	£20.00	—
	50	Song Birds of the World	£12.00	£600.00
L	50	Song Birds of the World	£25.00	—
	50	Types of All Nations	£22.00	—
	50	Wild Animals of the World	£15.00	—
	50	The World's Beauties, 1st series	£20.00	—
	50	The World's Beauties, 2nd series	£20.00	—
	50	The World's Champions, 1st series	£50.00	—
	50	The World's Champions, 2nd series	£50.00	—
L	50	The World's Champions, 2nd series	£90.00	—
	50	The World's Decorations	£13.00	£650.00
L	50	The World's Decorations	£25.00	—
	50	World's Dudes	£20.00	—
	50	The World's Racers	£25.00	—
	50	World's Smokers	£20.00	—
	50	World's Sovereigns	£27.00	—

ALLEN TOBACCO CO., USA

L	?	Views and Art Studies (c1910)	£5.00	—

THE AMERICAN CIGARETTE CO. LTD, China

	25	Beauties Group 1 (c1900)	£18.00	—
	? 15	Beauties Group 2 (c1900)	£24.00	—
	50	Flowers (c1900)	£14.00	—

THE AMERICAN TOBACCO COMPANY, USA

ALL SERIES ISSUED 1890-1902

A   *TYPESET BACK IN BLACK*

	28	Beauties Domino Girls	£20.00	—
	25	Beauties Group 1 RB18/4	£4.00	—
	? 1	Beauties Group 2 RB18/20	—	—
	25	Beauties Group 3 RB18/25	£4.00	—
	27	Beauties Group 3 RB18/26	£4.00	£110.00
	25	Beauties Group 3 RB18/27	£4.00	—
	25	Beauties Group 3 RB18/29	£4.00	—

Size Number in set		Price per card	Complete set

THE AMERICAN TOBACCO COMPANY, USA *(continued)*

Size Number in set		Price per card	Complete set
	Beauties Group 4 RB18/36:		
50	a Coloured	£4.00	£200.00
? 50	b Sepia	£15.00	—
52	Beauties PC Inset	£8.00	£420.00
25	Beauties — Star Girls	£15.00	—
25	Dancers	£12.00	—
50	Dancing Women	£20.00	—
50	Fancy Bathers	£20.00	—
36	Japanese Girls	£50.00	—
25	Military Uniforms RB18/101	£14.00	—
25	Military Uniforms RB18/102	£12.00	—
27	Military Uniforms RB18/103	£8.00	—
50	Musical Instruments	£14.00	—
50	National Flag and Arms	£9.00	—
25	National Flag and Flowers — Girls	£20.00	—
50	Savage Chiefs and Rulers	£22.00	—

B   NET DESIGN BACK IN GREEN

25	Beauties Black background RB18/62	£12.00	—
25	Beauties Curtain background RB18/65	£10.00	£250.00
25	Beauties Flower Girls RB18/67	£9.00	—
25	Beauties Group 1 RB18/1	£4.00	—
27	Beauties Group 1 RB18/2	£4.00	—
25	Beauties Group 1 RB18/3	£4.00	—
24	Beauties Group 1 RB18/4	£4.00	—
25	Beauties Group 1 RB18/5	£4.00	—
25	Beauties Group 1 RB18/6	£4.00	—
50	Beauties Group 1 RB18/10	£4.00	—
25	Beauties Group 2 RB18/16	£4.00	—
25	Beauties Group 2 RB18/17	£4.00	—
? 24	Beauties Group 2 RB18/18	£4.00	—
25	Beauties Group 2 RB18/19	£4.00	—
25	Beauties Group 2 RB18/20	£4.00	—
25	Beauties Group 2 RB18/21	£5.00	—
36	Beauties Group 2 RB18/22	£6.00	—
25	Beauties Group 3 RB18/25	£4.00	—
? 10	Beauties Group 3 RB18/28	—	—
25	Beauties Group 3 RB18/30	£4.00	—
25	Beauties Group 3 RB18/31	£8.00	—
25	Beauties Group 3 RB18/32	£4.00	—
50	Beauties Marine and Universe Girls	£30.00	—
25	Beauties Palette Girls	£9.00	—
25	Beauties Star Girls	£18.00	—
25	Beauties — Stippled background RB18/78	£10.00	—
20	Beauties — thick border RB18/79	£30.00	—
52	Beauties with Playing Card inset Set 1 RB18/85 (Head & Shoulder)	£9.00	—
52	Beauties with Playing Card inset Set 2 RB18/86 (Half Length)	£9.00	—
25	Boer War Series II — Series A:		
	a) numbered	£4.60	£115.00
	b) unnumbered	£6.00	—
	c) unnumbered and untitled "series A"	£7.00	—
22	Boer War Series II — Series B	£7.00	—
25	Chinese Girls	£12.00	—
25	Fish from American Waters	£8.00	—
25	International Code of Signals	£9.00	—
27	Military Uniforms numbered	£8.00	—
25	Military Uniforms unnumbered	£13.00	—

Size Number in set			Price per card	Complete set

THE AMERICAN TOBACCO COMPANY, USA (continued)

	50	National Flags and Arms	£10.00	—
	25	Old and Ancient Ships 1st Series	£5.00	£125.00
	25	Old and Ancient Ships 2nd Series	£8.00	£200.00
	25	Star Series — Beauties	£16.00	—

C NET DESIGN BACK IN BLUE

Actresses:

P	? 300	A	Large Letter Back	£4.00	—
P	? 300	B	Small Letter Back	£5.00	—
	25	Beauties blue frameline:			
		A	Matt	£20.00	—
		B	Varnished	£20.00	—
	28	Beauties — Domino Girls		£20.00	—
	25	Beauties Group 1 dull backgrounds RB18/7.2		£12.00	—
	25	Beauties Group 1 vivid coloured backgrounds set 1 RB18/7.3		£12.00	—
	25	Beauties Group 1 vivid coloured backgrounds set 2 RB18/9		£12.00	—
	25	Beauties numbered:			
		A	Front in black and white	£18.00	—
		B	Front in mauve	£14.00	—
	24	Beauties — orange framelines		£27.00	—
		Beauties — playing cards:			
	52	A	Inscribed 52 subjects	£9.00	—
	53	B	Inscribed 53 subjects	£9.00	—
	32	Celebrities		£6.00	—
	25	Comic Scenes		£8.00	—
P	? 149	Views		£3.00	—

D "OLD GOLD" BACK

25	Beauties Group 1 RB18/1	£4.00	—
27	Beauties Group 1 RB18/2	£4.00	—
25	Beauties Group 1 RB18/3	£4.00	—
24	Beauties Group 1 RB18/4	£4.00	—
25	Beauties Group 1 RB18/5	£4.00	—
25	Beauties Group 1 RB18/6	£4.00	—
? 47	Beauties Group 2 RB18/16, 17, 18	£4.00	—
25	Beauties Group 2 RB18/22	£4.00	—
25	Beauties Group 3 RB18/25	£4.00	—
27	Beauties Group 3 RB18/26	£4.00	—
25	Beauties Group 3 RB18/27	£4.00	—
25	Beauties Group 3 RB18/28	£4.00	—
25	Beauties Group 3 RB18/30	£4.00	—
25	Flowers Inset on Beauties	£8.00	£200.00
25	International Code of Signals:		
	A With series title	£8.00	£200.00
	B Without series title	£8.00	£200.00

E LABELS BACK

35	Beauties Group 1 RB18/2-3	£4.00	—
25	Beauties Group 2 1st Set RB18/15	£4.00	—
25	Beauties Group 2 2nd Set RB18/16	£4.00	—
	Beauties Group 3 RB18/25-26:		
27	A Old Gold Label	£4.00	—
26	B Brands Label	£4.00	—

F OTHER BACKS WITH NAME OF FIRM

P	100	Actresses RB18/91	£4.00	—
	44	Australian Parliament	£4.00	£170.00
	25	Battle Scenes	£12.00	—
	1	Columbian and Other Postage Stamps (1892)	—	£12.00
	50	Congress of Beauty — Worlds Fair	£20.00	—

Size	Number in set		Price per card	Complete set

THE AMERICAN TOBACCO COMPANY, USA *(continued)*

Size	Number in set	Description	Price per card	Complete set
	25	Constellation Girls	£25.00	—
	50	Fish from American Waters	£12.00	—
	50	Flags of All Nations	£10.00	—
	25	Flower Inset on Beauties	£9.00	£225.00
	25	International Code of Signals	£9.00	£225.00
	25	Songs A (1896):		
		A Thicker board size 70 × 39mm	£13.00	—
		B Thinner board size 67 × 39mm	£13.00	£325.00
	25	Songs B (1898):		
		A Size 70 × 39mm	£13.00	£325.00
		B Size 67 × 39mm	£13.00	—
	25	Songs C 1st series (1900)	£8.00	—
	25	Songs C 2nd series (1900)	£11.00	—
	25	Songs D (1899)	£8.00	£200.00
	27	Songs E (1901)	£11.00	—
	25	Songs F (1897)	£11.00	—
	25	Songs G (1899)	£10.00	—
	25	Songs H (1901)	£18.00	—
	25	Songs I (1895)	£22.00	—

ISSUES 1903-1940

Size	Number in set	Description	Price per card	Complete set
L	50	Actors	£6.00	—
	85	Actress Series	£6.50	—
L	50	Actresses	£9.00	—
		Animals:		
L	40	A Descriptive back	£2.00	—
L	40	B Non descriptive back	£2.00	—
L	25	Arctic Scenes	£5.40	—
M	15	Art Gallery Pictures	£5.00	—
M	50	Art Reproductions	£5.00	—
	21	Art Series	£15.00	—
	18	Ask Dad	£12.00	—
L	50	Assorted Standard Bearers of Different Countries	£5.50	—
	25	Auto-drivers	£14.00	—
M	50	Automobile Series	£13.00	—
L	50	Baseball Folder series (T201) (1911)	£30.00	—
M	121	Baseball series (T204)	£40.00	—
	208	Baseball series (T205) (1911)	£20.00	—
	522	Baseball series (T206)	£18.00	—
	200	Baseball series (T207) (1910)	£25.00	—
	565	Baseball series (T210)	£25.00	—
	75	Baseball series (T211)	£25.00	—
	426	Baseball series (T212)	£25.00	—
	180	Baseball series (T213)	£25.00	—
	90	Baseball series (T214)	£100.00	—
	100	Baseball series (T215)	£30.00	—
L	76	Baseball Triple Folders (T202) (1912)	£40.00	—
		Bird series:		
	50	A With white borders	£2.50	—
	50	B With gold borders	£2.50	—
	30	Bird Series with Fancy Gold Frame	£2.50	—
M	360	Birthday Horoscopes	£2.00	—
M	24	British Buildings "Tareyton" issue	£3.00	—
M	42	British Sovereigns "Tareyton" issue	£3.00	—
M	50	Butterfly Series	£4.00	—
L	153	Champion Athlete & Prize Fighter series (size 73 × 64mm)	£7.00	—
L	50	Champion Athlete and Prize Fighter series (size 83 × 63 mm)	£10.00	—
L	50	Champion Pugilists	£18.00	—

139

Size	Number in set		Price per card	Complete set
		THE AMERICAN TOBACCO COMPANY, USA *(continued)*		
EL	100	Champion Women Swimmers	£8.00	—
M	150	College series	£2.50	—
M	50	Costumes and Scenery for All Countries of the World	£3.50	—
L	49	Cowboy series	£6.50	—
M	38	Cross Stitch	£9.00	—
M	17	Embarrassing Moments or Emotional Moments	£25.00	—
M	50	Emblem Series	£3.00	—
L	100	Fable Series	£2.70	—
LP	53	Famous Baseball Players, American Athletic Champions and Photoplay Stars	£40.00	—
	50	Fish Series inscribed "1 to 50" — 1st 50 subjects	£2.50	—
	50	Fish Series inscribed "1 to 100" — 2nd 50 subjects	£2.50	—
	200	Flags of All Nations	£1.50	—
M	100	Flags of All Nations	£12.00	—
	50	Foreign Stamp Series	£6.00	—
L	505	Fortune Series	£2.00	—
M	79	Henry "Tareyton" issue	£2.50	—
L	50	Heroes of History	£7.00	—
M	50	Historic Homes	£4.00	—
L	25	Historical Events Series	£7.00	—
M	25	Hudson — Fulton Series	£6.00	—
L	50	Indian Life in the 60s (1910)	£7.00	—
L	221	Jig Saw Puzzle Pictures	£10.00	—
L	50	Light House Series	£7.00	—
L	50	Men of History	£6.50	—
M	100	Military Series white borders	£4.50	—
	50	Military Series gilt borders	£5.00	—
	50	Military Series "Recruit" issue:		
		A Uncut cards	£4.50	—
		B Die-cut cards	£4.50	—
	50	Movie Stars	£5.00	—
L	100	Movie Stars	£5.00	—
	33	Moving Picture Stars	£20.00	—
EL	50	Murad Post Card Series	£7.50	—
	100	Mutt & Jeff Series (black and white)	£4.50	—
	100	Mutt & Jeff Series (coloured)	£4.50	—
EL	16	National League and American League Teams	£50.00	—
	50	Pugilistic Subjects	£20.00	—
EL	18	Puzzle Picture Cards	£15.00	—
M	200	Riddle Series	£2.50	—
EL	60	Royal Bengal Souvenir Cards	£8.00	—
M	150	Seals of the United States and Coats of Arms of the World	£2.00	—
L	25	Series of Champions	£25.00	—
L	50	Sights and Scenes of the World	£3.50	—
L	50	Silhouettes	£8.00	—
L	25	Song Bird Series	£30.00	—
	39	Sports Champions	£20.00	—
	45	Stage Stars	£8.00	—
	25	State Girl Series	£6.50	—
L	50	Theatres Old and New Series	£7.00	—
M	50	Toast Series	£7.50	—
M	550	Toast Series	£2.00	—
L	25	Toasts	£12.00	—
	50	Types of Nations:		
		A Without series title	£2.50	—
		B With series title	£2.50	—
		C Anonymous back	£2.50	—

Size	Number in set		Price per card	Complete set

THE AMERICAN TOBACCO COMPANY, USA *(continued)*

L	25	Up to Date Baseball Comics	£20.00	—
L	25	Up to Date Comics	£8.00	—
P	340	World Scenes and Portraits	£3.00	—
	250	World War I Scenes	£2.25	—
L	50	World's Champion Athletes	£10.00	—
L	25	The World's Greatest Explorers	£5.60	—

THE AMERICAN TOBACCO CO. OF NEW SOUTH WALES LTD, Australia

	25	Beauties Group 1 RB18/8 (c1900)	£12.00	—
	25	Beauties Group 2 (c1900)	£12.00	—

THE AMERICAN TOBACCO CO. OF VICTORIA LTD, Australia

	? 98	Beauties Group 2 (c1900)	£12.00	—

ATLAM CIGARETTE FACTORY, Malta

M	65	Beauties back in blue (c1925)	£2.50	—
	150	Beauties back in brown (c1925)	£5.00	—
M	519	Celebrities (c1925)	£1.20	—
L	50	Views of Malta (c1925)	£5.00	—
M	128	Views of the World (c1925)	£5.00	—

BANNER TOBACCO CO., USA

EL	25	Girls (c1890)	£32.00	—

THOMAS BEAR & SONS LTD

	50	Aeroplanes (1926)	£4.00	—
	50	Cinema Artistes Set 2 (c1935)	£3.50	—
	50	Cinema Artistes Set 4 (c1935)	£3.50	—
	50	Cinema Stars coloured (1930)	£2.50	£125.00
	50	Do You Know (1923)	£1.70	£85.00
	270	Javanese series 1 blue background (c1925)	£1.50	—
	100	Javanese series 4 yellow background (c1925)	£8.00	—
	50	Stage and Film Stars (1926)	£3.60	—

AUG BECK & CO. USA

	? 34	Picture Cards (c1890)	£60.00	—

J. & F. BELL LTD, Denmark

	60	Rigsvaabner (Arms of Countries) (c1925)	£30.00	—
	60	Women of Nations (1924)	£30.00	—

BENSON & HEDGES (CANADA) LTD

	48	Ancient and Modern Fire Fighting Equipment (1947)	£6.00	—

BRITISH AMERICAN TOBACCO CO. LTD

A *WITH MAKER'S NAME NET DESIGN IN GREEN (ISSUES 1902-05)*

	25	Beauties Art series RB18/61	£12.00	—
	25	Beauties — Black background RB18/62	£11.00	—
	25	Beauties — Blossom Girls RB18/63	£38.00	—
	25	Beauties — Flower Girls RB18/67	£9.00	—

Size	Number in set		Price per card	Complete set

BRITISH AMERICAN TOBACCO CO. LTD *(continued)*

Size	Number in set		Price per card	Complete set
	25	Beauties — Fruit Girls RB18/68	£12.00	—
	25	Beauties — Girls in Costumes RB18/69	£12.00	—
	20	Beauties Group 1 RB18/9	£10.00	—
	25	Beauties — Lantern Girls RB18/70	£10.00	£250.00
	50	Beauties — Marine and Universe Girls RB18/71	£11.00	—
	25	Beauties — Palette Girls RB18/74:		
		A Plain border to front	£9.00	—
		B Red border to front	£13.00	—
	24	Beauties — Smoke Girls RB18/75	£15.00	—
	25	Beauties — Star Girls RB18/76	£15.00	—
	25	Beauties — Stippled background RB18/78	£9.00	£225.00
	25	Beauties — Water Girls RB18/80	£9.00	£225.00
	50	Buildings RB18/131	£9.00	—
	25	Chinese Girls 'A' RB18/111	£9.00	—
	25	Chinese Girls 'B' RB18/112:		
		A Background plain	£9.00	—
		B Background with Chinese letters	£9.00	—
	25	Chinese Girls 'C' RB18/113	£9.00	—
	25	Chinese Girls 'D' RB18/114	£9.00	—
	25	Chinese Girls 'E' RB18/115	£9.00	—
	25	Chinese Girls 'F' Set 1 RB18/116	£9.00	—
	25	Chinese Girls 'F' Set 2 RB18/116:		
		A Yellow border	£9.00	—
		B Gold border	£12.00	—
	50	Chinese Girls 'F' Set 3:		
		A Plain background	£9.00	—
		B Chinese characters background	£10.00	—
	40	Chinese Trades	£7.00	—

B WITH MAKER'S NAME NET DESIGN IN BLUE (ISSUES 1902-05)

	25	Beauties — numbered	£18.00	—
	53	Beauties — Playing Cards	£8.00	—

C WITH MAKER'S NAME OTHER BACKS

MP	50	Beauties (1925)	£2.50	—
MP	40	Beauties (1926)	£2.50	—
M	50	Birds, Beasts and Fishes (1925)	£2.00	£100.00
	50	Danish Athletes (1905)	£11.00	—
	28	Dominoes (1905)	£6.00	—
	48	Fairy Tales (1926)	£4.00	—
	48	A Famous Picture — The Toast (c1930)	£3.00	—
	25	New York Views (c1908)	£10.00	—
	53	Playing Cards (1905)	£10.00	—
M	50	Wild Animals (c1930)	£2.00	—

D SERIES WITH BRAND NAMES

ALBERT CIGARETTES

M	50	Aeroplanes (Civils) (1935)	£12.00	—
	50	Artistes de Cinema Nd 1-50 (1932)	£3.00	—
	50	Artistes de Cinema Nd 51-100 (1933)	£3.00	—
	50	Artistes de Cinema Nd 101-150 (1934)	£3.00	—
MP	? 67	Beauties (c1928)	£4.00	—
M	75	Belles Vues de Belgique (c1930)	£2.70	—
M	50	Birds, Beasts & Fishes (c1930)	£4.00	—
M	50	Butterflies (Girls) (1926)	£6.00	—
M	50	Cinema Stars (brown photogravure) (c1927)	£3.00	—
M	100	Cinema Stars (numbered, coloured) (c1928)	£3.00	—
M	208	Cinema Stars (unnumbered, coloured) (c1929)	£3.00	—

Size	Number in set		Price per card	Complete set

BRITISH AMERICAN TOBACCO CO. LTD *(continued)*

Size	Number in set		Price per card	Complete set
M	100	Circus Scenes (c1930)	£3.50	—
M	100	Famous Beauties (1916)	£3.50	—
M	50	L'Afrique Equitoriale de l'Est a l'Ouest (c1930)	£2.50	—
M	100	La Faune Congolaise (c1930)	£1.50	—
M	50	Les Grandes Paquebots du Monde (1924)	£6.00	—
M	50	Merveilles du Monde (1927)	£3.50	—
M	50	Women of Nations (Flag Girls) (1922)	£4.00	—

ATLAS CIGARETTES

	50	Buildings (1907)	£5.00	—
	25	Chinese Beauties (1912)	£2.80	—
	50	Chinese Trades Set IV (1908)	£2.50	—
	85	Chinese Trades Set VI (1912)	£2.50	—

BATTLE AX CIGARETTES

M	100	Famous Beauties (1916)	£4.50	—
M	50	Women of Nations (Flag Girls) (1917)	£5.50	—

COPAIN CIGARETTES

	52	Birds of Brilliant Plumage (1927)	£5.50	—

DOMINO CIGARETTES

	25	Animaux et Reptiles (1961)	20p	£4.00
	25	Corsaires et Boucaniers (1961)	20p	£2.50
	25	Figures Historiques 1st series (1961)	30p	£7.50
	25	Figures Historiques 2nd series (1961)	70p	£17.50
	25	Fleurs de Culture (1961)	20p	£2.50
	25	Les Oiseaux et l'Art Japonais (1961)	£1.00	—
	25	Les Produits du Monde (1961)	20p	£2.50
	50	Voitures Antiques (1961)	£1.20	—

EAGLE BIRD CIGARETTES

	50	Animals and Birds (1909)	£2.00	—
	50	Aviation series (1912)	£4.00	—
	25	Birds of the East (1912)	£2.00	£50.00
	25	China's Famous Warriors (1911)	£3.00	£75.00
	25	Chinese Beauties 1st series (1908):		
		A Vertical back	£3.00	—
		B Horizontal back	£3.00	—
	25	Chinese Beauties 2nd series (1909):		
		A Front without framelines	£2.40	—
		B Front with framelines	£2.40	—
	50	Chinese Trades (1908)	£2.20	£110.00
	25	Cock Fighting (1911)	£10.00	—
	60	Flags and Pennons (1926)	£1.30	£80.00
	50	Romance of the Heavens (1929)	£2.00	—
	50	Siamese Alphabet (1922)	£1.40	£70.00
	50	Siamese Dreams and Their Meanings (1923)	£1.10	£55.00
	50	Siamese Horoscopes (c1915)	£1.10	£55.00
	50	Siamese Play-Inao (c1915)	£1.40	£70.00
	50	Siamese Play-Khun Chang Khun Phaen 1st series (c1915)	£1.40	£70.00
	50	Siamese Play-Khun Chang Khun Phaen 2nd series (c1915)	£1.40	£70.00
	36	Siamese Play-Phra Aphaiu 1st series (c1918)	£1.50	£55.00
	36	Siamese Play-Phra Aphaiu 2nd series (1919)	£1.50	£55.00
	150	Siamese Play — Ramakien I (c1913)	£1.40	—
	50	Siamese Play — Ramakien II (1914)	£1.40	£70.00
	50	Siamese Uniforms (1915)	£2.00	£100.00
	50	Views of Siam (1928)	£3.00	£150.00
	50	Views of Siam (Bangkok) (1928)	£4.00	£200.00
	30	War Weapons (1914)	£2.00	£60.00

Size	Number in set		Price per card	Complete set

BRITISH AMERICAN TOBACCO CO. LTD *(continued)*

KONG BENG CIGARETTES
- 60   Animals (cut-outs) (1912) .... £7.00   —

MASCOT CIGARETTES
- 100   Cinema Stars (Nd 201-300) (1931) .... £3.00   —
- M   208   Cinema Stars unnumbered (1924) .... £2.40   —

MILLBANK CIGARETTES
- 60   Animals (cut-outs):
  - A   '1516' at base of back (1922) .... £1.20   —
  - B   '3971' at base of back (1923) .... £1.20   —

NASSA CIGARETTES
- M   50   Birds, Beasts and Fishes (1924) .... £4.00   —

PEDRO CIGARETTES *(see also Imperial Tobacco Co. of India)*
- 50   Actors and Actresses (c1905) .... £3.50   —
- 40   Nautch Girls. Coloured (1905) .... £2.50   —
- 37   Nautch Girls. Red border (c1905) .... £2.50   —

PINHEAD CIGARETTES
- 50   Chinese Modern Beauties (1912) .... £3.00   —
- 33   Chinese Heroes Set 1 (1912) .... £3.00   —
- 50   Chinese Heroes Set 2 (1913) .... £3.00   —
- 50   Chinese Trades Set III (1908) £3.00   £150.00
- 50   Chinese Trades Set IV (1909) £3.00   £150.00
- 50   Chinese Trades Set V (1910) £3.00   £150.00
- 50   Types of the British Army (1909) .... £4.00   —

RAILWAY CIGARETTES *(see also Imperial Tobacco Co. of India)*
- 37   Nautch Girls series (1907) .... £2.50   —

TEAL CIGARETTES
- 30   Chinese Beauties (c1915) .... £5.00   —
- 50   Cinema Stars (1930):
  - A   Back in blue .... £2.00   —
  - B   Back in red brown .... £2.00   —
- 30   Fish series (1916) £3.00   £90.00
- 50   War Incidents (1916) £2.50   £125.00

TIGER CIGARETTES
- 52   Nautch Girls series (1911):
  - A   Without frameline to front .... £2.50   —
  - B   With frameline to front:
    - i   With crossed cigarettes on back .... £2.50   —
    - ii   Without crossed cigarettes on back .... £2.50   —

E   PRINTED ON BACK NO MAKER'S NAME OR BRAND

(See also Imperial Tobacco Co. of Canada Ltd and United Tobacco Companies (South) Ltd)

Actresses 'ALWICS' (c1905):
- 175   A   Portrait in black .... £3.50   —
- 50   B   Portrait in red .... £4.00   —
- 50   Aeroplanes (1926) £3.00   £150.00
- 50   Aeroplanes of Today (1936) £1.00   £50.00
- 25   Angling (1930) .... £5.00   —
- 50   Arms and Armour (1910) .... £6.00   —
- 25   Army Life (c1910) .... £6.40   —
- 50   Art Photogravures (1913) .... £1.10   —
- 1   Australia Day (1915) .... —   £15.00
- 22   Automobielen (c1925) .... £7.00   —
- 75   Aviation (1910) .... £4.00   —

Size	Number in set		Price per card	Complete set
	50	Aviation series (1911):		
		A With album clause	£3.75	—
		B Without album clause	£3.50	—
		Beauties Set I (1925):		
P	50	A Black and white	£2.30	£115.00
MP	50	B Coloured	£2.00	—
P	50	Beauties 2nd series (1925):		
		A Black and white	£2.30	£115.00
		B Coloured	£2.00	—
P	50	Beauties 3rd series (1926)	£1.50	£75.00
	50	Beauties red tinted (c1906)	£3.00	—
		Beauties tobacco leaf back (c1908):		
	52	A With PC inset	£3.20	£160.00
	50	B Without PC inset	£4.00	£200.00
P	50	Beauties of Great Britain (1930):		
		A Non-stereoscopic	70p	£35.00
		B Stereoscopic	£2.50	—
P	50	Beautiful England (1928)	50p	£25.00
MP	60	La Belgique Monumentale et Pittoresque (c1925)	£3.25	—
	50	Best Dogs of Their Breed (1916)	£4.20	—
	50	Billiards (1929)	£2.00	—
	50	Birds, Beasts and Fishes (1937)	70p	£35.00
M	50	Birds, Beasts and Fishes (1929)	£1.20	£60.00
	24	Birds of England (1924)	£2.60	£65.00
	50	Boy Scouts (1930) — without album clause	£2.50	£125.00
	50	Britain's Defenders (1915):		
		A Blue grey fronts	£2.00	—
		B Mauve fronts	£1.50	£75.00
	50	British Butterflies (1930)	£1.10	£55.00
	50	British Empire series (1913)	£2.50	—
	25	British Trees and Their Uses (1930)	£2.00	£50.00
	50	British Warships and Admirals (1915)	£3.50	—
	50	Butterflies and Moths (1911):		
		A With album clause	£3.00	—
		B Without album clause	£1.80	—
	50	Butterflies (Girls) (1928)	£5.50	£275.00
M	50	Butterflies (Girls) (1928)	£7.00	£350.00
M	50	Celebrities of Film and Stage (1930):		
		A Title on back in box	£2.00	£100.00
		B Title on back not in box	£2.00	£100.00
LP	48	Channel Islands Past and Present (1939):		
		A Without '3rd Series'	£1.20	—
		B With '3rd Series'	32p	£16.00
	40	Characters from the Works of Charles Dickens (1919):		
		A Complete set	—	£45.00
		B 38 different (— Nos 33, 39)	60p	£23.00
	50	Cinema Artistes, black and white set 1 (Nd 1-50) (c1928)	£1.80	£90.00
	50	Cinema Artistes black and white set 4 (Nd 101-150) (c1928)	£1.80	£90.00
		Cinema Artistes brown set 1 (c1930):		
	60	A With 'Metro Golden Mayer'	£2.50	—
	50	B Without 'Metro Golden Mayer'	£2.50	—
	50	Cinema Artistes brown set 2 (c1931):		
		A Oblong panel at top back	£2.00	£100.00
		B Oval panel at top back	£2.00	£100.00
L	48	Cinema Artistes set 3 (c1931)	£2.00	£100.00
	48	Cinema Celebrities (C) (1935)	£1.10	£55.00
L	48	Cinema Celebrities (C) (1935)	£1.50	£75.00

Size	Number in set		Price per card	Complete set

BRITISH AMERICAN TOBACCO CO. LTD *(continued)*

Size	Number in set	Title	Price per card	Complete set
L	56	Cinema Celebrities (D) (1936)	£2.70	—
	50	Cinema Favourites (1929)	£2.20	£110.00
	50	Cinema Stars Set 2 (Nd 1-50) (1928)	£1.20	£60.00
	50	Cinema Stars Set 3 (Nd 51-100) (1929)	£3.00	—
	50	Cinema Stars Set 4 (Nd 101-150) (1930)	£1.20	—
	100	Cinema Stars 'BAMT' (coloured) (1931)	£2.30	—
P	50	Cinema Stars Set 1 (c1928)	£1.50	—
P	50	Cinema Stars Set 2 (c1928)	£1.20	£60.00
P	50	Cinema Stars Set 3 (c1928)	£1.50	—
MP	52	Cinema Stars Set 4 (c1928)	£1.80	—
MP	52	Cinema Stars Set 5 (c1928)	£1.80	—
MP	52	Cinema Stars Set 6 (c1928)	£2.50	—
LP	48	Cinema Stars Set 7 (c1928)	£3.00	—
P	50	Cinema Stars Set 8 (Nd 1-50) (c1928)	£1.20	£60.00
P	50	Cinema Stars Set 9 (Nd 51-100) (c1928)	£2.50	—
P	50	Cinema Stars Set 10 (Nd 101-150) (c1928)	£2.50	—
P	50	Cinema Stars Set 11 (Nd 151-200) (c1928)	£2.50	—
	25	Derby Day series (1914)	£9.00	—
	50	Do You Know? (1923)	50p	£25.00
	50	Do You Know? 2nd series (1931)	50p	£25.00
	25	Dracones Posthistorici (c1930)	£8.00	—
	25	Dutch Scenes (1928)	£3.00	£75.00
	50	Engineering Wonders (1930)	60p	£30.00
	40	English Costumes of Ten Centuries (1919)	£1.50	£60.00
P	25	English Cricketers (1926)	£2.80	£70.00
	26	Etchings (of Dogs) (1926)	£2.50	£65.00
P	50	Famous Bridges (1935)	£1.00	£50.00
	50	Famous Footballers Set 1 (1923)	£3.50	—
	50	Famous Footballers Set 2 (1924)	£3.50	—
	50	Famous Footballers Set 3 (1925)	£3.50	—
	25	Famous Racehorses (1926)	£3.00	£75.00
	25	Famous Railway Trains (1929)	£2.00	£50.00
	50	Favourite Flowers (c1925)	70p	£35.00
	50	Film and Stage Favourites (c1925)	£1.60	£80.00
	75	Film Favourites (1928)	£1.30	£100.00
	50	Flags of the Empire (1928)	80p	£40.00
	50	Foreign Birds (1930)	80p	£40.00
	50	Game Birds and Wild Fowl (1929)	£1.40	£70.00
LP	45	Grace and Beauty (Nos 1-45) (1938)	40p	£18.00
LP	45	Grace and Beauty (Nos 46-90) (1939)	30p	£13.50
LP	48	Guernsey, Alderney and Sark Past and Present 1st series (1937)	40p	£20.00
LP	48	Guernsey, Alderney and Sark Past and Present 2nd series (1938)	35p	£17.50
L	80	Guernsey Footballers Priaulx League (1938)	50p	£40.00
P	52	Here There and Everywhere:		
		A Non stereoscopic (1929)	40p	£20.00
		B Stereoscopic (1930)	80p	£40.00
	25	Hints and Tips for Motorists (1929)	£2.60	£65.00
P	50	Homeland Events (1928)	80p	£40.00
	50	Horses of Today (1906)	£5.00	—
	32	Houses of Parliament (red back) (1912)	£1.75	—
	32	Houses of Parliament (brown backs with verse) (1912)	£9.00	—
	50	Indian Chiefs (1930)	£9.00	—
	50	Indian Regiment series (1912)	£9.00	—
	50	International Airliners (1937)	80p	£40.00
	25	Java Scenes (1929)	£9.00	—
LP	48	Jersey Then and Now 1st series (1935)	£1.00	£50.00
LP	48	Jersey Then and Now 2nd series (1937)	80p	£40.00

Size	Number in set		Price per card	Complete set

BRITISH AMERICAN TOBACCO CO. LTD *(continued)*

Size	Number in set	Title	Price per card	Complete set
	50	Jiu Jitsu (1911)	£3.00	—
	50	Keep Fit (1939)	90p	£45.00
	50	Leaders of Men (1929)	£3.50	—
	50	Life in the Tree Tops (1931)	50p	£25.00
	50	Lighthouses (1926)	£1.60	£80.00
	40	London Ceremonials (1929)	£1.50	£60.00
P	50	London Zoo (1927)	70p	£35.00
	50	Lucky Charms (1930)	£1.50	£75.00
	25	Marvels of the Universe series (c1925)	£2.60	£65.00
	45	Melbourne Cup Winners (1906)	£7.00	—
	50	Merchant Ships of the World (1925)	£5.00	—
	25	Merchant Ships of the World (1925)	£3.50	—
	25	Military Portraits (1917)	£2.80	—
	36	Modern Beauties 1st series (1938)	£1.10	£40.00
	36	Modern Beauties 2nd series (1939)	60p	£22.00
MP	54	Modern Beauties 1st series (1937)	£1.00	£55.00
MP	54	Modern Beauties 2nd series (1938)	£1.00	£55.00
MP	36	Modern Beauties 3rd series (1938)	£1.50	£55.00
MP	36	Modern Beauties 4th series (1939)	£1.00	£36.00
ELP	36	Modern Beauties 1st series (1936)	£1.10	£40.00
ELP	36	Modern Beauties 2nd series (1936)	75p	£27.00
ELP	36	Modern Beauties 3rd series (1937)	85p	£30.00
ELP	36	Modern Beauties 4th series (1937)	£1.50	£55.00
ELP	36	Modern Beauties 5th series (1938)	£1.00	£36.00
ELP	36	Modern Beauties 6th series (1938)	85p	£30.00
ELP	36	Modern Beauties 7th series (1938)	£1.25	£45.00
LP	36	Modern Beauties 8th series (1939)	£1.50	£55.00
LP	36	Modern Beauties 9th Series (1939)	£1.50	£55.00
LP	36	Modern Beauties (1939)	£1.25	£45.00
	50	Modern Warfare (1936)	£1.10	£55.00
M	48	Modern Wonders (1938)	£3.00	—
	25	Modes of Conveyance (1928)	£1.80	£45.00
	48	Motor Cars green back (1926)	£4.00	—
	36	Motor Cars brown back (1929)	£5.50	—
	50	Motorcycles (1927)	£3.50	—
P	50	Native Life in Many Lands (1932)	£1.50	£75.00
P	50	Natural and Man Made Wonders of the World (1937)	60p	£30.00
P	50	Nature Studies stereoscopic (1928)	60p	£30.00
P	48	Nature Studies stereoscopic (1930)	80p	£40.00
	50	Naval Portraits (1917)	£2.50	—
	25	Notabilities (1917)	£2.60	£65.00
	25	Past and Present (1929)	£1.80	£45.00
P	48	Pictures of the East (1930):		
		A 'A Series of 48' 17mm long	£1.50	£75.00
		B 'A Series of 48' 14mm long	£1.50	£75.00
M	48	Picturesque China (c1925):		
		A With 'P' at left of base	£1.25	£60.00
		B Without 'P' at left of base	£1.25	£60.00
M	53	Playing Cards Ace of Hearts Back (c1935)	22p	£11.00
K	53	Playing Cards designed back (c1935):		
		A Blue back	£1.00	—
		B Red back	£1.00	—
	36	Popular Stage, Cinema and Society Celebrities (c1928)	£3.50	—
	25	Prehistoric Animals (1931)	£3.00	£75.00
	50	Prominent Australian and English Cricketers (1911)	£35.00	—
	25	Puzzle series (1916)	£5.00	—
	50	Railway Working (1927)	£1.60	£80.00

Size	Number in set		Price per card	Complete set
		BRITISH AMERICAN TOBACCO CO. LTD *(continued)*		
	10	Recruiting Posters (1915)	£7.00	—
	33	Regimental Pets (1911)	£6.00	—
	50	Regimental Uniforms (1936)	£1.50	£75.00
	50	Romance of the Heavens (1929)	90p	£45.00
P	50	Round the World in Pictures stereoscopic (1931)	£1.20	£60.00
	50	Royal Mail (1912)	£3.60	—
P	50	Royal Navy (1930)	£2.00	—
	27	Rulers of the World (1911)	£7.50	—
	40	Safety First (1931)	£2.00	£80.00
	25	Ships' Flags and Cap Badges 1st series (1930)	£2.80	£70.00
	25	Ships' Flags and Cap Badges 2nd series (1930)	£2.80	£70.00
P	50	Ships and Shipping (1928)	70p	£35.00
	50	Signalling series (1913)	£3.50	—
	100	Soldiers of the World (tobacco leaf back) (c1902)	£11.00	—
	50	Speed (1938)	70p	£35.00
	25	Sports and Games in Many Lands (1930)	£5.00	£125.00
	50	Stage and Film Stars (1926)	£1.50	—
M	50	Stars of Filmland (1927)	£2.30	—
	48	Transport Then and Now (1940)	45p	£22.00
	32	Transport of the World (1917)	£9.00	—
	20	Types of North American Indians (c1930)	£13.00	—
P	50	Types of the World (1936)	70p	£35.00
P	270	Views of the World stereoscopic (1908)	£3.00	—
	25	Warriors of All Nations (gold panel) (1937)	£1.60	£40.00
	50	War Incidents (brown back) (1915)	£1.60	£80.00
	50	War Incidents (blue back) (1916)	£1.60	£80.00
	50	Warships (1926)	£5.00	—
	25	Whaling (1930)	£2.40	£60.00
P	50	Who's Who in Sport (1926)	£2.50	£125.00
	50	Wild Animals of the World (tobacco leaf back) (1902)	£7.50	—
	25	Wireless (1923)	£4.00	—
	50	Wonders of the Past (1930)	80p	£40.00
	50	Wonders of the Sea (1929)	70p	£35.00
	25	Wonders of the World (c1928)	80p	£20.00
	40	World Famous Cinema Artistes (1933)	£1.25	£50.00
M	40	World Famous Cinema Artistes (1933)	£1.50	£60.00
	50	World's Products (1929)	50p	£25.00
P	50	The World of Sport (1927)	£2.00	£100.00
P	50	Zoo (1935)	60p	£30.00
	50	Zoological Studies (1928):		
		A Brown back	50p	£25.00
		B Black back	£1.50	—
F		**PLAIN BACKS**		
	50	Actors and Actresses 'WALP' (c1905):		
		A Portraits in black and white, glossy	£2.00	£100.00
		B Portraits flesh tinted, matt	£2.00	£100.00
	50	Actresses 'ALWICS' (c1905)	£2.00	—
	50	Actresses, four colours surround (c1905)	£2.00	£100.00
	30	Actresses unicoloured (c1910):		
		A Fronts in purple brown	£1.00	£30.00
		B Fronts in light brown	£1.00	£30.00
	50	Animals and Birds (1912)	£2.00	—
	60	Animals — cut-outs (1912)	£1.10	—
	50	Art Photogravures (1912)	£2.00	—
	50	Aviation series (1911)	£3.60	—
	40	Beauties — brown tinted (1913)	£2.20	—
	50	Beauties with backgrounds (1911)	£2.30	—

Size	Number in set		Price per card	Complete set

BRITISH AMERICAN TOBACCO CO. LTD *(continued)*

Size	Number in set	Title	Price per card	Complete set
	32	Beauties Picture Hats I with borders (1914)	£3.00	—
	45	Beauties Picture Hats II without borders (1914)	£3.00	—
	30	Beauties and Children (c1910)	£5.00	—
	30	Beauties 'Celebrated Actresses' (c1910)	£3.00	—
	52	Birds of Brilliant Plumage — PC inset (1914)	£2.60	—
	25	Bonzo series (1923):		
		A With series title	£3.60	—
		B Without series title	£3.60	—
	30	Boy Scouts Signalling (c1920):		
		A Captions in English	£3.00	£90.00
		B Captions in Siamese	£3.00	£90.00
	50	British Man of War series (1910)	£10.00	—
	50	Butterflies and Moths (1910)	£1.60	—
	50	Cinema Artistes (c1928)	£2.50	—
	50	Cinema Stars RB21/259 (c1930):		
		A Front matt	£1.50	£75.00
		B Front glossy	£1.50	—
	50	Cinema Stars RB21/260 (Nd 1-50) (c1930)	£1.50	—
	50	Cinema Stars RB21/260 (Nd 51-100) (c1930)	£1.50	—
	50	Cinema Stars RB21/260 (Nd 101-150) (c1930)	£1.50	—
	100	Cinema Stars RB21/260 (Nd 201-300) (c1930)	£1.20	£120.00
	50	Cinema Stars 'FLAG' (c1930)	£1.40	—
	27	Dancing Girls (1913)	£1.50	—
	32	Drum Horses (1910)	£5.00	—
	50	English Period Costumes	80p	£40.00
	50	Flag Girls of All Nations (1911)	£1.60	—
		Flags, Pennons and Signals (c1910):		
	70	A Numbered 1-70	90p	—
	70	B Unnumbered	90p	—
	50	C Numbered 71-120	90p	—
	45	D Numbered 121-165	90p	—
	20	Flowers (1915)	£1.25	£25.00
	50	Girls of All Nations (1908)	£2.00	—
	30	Heroic Deeds (1913)	£2.00	—
	25	Hindou Gods (1909)	£8.00	—
	32	Houses of Parliament (1914)	£3.00	—
	25	Indian Mogul Paintings (1909)	£9.00	—
	53	Jockeys and Owners Colours — PC inset (c1914)	£3.00	—
	30	Merrie England Female Studies (1922)	£5.00	—
K	36	Modern Beauties 1st series (1938)	£3.00	—
	36	Modern Beauties 2nd series (1939)	£3.00	—
P	48	Movie Stars (c1930)	£1.50	—
	50	Music Hall Celebrities (1911):		
		A Blue border	£2.20	—
		B Gilt border	£2.20	—
		C Red border	£2.20	—
		D Yellow border	£4.00	—
P	50	New Zealand, Early Scenes and Maori Life (c1928)	£1.60	—
	50	Poultry and Pidgeons (c1926)	£5.00	—
	25	Products of the World (1914)	£1.00	£25.00
	50	Royal Mail (1912)	£5.00	—
	36	Ships and Their Pennants (1913)	£2.25	—
	75	Soldiers of the World (c1902)	£8.00	—
	30	Sporting Girls (1913)	£5.50	—
	50	Sports of the World (1917):		
		A Brown front	£3.50	—
		B Coloured front	£3.50	—

Size	Number in set		Price per card	Complete set

BRITISH AMERICAN TOBACCO CO. LTD *(continued)*

Size	Number		Price	Complete
M	50	Stars of Filmland (1927)	£2.00	—
	32	Transport of the World (1917)	£1.30	—
	50	Types of the British Army (1908):		
		A Numbered	£3.20	—
		B Unnumbered	£3.20	—
P	50	Types of the World (1936)	£2.50	—
P	50	Units of the British Army and RAF (c1930)	£2.00	—
M	50	Women of Nations (Flag Girls) (1922)	£3.00	—

G PAPER BACKED SILKS ISSUED 1910-1917

Size	Number		Price	Complete
M	25	Arabic Proverbs	£13.00	—
M	50	Arms of the British Empire:		
		A Back in blue	£3.00	—
		B Back in brown	£4.00	—
M	50	Australian Wild Flowers	£3.50	—
M	50	Best Dogs of Their Breed	£6.00	—
	110	Crests and Badges of the British Army	£2.50	—
M	108	Crests and Badges of the British Army	£2.00	—
M	50	Crests and Colours of Australian Universities, Colleges and Schools	£2.50	—

BRITISH AMERICAN TOBACCO COMPANY (CHINA) LTD

	32	Sectional Picture — 'Beauties of Old China' (1934)	£5.00	—

BRITISH AMERICAN TOBACCO CO. LTD, Switzerland

	30	Series Actrices (1921)	£6.00	—

BRITISH CIGARETTE CO. LTD, China

	25	British and Foreign Actresses and Beauties (c1900)	£70.00	—
	25	South African War Scenes (c1900)	£28.00	—

BROWN & WILLIAMSON TOBACCO CORP, USA (Wings Cigarettes)

Size	Number		Price	Complete
M	50	Modern American Airplanes (c1938):		
		A Inscribed 'Series A'	£4.00	—
		B Without 'Series A'	£3.00	—
M	50	Modern American Airplanes 'Series B' (c1938)	£3.00	—
M	50	Modern American Airplanes 'Series C' (c1938)	£3.00	—
	50	Movie Stars (1940) (Golden Grain Tobacco)	£5.00	—

D. BUCHNER & CO., USA

Size	Number		Price	Complete
	48	Actors (1887)	£28.00	—
L	50	Actresses (c1890)	£25.00	—
	144	Baseball Players (c1890)	£90.00	—
L	28	Butterflies and Bugs (c1890)	£60.00	—
L	52	Morning Glory Maidens (c1890)	£40.00	—
L	23	Musical Instruments (c1890)	£50.00	—
L	21	Yacht Club Colours (c1890)	£55.00	—

BUCKTROUT & CO. LTD, Guernsey, Channel Islands

Size	Number		Price	Complete
M	416	Around the World (1926):		
		A Inscribed 'Places of Interest' Nd. 1-104	50p	£52.00
		B Inscribed 'Around the World' Nd. 105-208	50p	£52.00
		C Inscribed 'Around the World' Nd. 209-312	50p	£52.00
		D Inscribed 'Around the World' Nd. 313-416	50p	£52.00

Size	Number in set		Price per card	Complete set
		BUCKTROUT & CO. LTD, Guernsey, Channel Islands *(continued)*		
	24	Birds of England (1923)	£3.00	£75.00
	50	Cinema Stars, 1st series (1921)	£2.00	£100.00
	50	Cinema Stars, 2nd series (1922)	£2.20	£110.00
M	50	Football Teams (1924)	£3.20	—
M	22	Football Teams of the Bailiwick (1924)	90p	£20.00
	123	Guernsey Footballers (c1925)	£3.00	—
	20	Inventors Series (1924)	£1.25	£25.00
	25	Marvels of the Universe Series (1923)	£2.60	£65.00
M	54	Playing Cards (1928)	80p	£42.00
	25	Sports and Pastimes (1925)	£5.00	—

CALCUTTA CIGARETTE CO., India

	25	Actresses — 'ALWICS' (c1905):		
		A Fronts in blue	£25.00	—
		B Fronts in chocolate	£30.00	—

A. G. CAMERON & SIZER, USA (including Cameron & Cameron)

	25	The New Discovery (1889):		
		A Without overprint	£32.00	—
		B With overprint	£32.00	—
	24	Occupations for Women (1895)	£45.00	—
		Photographic Cards (c1895):		
	? 230	Actresses	£17.00	—
L	? 6	Actresses	£20.00	—
	75	Framed Paintings	£12.00	—

V. CAMILLERI, Malta

MP	104	Popes of Rome (1922):		
		A Nd. 1-52	£1.70	£85.00
		B Nd. 53-104	£1.70	£85.00

CAMLER TOBACCO COY, Malta

P	? 247	Footballers (c1925)	£8.00	—
M	96	Maltese Families Coats of Arms:		
		A Thick board (c1925)	£1.20	—
		B Thin board (1958)	£1.20	—

CARRERAS LTD, Australia & Canada

M	20	Canadian Fish (1985)	£1.50	—
M	20	Canadian Wild Animals (1984):		
		A Complete set	—	—
		B 15 Different	30p	£4.50
	72	Film Star Series (1933)	£1.50	—
	72	Football Series (1933)	£2.25	—
	24	Personality Series (1933)	£2.25	—
	72	Personality Series Film Stars (1933)	£1.50	—
	72	Personality Series Footballers (1933)	£2.25	—

CHING & CO., Jersey, Channel Islands

L	24	Around and About in Jersey, 1st series (1964)	30p	£7.50
L	24	Around and About in Jersey, 2nd series (1964)	80p	£20.00
	25	Do You Know? (1962)	20p	£2.50
	48	Flowers (1962)	90p	£45.00
L	24	Jersey Past and Present, 1st series (1960)	25p	£6.00

Size	Number in set		Price per card	Complete set

CHING & CO., Jersey, Channel Islands *(continued)*

Size	Number in set		Price per card	Complete set
L	24	Jersey Past and Present, 2nd series (1962)	60p	£15.00
L	24	Jersey Past and Present, 3rd series (1963)	20p	£5.00
	25	Ships and Their Workings (1961)	20p	£2.50
	50	Veteran and Vintage Cars (1960)	40p	£20.00

W.A. & A.C. CHURCHMAN, Channel Islands

(All cards without ITC clause)

Size	Number in set		Price per card	Complete set
M	48	Air Raid Precautions (1938)	£1.80	—
M	48	Holidays in Britain (sepia) (1937)	£1.80	—
M	48	Holidays in Britain (coloured) (1938)	£1.80	—
M	48	Modern Wonders (1938):		
		A ITC clause blocked out in silver	£5.00	—
		B Reprinted without ITC clause	£1.80	—
M	48	The Navy at Work (1937)	£1.80	—
M	48	The RAF at Work (1939)	£1.80	—
M	48	Wings Over the Empire (1939)	£1.80	—

THE CIGARETTE COMPANY, Jersey, Channel Islands

Size	Number in set		Price per card	Complete set
	72	Jersey Footballers (c1910)	£7.00	—

LA CIGARETTE ORIENTAL DE BELGIQUE, Belgium

Size	Number in set		Price per card	Complete set
L	100	Famous Men Throughout the Ages (c1940)	50p	—

C. COLOMBOS, Malta

Size	Number in set		Price per card	Complete set
MP	200	Actresses (c1900)	£3.50	—
MP	59	Actresses (c1900)	£15.00	—
	50	Actresses (coloured) (c1900)	£13.00	—
MP	57	Celebrities (c1900)	£17.00	—
P	136	Dante's Divine Comedy (c1914)	£2.20	—
		Famous Oil Paintings (c1910):		
MP	72	1 Series A	£1.00	—
MP	108	2 Series B	£1.00	—
MP	240	3 Series C	£1.00	—
MP	100	4 Series D	£1.00	—
LP	91	5 Large size	£6.50	—
MP	100	Life of Napoleon Bonaparte (c1914)	£3.00	—
MP	70	Life of Nelson (c1914)	£3.00	—
MP	70	Life of Wellington (c1914)	£3.00	—
MP	100	National Types and Costumes (c1910)	£3.00	—
MP	30	Opera Singers (c1900)	£30.00	—
	120	Paintings and Statues (c1912)	£1.00	—
M	112	Royalty and Celebrities (c1910)	£3.00	—

COLONIAL TOBACCOS (PTY) LTD, South Africa

Size	Number in set		Price per card	Complete set
EL	150	World's Fairy Tales (c1930)	£4.00	—

D. CONDACHI & SON, Malta

Size	Number in set		Price per card	Complete set
?	15	Artistes & Beauties (c1905)	£20.00	—

CONSOLIDATED CIGARETTE CO., USA

Size	Number in set		Price per card	Complete set
		Ladies of the White House (c1895):		
	14	A Size 73 × 43mm, white borders	£35.00	—
	25	B Size 70 × 38mm, no borders	£30.00	—

Size	Number in set		Price per card	Complete set

COPE BROS. & CO. LTD

A INDIAN ISSUE
| | 30 | Flags of Nations (c1903) | £75.00 | — |

B DANISH ISSUES
	50	Jordklodens Hunde (1912)	£35.00	—
	30	Scandinavian Actors and Actresses (1910)	£40.00	—
	35	Speider Billeder I Hver Pakke (1910)	£35.00	—
	25	Uniformer A F Fremragende Britiske Regimenter (1908)	£30.00	—
	25	Vilde Dyr Og Fugle (1907)	£35.00	—

A.G. COUSIS & CO., Malta

		Actors and Actresses (c1910):		
P	100	A Back with framework	£2.00	—
KP	100	B Back without framework	£2.00	—
K	254	Actors and Actresses (c1925)	£1.00	—
KP	100	Actresses Series I (c1910)	£1.80	—
KP	80	Actresses Series II (c1910)	£1.80	—
P	100	Actresses (c1910):		
		A Series I	£1.80	—
		B Series II	£1.80	—
		C Series III	£1.80	—
		D Series IV	£1.80	—
		E Series V	£1.80	—
		F Series VI	£1.80	—
		G Series VII	£1.80	—
		H Series VIII	£1.80	—
		I Series IX	£1.80	—
		J Series X	£1.80	—
		K Series XI	£1.80	—
		L Series XII	£1.80	—
		M Series XIII	£1.80	—
		N Series XIV	£1.80	—
		O Series XV	£1.80	—
		P Series XVI	£1.80	—
		Q Series XVII	£1.80	—
		R Series XVIII	£1.80	—
		S Series XIX	£1.80	—
		Actresses (c1910):		
KP	2281	A Miniature size 50 × 30mm	£1.00	—
P	1283	B Small size 58 × 39mm	£1.00	—
MP	325	Actresses, Celebrities and Warships (c1910)	£9.00	—
		Actresses, Partners and National Costumes (c1910):		
KP	200	A Miniature size 50 × 30mm	£2.00	—
P	100	B Small size 60 × 39mm	£2.00	—
MP	50	Beauties, Couples and Children (c1908):		
		A Back inscribed 'Collection No. 1'	£3.00	—
		B Back inscribed 'Collection No. 2'	£3.00	—
		C Back inscribed 'Collection No. 3'	£3.00	—
K	50	Beauties, Couples and Children (red back) (c1925)	£2.20	—
P	402	Celebrities numbered matt (c1910):		
		A Front inscribed 'Cousis' Dubec Cigarettes', Nd. 1-300	£1.60	—
		B Front inscribed 'Cousis' Cigarettes', Nd. 301-402	£1.60	—
P	2162	Celebrities unnumbered (c1910):		
		A Miniature size 50 × 30mm	£1.00	—
		B Small size 59 × 39mm	£1.00	—
MP	72	Grand Masters of the Order of Jerusalem (c1910)	£3.00	—
P	100	National Costumes (c1910)	£2.50	—

Size	Number in set			Price per card	Complete set

A.G. COUSIS & CO., Malta *(continued)*

Size	Number			Price	Complete
MP	? 57	Paris Exhibition 1900 (c1901)		£28.00	—
MP	102	Paris Series (1902)		£28.00	—
		Popes of Rome (c1910):			
MP	182	A	Back inscribed 'A.G. Cousis & Co'	£1.80	—
MP	81	B	Back inscribed 'Cousis' Dubec Cigarettes'	£3.00	—
P	100	Statues and Monuments (c1910):			
		A	Numbered	£1.80	—
		B	Unnumbered	£1.80	—
KP	127	Views of Malta (c1910)		£2.20	—
P	115	Views of Malta numbered (c1910)		£1.40	—
MP	127	Views of Malta numbered (c1910)		£1.40	—
MP	? 65	Views of Malta unnumbered (c1910)		£1.40	—
P	559	Views of the World (c1910):			
		A	Small size 59 × 39mm	£1.30	—
		B	Medium size 65 × 45mm	£1.30	—
P	99	Warships, white border (c1910)		£3.20	—
		Warships, Liners and Other Vessels (c1904):			
MP	105	A	'Cousis' Dubec Cigarettes'	£6.00	—
MP	22	B	'Cousis' Excelsior Cigarettes'	£6.00	—
MP	40	C	'Cousis' Superior Cigarettes'	£6.00	—
MP	851	D	'Cousis' Cigarettes'	£1.80	—
KP	851	E	'Cousis' Cigarettes'	£1.80	—

CROWN TOBACCO CO., India

		National Types, Costumes and Flags (c1900):			
	? 19	A	Size 70 × 40mm	£40.00	—
	? 14	B	Size 88 × 49mm	£42.00	—

DIXSON, Australia

	50	Australian MPs and Celebrities (c1900)	£17.00	—

DOMINION TOBACCO CO., Canada

	50	The Smokers of the World (c1905)	£50.00	—

DOMINION TOBACCO CO. LTD, New Zealand

	50	Coaches and Coaching Days (c1928)	£2.50	—
	50	People and Places Famous in New Zealand History (c1928)	£1.80	—
	50	Products of the World (c1928)	£1.00	£50.00
	50	USS Co's Steamers (c1928)	£2.50	—

DUDGEON & ARNELL, Australia

K	16	1934 Australian Test Team (1934)	£8.00	—
K	55	Famous Ships (1933)	£3.80	—

W. DUKE, SONS & CO., USA

ALL SERIES ISSUED 1885-95

	50	Actors and Actresses Series No. 1	£16.00	—
	50	Actors and Actresses Series No. 2	£16.00	—
	25	Actresses RB18/27	£11.00	—
EL	25	Albums of American Stars	£50.00	—
EL	25	Battle Scenes	£36.00	—
EL	25	Breeds of Horses	£34.00	—

Size	Number in set		Price per card	Complete set

W. DUKE, SONS & CO., USA *(continued)*

Size	Number in set		Price per card	Complete set
EL	25	Bridges	£25.00	—
	50	Coins of All Nations	£16.00	—
EL	25	Comic Characters	£26.00	—
EL	25	Cowboys Scenes	£36.00	—
EL	50	Fairest Flowers in the World	£26.00	—
	50	Fancy Dress Ball Costumes	£15.00	—
EL	50	Fancy Dress Ball Costumes	£26.00	—
	50	Fishers and Fish	£16.00	—
EL	25	Flags and Costumes	£30.00	—
	50	Floral Beauties and Language of Flowers	£15.00	—
EL	25	French Novelties	£28.00	—
EL	25	Gems of Beauty	£28.00	—
	50	Great Americans	£22.00	—
	25	Gymnastic Exercises	£30.00	—
EL	25	Habitations of Man	£26.00	—
	50	Histories of Generals (Booklets) (1888)	£35.00	—
	50	Histories of Poor Boys who have become rich and other famous people	£28.00	—
	50	Holidays	£15.00	£750.00
EL	25	Illustrated Songs	£28.00	—
EL	25	Industries of the States	£30.00	—
	50	Jokes	£16.00	—
EL	25	Lighthouses (die cut)	£26.00	—
EL	25	Miniature Novelties	£25.00	—
	50	Musical Instruments	£20.00	—
	36	Ocean and River Steamers	£26.00	—
M	240	Photographs from Life RB23/D76-84	£6.00	—
	53	Playing Cards	£12.00	—
	50	Popular Songs and Dancers	£22.00	—
	50	Postage Stamps	£16.00	—
		Rulers, Flags and Coats of Arms (1888):		
EL	50	A Thick card type	£24.00	—
EL	50	B Thin folders (titled Rulers, Coats of Arms & Flags)	£15.00	—
	50	Scenes of Perilous Occupations	£22.00	—
EL	25	Sea Captains	£32.00	—
	50	Shadows	£16.00	£800.00
EL	25	Snap Shots from Puck	£25.00	—
EL	25	Stars of the Stage, 1st series:		
		A With Duke	£28.00	£700.00
		B Inscribed 'Third Series'	£28.00	—
EL	25	Stars of the Stage, 2nd series	£28.00	—
EL	25	Stars of the Stage, 3rd series	£28.00	£700.00
EL	25	Stars of the Stage, 4th series (die cut)	£28.00	—
EL	48	State Governors' Coats of Arms	£25.00	—
EL	48	State Governors' Coats of Arms (folders)	£15.00	—
	50	The Terrors of America and Their Doings	£16.00	—
EL	50	The Terrors of America and Their Doings	£28.00	—
	50	Tinted Photos:		
		A Standard size	£20.00	—
		B Die cut to shape	£17.00	—
EL	25	Types of Vessels (die cut)	£26.00	—
	50	Vehicles of the World	£22.00	—
	50	Yacht Colors of the World	£16.00	—

PHOTOGRAPHIC CARDS

	340	Actors and Actresses, 'Cross-Cut Cigarettes' with number and caption in design, Group 1	£4.00	—
	260	Actors and Actresses, 'Cross-Cut Cigarettes' in design, number and caption at base, Group 2	£4.00	—

Size	Number in set		Price per card	Complete set

W. DUKE, SONS & CO., USA *(continued)*

Size	Number in set		Price per card	Complete set
	?	Actors and Actresses, 'Cross-Cut Cigarettes' and all wording at base, Group	£4.00	—
	148	Actors and Actresses, 'Dukes Cameo Cigarettes' in design, number and caption at base, Group 4	£4.00	—
	?	Actors and Actresses, 'Dukes Cameo Cigarettes', number and caption at base, Group 5	£4.00	—
	?	Actors and Actresses, 'Dukes Cigarettes' in design, number and caption at base, Group 6	£4.00	—
	?	Actors and Actresses, 'Dukes Cigarettes' and all wording at base, Group 7	£4.00	—
	?	Actors, Actresses and Celebrities, printed back:		
		1 Horizontal 'Dukes Cameo Cigarettes' back	£4.00	—
		2 Vertical 'Sales 1858' back	£4.00	—
		3 Horizontal 'Dukes Cigarettes' back	£4.00	—
EL	?	Actors, Actresses, Celebrities etc	£5.00	—

H. ELLIS & CO., USA

Size	Number in set		Price per card	Complete set
	25	Breeds of Dogs (c1890)	£40.00	—
	25	Costumes of Women (c1890)	£60.00	—
	25	Generals of the Late Civil War (c1890)	£70.00	—
	25	Photographic Cards — Actresses (c1887)	£12.00	—

FOH CHONG, China

Size	Number in set		Price per card	Complete set
M	10	Chinese Series (c1930)	—	£20.00

G.W. GAIL & AX., USA

Size	Number in set		Price per card	Complete set
EL	25	Battle Scenes (c1890)	£35.00	—
EL	25	Bicycle and Trick Riders (c1890)	£38.00	—
EL	25	French Novelties (c1890)	£32.00	—
EL	25	Industries of the States (c1890)	£32.00	—
EL	25	Lighthouses (die cut) (c1890)	£28.00	—
EL	25	Novelties (die cut) (c1890)	£30.00	—
EL	?	Photographic Cards (c1890)	£5.00	—
EL	25	Stars of the Stage (c1890)	£30.00	—

GENERAL CIGAR COMPANY, Montreal, Canada

Size	Number in set		Price per card	Complete set
		Northern Birds:		
EL	24	A With series title Nd. 1-24 (1968)	£1.20	—
EL	12	B Without series title, Nd. 25-36 (1977)	£1.40	—

GOODWIN & CO, USA

Size	Number in set		Price per card	Complete set
	15	Beauties — 'PAC' (c1888)	£60.00	—
	50	Champions (c1888)	£40.00	—
	50	Dogs of the World (c1888)	£20.00	—
	50	Flowers (c1888)	£20.00	—
	50	Games and Sports Series (c1888)	£28.00	—
	50	Holidays (c1888)	£26.00	—
	50	Occupations for Women (c1888)	£55.00	—
		Photographic Cards (c1888):		
	?	Actors and Actresses	£6.00	—
	?	Baseball Players	£50.00	—
	?	Celebrities and Prizefighters	£25.00	—
	50	Vehicles of the World (c1888)	£26.00	—

Size	Number in set			Price per card	Complete set

GUERNSEY TOBACCO CO., Channel Islands

		A Famous Picture:			
	49	A And When Did You Last See Your Father? (1934)		£2.30	—
	48	B The Laughing Cavalier (1935)		£2.30	—
	48	C The Toast (1936)		£2.30	—
K	52	Miniature Playing Cards (1933)		£1.20	—

THOS. H. HALL, USA

	4	Actresses RB23/-H6-1 (1880)	£65.00	—
	14	Actresses RB23/-H6-2 (c1885)	£16.00	—
	140	Actors and Actresses RB23/-H6-3 (c1885)	£16.00	—
	112	Actresses and Actors RB23/-H6-4 (c1885)	£16.00	—
	?	Actresses and Actors RB23/-H6-5 (c1885)	£16.00	—
	? 158	Actresses and Actors RB23/-H6-6 (c1885)	£16.00	—
	52	Actresses RB23/-H6-7 (c1885)	£18.00	—
	12	Actresses RB23/-H6-8 (c1885)	£35.00	—
	25	Actresses RB23/-H6-9 (c1885)	£27.00	—
	11	Actresses RB23/-H6-10 (c1885)	£75.00	—
	12	Athletes RB23/-H6-3 (1881)	£60.00	—
	4	Presidential Candidates RB23/-H6-1 (1880)	£65.00	—
	22	Presidents of the United States RB23/-H6-11 (c1888)	£35.00	—
	25	Theatrical Types RB23/-H6-12 (c1890)	£35.00	—

HIGNETT BROS. & CO., New Zealand

MP	50	Beauties, Set 1 (1926):		
		A Back without framelines, no brand mentioned	£2.00	—
		B Back with framelines, 'Chess Cigarettes'	£1.50	£75.00
MP	50	Beauties, Set 2 (1927)	£1.80	£90.00

R. & J. HILL LTD

	10	Chinese Series (c1912)	£75.00	—

THE HILSON CO., USA

L	25	National Types (1900)	£24.00	—

IMPERIAL CIGARETTE & TOBACCO CO., Canada

	? 24	Actresses (c1900)	£60.00	—

IMPERIAL TOBACCO COMPANY OF CANADA LTD, Canada

A WITH FIRM'S NAME

	25	Beauties — Girls in Costume (c1903)	£50.00	—
	24	Beauties — Smoke Girls (c1903)	£50.00	—
M	50	Birds, Beasts and Fishes (1923)	£1.60	£80.00
L	100	Birds of Canada (1924)	£3.25	—
L	100	Birds of Canada (Western Canada) (1925)	£5.25	—
	50	British Birds (1923)	90p	£45.00
	48	Canadian History Series (1926)	£1.80	—
	50	Children of All Nations (1924)	£1.00	£50.00
	23	Dogs Series (1924)	£1.70	£40.00
	50	Dogs, 2nd series (1925)	£1.50	£75.00
	50	Famous English Actresses (1924)	£1.00	£50.00

Size	Number in set		Price per card	Complete set

IMPERIAL TOBACCO COMPANY OF CANADA LTD, Canada *(continued)*

Size	Number in set		Price per card	Complete set
	50	Film Favourites (1925):		
		A English Issue:		
		i Numbered	£3.00	—
		ii Unnumbered	£3.20	—
		B French Issue:		
		i Numbered	£6.00	—
		ii Unnumbered	£6.00	—
	50	Fish and Bait (1924)	£1.60	£80.00
	50	Fishes of the World (1924)	£2.20	£110.00
	50	Flower Culture in Pots (1925)	70p	£35.00
	30	Game Bird Series (1925)	£1.65	£50.00
	50	Gardening Hints (1923)	60p	£30.00
M	25	Heraldic Signs and Their Origins (1925)	£1.20	£30.00
	50	How to Play Golf (1925)	£8.00	—
	50	Infantry Training (1915):		
		A Glossy card	£2.40	—
		B Matt card	£2.40	—
L	48	Mail Carriers and Stamps (1903)	£27.00	—
	50	Merchant Ships of the World (1924)	£1.20	£60.00
	25	Military Portraits (1914)	£2.60	—
	50	Modern War Weapons, 'Sweet Caporal' issue (1914)	£3.50	—
	56	Motor Cars (1924)	£2.00	—
	50	Naval Portraits (1914)	£2.40	—
	25	Notabilities (1914)	£2.40	—
	53	Poker Hands (1924)	£1.50	—
	53	Poker Hands, New Series (1925)	£1.50	—
	25	Poultry Alphabet (1924)	£2.60	—
	50	Railway Engines (1924):		
		A With 'Wills' blanked out	£1.30	—
		B Without 'Wills'	£1.00	£50.00
	50	The Reason Why (1924)	£1.00	£50.00
	127	Smokers Golf Cards (1925)	£5.00	—

B *WITHOUT FIRM'S NAME*

Size	Number in set		Price per card	Complete set
	50	Arms of the British Empire (1911)	£2.50	—
	50	Around the World (c1910)	£3.50	—
	90	Baseball Series (1912)	£35.00	—
	30	Bird Series (c1910)	£2.50	—
	50	Boy Scouts (1911) — with album clause	£5.00	—
	50	Canadian Historical Portraits (1913)	£6.00	—
	50	Canadian History Series (1914)	£1.80	—
	50	Fish Series (c1910)	£2.40	—
	50	Fowls, Pigeons and Dogs (1911)	£3.50	—
	45	Hockey Players (1912)	£15.00	—
	36	Hockey Series (coloured) (1911)	£15.00	—
	50	How To Do It (c1910)	£2.75	—
	100	Lacrosse Series (coloured), Leading Players (c1910)	£6.00	—
	100	Lacrosse Series (coloured) (c1910)	£6.00	—
	50	Lacrosse Series (black and white) (c1910)	£6.00	—
	50	L'Historie du Canada (1926)	£1.50	—
	50	Movie Stars (c1930)	£1.80	—
L	50	Pictures of Canadian Life (c1910):		
		A Brown front	£7.00	—
		B Green front	£6.00	—
	50	Prominent Men of Canada (c1910)	£3.50	—
	50	Tricks and Puzzles (c1910)	£7.00	—
	50	Types of Nations (c1910)	£3.00	—

Size	Number in set		Price per card	Complete set

IMPERIAL TOBACCO COMPANY OF CANADA LTD, Canada *(continued)*

	25	Victoria Cross Heroes (blue back) (1915)	£3.00	£75.00
L	45	Views of the World (c1910)	£6.00	—
	25	The World's Dreadnoughts (1910)	£4.00	—

C SILKS ISSUED 1910-25

M	55	Animals with Flags	£3.50	—
EL	50	Canadian History Series	£11.00	—
M	121	Canadian Miscellany	£4.00	—
M	55	Garden Flowers of the World	£2.50	—
M	55	Orders and Military Medals	£2.50	—
M	55	Regimental Uniforms of Canada	£3.50	—
L	50	Yachts, Pennants and Views	£6.00	—

THE IMPERIAL TOBACCO CO. OF INDIA LTD, India

	25	Indian Historical Views (1915):		
		A Set 1, First Arrangement	£2.20	—
		B Set 2, Second Arrangement	£2.20	—
	40	Nautch Girl Series:		
		A 'Pedro Cigarettes' (c1905)	£2.50	—
		B 'Railway Cigarettes' (c1907)	£2.50	—
	52	Nautch Girl Series, PC inset:		
		A 'Pedro Cigarettes' (c1905)	£2.20	—
		B 'Railway Cigarettes' (c1907)	£2.20	—
K	53	Playing Cards, red back (1919)	£1.50	—
K	52	Playing Cards, blue back (1933)	£1.50	—

THE JERSEY TOBACCO CO. LTD, Channel Islands

K	53	Miniature Playing Cards (1933)	£1.00	—

JUST SO, USA

EL	?	Actresses (c1890)	£10.00	—

KENTUCKY TOBACCO PTY. LTD, South Africa

L	120	The March of Mankind (1940)	£2.00	—

WM. S. KIMBALL & CO., USA

ALL SERIES ISSUED 1885-95

	? 33	Actresses	£70.00	—
	72	Ancient Coins	£28.00	—
	48	Arms of Dominions	£20.00	—
	50	Ballet Queens	£22.00	—
	52	Beauties with Playing Card Insets	£22.00	—
EL	20	Beautiful Bathers	£45.00	—
	50	Butterflies	£22.00	—
	50	Champions of Games and Sports	£40.00	—
	50	Dancing Girls of the World	£20.00	—
	50	Dancing Women	£20.00	—
	50	Fancy Bathers	£20.00	—
	50	Goddesses of the Greeks & Romans	£25.00	—
EL	25	Household Pets	£30.00	—
	?	Photographic Actresses RB23/K26-15-2	£7.00	—
EL	20	Pretty Athletes	£35.00	—
	50	Savage and Semi Barbarous Chiefs and Rulers	£28.00	—

	Size	Number in set		Price per card	Complete set

KINNEY BROS, USA

ALL SERIES ISSUED 1885-95

		25	Actresses Group 1 Set 1 RB18/1	£7.50	—
		25	Actresses Group 1 Set 2 RB18/2	£12.00	—
		25	Actresses Group 1 Set 3 RB18/3	£13.00	—
		25	Actresses Group 1 Set 4	£15.00	—
		25	Actresses Group 1 Set 5	£15.00	—
		25	Actresses Group 2 RB18/15	£6.00	—
		25	Actresses Group 2 RB18/16:		
			A Subjects named	£6.00	—
			B Subjects unnamed	£6.00	—
		25	Actresses Group 3 RB18/26	£6.00	—
		25	Actresses Group 3 RB18/29	£6.00	—
		50	Actresses Group 4 RB18/36	£6.00	—
		150	Actresses Group 4	£6.00	—
		25	Animals	£20.00	—
		10	Butterflies of the World. Light background	£20.00	—
		50	Butterflies of the World. Gold background	£18.00	—
		25	Famous Gems of the World	£20.00	—
		52	Harlequin Cards 1st series	£20.00	—
		53	Harlequin Cards 2nd series (1889)	£20.00	—
L		50	International Cards	£38.00	—
K		24	Jocular Oculars	£36.00	—
		25	Leaders:		
			A Standard size	£22.00	£550.00
			B Narrow card — officially cut	£22.00	£550.00
		50	Magic Changing Cards (1881)	£22.00	—
		622	Military series	From £5.50	—
		50	National Dances:		
			A Front with white border	£18.00	£900.00
			B Front without border	£20.00	—
		25	Naval Vessels of the World	£20.00	—
		50	New Year 1890 (1889)	£20.00	—
		25	Novelties Type 1. Thick circular, no border	£24.00	—
		50	Novelties Type 2. Thin circular with border	£12.00	—
			Novelties Type 3. Die cut:		
		25	A Inscribed '25 Styles'	£8.00	—
		50	B Inscribed '50 Styles'	£8.00	—
		75	C Inscribed '75 Styles'	£8.00	—
		50	Novelties Type 5. Standard size cards	£11.00	—
		14	Novelties Type 6. Oval	£28.00	—
			Photographic Cards:		
		?	A Actors and Actresses. Horizontal back with Kinney's name	£4.00	—
		?	B Actors and Actresses. Vertical, Sweet Caporal backs	£4.00	—
		45	C Famous Ships	£12.00	—
			Racehorses (1889):		
		25	1 American Horses:		
			A Back with series title 'Famous Running Horses'	£24.00	—
			B Back 'Return 25 of these small cards' 11 lines of text	£22.00	—
		25	2 English Horses 'Return 25 of these cards' with 6 lines of text	£22.00	—
		25	3 Great American Trotters	£24.00	—
		50	Surf Beauties	£22.00	—
		52	Transparent Playing Cards	£14.00	—
		25	Types of Nationalities (folders)	£25.00	—

KRAMERS TOBACCO CO. (PTY) LTD, South Africa

		50	Badges of South African Rugby Football Clubs (1933)	£7.50	—

Size	Number in set		Price per card	Complete set

LAMBERT & BUTLER

Size	Number in set	Description	Price per card	Complete set
	50	Actors and Actresses — 'WALP' (1905)	£3.50	—
	250	Actresses — 'ALWICS' (1905):		
		A Portraits in black, border in red	£3.20	—
		B Portraits and border in black	£7.00	—
	50	Beauties red tinted (1908)	£3.50	—
	83	Danske Byvaabner (c1915)	£15.00	—
M	26	Etchings of Dogs (1926)	£30.00	—
	25	Flag Girls of All Nations (1908)	£12.00	—
P	50	Homeland Events (1928)	£2.20	£110.00
P	50	London Zoo (1927)	£1.30	—
	50	Merchant Ships of the World (1924)	£2.40	—
	30	Music Hall Celebrities (1916)	£6.00	—
P	50	Popular Film Stars (1926):		
		A Series title in one line, no brand quoted	£1.40	£70.00
		B Series title in two lines, inscribed 'Varsity Cigarettes'	£2.50	—
		C Series title in two lines, no brand quoted	£1.40	£70.00
P	50	The Royal Family at Home and Abroad (1927)	£1.40	£70.00
	100	Royalty, Notabilities and Events in Russia, China, Japan and South Africa (1902)	£14.00	—
	100	Russo Japanese series (1905)	£6.00	—
P	50	Types of Modern Beauty (1927)	£1.10	£60.00
P	50	Who's Who in Sport (1926)	£3.00	£150.00
P	50	The World of Sport (1927)	£1.80	£90.00

LEWIS & ALLEN CO. USA

Size	Number in set	Description	Price per card	Complete set
L	? 120	Views and Art Studies (c1910)	£6.00	—

LONE JACK CIGARETTE CO. USA

Size	Number in set	Description	Price per card	Complete set
	50	Language of Flowers (1888)	£28.00	—

P. LORILLARD CO., USA

ALL SERIES ISSUED 1885-98

Size	Number in set	Description	Price per card	Complete set
M	25	Actresses RB23/L70-4-3	£27.00	—
M	25	Actresses RB23/L70-5	£27.00	—
EL	25	Actresses RB23/L70-6:		
		A 'Red Cross' long cut	£27.00	—
		B 'Sensation Cut Plug' front and back	£27.00	—
		C 'Sensation Cut Plug' front only	£27.00	—
EL	25	Actresses RB23/L70-8	£27.00	—
EL	25	Actresses in Opera Roles RB23/L70-9	£38.00	—
M	25	Ancient Mythology Burlesqued RB23/L70-10	£25.00	—
M	50	Beautiful Women RB23/L70-11:		
		A '5c Ante' front and back	£24.00	—
		B 'Lorillard's Snuff' front and back	£24.00	—
		C 'Tiger' front and back	£24.00	—
EL	25	Circus Scenes	£70.00	—
EL	50	Prizefighters	£100.00	—
M	25	Types of the Stage	£25.00	—

W.C. MACDONALD INC., Canada

Size	Number in set	Description	Price per card	Complete set
	?	Aeroplanes and Warships (c1940)	£1.20	—
M	53	Playing Cards (different designs) (1926-47)	60p	—

Size	Number in set		Price per card	Complete set

B. & J.B. MACHADO, Jamaica

	25	British Naval series (1916)	£22.00	—
	50	The Great War — Victoria Cross Heroes (1916)	£22.00	—
P	50	Popular Film Stars (1926)	£6.00	—
P	50	The Royal Family at Home and Abroad (1927)	£5.00	—
P	52	Stars of the Cinema (1926)	£5.50	—
P	50	The World of Sport (1928)	£6.50	—

MACLIN-ZIMMER-MCGILL TOB. CO., USA

EL	53	Playing Cards — Actresses (c1890)	£22.00	—

MALTA CIGARETTE CO., Malta

	135	Dante's Divine Comedy (c1905)	£15.00	—
	M40	Maltese Families Arms & Letters (c1905)	£7.00	—
	? 44	Prominent People (c1905)	£15.00	—

H. MANDELBAUM, USA

	20	Types of People (c1890)	£50.00	—

MARBURG BROS, USA

	48	National Costume Cards (c1890)	£50.00	—

P.H. MAYO & BROTHER, USA

	25	Actresses RB23/M80-1 (c1890)	£28.00	—
M	25	Actresses RB23/M80-3 (c1890)	£28.00	—
L	12	Actresses RB23/M80-4 (c1890)	£65.00	—
	? 39	Actresses RB23/M80-5 (c1890)	£28.00	—
	40	Baseball Players (c1890)	£100.00	—
	20	Costumes and Flowers (c1890)	£30.00	—
	25	Head Dresses of Various Nations (c1890)	£30.00	—
M	25	National Flowers (Girl and Scene) (c1890)	£30.00	—
	20	Naval Uniforms (c1890)	£30.00	—
	35	Prizefighters (c1890)	£50.00	—
	20	Shakespeare Characters (c1890)	£30.00	—

M. MELACHRINO & CO., Switzerland

	52	Peuples Exotiques 1st series (c1925)	£1.00	—
	52	Peuples Exotiques 2nd series (c1925)	£1.00	—
	52	Peuples Exotiques 3rd series (c1925)	£1.00	—

MIFSUD & AZZOPARDI, Malta

KP	59	First Maltese Parliament (1922)	£8.00	

L. MILLER & SONS, USA

M	25	Battleships (c1900)	£28.00	—
M	25	Generals and Admirals (Spanish War) (c1900)	£28.00	—
M	24	Presidents of US (c1900)	£24.00	—
M	50	Rulers of the World (c1900)	£22.00	—

CHAS. J. MITCHELL & CO., Canada

	26	Actresses — 'FROGA A' (1900):		
		A Backs in brown	£36.00	—
		B Backs in green	£34.00	—

Size	Number in set		Price per card	Complete set

MITSUI & CO., Japan
| | ? | Japanese Women (c1908) | £8.00 | — |

MOORE & CALVI, USA
EL	53	Playing Cards — Actresses (c1890):		
		A 'Trumps Long Cut' back	£22.00	—
		B 'Hard-A-Port' with maker's name	£20.00	—
		C 'Hard-A-Port' without maker's name	£20.00	—

MURAI BROS & CO., Japan
	150	Actresses — 'ALWICS' (c1905)	£9.00	—
	100	Beauties — 'THIBS' (c1900)	£30.00	—
	50	Beauties Group 1 (c1902)	£12.00	—
	25	Chinese Beauties 1st series Peacock issue (c1910)	£3.00	£75.00
	25	Chinese Beauties 3rd series Peacock issue (c1910)	£4.50	—
	50	Chinese Beauties, back in red (c1908)	£5.00	—
	50	Chinese Children's Games without border Peacock issue (c1910)	£2.50	£125.00
	20	Chinese Children's Games with border Peacock issue (c1910)	£3.00	—
	54	Chinese Girls Set 3 (c1905)	£7.50	—
	50	Chinese Pagodas Peacock issue (c1910)	£3.50	—
	30	Chinese Series Peacock issue (c1910)	£3.25	—
	40	Chinese Trades I, back in black (c1905)	£25.00	—
	40	Chinese Trades II, back in olive, Peacock issue (c1910)	£5.00	—
	50	Dancing Girls of the World (c1900)	£35.00	—

NATIONAL CIGARETTE AND TOBACCO CO., USA
| | 25 | National Types (c1890) | £26.00 | — |
| | 44 | National Types (c1890) | £25.00 | — |

PHOTOGRAPHIC CARDS
	?	Actresses (c1888):		
		A Plain back	£7.00	—
		B Printed back	£8.00	—

NATIONAL TOBACCO WORKS, USA
| | EL13 | Art Miniatures (1892) | £25.00 | — |
| | EL ? | Cabinet Pictues (c1890) | £25.00 | — |

OGDENS LTD
	51	Actresses, black and white Polo issue (1906)	£3.00	—
	30	Actresses, unicoloured Polo issue (1908):		
		A Tin foil at back white	£2.50	£75.00
		B Tin foil at back shaded	£3.00	£90.00
	17	Animals Polo issue (1916)	£11.00	
	60	Animals — cut-outs:		
		A Ruler issue (1912)	£3.00	—
		B Tabs issue (1913):		
		i With captions	£3.00	—
		ii Without captions	£4.50	—
	50	Aviation series Tabs issue (1912):		
		A Ogdens at base	£7.00	—
		B Ogdens England at base	£8.00	—
		Beauties green net design back 1901:		
	? 66	A Front black & white	£15.00	—
	? 98	B Front coloured	£28.00	—

Size	Number in set		Price per card	Complete set
		OGDENS LTD *(continued)*		
	45	Beauties Picture Hats Polo issue (1911)	£6.50	—
	50	Best Dogs of Their Breed Polo issue (1916):		
		A Back in red	£8.00	—
		B Back in blue	£8.00	—
	52	Birds of Brilliant Plumage Ruler issue (1914):		
		A Fronts with framelines	£3.00	—
		B Fronts without framelines	£3.00	—
	25	British Trees and Their Uses, Guinea Gold issue (1927)	£2.00	£50.00
	25	China's Famous Warriors, Ruler issue (1913)	£6.00	—
	25	Famous Railway Trains, Guinea Gold issue (1928)	£2.80	£70.00
	20	Flowers, Polo issue (1915):		
		A Without Eastern inscription	£5.50	—
		B With Eastern inscription	£5.50	—
	25	Indian Women, Polo issue (1919):		
		A Framework in light apple green	£5.00	—
		B Framework in dark emerald green	£5.00	—
K	52	Miniature Playing Cards, Polo issue (1922)	£13.00	—
		Music Hall Celebrities (1911):		
	30	A Polo issue	£5.50	—
	50	B Tabs issue	£5.50	—
	50	Riders of the World, Polo issue (1911)	£4.00	—
	50	Russo-Japanese series (1905)	£22.00	—
	36	Ships and Their Pennants, Polo issue (1911)	£6.00	—
	32	Transport of the World, Polo issue (1917)	£5.50	—

OLD FASHION, USA

L	? 200	Photographic Cards — Actresses (c1890)	£13.00	—

PENINSULAR TOBACCO CO. LTD, India

	50	Animals and Birds (1910)	£2.00	—
	52	Birds of Brilliant Plumage (1916):		
		A Back with single large packings	£3.00	—
		B Back with two small packings	£3.00	—
	25	Birds of the East, 1st series (1912)	£2.00	—
	25	Birds of the East, 2nd series (1912)	£2.00	£50.00
	25	China's Famous Warriors:		
		A Back 'Monchyr India'	£3.40	£85.00
		B Back 'India' only	£3.40	£85.00
	25	Chinese Heroes (1913)	£2.60	£65.00
	50	Chinese Modern Beauties (1912)	£5.00	—
	50	Chinese Trades (1908):		
		A Back with 'Monchyr'	£3.00	—
		B Back without 'Monchyr'	£3.00	—
	30	Fish series (1916)	£2.50	—
	25	Hindoo Gods (1909)	£2.80	£70.00
	37	Nautch Girl series (1910)	£6.00	—
	25	Products of the World (1915)	£2.00	£50.00

PLANTERS' STORES & AGENCY CO. LTD, India

	? 47	Actresses — 'FROGA' (1900)	£35.00	—
	25	Beauties 'FECKSA' (1900)	£38.00	—

Size	Number in set		Price per card	Complete set

JOHN PLAYER & SONS

A CHANNEL ISLANDS ISSUES (WITHOUT ITC CLAUSE)

	50	Aircraft of the Royal Air Force (1938)	£1.40	£70.00
	50	Animals of the Countryside (1939)	70p	£35.00
	50	Birds and Their Young (1937)	70p	£35.00
	50	Coronation series Ceremonial Dress (1937)	£1.00	£50.00
	50	Cricketers (1938)	£1.80	£90.00
	50	Cycling (1939)	£1.40	£70.00
L	25	Famous Beauties (1937)	£2.40	£60.00
	50	Film Stars 3rd series (1938)	£1.50	£75.00
L	25	Golf (1939)	£7.00	£175.00
	50	International Air Liners (1936)	£1.00	£50.00
	50	Military Uniforms of the British Empire Overseas (1938):		
		A Adhesive backs	£1.40	£70.00
		B Non-adhesive backs	£1.40	£70.00
	50	Modern Naval Craft (1939)	90p	£45.00
	50	Motor Cars 1st series (1936)	£2.00	£100.00
	50	Motor Cars 2nd series (1937)	£1.70	£85.00
	50	National Flags and Arms (1936)	70p	£35.00
L	25	Old Hunting Prints (1938)	£4.00	—
L	25	Old Naval Prints (1936)	£3.60	—
L	25	Racing Yachts (1938)	£5.00	—
	50	RAF Badges (1937)	£1.00	£50.00
	50	Sea Fishes (1935)	70p	£35.00
L	25	Types of Horses (1939)	£4.60	—
L	25	Zoo Babies (1937)	£2.00	—

B GENERAL OVERSEAS ISSUES

	50	Aeroplane Series (1926)	£2.20	—
	50	Arms and Armour (1926)	£3.00	£150.00
MP	50	Beauties 1st series (1925):		
		A Black and white fronts	£1.60	£80.00
		B Coloured fronts	£1.80	£90.00
MP	50	Beauties 2nd series (1925)	£1.60	£80.00
	52	Birds of Brilliant Plumage (1927)	£3.50	—
	25	Bonzo Dogs (1923)	£5.00	—
	50	Boy Scouts (1924)	£3.20	—
M	25	British Live Stock (1924)	£7.20	—
	50	Butterflies (Girls) (1928)	£6.00	—
	25	Dogs (Heads) (1927)	£1.60	£40.00
	32	Drum Horses (1911)	£8.00	—
	25	Flag Girls of All Nations (1908)	£7.00	—
	50	Household Hints (1928-29)	90p	£45.00
	50	Lawn Tennis (1928)	£4.00	—
	50	Leaders of Men (1925)	£2.40	£120.00
	48	Pictures of the East (1931)	£2.40	£120.00
	25	Picturesque People of the Empire (1928)	£2.20	£55.00
M	53	Playing Cards (1929)	£1.20	—
	50	Pugilists in Action (1928)	£4.00	—
	50	Railway Working (1926)	£2.00	£100.00
P	50	The Royal Family at Home and Abroad (1927)	£2.50	—
	50	Ships Flags and Cap Badges (1930)	£2.00	£100.00
	50	Signalling series (1926)	£1.50	—
	25	Whaling (1930)	£2.80	£70.00

POLICANSKY BROS, South Africa

	50	Beautiful Illustrations of South African Fauna (1925)	£8.00	—

Size	Number in set		Price per card	Complete set

R.J. REYNOLDS (Doral) USA

	23	America's Backyard (plants) (2006)	£1.25	—
		America On The Road (2004):		
	25	A Set of 24 plus List Card	£1.25	—
	1	B Limited Edition Card	—	—
		American Treasures (2005):		
	25	A Set of 24 plus List Card	£1.25	—
	1	B Limited Edition Card	—	—
	52	The 50 States (2000) plus 2 List Cards	£1.25	—
		Great American Festivals (2003):		
	31	A Set of 30 plus List Card	£1.25	—
	1	B Limited Edition Card	—	—
		Snapshots of The Century (2001):		
	36	A Set of 35 plus Title Card	£1.25	—
	1	B Limited Edition Card	—	—
	1	C Special Edition Card	—	—
	4	Doral's Employees (2006)	£1.25	£5.00

RICHMOND CAVENDISH CO. LTD

	28	Chinese Actors and Actresses (1922)	£4.00	—
P	50	Cinema Stars (1926)	£3.50	—

RUGGIER BROS, Malta

M	50	Story of the Knights of Malta (c1925)	£6.00	—

SANTA FE NATURAL TOBACCO CO., USA

	36	A Tribute To The Endangered Set 1 (2001)	£1.25	—
	36	A Tribute To The Endangered Set 2 (2001)	£1.25	—
	36	Century of The Great American Spirit Set 1 (2000)	£1.25	—
	36	Century of The Great American Spirit Set 2 (2000)	£1.25	—
	36	Music of America (2003)	£1.25	—
	36	Spirit of The Old West Series 1 (1999)	£1.25	—
	36	Spirit of The Old West Series 2 (1999)	£1.25	—

SCERRI, Malta

		Beauties and Children (c1930):		
	150	A Black and white, no borders	£1.20	—
	? 86	B Black and white, white border	£13.00	—
	45	C Coloured	£1.70	—
MP	50	Beautiful Women (c1935)	£3.00	£150.00
MP	480	Cinema Artists (c1935)	£2.30	—
MP	180	Cinema Stars (c1935)	£2.70	—
MP	50	Famous London Buildings (c1935)	£3.50	—
MP	60	Film Stars 1st series Nos 1-60 (c1935)	£3.00	—
MP	60	Film Stars 2nd series Nos 61-120 (c1935)	£3.00	—
	52	Interesting Places of the World (c1936)	50p	£26.00
P	25	International Footballers (c1935)	£25.00	—
M	401	Malta Views (c1930)	70p	—
M	51	Members of Parliament — Malta (c1930)	44p	£22.00
	146	Prominent People (c1930)	£1.40	—
MP	100	Scenes from Films (c1935)	£2.75	—
LP	100	Talkie Stars (c1930)	£2.75	—
M	100	World's Famous Buildings (c1930)	55p	£55.00

Size	Number in set		Price per card	Complete set

J.J. SCHUH TOBACCO CO. PTY LTD, Australia
ALL SERIES ISSUED 1920-25
	60	Australian Footballers series A (half-full length)	£8.00	—
	40	Australian Footballers series B (Rays)	£8.00	—
	59	Australian Footballers series C (oval frame)	£13.00	—
		Australian Jockeys:		
	30	A Numbered	£6.00	—
	30	B Unnumbered	£6.00	—
P	72	Cinema Stars	£2.30	—
	60	Cinema Stars	£2.50	—
L	12	Maxims of Success	£40.00	—
P	72	Official War Photographs	£3.00	—
P	96	Portraits of Our Leading Footballers	£5.00	—

G. SCLIVAGNOTI, Malta
	50	Actresses and Cinema Stars (1923)	£2.80	—
MP	71	Grand Masters of the Orders of Jerusalem (1897)	£11.00	—
P	102	Opera Singers (1897)	£12.00	—
M	100	Opera Singers (1897)	£12.00	—

SIMONETS LTD, Jersey, Channel Islands
MP	36	Beautiful Women (c1925)	£6.00	—
P	24	Cinema Scenes series (c1925)	£7.00	—
P	27	Famous Actors and Actresses (c1925)	£6.00	—
	50	Local Footballers (c1914)	£5.00	—
	25	Picture Series (c1920)	£4.00	—
P	27	Sporting Celebrities (c1930)	£10.00	—
LP	50	Views of Jersey (plain back) (c1940)	£2.25	—

THE SINSOCK & CO., Korea
	20	Korean Girls (c1905)	£16.00	—

SNIDERS & ABRAHAMS PTY LTD, Australia
		Actresses (c1905):		
	30	A Gold background	£6.00	—
	14	B White Borders	£6.00	—
	20	Admirals and Warships of USA (1908)	£8.00	—
	60	Animals (c1912)	£3.50	—
	60	Animals and Birds (c1912):		
		A 'Advertising Gifts' issue	£2.75	—
		B 'Peter Pan' issue	£3.20	—
	15	Australian Cricket Team (1905)	£40.00	—
	16	Australian Football Incidents in Play (c1906)	£12.00	—
	24	Australian Footballers (full length) series AI with blue framelines (1905)	£13.00	—
	50	Australian Footballers (full length) series AII without framelines (1905)	£13.00	—
	76	Australian Footballers (½ length) series B (1906)	£11.00	—
	76	Australian Footballers (½ length) series C (1907)	£10.00	—
	140	Australian Footballers (head and shoulders) series D (1908)	£9.00	—
	60	Australian Footballers (head in oval) series E (1910)	£9.00	—
	60	Australian Footballers (head in rays) series F (1911)	£9.00	—
	60	Australian Footballers (with pennant) series G (1912)	£9.00	—
	60	Australian Footballers (head in star) series H (1913)	£9.00	—
	60	Australian Footballers (head in shield) series I (1914)	£9.00	—
	56	Australian Footballers (½-¾ length) series J (1910)	£13.00	—
	48	Australian Jockeys, back in blue (1907)	£4.50	—
	83	Australian Jockeys, back in brown (1908)	£5.00	—

Size	Number in set		Price per card	Complete set
		SNIDERS & ABRAHAMS PTY LTD, Australia *(continued)*		
	56	Australian Racehorses, horizontal back (1906)	£5.00	—
	56	Australian Racehorses, vertical back (1907)	£5.00	—
	40	Australian Racing Scenes (1911)	£4.50	—
	? 133	Australian VCs and Officers (1917)	£6.00	—
	12	Billiard Tricks (c1910)	£18.00	—
	60	Butterflies and Moths, captions in small letters (c1912)	£1.80	—
	60	Butterflies and Moths, captions in block letters (c1912)	£1.80	—
	60	Cartoons and Caricatures (c1908)	£6.00	—
	12	Coin Tricks (c1910)	£12.00	—
	64	Crests of British Warships (1915)	£4.50	—
	40	Cricketers in Action (1906)	£50.00	—
	12	Cricket Terms (c1906)	£30.00	—
	32	Dickens series (c1910)	£5.00	—
	16	Dogs (c1910):		
		A 'Standard' issue	£9.00	—
		B 'Peter Pan' issue:		
		1 White panel	£9.00	—
		2 Gilt panel	£9.00	—
		C 'Coronet' issue	£9.00	—
	6	Flags (shaped metal) (c1910)	£6.00	—
	6	Flags (shaped card) (c1910)	£6.00	—
	60	Great War Leaders and Warships (c1915):		
		A Front in green	£4.00	—
		B Front in sepia brown	£4.00	—
	30	How to Keep Fit (c1908)	£6.00	—
	60	Jokes (c1906):		
		A 'Aristocratica' issue	£4.00	—
		B 'Standard' issue	£4.00	—
	12	Match Puzzles (c1910)	£12.00	—
	48	Medals and Decorations (c1915)	£6.00	—
M	48	Melbourne Buildings (c1915)	£8.00	—
	25	Natives of the World (c1906)	£16.00	—
	12	Naval Terms (c1906)	£8.00	—
	29	Oscar Ashe, Lily Brayton and Lady Smokers (1911)	£6.00	—
	40	Shakespeare Characters (c1908)	£5.50	—
	30	Signalling — Semaphore and Morse (c1916)	£7.00	—
	14	Statuary (c1906)	£8.50	—
	60	Street Criers in London, 1707 (c1916)	£8.00	—
	32	Views of Victoria in 1857 (c1908)	£8.50	—
P	250	Views of the World 1908	£3.25	—

STAR TOBACCO CO., India

	52	Beauties (PC inset) (c1898)	£25.00	—
	52	Indian Native Types (PC inset) (c1898)	£25.00	—

TEOFANI & CO. LTD, Iceland

LP	50	Teofani's Icelandic Employees (1930)	£6.00	—

TOBACCO PRODUCTS CORPORATION, USA

	220	Movie Stars (1915)	£3.00	—

TOBACCO PRODUCTS CORPORATION OF CANADA LTD

	? 45	Canadian Sports Champions (c1920)	£12.00	—
	60	Do You Know (1924)	£5.50	—

Size	Number in set		Price per card	Complete set

TOBACCO PRODUCTS CORPORATION OF CANADA LTD *(continued)*

	60	Hockey Players (1926)	£25.00	—
	120	Movie Stars (c1920)	£2.50	—
	? 163	Movie Stars Set 4 (c1920)	£3.50	—

TUCKETT LIMITED, Canada

	25	Autograph series (c1913)	£28.00	—
	? 210	Beauties and Scenes (c1910)	£8.00	—
	25	Boy Scout series (c1915)	£22.00	—
P	100	British Views without Tucketts on front (c1912)	£2.00	—
P	? 224	British Views with Tucketts on front (c1912)	£2.00	—
P	80	British Warships (c1915)	£8.00	—
P	50	Canadian Scenes (c1912)	£2.00	—
	53	Playing Card Premium Certificates (c1930)	£7.50	—
	52	Tucketts Aeroplane series (1930)	£4.50	—
	52	Tucketts Aviation series (1929)	£4.50	—
	52	Tucketts Auction Bridge series (1930)	£6.00	—

UNITED TOBACCO COMPANIES (SOUTH) LTD, South Africa

A WITH FIRM'S NAME

	50	Aeroplanes of Today (1936):		
		A 'Box 78 Capetown'	£1.60	£80.00
		B 'Box 1006 Capetown'	£1.60	£80.00
	50	Animals and Birds Koodoo issue (1923)	£6.50	—
L	24	Arms and Crests of Universities and Schools of South Africa (1930)	£1.40	£35.00
L	52	Boy Scouts, Girl Guide and Voortrekker Badges (1932)	£2.00	£100.00
L	62	British Rugby Tour of South Africa (1938)	£1.80	—
	50	Children of All Nations (1928)	£1.00	—
	50	Cinema Stars 'Flag Cigarettes' (1924)	£2.20	£110.00
	60	Do You Know? (1929)	60p	£36.00
	50	Do You Know 2nd series (1930)	60p	£30.00
	50	Do You Know 3rd series (1931)	60p	£30.00
K	28	Dominoes 'Ruger Cigarettes' (1934)	£6.00	—
L	50	Exercises for Men and Women (1932)	£1.00	£50.00
	48	Fairy Tales 1st series Flag issue (1928)	£1.80	—
	48	Fairy Tales 2nd series Flag issue (1928)	£1.80	—
	24	Fairy Tales (1926) (booklets)	£10.00	—
L	120	Farmyards of South Africa (1934)	£1.50	—
M	50	Household Hints (1926)	£2.00	—
	25	Interesting Experiments (1930)	£1.40	£35.00
L	100	Medals and Decorations of the British Commonwealth of Nations (1941)	90p	—
	50	Merchant Ships of the World (1925)	£1.20	£60.00
	50	Motor Cars (1923)	£3.70	—
L	100	Our Land (1938)	22p	£22.00
L	200	Our South Africa Past and Present (1938)	20p	£40.00
L	24	Pastel Plates (1938)	£1.20	£30.00
L	88	Philosophical Sayings (1938)	£1.20	—
	25	Picturesque People of the Empire (1929)	£1.40	£35.00
K	53	Playing Cards 'Flag' Cigarettes	£1.80	—
K	53	Playing Cards 'Lifeboat' Cigarettes (1934)	£2.00	—
M	53	Playing Cards 'Lotus Cigarettes' (1934)	£2.25	—
L	53	Playing Cards 'Loyalist Cigarettes' (1934)	£2.00	—
K	53	Playing Cards 'MP Cigarettes' (1934)	£2.00	—
K	53	Playing Cards 'Rugger Cigarettes' (1934)	£3.00	—
L	50	Racehorses South Africa Set 1 (1929)	£2.00	—

Size	Number in set		Price per card	Complete set

UNITED TOBACCO COMPANIES (SOUTH) LTD, South Africa *(continued)*

Size	Number in set		Price per card	Complete set
L	52	Racehorses South Africa Set 2 (1930):		
		A Inscribed 'a series of 50'	£2.00	—
		B Inscribed 'a series of 52'	£2.00	—
	50	Regimental Uniforms (1937)	£1.80	£90.00
	50	Riders of the World (1931)	£1.30	£65.00
L	52	S. A. Flora (1935):		
		A With 'CT Ltd'	50p	—
		B Without 'CT Ltd'	40p	£22.00
	25	South African Birds 1st series (1927)	£1.40	—
	25	South African Birds 2nd series (1927)	£1.40	—
L	52	South African Butterflies (1937)	80p	£42.00
L	52	South African Coats of Arms (1931)	50p	£26.00
L	65	South African Rugby Football Clubs (1933)	£2.00	—
L	52	Sports and Pastimes in South Africa (1936)	£1.80	£90.00
L	47	Springbok Rugby and Cricket Teams (1931)	£3.00	—
L	28	1912-13 Springboks (1913)	£50.00	—
	25	Studdy Dogs (1925)	£4.60	—
?	98	Transfers (c1925)	£6.00	—
L	40	Views of South African Scenery 1st series (1918):		
		A Text back	£4.50	—
		B Anonymous plain back	£4.50	—
L	36	Views of South African Scenery 2nd series (1920)	£4.50	—
	25	Wild Flowers of South Africa 1st series (1925)	£1.40	—
	25	Wild Flowers of South Africa 2nd series (1926)	£1.40	—
	50	The World of Tomorrow (1938)	£1.00	£50.00

B WITHOUT FIRM'S NAME

Size	Number in set		Price per card	Complete set
	50	African Fish (1937)	£1.50	£75.00
	50	British Aeroplanes (1933)	£1.60	—
EL	25	Champion Dogs (1934)	£5.00	—
	30	Do You Know (1933)	80p	£24.00
	50	Eminent Film Personalities (1930)	£2.20	—
	50	English Period Costumes (1932)	£1.00	£50.00
	25	Famous Figures from South African History (1932)	£2.00	—
L	100	Famous Works of Art (1939)	25p	£25.00
	25	Flowers of South Africa (1932)	£2.00	—
M	50	Humour in Sport (1929)	£3.50	—
L	100	Our Land (1938)	30p	—
M	150	Our South African Birds (1942)	40p	£60.00
L	150	Our South African Birds (1942)	30p	£45.00
M	100	Our South African Flora (1940)	20p	£20.00
L	100	Our South African Flora (1940)	20p	£17.00
M	100	Our South African National Parks (1941)	22p	£22.00
L	100	Our South African National Parks (1941)	22p	£22.00
L	50	Pictures of South Africa's War Effort (1942)	30p	£15.00
	50	Riders of the World (1931)	£1.30	£65.00
	50	Safety First (1936)	£1.10	£55.00
	40	Ships of All Times (1931)	£1.80	—
	25	South African Birds 2nd series	£2.60	—
L	17	South African Cricket Touring Team (1929):		
		A Fronts with autographs	£20.00	—
		B Fronts without autographs	£20.00	—
M	100	South African Defence (1939)	25p	£25.00
L	50	South African Places of Interest (1934)	35p	£17.50
P	50	Stereoscopic Photographs Assorted Subjects (1928)	£1.00	—
P	50	Stereoscopic Photographs of South Africa (1929)	£1.00	—
	50	The Story of Sand (1934)	£1.00	£50.00

Size	Number in set		Price per card	Complete set
\multicolumn{5}{l}{**UNITED TOBACCO COMPANIES (SOUTH) LTD, South Africa** *(continued)*}
M	50	Tavern of the Seas (1939)	50p	£25.00
	25	Warriors of All Nations (crossed swords at base) (1937)	£1.80	£45.00
	25	What's This (1929)	£1.60	£40.00
	50	Wild Animals of the World (1932)	£1.30	£65.00
M	40	Wonders of the World (1931)	£1.00	—
M	100	World Famous Boxers (c1935)	£6.00	—
C	*SILK ISSUES*			
M	20	British Butterflies (c1920)	£10.00	—
M	30	British Roses (c1920)	£10.00	—
M	65	Flags of All Nations (c1920)	£3.00	—
M	25	Old Masters (c1920)	£8.00	—
M	50	Pottery Types (c1920)	£7.00	—
M	50	South African Flowers Nd 1-50 (c1920)	£3.75	—
M	50	South African Flowers Nd 51-100 (c1920)	£3.75	—

UNIVERSAL TOBACCO CO. PTY LTD, South Africa

	835	Flags of All Nations (1935)	£1.20	—

S.W. VENABLE TOBACCO CO., USA

EL	?	Actresses (c1890)	£35.00	—

WESTMINSTER TOBACCO CO. LTD

A	*CARD ISSUES*			
M	332	Adamsons Oplevelser (1930)	£20.00	—
M	50	Beauties (1924)	£3.00	—
MP	100	Beautiful Women (1915)	£2.80	—
M	50	Birds, Beasts and Fishes (1923)	£2.60	—
		British Beauties (1915):		
M	102	A Coloured	£4.00	—
M	86	B Uncoloured	£4.00	—
P	48	British Royal and Ancient Buildings (1925)	£1.00	£50.00
M	50	Butterflies and Moths (1920)	£2.80	—
P	36	Canada 1st series (1926)	£1.00	£36.00
P	36	Canada 2nd series (1928)	£1.00	£36.00
	30	Celebrated Actresses (1921)	£5.00	—
	100	Cinema Artistes green back (1929-33)	£3.00	—
	50	Cinema Artistes grey back (1929-33)	£3.00	—
	48	Cinema Celebrities (1935)	£3.00	—
P	50	Cinema Stars (1926)	£3.00	—
MP	50	Cinema Stars black and white (1930)	£3.20	—
MP	50	Cinema Stars (1930) hand coloured	£3.20	—
M	27	Dancing Girls (1917)	£5.50	—
	50	Do You Know (1922)	£2.50	—
	24	Fairy Tale (booklets) (1926)	£6.50	—
M	100	Famous Beauties (1916):		
		A Captions in brown	£2.30	—
		B Captions in blue	£2.50	—
MP	52	Film Favourites (1927):		
		A Uncoloured	£4.00	—
		B Coloured	£4.00	—
M	50	Film Personalities (1931)	£4.00	—
M	50	Garden Flowers of the World (1917)	£3.00	—
	40	The Great War Celebrities (1914)	£8.00	—
P	48	Indian Empire 1st series (1925)	£1.00	£50.00
P	48	Indian Empire 2nd series (1926)	£1.00	£50.00

Size	Number in set		Price per card	Complete set

WESTMINSTER TOBACCO CO. LTD *(continued)*

Size	Number in set		Price per card	Complete set
LP	50	Islenzkar Eimskipamyndir (Trawlers) (1931)	£3.00	£150.00
LP	50	Islenzkar Landslagmyndir (Views) (1928)	£2.20	£110.00
LP	50	Islenzkar Landslagmyndir 2nd series (Views) (1929)	£2.20	£110.00
	40	Merrie England Studies (1914)	£8.00	—
	36	Modern Beauties (1938)	£3.50	—
MP	52	Movie Stars (1925)	£3.50	—
P	36	New Zealand 1st series (1928)	£1.25	£42.00
P	36	New Zealand 2nd series (1929)	£1.25	£42.00
K	53	Playing Cards (1934)	£2.00	—
M	55	Playing Cards (1934):		
		A Blue back	£2.00	—
		B Red back	£2.00	—
P	50	Popular Film Stars (1926)	£3.20	—
P	36	South Africa 1st series (1928)	£1.00	£36.00
P	36	South Africa 2nd series (1928)	£1.00	£36.00
M	49	South African Succulents (1936)	25p	£12.50
M	100	Stage and Cinema Stars, captions in grey (1921)	£2.00	—
M	100	Stage and Cinema Stars, captions in black (1921)	£2.80	—
M	50	Stars of Filmland (1927)	£3.30	—
	50	Steamships of the World (1920)	£9.00	—
M	50	Uniforms of All Ages (1917)	£10.00	—
P	50	Views of Malaya (1930)	£7.00	—
	25	Wireless (1923)	£5.00	—
M	50	Women of Nations (1922)	£4.00	—
	50	The World of Tomorrow (1938)	£1.30	£65.00
B	**SILK ISSUES**			
M	50	Garden Flowers of the World (c1914)	£5.00	—
M	24	Miniature Rugs (c1925)	£16.00	—

W.D. & H.O. WILLS

A   CHANNEL ISLAND ISSUES *(without ITC clause)*

	Number		Price	Complete
	50	Air Raid Precautions (1938)	£1.20	£60.00
	50	Association Footballers (1936)	£2.20	£110.00
	50	Dogs (1937)	£1.00	£50.00
	50	Garden Flowers by Richard Sudell (1939)	50p	£25.00
	50	Garden Hints (1938)	50p	£25.00
	50	Household Hints (1936)	50p	£25.00
	50	Life in the Royal Navy (1939)	40p	£20.00
	50	Our King and Queen (1937)	50p	£25.00
	50	Railway Equipment (1939)	60p	£30.00
	50	The Sea Shore (1938)	50p	£25.00
	50	Speed (1938)	50p	£25.00
	50	Wild Flowers 1st series (1936)	60p	£30.00
	50	Wild Flowers 2nd series (1937)	50p	£25.00

B   GENERAL OVERSEAS ISSUES

	Number		Price	Complete
	50	Actors and Actresses, scroll backs in green (c1905) Ref. 32:		
		A Portraits in black and white	£3.50	—
		B Portraits flesh tinted	£2.50	—
	30	Actresses — brown and green (1905) Ref. 116. Scissors issue	£3.30	£100.00
	50	Actresses — four colours surround (c1904) Ref. 117:		
		A Scissors issue	£7.00	—
		B Green scroll back issue	£2.50	—
	30	Actresses — orange/mauve surround (c1915) Scissors issue Ref. 118:		
		A Surround in Orange	£2.50	£75.00
		B Surround in mauve	£1.50	£45.00

Size	Number in set		Price per card	Complete set

W.D. & H.O. WILLS (continued)

	Number in set		Price per card	Complete set
	100	Actresses (c1903) Ref. 34:		
		A Capstan issue	£3.00	—
		B Vice Regal issue	£3.00	—
	250	Actresses (c1903) Ref. 33:		
		A Front portrait in black	£3.00	—
		B Front portrait in red	£3.00	—
	25	Actresses — Tabs type numbered Ref. 16 (1902)	£18.00	—
	50	Actresses — Tabs type unnumbered Ref. 119 Scissors issue (c1905)	£12.00	—
	30	Actresses unicoloured 1 (c1908) Ref. 120:		
		A Scissors issue, back in red	£1.70	£50.00
		B Scissors issue, back in purple brown	£2.50	£75.00
	30	Actresses — unicoloured 11 (c1908) Ref. 121 Scissors issue	£2.00	£60.00
	50	Aeroplanes (1925)	£3.20	—
	60	Animals (cut-outs) (1913):		
		A Havelock issue	£1.80	—
		B Wills' Specialities issue	£1.00	£60.00
	50	Animals and Birds (1912):		
		A With text, without title	£4.50	—
		B Without text, with title	£4.50	—
		C Without text or title	£5.50	—
	50	Arms and Armour (1910):		
		A Capstan issue	£2.00	—
		B Havelock issue	£3.00	—
		C Vice Regal issue	£2.00	—
		D United Service issue	£3.00	£150.00
	50	Arms of the British Empire (1910):		
		A Backs in black	£1.10	£55.00
		B Wills' Specialities issue	£1.10	—
		C Havelock issue	£7.00	—
	25	Army Life 1910 Scissors issue	£2.40	£60.00
	50	Art Photogravures 1st series (1913):		
		A Size 67 × 33mm	80p	—
		B Size 67 × 44mm	80p	—
	50	Art Photogravures 2nd series (1913)	80p	—
	42	Australian Club Cricketers (1905) Ref. 59A:		
		A Dark blue backs	£18.00	—
		B Green backs	£18.00	—
		C Pale blue backs	£18.00	—
	25	Australian and English Cricketers (1903) Ref. 59B	£16.00	—
	25	Australian and English Cricketers (1909) Ref. 59C:		
		A Capstan issue:		
		i Framework in scarlet	£15.00	—
		ii Framework in blue	£15.00	—
		B Vice Regal issue:		
		i Framework in scarlet	£15.00	—
		ii Framework in blue	£15.00	—
	60	Australian and South African Cricketers (1910) Ref. 59D:		
		A Capstan issue:		
		i Framework in scarlet	£16.00	—
		ii Framework in blue	£16.00	—
		B Havelock issue:		
		i Framework in scarlet	£38.00	—
		ii Framework in blue	£38.00	—
		C Vice Regal issue:		
		i Framework in scarlet	£16.00	—
		ii Framework in blue	£16.00	—

Size	Number in set			Price per card	Complete set

W.D. & H.O. WILLS (continued)

Size	Number in set	Description	Price per card	Complete set
M	100	Australian Scenic series (1928)	80p	—
	50	Australian Wild Flowers (1913):		
		A Wills' Specialities issue, grey-brown back	90p	£45.00
		B Wills' Specialities issue, green back	£2.00	—
		C Havelock issue	£3.50	—
		Aviation (1910):		
	85	A Black backs 'Series of 85':		
		i Capstan issue	£2.50	—
		ii Vice Regal issue	£2.50	—
	75	B Black backs 'Series of 75':		
		i Capstan issue	£2.00	—
		ii Havelock issue	£3.00	—
		iii Vice Regal issue	£2.00	—
	75	C Green back 'Series of 75':		
		i Capstan issue	£2.30	—
		ii Havelock issue	£3.50	—
		iii Vice Regal issue	£2.30	—
	50	Aviation series (1910):		
		A W.D. and H.O. Wills back	£3.50	—
		B Anonymous backs with album clause	£3.20	—
		C Anonymous backs without album clause	£3.20	—
	? 97	Baseball series (1912) Pirate issue	£250.00	—
	40	Beauties — brown tinted (c1913):		
		A Scissors issue	£1.50	£60.00
		B Star circle and leaves issue	£3.00	—
	30	Beauties — 'Celebrated Actresses' Ref. 140 Scissors issue (1921)	£4.50	—
	52	Beauties — Heads and shoulders set in background Ref. 141 (1911):		
		A Scissors issue:		
		i Background to packets plain	£6.00	—
		ii Background to packets latticework design	£3.20	£170.00
		B Star circle and leaves issue	£5.00	—
P	25	Beauties 1st series (1924) Ref. 142	£3.00	—
P	50	Beauties 2nd series (1924) Ref. 143	£3.50	—
	32	Beauties — Picture Hats (c1914) Ref. 144:		
		A Scissors issue	£3.50	£115.00
		B Star circle and leaves issue	£5.50	—
MP	72	Beauties — red star and circle back (c1915) Ref. 145	£12.00	—
	50	Beauties — red tinted (1905) Ref. 146	£2.20	£110.00
	30	Beauties and Children (c1910) Ref. 147 Scissors issue	£2.50	£75.00
P	50	Beautiful New Zealand (c1928)	40p	£20.00
	50	Best Dogs of Their Breed (1916):		
		A Havelock issue	£7.00	—
		B Wills' Specialities issue	£4.50	—
		C Anonymous back, Wills' on front	£8.00	—
	30	Birds and Animals (1911) Ruby Queen issue	£2.50	—
	50	Birds, Beasts and Fishes (c1925)	40p	£20.00
	100	Birds of Australasia (1912):		
		A Green backs:		
		i Capstan issue	£1.20	£120.00
		ii Havelock issue	£2.50	—
		iii Vice Regal issue	£1.20	£120.00
		B Yellow backs:		
		i Havelock issue	£2.50	—
		ii Wills' Specialities issue	£1.20	—

Size	Number in set				Price per card	Complete set

W.D. & H.O. WILLS (continued)

Size	Number in set				Price per card	Complete set
	52	Birds of Brilliant Plumage:				
		A	Four Aces issue (1924)		£3.00	—
		B	Pirate Issue:			
			i	With border on front (1914)	£4.00	—
			ii	Without border on front (1916)	£4.00	—
		C	Red star, circle and leaves issue (1914)		£4.50	—
	25	Birds of the East 1st series Ruby Queen issue (1912)			£1.40	£35.00
	25	Birds of the East 2nd series Ruby Queen issue (1912)			£1.40	£35.00
	36	Boxers (1911):				
		A	Scissors issue		£9.00	—
		B	Green star and circle issue		£9.00	—
		Britain's Defenders (1915):				
		A	Wills' Specialities issue:			
	50		i	Inscribed 'A Series of 50'	£1.50	£75.00
	8		ii	Without inscription 'A Series of 50'	£9.00	—
	50	B	Havelock issue		£2.50	—
	50	C	Scissors issue:			
			i	Red upright 'Scissors' packet	£1.60	£80.00
			ii	Green upright 'Scissors' packet	£1.70	£85.00
			iii	Red slanting 'Scissors' packet	£1.60	£80.00
	50	D	Green star and circle issue		£1.80	—
	43	British Army Boxers (1913) Scissors issue			£5.00	—
	50	British Army Uniforms (c1910):				
		A	Wild Woodbine issue		£6.00	£300.00
		B	Flag issue		£5.00	—
		C	Scissors issue		£5.00	£250.00
	101	British Beauties (c1915)			£2.00	—
	50	British Empire series (1913):				
		A	Capstan issue		90p	£45.00
		B	Havelock issue		£1.80	—
		C	Vice Regal issue		90p	£45.00
P	48	British Royal and Ancient Buildings (1925)			50p	£25.00
	45	British Rugby Players (1930)			£2.40	—
	50	Chateaux (1925)			£5.00	—
	50	Children of All Nations (1925)			70p	£35.00
	100	China's Famous Warriors (1911) Pirate issue Ref. 357:				
		A	First 25 subjects		£2.80	£70.00
		B	Second 25 subjects		£2.80	£70.00
		C	Third 25 subjects		£2.80	£70.00
		D	Fourth 25 subjects		£2.80	£70.00
	28	Chinese Actors and Actresses (1907) Pirate issue Ref. 361			£3.00	—
	25	Chinese Beauties 1st Series (1907) Pirate issue Ref. 362:				
		A	Vertical back		£1.60	£40.00
		B	Horizontal back		£1.80	£45.00
	25	Chinese Beauties 2nd series (1909) Pirate issue Ref. 363:				
		A	With framelines on front		£1.60	£40.00
		B	Without framelines on front		£1.60	£40.00
	30	Chinese Children's Games (1911) Ruby Queen issue Ref. 364			£2.00	—
	50	Chinese Costumes Pirate issue (1928) Ref. 365			£4.00	—
EL	25	Chinese Pagodas (1905-10) Pirate issue Ref. 366			£45.00	—
	50	Chinese Proverbs brown Ref. 367 (1928):				
		A	Pirate issue		£1.25	—
		B	Ruby Queen issue		£4.00	—
	50	Chinese Proverbs coloured (1914-16) Pirate issue Ref. 368:				
		A	Back in blue:			
			i	Without overprint	£1.25	—
			ii	With overprint	£1.25	—
		B	Back in olive green		£1.50	—

Size	Number in set				Price per card	Complete set

W.D. & H.O. WILLS *(continued)*

Size	Number in set	Description	Price per card	Complete set
	40	Chinese Trades (c1905) Autocar issue	£7.00	—
	50	Chinese Transport (1914) Ref. 370 Ruby Queen issue	£3.00	—
	50	Cinema Stars Four Aces issue (c1926):		
		A Numbered	£1.60	£80.00
		B Unnumbered	£1.80	£90.00
	25	Cinema Stars (c1922) Scissors issue	£2.40	£60.00
	50	Coaches and Coaching Days (1925)	£2.00	£100.00
		Conundrums (c1900):		
	25	A With album clause	£12.00	—
	25	B Without album clause	£12.00	—
	25	C Without album clause redrawn	£12.00	—
	50	D Without album clause inscribed '50 Different'	£12.00	—
M	68	Crests and Colours of Australian Universities, Colleges and Schools (1922)	80p	£55.00
P	63	Cricketers Ref. 59E (c1925)	£8.00	—
	25	Cricketer series Ref. 59F (1902)	£120.00	—
	50	Cricketer series (1901) Ref. 59G	£120.00	—
P	48	Cricket Season 1928-29	£3.40	—
	27	Dancing Girls (1915) Scissors issue:		
		A Inscribed '28 Subjects' (No. 3 not issued)	£2.50	—
		B Inscribed '27 Subjects'	£2.50	—
	25	Derby Day series (1914):		
		A Scissors issue:		
		i With title	£7.00	—
		ii Without title	£9.00	—
		B Star and circle issue	£9.00	—
	50	Dogs — Scenic backgrounds (1925)	90p	£45.00
M	20	Dogs — Heads 1st series (1927):		
		A Wills' World Renown Cigarettes issue:		
		i With album clause	£3.00	—
		ii Without album clause	£3.00	—
		B Three Castles and Vice Regal Cigarettes issue	£3.00	—
M	20	Dogs-Heads 2nd series (1927)	£3.25	—
	32	Drum Horses (c1909):		
		A Scissors issue:		
		i Vertical format, open Scissors packet	£8.00	—
		ii Horizontal format, closed Scissors packet	£6.50	£200.00
		B United Service issue	£6.00	—
		C Green star, circle and leaves issue	£7.00	—
P	25	English Cricketers (1926)	£2.80	£70.00
M	25	English Period Costumes (1928):		
		A White card	£1.80	—
		B Cream card	£1.80	£45.00
ELP	10	English Views & Buildings (c1928)	£12.00	—
		Etchings (of Dogs) (1925):		
	26	A Small size English language issues:		
		i With 'Gold Flake Cigarettes'	£7.00	—
		ii Without 'Gold Flake Cigarettes'	£2.50	—
	26	B Small size Dutch language issues:		
		i With framelines to back	£8.00	—
		ii Without framelines to back	£8.00	—
M	26	C Medium size	£5.00	—
	25	The Evolution of the British Navy (c1915)	£3.00	£75.00
ELP	10	Famous Castles (c1928)	£10.00	—
		Famous Film Stars (1934):		
	100	A Small size	£1.20	—
M	100	B Medium size:		
		i White card	£2.20	—
		ii Cream card	£2.20	—

Size	Number in set				Price per card	Complete set

W.D. & H.O. WILLS *(continued)*

Size	Number in set	Title			Price per card	Complete set
MP	100	Famous Film Stars (c1936)			£3.20	—
	50	Famous Footballers (1914):				
		A	Scissors issue		£9.00	—
		B	Star and circle issue		£9.00	—
	50	Famous Inventions (without ITC clause) (1927)			90p	£45.00
	75	Film Favourites Four Aces issue (1928)			£1.70	—
	50	Fish of Australasia (1912):				
		A	Capstan issue		£1.00	£50.00
		B	Havelock issue		£2.30	—
		C	Vice Regal issue		£1.00	£50.00
		Flag Girls of All Nations (1908):				
	50	A	Capstan issue		£2.00	—
	50	B	Vice Regal issue		£2.00	—
	25	C	United Service issue		£2.80	£70.00
	25	D	Scissors issue:			
			i	Numbered	£10.00	—
			ii	Unnumbered	£10.00	—
	25	E	Green star, circle and leaves issue		£2.80	£70.00
	8	Flags, shaped metal (1915)			£8.50	—
	126	Flags and Ensigns (1903)			£1.50	—
	25	Flags of the Empire (no ITC clause) (1926)			£7.00	—
		Flowers Purple Mountain issue (1914):				
	20	A	Numbered		£11.00	—
	100	B	Unnumbered		£11.00	—
	50	Football Club Colours Scissors/Special Army Quality issue (1905)			£9.00	—
	28	Football Club Colours and Flags (1913):				
		A	Capstan issue		£4.50	—
		B	Havelock issue		£6.50	—
	200	Footballers (1933):				
		A	Small size		£1.40	—
		B	Medium size		£2.80	—
	50	Girls of All Nations (1908):				
		A	Capstan issue		£2.50	—
		B	Vice Regal issue		£2.50	—
		C	Green star, circle and leaves issue		£2.60	—
	25	Governor-General of India, Scissors issue (1911)			£6.50	—
M	25	Heraldic Signs and Their Origins (1925)			£1.60	£40.00
	30	Heroic Deeds (1914) Scissors issue			£4.00	—
	50	Historic Events (1912):				
		A	Wills' Specialities issue		£1.00	£50.00
		B	Havelock issue		£2.00	—
M	25	History of Naval Dress (1930)			£25.00	—
P	50	Homeland Events (1927)			70p	£35.00
	50	Horses of Today (1906):				
		A	Capstan issue		£2.80	—
		B	Havelock issue		£5.00	—
		C	Vice Regal issue		£2.80	—
	50	Household Hints (1927):				
		A	With 'Wills' Cigarettes' at top back		50p	—
		B	Without 'Wills' Cigarettes' at top back		£1.50	—
		Houses of Parliament (c1912):				
	33	A	Pirate issue		£1.40	£45.00
	32	B	Star and circle issue		£2.00	£65.00
	50	Indian Regiments (c1912):				
		A	Scissors issue		£8.00	—
		B	Star and circle issue		£9.00	—
	50	Interesting Buildings (1905)			£2.20	£110.00

Size	Number in set			Price per card	Complete set

W.D. & H.O. WILLS *(continued)*

Size	Number in set	Description	Price per card	Complete set
	67	International Footballers Season 1909-1910:		
		A Scissors issue (1910)	£10.00	—
		B United Services issue (1910)	£10.00	—
		C Flag issue (1911)	£10.00	—
	5	Islands of the Pacific (c1916)	£200.00	—
	50	Jiu-Jitsu (c1910):		
		A Scissors issue	£6.00	—
		B Flag issue	£5.00	—
	53	Jockeys and Owners Colours with PC inset Scissors issue (1914)	£8.00	—
	50	Lighthouses (1925)	£1.80	£90.00
		Maori Series (c1900):		
	100	A White border	£90.00	—
	? 44	B Green border. Numbered bottom left	£90.00	—
	? 3	C Green border. Numbered top left	£175.00	—
	? 4	D Green border. Unnumbered	£175.00	—
	? 100	E White border. Plain back (anonymous)	£75.00	—
	45	Melbourne Cup Winners (1906)	£8.00	—
	50	Merchant Ships of the World (1925) (without ITC clause)	£1.10	£55.00
	40	Merrie England Studies (Male) (1916)	£6.50	—
	24	Merveilles du Monde (1927)	£6.50	—
	25	Military Portraits (1917) Scissors issue	£4.00	—
M	25	Miniatures — oval medallions (1914)	£50.00	—
K	52	Miniature Playing Cards Scissors issue (1906)	£11.00	—
	50	Modern War Weapons (1916):		
		A Wills' Specialities issue	£1.70	—
		B Havelock issue	£2.80	—
	25	Modes of Conveyance (1928) Four Aces issue	£2.00	£50.00
	48	Motor Cars (1924)	£2.00	£100.00
P	50	Motor Cars (1928)	£1.50	£75.00
	50	Motor Cycles (1926)	£3.20	£160.00
P	48	Movie Stars (1927)	£3.50	—
	50	Music Hall Celebrities (1911) Scissors issue	£6.50	—
	50	National Flags and Arms (1936)	£1.50	—
M	25	The Nation's Shrines (1928)	£1.40	£35.00
P	50	Nature Studies (1928)	£1.50	—
	50	New Zealand Birds (1925)	70p	£35.00
P	50	New Zealand — Early Scenes and Maori Life (1926)	40p	£20.00
	50	New Zealand Footballers (1928)	£1.30	£65.00
	50	New Zealand Race Horses (1928):		
		A Cream card	90p	£45.00
		B White card	£1.00	—
	50	N.Z. Butterflies, Moths and Beetles (1925)	70p	£35.00
	25	Past and Present (1929)	£1.20	£30.00
	50	Past and Present Champions (1908):		
		A Capstan Cigarette issue	£7.50	—
		B Capstan Tobacco issue	£7.50	—
	25	Picturesque People of the Empire (1928)	£1.20	£30.00
	25	Pirates and Highwaymen (1925)	£1.60	£40.00
	25	Police of the World (1910)	£10.00	—
M	70	Practical Wireless (1923)	£7.50	—
		Products of the World — Maps and Scenes (1913):		
	50	A Pirate issue	£1.20	—
	25	B Green star, circle and leaves issue	£1.80	—
	50	Products of the World — Scenes only (1929)	40p	£20.00
	50	Prominent Australian and English Cricketers (1907) Ref. 59H	£13.00	—
	23	Prominent Australian and English Cricketers (1907) Ref. 59I	£18.00	—

Size	Number in set					Price per card	Complete set

W.D. & H.O. WILLS (continued)

	59	Prominent Australian and English Cricketers (1911) Ref. 59J:					
		A	Capstan issue:				
				i	'A Series of 50'	£13.00	—
				ii	'A Series of .../A Series of 59'	£13.00	—
		B	Vice Regal issue:				
				i	'A Series of 50'	£13.00	—
				ii	'A Series of .../A Series of 59'	£13.00	—
		C	Havelock issue			£40.00	—
	25	Puzzle series (1910) Scissors/United Service issue				£7.00	—
	50	Races of Mankind (1910)				£12.00	—
	50	Railway Engines (1924)				£1.20	£60.00
	50	Railway Working (1927)				£2.20	—
	50	Regimental Colours and Cap Badges (c1910):					
		A	Scissors issue			£1.40	£70.00
		B	United Service issue:				
				i	Red back	£1.40	£70.00
				ii	Blue back	£1.40	£70.00
	33	Regimental Pets (1911) Scissors issue				£6.00	—
	50	Regimental Standards and Cap Badges (1930)				70p	£35.00
	50	Riders of the World:					
		A	Capstan/Vice Regal/Pennant/Wills' Specialities issue (1913)			£1.60	—
		B	Havelock issue (1913)			£3.00	—
		C	Back in red-brown (1925)			£1.00	£50.00
	50	Romance of the Heavens (1928) (No ITC clause)				£1.50	—
	25	Roses (1912):					
		A	Purple Mountain issues:				
				i	With Wills' Cigarettes on front	£6.00	—
				ii	Without Wills' Cigarettes on front	£6.00	—
		B	Plain backs with Wills' Cigarettes on front			£6.00	—
P	50	The Royal Family at Home and Abroad (1927)				£1.50	—
	50	Royal Mail (with Wills' Cigarettes on fronts) (1913):					
		A	Capstan issue			£3.80	£190.00
		B	Havelock issue (without Wills' Cigarettes on fronts)			£5.00	—
		C	Vice Regal issue			£3.80	£190.00
		D	With anonymous backs			£6.00	—
		E	With plain back			£6.00	—
P	50	The Royal Navy (c1930)				£1.60	£80.00
	100	Royalty, Notabilities and Events in Russia, China and South Africa (1902)				£2.40	—
	27	Rulers of the World (1911)				£7.50	—
		Russo-Japanese series (1905):					
	100	A	Fronts in black			£1.80	£180.00
	50	B	Fronts in red			£7.50	—
	50	Safety First (1937)				80p	£40.00
LP	48	Scenes from the Empire (1939)				£1.80	£90.00
	30	Semaphore Signalling (1910)				£3.30	£100.00
P	50	Ships and Shipping (1928)				90p	£45.00
	36	Ships and Their Pennants (1913)				£5.50	—
	50	Ships' Badges (1926)				90p	£45.00
	50	Signalling series (1913):					
		A	Capstan issue			£1.10	£55.00
		B	Havelock issue			£2.30	—
		C	Vice Regal issue			£1.10	£55.00
	40	Sketches in black and white (1905)				£2.30	—
		Soldiers of the World (1903):					
	50	A	Numbered			£9.00	—
	75	B	Unnumbered			£10.00	—

Size	Number in set		Price per card	Complete set

W.D. & H.O. WILLS *(continued)*

Size	Number in set	Description	Price per card	Complete set
	99	South African Personalities (1900)	£125.00	—
ELP	10	Splendours of New Zealand (c1928)	£10.00	—
	30	Sporting Girls (1913) Scissors issue	£8.00	—
P	50	A Sporting Holiday in New Zealand (1928):		
		A Small size	70p	£35.00
		B Medium size	90p	£45.00
	25	Sporting Terms (1905):		
		A Capstan issue	£13.00	—
		B Vice Regal issue	£13.00	—
	50	Sports of the World (1917)	£5.00	—
	50	Stage and Music Hall Celebrities (1904) (Portrait in oval frame):		
		A Capstan issue	£3.00	—
		B Vice Regal issue	£3.00	—
		C Havelock issue	£4.50	—
	50	Stage and Music Hall Celebrities (1904) (Portrait in oblong frame)	£3.50	—
P	52	Stars of the Cinema (1925):		
		A Text back	£5.00	—
		B Four Aces issue	£5.00	—
	50	Time and Money in Different Countries (1908):		
		A Capstan issue	£1.50	—
		B Havelock issue	£2.70	—
		C Vice Regal issue:		
		i With album clause	£1.40	£70.00
		ii Without album clause	£1.40	£70.00
	50	A Tour Round the World (1907)	£2.70	—
	50	Types of the British Army (1912):		
		A Capstan issue	£2.00	—
		B Vice Regal issue	£2.00	—
	50	Types of the Commonwealth Forces (1910):		
		A Capstan issue	£2.20	—
		B Vice Regal issue	£2.20	—
		C Havelock issue	£4.50	—
	25	United States Warships (1911):		
		A Capstan issue	£2.80	—
		B Havelock issue	£5.00	—
		C Vice Regal issue	£2.80	—
P	50	Units of the British Army and RAF (1928)	60p	£30.00
	50	USS Co's Steamers (1930)	£2.60	—
	50	VCs (1925)	£1.80	£90.00
	25	Victoria Cross Heroes (c1915):		
		A Havelock issue	£4.00	—
		B Wills' Specialities issue	£2.40	£60.00
		C Scissors issue	£3.00	£75.00
	10	Victorian Football Association (c1910):		
		A Capstan on front	£4.00	—
		B Havelock on front	£6.00	—
	19	Victorian Football League (c1910):		
		A Capstan on front	£4.00	—
		B Havelock on front	£6.00	—
	215	Views of the World (1908):		
		A Numbers 1-50 plain backs (anonymous)	80p	—
		B Numbers 51-215 blue back Capstan issue	80p	—
		C Numbers 51-215 green back Vice Regal issue	80p	—
	25	Village Models series (1925):		
		A Small size	£1.40	£35.00
		B Medium size	£6.00	—

Size	Number in set		Price per card	Complete set

W.D. & H.O. WILLS (continued)

Size	Number in set		Price per card	Complete set
	50	War Incidents 1st series (1916):		
		A Wills' Specialities issue	£2.20	—
		B Havelock issue	£3.00	—
		C Scissors issue	£2.50	£125.00
	50	War Incidents 2nd series (1917):		
		A Wills' Specialities issue	£3.00	£150.00
		B Havelock issue	£5.00	—
	50	War Pictures (1915):		
		A Wills' Specialities issue	£1.30	£65.00
		B Havelock issue	£2.20	—
	50	Warships (1925)	£1.60	£80.00
	30	What It Means (1916) Scissors issue	£1.40	£42.00
		Wild Animals (c1935):		
	50	A Small size titled 'Wild Animals' Heads	70p	£35.00
M	25	B Medium size titled 'Wild Animals'	£1.40	£35.00
	50	Wild Animals of the World (1906):		
		A Bristol and London issue	£11.00	—
		B Celebrated Cigarettes issue	£5.50	£275.00
		C Star, circle and leaves issue	£8.00	—
	25	Wonders of the World (1926)	£1.20	£30.00
	25	The World's Dreadnoughts (1910):		
		A Capstan issue	£2.00	—
		B Vice Regal issue	£2.00	—
		C No ITC clause	£2.60	£65.00
P	50	Zoo (1927):		
		A Scissors issue without descriptive back	£4.00	—
		B Wills' issue with descriptive back	30p	£15.00
MP	50	Zoological series (1922)	£1.80	—
C		***SILK ISSUES 1911-17***		
M	50	Arms of the British Empire	£3.00	—
M	50	Australian Butterflies	£3.00	—
M	50	Birds and Animals of Australia	£3.00	—
		Crests and Colours of Australian Universities, Colleges and Schools:		
M	50	A Numbered	£3.00	—
M	1	B Unnumbered	£25.00	—
EL	1	Flag (Union Jack)	£28.00	—
	28	Flags of 1914-18 Allies:		
		A Backs with letterpress in capitals	£2.00	—
		B Backs with letterpress in small lettering	£2.00	—
	38	Kings and Queens of England	£4.50	—
M	50	Popular Flowers:		
		A Backs inscribed 'Now being inserted in the large packets'	£4.50	—
		B Backs inscribed 'Now being inserted in the 1/- packets'	£4.50	—
M	67	War Medals	£3.25	—

J. WIX & SONS LTD

P	24	Royal Tour in New Zealand (1928)	£13.00	—

GEO. F. YOUNG & BRO., USA

L	?	Actresses (c1890)	£30.00	—

ANONYMOUS SERIES — Chinese Language

M	10	Chinese Beauties (Ref ZE2-11) (c1930)	—	£20.00
M	10	Chinese Series (Ref ZE9-31) (c1930)	—	£20.00
	10	Chinese Views & Scenes (Ref ZE9-49) (c1930) (San Shing)	—	£20.00
	48	Hints on Association Football (Ref ZE3-2) (c1930)	—	£10.00
	30	Safety First (Ref ZE9-41) (c1930) (Hwa Ching)	—	£45.00

SECTION III
REPRINT SERIES

During the past twenty years or so, around 350 classic cigarette and trade card series have been reprinted. Many of the originals are extremely rare and do not often turn up in collections, so reprints provide an opportunity to enjoy cards rarely seen. At such low prices, reprints have established a following in their own right, and have also become popular for framing to make an interesting decorative feature. The quality of reproduction is very good, and they are clearly marked as reprints to avoid confusion.

NOTE: C.C.S. = Card Collectors Society

Size	Print-ing	Number in set		Complete set
ADKIN & SONS				
—	C	4	Games by Tom Browne (135 × 83mm) c1900 (reprinted 2001)	£4.00
A.W. ALLEN LTD (Australia)				
D2	U	18	Bradman's Records (Cricketer) 1932 (reprinted 2002)	£7.00
ALLEN & GINTER/GOODWIN/KIMBALL (USA)				
A	C	28	Baseball Greats of 1890 (reprinted 1991)	£6.00
ALLEN & GINTER (USA)				
A	C	50	Celebrated American Indian Chiefs 1888 (reprinted 1989)	—
A	C	50	Fans of The Period 1890 (reprinted 2005)	£8.50
A	C	50	Fruits (Children) 1891 (reprinted 1989)	£8.50
A	C	50	Pirates of the Spanish Main 1888 (reprinted 1996)	—
A	C	50	Prize and Game Chickens c1890 (reprinted 2000)	£10.00
D2	U	9	Women Baseball Players c1888 (reprinted 2001)	£3.00
—	C	50	The World's Champions 2nd Series (82 × 73mm) c1890 (reprinted 2001)	£17.50
AMERICAN TOBACCO CO. (USA)				
B	C	50	Lighthouse Series 1912 (reprinted 2000)	£12.00
A	C	25	Military Uniforms — numbered (green net design back) 1900 (reprinted 2003)	£6.25
ARDATH TOBACCO CO. LTD				
A2	C	35	Hand Shadows c1930 (reprinted 2001)	£7.50
A. BAKER & CO. LTD				
A	C	25	Star Girls c1898 (reprinted 2001)	£6.00
BARBERS TEA LTD				
A	C	24	Cinema & Television Stars 1955 (reprinted 1993)	£6.25
FELIX BERLYN				
A	C	25	Golfing Series Humorous 1910 (reprinted 1989)	£6.00

Size	Printing	Number in set		Complete set
ALEXANDER BOGUSLAVSKY LTD				
—	C	12	Big Events on the Turf (133 × 70mm) 1924 (reprinted 1995)	—
A	C	25	Conan Doyle Characters 1923 (reprinted 1996)	£6.25
A	C	25	Winners on the Turf 1925 (reprinted 1995)	£6.25
BOWMAN GUM INC. (USA)				
—	C	108	Jets-Rockets-Spacemen (80 × 54mm) 1951 (reprinted 1985)	£9.00
WM BRADFORD				
D2	U	20	Boer War Cartoons c1901 (reprinted 2001)	£5.00
BRIGHAM & CO				
B2	BW	16	Down The Thames From Henley to Windsor c1912 (reprinted 2001)	£6.50
BRITISH AMERICAN TOBACCO CO. LTD				
A	C	50	Aeroplanes 1926 (reprinted 2001)	£8.50
D	C	25	Beauties — Blossom Girls c1904 (reprinted 2001)	£6.00
A	C	32	Drum Horses 1910 (reprinted 2001)	£6.25
A	C	50	Indian Regiments 1912 (reprinted 2001)	£8.50
A	C	50	Lighthouses 1926 (reprinted 2000)	£8.50
A	C	45	Melbourne Cup Winners 1906 (reprinted 1992)	£8.50
A	C	50	Motorcycles 1927 (reprinted 1991)	£8.50
A	C	33	Regimental Pets 1911 (reprinted 1998)	£6.25
CADBURY BROS. LTD				
—	C	6	Sports Series (109 × 35mm) c1905 (reprinted 2001)	£3.00
CARRERAS LTD				
A	C	50	Famous Airmen & Airwomen 1936 (reprinted 1996)	£8.50
A	C	75	Footballers 1934 (reprinted 1997)	£13.50
H. CHAPPEL & CO.				
A2	C	10	British Celebrities 1905 (reprinted 2001)	£3.00
W.A. & A.C. CHURCHMAN				
A	U	50	Boxing Personalities 1938 (reprinted 1990)	£8.50
A	C	50	Cricketers 1936 (C.C.S. reprinted 1999)	£10.00
A	C	52	Frisky 1935 (reprinted 1994)	£8.50
A	C	50	In Town To-Night 1938 (C.C.S. reprinted 1999)	£10.00
A	C	50	Landmarks in Railway Progress 1931 (reprinted 1994)	£8.50
A	C	50	Pioneers 1956 (reprinted 2000)	£9.50
A	C	25	Pipes of The World 1927 (C.C.S. reprinted 2000)	£6.50
A	C	50	Prominent Golfers 1931 (reprinted 1989)	£8.50
B	C	12	Prominent Golfers 1931 (reprinted 1989)	£6.00
A	C	50	Racing Greyhounds 1934 (reprinted 1989)	£8.50
—	C	48	The RAF at Work (68 × 53mm) 1938 (reprinted 1995)	£14.00
A	C	50	The Story of Navigation 1936 (C.C.S. reprinted 1999)	£10.00
WM. CLARKE & SON				
A	BW	30	Cricketer Series 1901 (reprinted 2001)	£7.50

Size	Printing	Number in set		Complete set

COHEN WEENEN & CO. LTD

A	C	60	Football Club Captains 1907-8 (reprinted 1998)	£10.00
A	C	40	Home & Colonial Regiments 1901 (reprinted 1998)	£8.50
A	C	50	Star Artistes 1905 (reprinted 1998)	£8.50
A	C	50	V.C. Heroes (of World War I) 1915 (reprinted 1998)	£8.50

CO-OPERATIVE WHOLESALE SOCIETY LTD (C.W.S.)

| A | C | 25 | Parrot Series 1910 (reprinted 1996) | £6.00 |
| A | C | 48 | Poultry 1927 (reprinted 1996) | £8.50 |

COPE BROS. & CO. LTD

A	C	50	British Warriors 1912 (reprinted 1996)	£8.50
A	C	50	Cope's Golfers 1900 (reprinted 1983)	£8.50
A	C	50	Dickens Gallery 1900 (reprinted 1989)	£8.50
—	C	7	The Seven Ages of Man (114 × 78mm) c1885 (reprinted 2001)	£6.00
A	C	50	Shakespeare Gallery 1900 (reprinted 1989)	—
A	C	25	Uniforms of Soldiers and Sailors 1898 (reprinted 1996)	£6.25
A	C	25	The World's Police 1935 (reprinted 2005)	£6.00

DAH TUNG NAN (China)

| — | C | 18 | Golf Girl Series (65 × 50mm) c1920 (reprinted 1997) | £6.00 |

W. DUKE, SONS & CO (USA)

| A | C | 25 | Fishers c1890 (reprinted 2002) | £6.00 |
| A | C | 30 | Generals of American Civil War (Histories of Generals) 1888 (reprinted 1995) | £6.25 |

J. DUNCAN & CO. LTD

| D1 | C | 50 | Evolution of The Steamship 1925 (reprinted 2002) | £8.50 |

H. ELLIS & CO. (USA)

| A | C | 25 | Generals of the Late Civil War 1890 (reprinted 1991) | £6.00 |

EMPIRE TOBACCO CO.

| D | C | 6 | Franco-British Exhibition 1907 (reprinted 2001) | £2.00 |

W. & F. FAULKNER

C	C	25	Beauties (coloured) c1898 (reprinted 2001)	£6.00
D	C	12	Cricket Terms 1899 (reprinted 1999)	£2.50
D	C	12	Football Terms 1st Series 1900 (reprinted 1999)	£2.50
D	C	12	Football Terms 2nd Series 1900 (reprinted 1999)	£2.50
D	C	12	Golf Terms (with "Faulkners" on front) 1901 (reprinted 1999)	£2.50
D2	C	12	Golf Terms (without "Faulkners" titled Golf Humour) 1901 (reprinted 1998)	£2.50
D	C	12	Grenadier Guards 1899 (reprinted 1999)	£2.50
D	C	12	Military Terms 1st Series 1899 (reprinted 1999)	£2.50
D	C	12	Military Terms 2nd Series 1899 (reprinted 1999)	£2.50
D	C	12	Nautical Terms 1st Series 1900 (reprinted 1999)	£2.50
D	C	12	Nautical Terms 2nd Series 1900 (reprinted 1999)	£2.50
D	C	12	Policemen of the World 1899 (reprinted 1999)	£2.50
D	C	12	Police Terms (with "Faulkners" on front) 1899 (reprinted 1999)	£2.50
D2	C	12	Police Terms (without "Faulkners" titled Police Humour) 1899 (reprinted 1998)	£2.50
A	C	25	Prominent Racehorses of the Present day 1923 (reprinted 1993)	£6.00
D	C	12	Puzzle Series 1897 (reprinted 1999)	£2.50
D	C	12	Sporting Terms 1900 (reprinted 1999)	£2.50
D	C	12	Street Cries 1902 (reprinted 1999)	£2.50

Size	Print-ing	Number in set		Complete set

FRANKLYN, DAVEY & CO.

| A | C | 25 | Boxing 1924 (reprinted 2002) | £6.00 |

J.S. FRY & SONS LTD

| A | C | 25 | Days of Nelson 1906 (reprinted 2003) | £6.25 |
| A | C | 25 | Days of Wellington 1906 (reprinted 2003) | £6.25 |

J. GABRIEL

| A | BW | 20 | Cricketers Series 1901 (reprinted 1992) | £5.00 |

GALLAHER LTD

A	C	48	Army Badges 1939 (reprinted 2001)	£8.50
A	C	50	The Great War Nos. 1-50 1915 (reprinted 2001)	£8.50
A	C	50	The Great War Nos. 51-100 1915 (reprinted 2003)	£8.50
A	C	25	The Great War Victoria Cross Heroes 1st Series 1915 (reprinted 2001)	£6.25
A	C	25	The Great War Victoria Cross Heroes 2nd Series 1915 (reprinted 2001)	£6.25
A	C	25	The Great War Victoria Cross Heroes 3rd Series 1915 (reprinted 2001)	£6.25
A	C	25	The Great War Victoria Cross Heroes 4th Series 1915 (reprinted 2001)	£6.25
A	C	25	The Great War Victoria Cross Heroes 5th Series 1915 (reprinted 2003)	£6.25
A	C	25	The Great War Victoria Cross Heroes 6th Series 1915 (not issued)	—
A	C	25	The Great War Victoria Cross Heroes 7th Series 1915 (reprinted 2003)	£6.25
A	C	25	The Great War Victoria Cross Heroes 8th Series 1915 (reprinted 2003)	£6.25
A	C	50	Lawn Tennis Celebrities 1928 (reprinted 1997)	£8.50
A	C	25	Motor Cars 1934 (reprinted 1995)	£6.25
A	C	50	Regimental Colours and Standards 1899 (reprinted 1995)	£8.50
A	C	48	Signed Portraits of Famous Stars 1935 (reprinted 1997)	£8.50
A	C	50	South African Series No. 101-150 (Boer War Uniforms) (reprinted 2000)	£8.50
A	C	50	South African Series No. 151-200 (Boer War Uniforms) (reprinted 2000)	£8.50
A	C	50	Types of the British Army No. 1-50 1900 (reprinted 1995)	£8.50
A	C	50	Types of the British Army No. 51-100 1900 (reprinted 1996)	£8.50

GLOBE CIGARETTE CO.

| D | BW | 25 | Actresses — French c1900 (reprinted 2001) | £6.00 |

GLOBE INSURANCE

| — | U | 11 | Famous Golfers (75 × 60mm) 1929 (reprinted 1996) | £6.00 |

G.G. GOODE LTD (Australia)

| D2 | U | 17 | Prominent Cricketer Series 1924 (reprinted 2001) | £5.00 |

THOS. H. HALL (USA)

| C1 | C | 8 | Presidential Candidates & Actresses 1880 (reprinted 2001) | £2.00 |

HIGNETT BROS & CO.

| A | C | 25 | Greetings of The World 1907 (C.C.S. reprinted 2000) | £6.50 |
| A | C | 50 | Prominent Racehorses of 1933 (C.C.S. reprinted 2000) | £10.00 |

R. & J. HILL LTD

| A | C | 25 | Battleships and Crests 1901 (reprinted 1995) | £6.25 |
| A | C | 20 | Types of The British Army 1914 (reprinted 2001) | £6.25 |

Size	Printing	Number in set		Complete set

HUDDEN & CO. LTD
| A | C | 25 | Famous Boxers 1927 (reprinted 1992) | £6.25 |

HUNTLEY & PALMER (France)
| — | C | 12 | Aviation (114 × 85mm) c1908 (reprinted 2001) | £7.50 |

IMPERIAL TOBACCO COMPANY OF CANADA LTD
| A | C | 45 | Hockey Players 1912 (reprinted 1987) | — |
| A | C | 36 | Hockey Series 1911 (reprinted 1987) | — |

JAMES & CO.
| — | C | 20 | Arms of Countries (70 × 52mm) c1915 (reprinted 2001) | £7.50 |

JONES BROS., Tottenham
| A | BW | 18 | Spurs Footballers 1912 (reprinted 1986) | £2.50 |

WM. S. KIMBALL & CO. (USA)
| A1 | C | 50 | Champions of Games & Sports c1890 (reprinted 2001) | £10.00 |

KINNEAR LTD
| D1 | BW | 15 | Australian Cricketers 1897 (reprinted 2001) | £4.00 |

KINNEY BROS. (USA)
| A | C | 25 | Famous English Running Horses 1889 (reprinted 1996) | £6.25 |
| A | C | 25 | Leaders 1889 (reprinted 1990) | £6.00 |

J. KNIGHT (HUSTLER SOAP)
| A | C | 30 | Regimental Nicknames 1924 (reprinted 1996) | £6.25 |

B. KRIEGSFELD & CO.
| A | C | 50 | Phrases and Advertisements c1900 (reprinted 2001) | £10.00 |

A. KUIT LTD
| A | U | 25 | Principal Streets of British Cities and Towns 1916 (reprinted 2001) | £6.00 |

LACY'S CHEWING GUM
| A | BW | 50 | Footballers c1925 (reprinted 2001) | £10.00 |

LAMBERT & BUTLER
A	C	25	Aviation 1915 (reprinted 1997)	£6.00
A	C	25	Dance Band Leaders 1936 (reprinted 1992)	£6.00
A	C	50	Empire Air Routes 1936 (C.C.S. reprinted 2000)	£10.00
A	C	25	Hints and Tips for Motorists 1929 (reprinted 1994)	£6.00
A	C	50	Horsemanship 1938 (reprinted 1994)	£8.50
A	C	50	Interesting Sidelights On The Work of The GPO 1939 (C.C.S. reprinted 1999)	£10.00
A	C	20	International Yachts 1902 (reprinted 2001)	£5.00
A	C	25	London Characters 1934 (reprinted 1992)	£6.00
A	C	25	Motor Cars 1st series 1922 (reprinted 1988)	£6.25
A	C	25	Motor Cars 2nd series 1923 (reprinted 1988)	£6.25
A	C	25	Motor Cars 1934 (reprinted 1992)	£6.25

Size	Printing	Number in set		Complete set

LAMBERT AND BUTLER *(continued)*

A	C	50	Motor Cycles 1923 (reprinted 1990)	£8.50
A	C	25	Motors 1908 (reprinted 1992)	£6.00
A	C	25	Winter Sports 1914 (reprinted 1998)	£6.00
A	C	50	World's Locomotives 1912 (reprinted 1988)	£8.50

R. J. LEA LTD

A	C	50	Flowers to Grow 1913 (reprinted 1997)	£8.50

LEAF GUM CO. (USA)

—	BW	72	Star Trek (87 × 61mm) 1967 (reprinted 1981)	£12.50

J. LEES

A	C	20	Northampton Town Football Club c1912 (reprinted 2001)	£5.00

LIEBIG (France)

J2	C	6	Famous Explorers (F1088) 1914 (reprinted 2001)	£5.00

LUSBY LTD

D	C	25	Scenes From Circus Life c1900 (reprinted 2001)	£6.00

MARBURG BROS. (USA)

A	C	15	Beauties "PAC" c1890 (reprinted 2001)	£4.00

P.H. MAYO & BROTHER (USA)

C	U	35	Prizefighters c1890 (reprinted 2001)	£7.50

STEPHEN MITCHELL & SON

A	C	25	Angling 1928 (reprinted 1993)	£6.00
A	C	50	Famous Scots 1933 (C.C.S. reprinted 1999)	£10.00
A	C	50	A Gallery of 1935 (C.C.S. reprinted 1999)	£10.00
A	C	50	Humorous Drawings 1924 (C.C.S. reprinted 1999)	£10.00
A	C	25	Money 1913 (C.C.S. reprinted 2000)	£6.50
A	C	25	Regimental Crests, Nicknames and Collar Badges 1900 (reprinted 1993)	£6.50
A	C	50	Scotland's Story (C.C.S. reprinted 2000)	£10.00

MURRAY, SONS & CO. LTD

A	BW	20	Cricketers 1912 (reprinted 1991)	£7.50
A	C	20	War Series K — Uniforms 1915 (reprinted 2000)	£6.25
A	C	15	War Series K — World War I Leaders & Generals 1915 (reprinted 2000)	—

NATIONAL CIGARETTE CO. (Australia)

A	BW	13	English Cricket Team 1897-8 (reprinted 2001)	£4.00

NATIONAL EXCHANGE BANK, USA

—	C	9	Seven Ages of Golf (85 × 57mm) c1885 (reprinted 1995)	£4.50

OGDENS LTD

A	C	50	A.F.C. Nicknames 1933 (reprinted 1996)	£8.50
A	C	50	Air Raid Precautions 1938 (C.C.S. reprinted 1999)	£10.00
A	C	50	British Birds 1905 (C.C.S. reprinted 2000)	£10.00

Size	Print-ing	Number in set		Complete set
			OGDENS LTD *(continued)*	
A	C	50	By The Roadside 1932 (C.C.S. reprinted 2000)	£10.00
A	C	50	Champions of 1936 (C.C.S. reprinted 2000)	£10.00
D2	U	50	Cricketers and Sportsmen c1898 (reprinted 2001)	£10.00
A	C	50	Flags and Funnels of Leading Steamship Lines 1906 (reprinted 1997)	£8.50
A	C	50	Jockeys 1930 (reprinted 1990)	—
A	C	50	Modern Railways 1936 (reprinted 1996)	£8.50
A	C	50	Motor Races 1931 (reprinted 1993)	£8.50
A	C	25	Poultry 1st Series 1915 (reprinted 1998)	£6.00
A	C	25	Poultry 2nd Series 1916 (reprinted 2000)	£6.00
A	C	50	Shakespeare Series 1903 (C.C.S. reprinted 2000)	£10.00
A	C	50	Smugglers & Smuggling 1931 (C.C.S. reprinted 1999)	£10.00
A	C	50	Soldiers of the King 1909 (reprinted 1993)	£8.50
A	C	50	The Story of the Life Boat 1940 (reprinted 1989)	—
A	C	50	The Story of The Lifeboat 1940 (without "Ogdens") (reprinted 2001)	£8.50
A	C	50	Swimming, Diving and Life-Saving 1931 (C.C.S. reprinted 2000)	£10.00

OLD CALABAR BISCUIT CO. LTD

Size	Print-ing	Number in set		Complete set
J2	C	16	Sports and Games c1900 (reprinted 2001)	£7.50

THE ORLANDO CIGARETTE & CIGAR CO.

Size	Print-ing	Number in set		Complete set
A	C	40	Home & Colonial Regiments c1901 (reprinted 2001)	£8.50

PALMER MANN & CO (Sifta Sam)

Size	Print-ing	Number in set		Complete set
A	C	25	Famous Cricketers (set 24 plus 1 variety) 1950 (reprinted 2001)	£6.00

J.A. PATTREIOUEX, Manchester

Size	Print-ing	Number in set		Complete set
A	C	75	Cricketers Series 1926 (reprinted 1997)	£13.50

GODFREY PHILLIPS LTD

Size	Print-ing	Number in set		Complete set
A	C	30	Beauties "Nymphs" c1896 (reprinted 2001)	£7.50
A	C	25	Railway Engines 1924 (reprinted 1997)	
A	C	20	Russo-Japanese War Series 1904 (reprinted 2001)	£5.00
A	C	25	Territorial Series 1908 (reprinted 2001)	£6.25
A	C	25	Types of British Soldiers 1900 (reprinted 1997)	£6.25

JOHN PLAYER & SONS

Size	Print-ing	Number in set		Complete set
A	C	50	Aeroplanes (Civil) 1935 (reprinted 1990)	£8.50
A	C	50	Aircraft of The Royal Air Force 1938 (reprinted 1990)	£8.50
A	C	50	Animals of The Countryside 1939 (C.C.S. reprinted 1999)	£10.00
A	C	50	Aviary & Cage Birds 1933 (reprinted 1989)	£8.50
B	C	25	Aviary and Cage Birds 1935 (reprinted 1987)	£8.50
A	C	50	British Empire Series 1904 (C.C.S. reprinted 1999)	£10.00
A	C	50	Butterflies & Moths 1904 (C.C.S. reprinted 2000)	£10.00
B	C	24	Cats 1936 (reprinted 1986)	£8.50
A	C	25	Characters from Dickens 1912 (reprinted 1990)	£6.00
A	C	25	Characters from Dickens 2nd series 1914 (reprinted 1990)	£6.00
A	C	50	Cities of The World 1900 (C.C.S. reprinted 1999)	£10.00
B	C	25	Country Sports 1930 (reprinted 2000)	£8.50
A	C	50	Cricketers 1930 (reprinted 2000)	£8.50
A	C	50	Cricketers 1934 (reprinted 1990)	£8.50
A	C	50	Cricketers 1938 (C.C.S. reprinted 2000)	£10.00
A	C	50	Cricketers Caricatures by "Rip" 1926 (reprinted 1993)	£8.50
A	C	50	Derby and Grand National Winners 1933 (reprinted 1988)	£8.50

Size	Print-ing	Number in set		Complete set
			JOHN PLAYER & SONS *(continued)*	
A	C	50	Dogs' Heads (silver-grey backgrounds) 1940 (reprinted 1994)	£8.50
A2	C	25	England's Naval Heroes 1898 descriptive (reprinted 1987)	—
A	C	50	Film Stars 1st Series 1934 (C.C.S. reprinted 2000)	£10.00
A	C	50	Film Stars 3rd series 1938 (reprinted 1989)	£8.50
A	C	50	Fire-Fighting Appliances 1930 (reprinted 1991)	£8.50
A	C	50	Game Birds and Wild Fowl 1927 (C.C.S. reprinted 1999)	£10.00
B	C	25	Game Birds and Wild Fowl 1928 (reprinted 1987)	£8.50
A	C	50	Gilbert & Sullivan 2nd series 1927 (reprinted 1990)	£8.50
B	C	25	Golf 1939 (reprinted 1986)	£8.50
A	C	25	Highland Clans 1908 (reprinted 1997)	£6.00
A	C	50	Kings & Queens 1935 (reprinted 1990)	£8.50
A	C	50	Military Head-Dress 1931 (C.C.S. reprinted 1999)	£10.00
A	C	50	Military Series 1900 (reprinted 1983)	£8.50
A	C	50	Motor Cars 1st series 1936 (reprinted 1990)	£8.50
A	C	25	Napoleon 1916 (reprinted 1989)	£6.00
A	C	50	Nature Series 1909 (C.C.S. reprinted 2000)	£10.00
A	C	50	Old England's Defenders 1898 (reprinted 1987)	—
B	C	25	Old Hunting Prints 1938 (reprinted 1989)	£8.50
B	C	25	Old Naval Prints 1936 (reprinted 1989)	£8.50
B	C	25	Picturesque London 1931 (reprinted 1997)	£8.50
A	C	50	Poultry 1931 (reprinted 1993)	£8.50
A	C	50	Products of The World 1928 (C.C.S. reprinted 1999)	£10.00
B	C	25	Racing Yachts 1938 (reprinted 1987)	£8.50
A	C	50	Regimental Standards & Cap Badges 1930 (reprinted 1993)	£8.50
A	C	50	Regimental Uniforms Nd. 51-100 1914 (reprinted 1995)	£8.50
A	C	50	Speedway Riders 1937 (C.C.S. reprinted 2000)	£10.00
A	C	50	Tennis 1936 (C.C.S. reprinted 1999)	£10.00
B	C	24	Treasures of Britain 1931 (reprinted 1996)	£8.50
B	C	25	Types of Horses 1939 (reprinted 1998)	£8.50
A	C	50	Uniforms of the Territorial Army 1939 (reprinted 1990)	£8.50
B	C	25	Wild Birds 1934 (reprinted 1997)	£8.50

JOHN PLAYER & SONS (OVERSEAS)

A	C	50	Ships, Flags and Cap Badges 1930 (reprinted 1997)	—

REEVES LTD

D	C	25	Cricketers 1912 (reprinted 1993)	£8.00

RICHMOND CAVENDISH CO. LTD

A	C	20	Yachts c1900 (reprinted 2001)	£5.00

E. ROBINSON & SONS LTD

A	C	6	Medals & Decorations of Great Britain c1905 (reprinted 2001)	£2.00
A2	C	25	Regimental Mascots 1916 (reprinted 2001)	£6.00

S.D.V. TOBACCO CO. LTD

A1	BW	16	British Royal Family c1901 (reprinted 2001)	£4.00

SALMON & GLUCKSTEIN LTD

A	C	15	Billiard Terms 1905 (reprinted 1997)	£5.00
A	C	25	Coronation Series 1911 (C.C.S. reprinted 2000)	£6.50
C2	C	30	Music Hall Celebrities c1902 (reprinted 2001)	£7.50

Size	Print-ing	Number in set		Complete set

JOHN SINCLAIR LTD

A	C	50	British Sea Dogs 1926 (reprinted 1997)	£8.50

SINGLETON & COLE LTD

A	BW	35	Famous Boxers 1930 (reprinted 1992)	£6.25
D	BW	50	Footballers c1905 (reprinted 2001)	£10.00

F. & J. SMITH

A	C	25	Advertisement Cards 1899 (reprinted 2001)	£6.00
D	BW	50	Champions of Sport (unnumbered) 1902 (reprinted 2001)	£10.00
A	C	25	Cinema Stars 1920 (reprinted 1987)	£6.50
A	C	50	Fowls, Pigeons and Dogs 1908 (C.C.S. reprinted 2000)	£10.00
A	C	25	Holiday Resorts 1925 (C.C.S. reprinted 2000)	£6.50
A	C	25	Prominent Rugby Players 1924 (reprinted 1992)	£8.00

SPIRO VALLERI & CO.

A1	U	10	Noted Footballers c1905 (reprinted 2001)	£3.00

SPRATTS PATENT LTD

C2	C	12	Prize Dogs c1910 (reprinted 2001)	£3.50

TADDY & CO.

A	C	20	Clowns & Circus Artists 1920 (reprinted 1991)	£6.00
A	BW	238	County Cricketers 1907 (reprinted 1987)	£32.00
			Individual Counties of the above set:	
		15	Derbyshire	£2.50
		15	Essex	£2.50
		16	Gloucestershire	£2.50
		15	Hampshire	£2.50
		15	Kent	£2.50
		15	Lancashire	£2.50
		14	Leicestershire	£2.50
		15	Middlesex	£2.50
		15	Northamptonshire	£2.50
		14	Nottinghamshire	£2.50
		15	Somersetshire	£2.50
		15	Surrey	£2.50
		15	Sussex	£2.50
		15	Warwickshire	£2.50
		14	Worcestershire	£2.50
		15	Yorkshire	£2.50
A	U	5	English Royalty c1898 (reprinted 2001)	£2.00
A	C	25	Famous Jockeys 1910 (reprinted 1996)	£6.25
A	C	25	Natives of the World c1900 (reprinted 1999)	£6.00
A	BW	15	Prominent Footballers Aston Villa 1907 (reprinted 1992)	£2.50
A	BW	15	Prominent Footballers Chelsea 1907 (reprinted 1998)	£2.50
A	BW	15	Prominent Footballers Everton 1907 (reprinted 1998)	£2.50
A	BW	15	Prominent Footballers Leeds 1907 (reprinted 1992)	£2.50
A	BW	15	Prominent Footballers Liverpool 1907 (reprinted 1992)	£2.50
A	BW	15	Prominent Footballers Manchester Utd 1907 (reprinted 1992)	£2.50
A	BW	15	Prominent Footballers Middlesbrough 1907 (reprinted 1998)	£2.50
A	BW	15	Prominent Footballers Newcastle Utd 1907 (reprinted 1992)	£2.50
A	BW	15	Prominent Footballers Queens Park Rangers 1907 (reprinted 1992)	—
A	BW	15	Prominent Footballers Sunderland 1907 (reprinted 1998)	£2.50
A	BW	15	Prominent Footballers Tottenham Hotspur 1907 (reprinted 1998)	£2.50

Size	Printing	Number in set		Complete set
			TADDY & CO. *(continued)*	
A	BW	15	Prominent Footballers West Ham Utd 1907 (reprinted 1998)	£2.50
A	BW	15	Prominent Footballers Woolwich Arsenal 1907 (reprinted 1992)	£2.50
A2	C	20	Royalty, Actresses, Soldiers c1898 (reprinted 2001)	£5.00
A	C	25	Royalty Series 1908 (reprinted 1998)	£6.25
A	BW	15	South African Cricket Team 1907 (reprinted 1992)	—
A	C	25	Territorial Regiments 1908 (reprinted 1996)	£6.25
A	C	25	Thames Series 1903 (reprinted 1996)	£6.25
A	C	20	Victoria Cross Heroes (Nos 1-20) 1900 (reprinted 1996)	£6.25
A	C	20	Victoria Cross Heroes (Nos 21-40) 1900 (reprinted 1996)	£6.25
A	C	20	VC Heroes — Boer War (Nos 41-60) 1901 (reprinted 1997)	£6.25
A	C	20	VC Heroes — Boer War (Nos 61-80) 1901 (reprinted 1997)	£6.25
A	C	20	VC Heroes — Boer War (Nos 81-100) 1902 (reprinted 1997)	£6.25
A	C	25	Victoria Cross Heroes (Nos 101-125) 1905 (reprinted 1996)	£6.25

TEOFANI & CO. LTD

A	C	24	Past and Present The Army 1938 (reprinted 2001)	£6.25
A	C	24	Past and Present Weapons of War 1938 (reprinted 2001)	£6.25

D. C. THOMSON

A	C	24	Motor Bike Cards 1929 (reprinted 1993)	£6.00
A	C	20	Motor Cycles 1923 (Wizard Series) (reprinted 1993)	£6.00

TOPPS CHEWING GUM INC. (USA)

—	C	56	Mars Attacks (90 × 64mm) 1962 (reprinted 1987)	£12.50

UNION JACK

—	C	8	Police of All Nations (70 × 45mm) 1922 (reprinted 2005)	£4.00

UNITED TOBACCONISTS' ASSOCIATION LTD

A	C	10	Actresses "MUTA" c1900 (reprinted 2001)	£3.00

HENRY WELFARE & CO.

D	BW	22	Prominent Politicians c1911 (reprinted 2001)	£6.00

W.D. & H.O. WILLS

A	C	50	Allied Army Leaders 1917 (C.C.S reprinted 2000)	£10.00
A	C	50	Arms of Companies 1913 (C.C.S reprinted 1999)	£10.00
A	C	50	Builders of The Empire 1898 (C.C.S. reprinted 1999)	£10.00
B	C	7	Cathedrals 1933 (from set of 25) (reprinted 2000)	£2.50
A	C	50	Cricketers 1896 (reprinted 1982)	£8.50
A	C	50	Cricketers 1901 (reprinted 1983)	—
B	C	25	Dogs 1914 (reprinted 1987)	£8.50
A	C	50	Double Meaning 1898 (C.C.S. reprinted 1999)	£10.00
A	C	50	Engineering Wonders 1927 (C.C.S. reprinted 1999)	£10.00
B	C	25	Famous Golfers 1930 (reprinted 1987)	£8.50
A	C	50	Fish & Bait 1910 (reprinted 1990)	£8.50
A	C	50	Flower Culture In Pots 1925 (C.C.S. reprinted 2000)	£10.00
A	C	50	Household Hints 1st Series 1927 (C.C.S. reprinted 1999)	£10.00
B	C	25	Lawn Tennis 1931 (reprinted 1988)	£8.50
A	C	50	Life in the Hedgerow 1950 (reprinted 1991, Swan Vestas)	£12.50
A	C	50	Life In The Royal Navy 1939 (C.C.S. reprinted 1999)	£10.00
A	C	50	Military Aircraft (unissued c1967) (reprinted 1991)	£8.50
A	C	50	Military Motors 1916 (reprinted 1994)	£8.50

Size	Printing	Number in set		Complete set

W.D. & H.O. WILLS (continued)

Size	Printing	Number in set	Description	Complete set
A	C	58	Musical Celebrities 2nd series including 8 substituted cards 1914 (reprinted 1987)	£9.50
A	C	25	National Costumes c1895 (reprinted 1999)	£6.00
A	C	50	Naval Dress & Badges 1909 (reprinted 1997)	£8.50
A	C	50	Old English Garden Flowers 2nd Series 1913 (reprinted 1994)	£8.50
B	C	40	Puppies by Lucy Dawson (unissued) (reprinted 1990)	£12.50
A	C	50	Railway Engines 1924 (reprinted 1995)	£8.50
A	C	50	Railway Engines 1936 (reprinted 1992)	£8.50
A	C	50	Railway Equipment 1939 (reprinted 1993)	£8.50
A	C	50	Railway Locomotives 1930 (reprinted 1993)	£8.50
A	C	12	Recruiting Posters 1915 (reprinted 1987)	£3.00
B	C	25	Rigs of Ships 1929 (reprinted 1987)	£8.50
A	C	50	Roses 1st series 1912 (reprinted 1994)	£8.50
A	C	50	Rugby Internationals 1929 (reprinted 1996)	£8.50
A	C	50	School Arms 1906 (C.C.S. reprinted 2000)	£10.00
A	C	50	Ships Badges 1925 (C.C.S. reprinted 2000)	£10.00
A	C	50	Waterloo 1915 (reprinted 1987)	£10.00
A	C	50	Wild Flowers 1923 (C.C.S. reprinted 1999)	£10.00
A	C	50	Wild Flowers 1st series 1936 (reprinted 1993)	—
A	C	50	Wonders of The Sea 1928 (C.C.S. reprinted 2000)	£10.00
A	C	25	World's Dreadnoughts 1910 (reprinted 1994)	£6.00

W.D. & H.O. WILLS (Australia)

Size	Printing	Number in set	Description	Complete set
—	C	4	Advert Postcards of Packings (140 × 90mm) 1902 (reprinted 1988)	£5.00
A	C	50	Types of the British Army 1912 (reprinted 1995)	£8.50
A	C	50	War Incidents 2nd Series 1917 (reprinted 1995)	£8.50

W.H. & J. WOODS LTD

Size	Printing	Number in set	Description	Complete set
A	C	25	Types of Volunteers & Yeomanry 1902 (reprinted 1996)	£6.25

TRADE CARD CATALOGUE 2009 EDITION

This is the only major catalogue devoted to trade cards. It gives details of a magnificent selection of over 6,000 different series issued by non-tobacco companies, with prices for sets, odd cards and makers' albums. The new 34th edition features the issues of Brooke Bond, Bassett, Topps, Typhoo, Inkworks, Rittenhouse, Comic Images and hundreds of other firms, with prices from £2.25 a set. Contains eight-page section with 61 colour illustrations. **£5.50 Post Free**

LONDON CIGARETTE CARD CO LTD WEBSITE

www.londoncigcard.co.uk

Our website is a secure site so there are no worries about using your credit/debit card to place an order. The website now has over 100 pages for you to browse through.

New Issues and additions to stock from September 1999.
Sample card from each of more than 4000 series shown in colour.
36 Thematic Lists containing thousands of sets covering many subjects such as Football, Cricket, Motoring, Royalty, Military, Sci Fi & Films, etc.
Full range of storage albums illustrated.
Details of around 50 books on the subject of card collecting.
Sets of the month from September 2000 onwards with description of each set.
Article on the auction with a taster of what's up for sale each month.
Details on Card Collectors News Magazine, Our Shop in West Street, Somerton, Framing Kits, Who's Who at the LCCC etc. Plus special offers pages changed each month.